THE GUIDE TO CAREERS IN SPORTS

LEN KARLIN

A Careers & Colleges Publication

New York

D0764854

The Guide to Careers in Sports

Published by E.M. Guild, Inc., 989 Avenue of the Americas, New York, NY 10018; (212) 563-4688.

Copyright © 1997 by Len Karlin. Previous edition © 1995 by Len Karlin. All rights reserved. No part of this book may be reproduced or utilized in any form or by any means, electronic or mechanical, including photocopying, recording, or by any information storage and retrieval systems, without permission in writing from the publisher, except in the case of brief quotations embodied in critical articles and reviews.

A Careers & Colleges Publication

PHOTO CREDITS

p.1 David Black/Sports Photo Masters, Inc.

p.2 (College) Chip Henderson/Tony Stone Images Inc.; (Desk) David Rigg/Tony Stone Images Inc.

p.20 (Baseball) Kirk Schlea/Sports Photo Masters, Inc.; (Football) Mitchell B. Reibel/Sports Photo Masters, Inc.; (Basketball) Brian Drake/Sports Photo Masters, Inc.; (Hockey) Don Smith/Sports Photo Masters, Inc.

p.64 Mitchell B. Reibel/Sports Photo Masters, Inc.

p.98 Focus On Sports

p.130 Robert J. Rodgers/Sports Photo Masters, Inc.

p.160 Mitchell B. Reibel/Sports Photo Masters, Inc.

p.177 Courtesy of Michigan State University

p.188 Jonathan Kirn/Sports Photo Masters, Inc.

p.204 Kirk Schlea/Sports Photo Masters, Inc.

p.214 Mitchell B. Reibel/Sports Photo Masters, Inc.

p.224 (Greenspan) Frode Nielsen

p.233 Beth Green Studios

Library of Congress Catalog Card Number 96-078606
ISBN 0-9647594-1-1

Printed in the United States of America

About the author: Len Karlin has been a newspaper editor, a professor of journalism, and head of a book publishing firm. He founded two magazines: *Careers & Colleges* and *Sports inc., The Sports Business Weekly.*

———————————————

Acknowledgments: Cynthia Cannon, Dan Navarro, Marya Kazakova, and intern Traci Mosser provided valuable research assistance for this book. Jane Lincoln Taylor was a wise and patient editor.

CONTENTS

How to get

in the game

Sports events occupy more space in the newspapers and more time on television than any other human activity, except, possibly, wars.

Yet for all its visibility, the sports industry is only dimly understood.

This book will take you inside the industry and show you where the jobs are, what they are—and how to connect, which we'll deal with right now.

What you must understand right off the bat (excuse, please) is that it is next to impossible to break into this industry without first serving an internship.

True, the sports industry is growing, but everywhere the availability of jobs depends on experience. Entry-level jobs are like left-handed catchers: scarce.

Not scarce, however, are the internships that can give you the experience you need.

Internships are available by the thousands. They're offered by professional teams, sports marketing agencies, college athletics programs, corporate sports sponsors, sports resorts, stadiums and arenas and racetracks, sports radio stations, and just about every other part of the industry.

You will need an internship to get in the game.

We'll give you the phone numbers.

—LK

COLLEGE PROGRAMS IN SPORTS MANAGEMENT

Courses differ in content and quality,

but common to all programs

is the emphasis on internships.

PAGE 18: EVERYTHING YOU NEED TO KNOW ABOUT INTERNSHIPS

Something O'Malley Said

It was Walter O'Malley, late owner of the Los Angeles Dodgers, who was responsible for bringing the business of sports into the college classroom.

The time was the mid 1960s, when television was beginning to signal a new era of prosperity for professional sports. But was baseball ready to break out of its moth-eaten way of conducting business? In a conversation one day with Professor James Mason of Biscayne College, O'Malley expressed his frustration with baseball's front-office personnel, many of them retreads from the ballfield. What baseball desperately needed, said O'Malley, was an infusion of sports-wise administrators with up-to-date business smarts.

Mason didn't need a batting cage to fall on him. A short time after hearing O'Malley's plaint, he left Biscayne for a position at Ohio University, where he drew up a new master's degree curriculum that would provide the kind of training O'Malley had talked about. The university announced its new sports management program—the nation's first—in its 1966 catalog.

It did not set the academic world afire.

Actually, several years passed before the program caught on at a few other campuses. Then, quite suddenly in the '80s, when it became clear to college administrators that sports was indeed a major industry and that many young people were attracted to the idea of working in it, adaptations of Mason's program began sprouting up all over the country.

Today a program in sports management—variously called sport management or sport administration or athletics administration—is available at more than 190 colleges and universities.

At most schools it is given at the bachelor's degree level. Some schools offer both bachelor's and master's programs, and some, like Ohio University, offer it at the master's level only. A few—11, to be exact—offer doctorates.

The Quest for Standards

The popularity of sports management programs continues, but there's a problem. The quality of the programs around the country is, to put it gently, uneven.

All programs subscribe to this twofold purpose: (1) to give students an understanding of the sports industry, and (2) to teach them skills that will help them make their way in the industry. But while the purpose is a common one, the methods of achieving it aren't. Courses vary widely from campus to campus, and so do the credentials of the teaching staffs.

Inconsistencies are especially visible in the quality of business courses. Programs at some institutions stress rigorous courses in business administration; at other institutions, where the teaching burden may fall mainly on members of the phys ed faculty, business courses get only a superficial airing.

Into the picture of late have come two professional organizations—the National Association for Sport and Physical Education (NASPE) and the North American Society for Sport Management (NASSM). Long concerned about the inconsistencies (and occasional spuriousness) of courses in sports management, these organizations have taken joint action to establish national standards by providing precise guidelines for the content and depth of the courses.

The guidelines place emphasis on such courses as management and organizational skills, marketing and sales, communications, finance, sports law, and ethics.

A roster of approved programs is to appear annually in NASPE and NASSM publications. Collecting information for NASPE and NASSM is a panel of reviewers bearing still another set of initials: SMPRC—the Sport Management Program Review Council.

On the Subject of Jobs

Most graduates of sports management programs find their way into these areas of the sports industry: professional sports, college sports, stadium and arena operations, and the business of sports marketing and management.

The range of occupations within each of those areas is as wide as Hakeem Olajuwon's wingspread, but it needs to be understood that sports is a mighty magnet for jobseekers and competition for jobs is pretty tough.

A degree in sports management, however, gives an applicant a distinct advantage. It is widely recognized by employers in the industry. For that matter, many employers are themselves sports management graduates. Especially important: all sports management programs include placing students in internships.

꙳ ꙳ ꙳ ꙳

The list that follows is a sampling of positions held by sports management graduates of several college programs we looked at.

Professional sports operations.
•Vice president, business affairs—Baltimore Orioles
•Director of media relations—Buffalo Bills
•General manager—Yakima Bears (Northwest League)
•Director of communications & community relations—Minnesota Vikings
•Senior vice president, business operations—Pittsburgh Pirates
•Executive vice president, corporate sales—Detroit Pistons
•Vice president, marketing—Texas Rangers
•Executive vice president—Oakland Athletics
•Director of public relations—Pittsburgh Pirates
•Vice president, sales & marketing—Colorado Rockies
•Vice president—Providence Bruins
•Manager, promotions & publications—Cleveland Indians
•Director, retail licensing—NFL Properties

•Executive vice president—Detroit Pistons
•Director of publications—Charlotte Hornets
•Senior vice president, sales & marketing—Cleveland Cavaliers
•Information director—PGA Tour
•Scouting director—Houston Astros
•Executive director, general sales manager—Detroit Red Wings & Tigers
•Director of public relations—Miami Heat
•Vice president, tournament & sponsor relations—PGA Tour
•General manager—Vero Beach Dodgers (Florida State League)
•Vice president, operations—Dallas Mavericks
•Tournament manager—U.S. Pro Indoor Tennis Championship
•President & general manager—Erie Sailors (New York–Pennsylvania League)
•Director of operations—U.S. Open (golf)
•Director of statistics—Boston Red Sox
•Broadcast coordinator—Chicago White Sox
•Promotions director—Philadelphia Phillies
•Director of media relations—Miami Dolphins
•General manager—Pawtucket Red Sox (International League)
•Director of ticket operations—New York Mets
•Director, corporate marketing—Major League Baseball
•Director, suite & season ticket sales—Colorado Rockies

College sports operations:
•Director of marketing—College Football Association
•Director, athletic programs development—Virginia Tech
•Commissioner—Missouri Valley Conference
•Assistant commissioner—Southwest Conference
•Director of athletics—University of Arkansas

•Public relations director—Sun Belt Conference
•Sports information director—Wake Forest University
•Director, ticket operations—University of North Carolina
•Publicity director—Pac-10 Conference
•Commissioner—Rocky Mountain Conference
•Director of athletics—University of North Carolina
•Director of compliance services—NCAA
•Business manager of athletics—Dartmouth College
•Athletic event coordinator—Penn State University
•Athletics business manager—University of Michigan
•Director, athletics marketing—University of Connecticut

Stadium and arena operations:
•Director, operations & marketing—Cotton Bowl Classic
•Director of marketing—Knickerbocker Arena (Albany, N.Y.)
•Director, financial operations—Charlotte Coliseum (N.C.)
•Business manager—Market Square Arena (Indianapolis)
•Executive director—Hoosier Dome (Indianapolis)
•Vice president, athletics—Madison Square Garden (N.Y.)
•Manager—Fargo Dome (N.D.)
•Administrative manager—Georgia Dome
•President—Centre Management (managers of sports facilities)
•President—Riverfront Stadium (Cincinnati)
•Box office manager—Meadowlands Arena & Giants Stadium (N.J.)
•Events & marketing director—Pontiac Silverdome (Mich.)
•Vice president, event development & promotions—Madison Square Garden
•President & CEO—Spectrum (Philadelphia)

•Director of administration—Charlotte Coliseum
•Vice president—Lake Placid Olympic Training Center (N.Y.)
•Marketing consultant—New Jersey Sports Exposition Authority
•Supervisor, marketing & promotion—Busch Stadium (St. Louis)
•Superintendent of special facilities—City of Fort Lauderdale

Sports marketing and management operations:
•Account executive—Kemper Sports Marketing
•Associate executive director—Atlanta Sports Council
•Manager, pro sports marketing—Miller Brewing
•Project coordinator—Coca-Cola USA
•Manager—The Greenbrier (W.Va.)
•Director, media relations—Raycom Management Group
•Senior account executive—Advantage International
•Manager—Nashua Country Club (N.H.)
•Executive director—National Golf Course Owners Association
•Director, footwear sales—Nike
•Consultant, sports & entertainment—KPMG Peat Marwick
•Public relations consultant—USGA Foundation
•Manager, sports promotions—Met Life
•Coordinator, sports marketing—Anheuser-Busch
•Media relations coordinator—Spalding Sports Worldwide
•Public relations director—Advantage International
•Vice president—International Management Group

The Doctoral Programs
   Among the 200-plus colleges and universities that offer programs in the business of

sports are 11 institutions that report they are now conferring doctorates in this discipline (though in a few cases the actual degree reads doctor of philosophy or doctor of education). A doctorate on your resume is reasonable evidence of a mind with a capacity for knowledge and perception, and it makes a fine impression on employers in all areas of sports, especially those engaged in market research or other projects requiring trained analysts.

These are the institutions with doctoral programs:

University of Connecticut
Florida State University
University of Massachusetts at Amherst
University of Miami (Florida)
University of New Mexico
University of Northern Colorado
Ohio State University
University of Southern Illinois at Carbondale
University of Southern Mississippi
Temple University
United States Sports Academy

Sports psychology. It's not too much of a stretch to add to the elite company above the University of Virginia and the University of Iowa, which offer doctoral degrees in sports psychology.

The job of a sports psychologist is to help athletes overcome psychological problems that affect their performance. The work may involve counseling an athlete whose motivation has turned to sloth or whose self-confidence has suddenly unraveled. It may also include helping an athlete who is distracted by domestic troubles, or who can't say no to booze or drugs, or who is in the grip of some other compulsion, like gambling.

Normally, you won't find the sports psychologist listed in the published rosters of college or professional teams, but you can bet his or her phone number is handy. The New York Rangers hockey club is one organization that doesn't shrink from such a listing. In fact, its 1994 press book identified not one but two club psychologists. That was the year the Rangers won the Stanley Cup. Does that tell you something?

SPECIAL PROGRAMS

Professional Golf Management

Penn State has two labs that are bigger than many college campuses.

The labs are a pair of 18-hole golf courses, the training ground for students in the university's Professional Golf Management program.

Penn State is the latest of four universities to offer the program, which trains students in the operation of golf facilities at country clubs, sports resorts, and public parks. The other institutions are Ferris University (Michigan), New Mexico State University, and Mississippi State University. Each has an 18-hole course.

The program, similar in content at all four institutions, leads to a baccalaureate degree. At Ferris, New Mexico State, and Mississippi State, it is given in their colleges of business; at Penn State it is in the School of Hotel, Restaurant, and Recreation Management.

The curriculum, aside from required general courses, is business-oriented, covering such areas as marketing, merchandising, managerial accounting, operations management, and business law.

Closely associated with the program is the Professional Golfers Association of America (the PGA), which supervises 16 months of on-the-job training at courses away from campus. The PGA also conducts mandatory on-campus workshops on facilities maintenance, golf instruction techniques, pro shop operations, and other aspects of the job, including the art of repairing clubs.

That's the good news. Here's the bad news: to be considered for the program an applicant has to be an 8-handicap player or better.

Professional Tennis Management

Not only is Michigan's Ferris University one of the few schools that have professional golf management programs, it also owns the distinction of having been the first four-year institution to offer a degree program in professional tennis management.

The Ferris tennis program, introduced in 1986, was followed six years later by a parallel program set up at Hampton University, the historically black institution in Virginia. Both programs are approved by the United States Professional Tennis Association.

Most students in the programs are interested in careers as teaching professionals (it takes a 4.5 NTRP rating to get into either program), but academic work at both schools focuses on business courses that give students other career options in the tennis industry. Options include management positions at tennis clubs, country clubs, and resorts; administrative positions with tennis associations; and marketing jobs with manufacturers of tennis products.

The Ferris program has placed 100 percent of its graduates in jobs. At Hampton the program was too new, at this writing, to have produced graduates, but officials there are looking forward to getting more African Americans into the tennis industry.

Ferris and Hampton are not the only players in the game. In Texas, Tyler Junior College has a well-established two-year tennis program that also has a high rate of placement. Here, too, classroom work leans heavily on business courses.

Racetrack Management

Talk with horse racing people about preparing for a career in their industry and you can bet they'll bring up the undergraduate programs at the University of Arizona and the University of Louisville. Both programs have excellent reputations.

The Race Track Industry Program at the U. of Arizona. The RTIP, as it's known, has had a close connection with the racetrack industry ever since the program was established in 1974. Industry dollars helped get it started, and financial support by the industry continues (some of it for scholarships). The program is housed in the university's College of Agriculture and leads to a B.S. degree. Its purpose is to turn out graduates with management skills for jobs in racetrack operations, regulatory agencies, breed registries, and other businesses related to racing. Student interns are placed with tracks throughout the country. Some interns are placed with such organizations as the American Quarter Horse Association, the Jockey Club, the U.S. Trotting Association, and the New York Racing Association. RTIP graduates become stewards, racing secretaries, general managers, racing officials, publicists, marketing directors, wagering managers, breed registry officials, farm managers, and trainers.

The RTIP faculty and staff, with student assistance, each year run a "Symposium on Racing," the largest industrywide conference in the country. The event draws about a thousand industry leaders from the U.S. and abroad. Students help set it up.

The Equine Industry Program at the U. of Louisville. Introduced by the university's School of Business only a few years ago, the program has run a fast race to prominence. The location of its campus—in the heart of Kentucky horse country and just a few furlongs from Churchill Downs—is a factor in its success. So is the quality of its curriculum, which includes such traditional business courses as accounting, economics, finance, management, and marketing, plus business courses tailored to the equine industry and seminars conducted by industry executives. Interns are placed with racetracks, breeding farms, bloodstock agencies, auction sale companies, breed associations, and training centers. Graduates receive a bachelor of business administration degree and head for careers in racing, showing, breeding, and oth-erequine-related businesses.

The Global Business of Sports

Jumping ahead of the parade of colleges offering courses on the U.S. sports industry, the Georgia Institute of Technology has established a center of training and research in the worldwide business of sports.

The new center is known as the Institute for World Sports Management and will be administered by Georgia Tech's Ivan Allen College of Management, Policy, and International Affairs. Much of the funding is expected to come from corporate grants. Malcolm J. MacKenzie heads the project.

The incentive for the new institute, said MacKenzie, was the recognition that sports and its related businesses "are among the fastest-growing industries in the United States and have become a major and dynamic industry in Western Europe, Japan, and most middle-tier countries." However, he said, the growth is "unplannedand hap hazard."

He said that the institute will help train industry leaders, provide direction for the successful management of events around the world, and set up a research center for the benefit of educators, social scientists, and business interests. Its activities will include an annual international conference on sports business and management.

In a first step, Georgia Tech announced the introduction of a master's program in world sports management.

SIDELINES

Women Show Strong Numbers

A random survey we made of 20 sports management programs showed that approximately one-third of the more than 2,250 students enrolled in those programs were women.

The largest percentage was at Temple University, where women constituted about 50 percent of the 300-plus enrollment.

If those numbers are surprising, consider this: Of the 202 sports management programs we were able to identify, 53 are headed by women.

Stretching Exercises

Most sports management programs are conducted within the borders of what were once universally known as departments of physical education. But on many campuses today the departments have taken on the plumage of new, elongated names intended to show that they're offering more than plain old phys ed. Example: Department of Health, Physical Education, Sport Science, and Leisure Studies.

To ease the nomenclatural clutter, however, colleges usually refer to these wordy titles by their initials—which sort of defeats the original purpose. (Does "Department of HPESSLS" explain what the department offers?)

It would help if the initials were acronymic—if they formed a pronounceable word—but they aren't. Closest to an acronym is the Department of Health, Physical Education, Sports Medicine, and Sport Management at Mount Union College in Ohio. The initials are HPESMSM, almost pronounceable as "pessimism"—not an appropriate word for Mount Union's upbeat department.

In any case, departments are given their full names in the directory that follows.

Professional Organizations

North American Society for Sport Management (NASSM)
106 Main St., Suite 344
Houlton, ME 04730-9001
Contact: Garth Patton (506) 453-5010

NASSM is a scholarly organization for teachers of sports management. Membership also is open to students at a cost of $25 a year. Members receive the *Journal of Sport Management*, published three times a year, and an invitation to NASSM's annual conference, where job tips are floated.

National Association for Sport and Physical Education (NASPE)
1900 Association Dr.
Reston, VA 20191-1599
Phone: (703) 476-3414

NASPE is devoted to improving the quality of physical education and the teaching of sports. It has a national membership of more than 28,000 professionals and students and is one of six professional associations that form the American Alliance for Health, Physical Education, Recreation, and Dance.

Administrator of NASPE/NASSM's Sport Management Program Review Council is Mary Ellen Saville.

PROGRAMS IN CANADA
Sports management programs are available at the following Canadian universities:

Concordia University
Montreal, Quebec H4B 1R6

Laurentian University
Sudbury, Ontario P3E 2C6

McMaster University
Hamilton, Ontario L8S 4K1

Queens University
Kingston, Ontario K7L 3N6

University of Alberta
Edmonton, Alberta T6G 2H9

University of British Columbia
Vancouver, British Columbia V6T 1V1

University of New Brunswick
Fredericton, New Brunswick E3B 5A3

University of Ottawa
Ottawa, Ontario K1N 6N5

University of Regina
Regina, Saskatchewan S4S 0A2

University of Saskatchewan
Saskatoon, Saskatchewan S7N 0W0

University of Waterloo
Waterloo, Ontario N2L 3G1

University of Western Ontario
London, Ontario N6A 3K7

University of Windsor
Windsor, Ontario N9B 3P4

York University
North York, Ontario M3J 1P3

The term *sports management,* which we favor, is not the term of choice at many—actually, most—colleges, where the preference is *sport management,* or *sport administration.* We've used the term preferred by each college.

The letters *U* and *G* denote programs leading to undergraduate and graduate degrees, respectively. The letter *A* indicates a two-year associate's degree program.

ALABAMA

Faulkner University — U
Montgomery, AL 36109
Sports Management
Terry Brown
Dep't of Physical Education &
Sports Management
(205) 260-6286

United States Sports Academy — U, G
Daphne, AL 36526
Sport Management
Hal Walker, Chair
Dep't of Sport Management
(334) 626-3303

ARIZONA

University of Arizona — U
Tucson, AZ 85721
Special program: Race Track Management
F. Douglas Reed, Program
Coordinator
Race Track Industry Program
(520) 621-5660

ARKANSAS

Arkansas State University — U
State University, AR 72467
Sports Management
Jack Sugg
Dep't of Health, Physical Education
& Recreation
(501) 972-3066

Harding University — U
Searcy, AR 72149
Sports Management
Wilt Martin, Chair
Dep't of Kinesiology
(501) 279-4761

University of Arkansas — G
Fayetteville, AR 72701
Sport Management
Sharon Hunt
Dep't of Health Sciences,
Kinesiology, Recreation &
Dance
(501) 575-2857

CALIFORNIA

**California State University
at Fullerton — U, G**
Fullerton, CA 92634
Sport Management
Anne Marie Bird, Chair
Dep't of Kinesiology & Health
Promotion
(714) 773-3316

**California State University
at Long Beach — G**
Long Beach, CA 90840
Sports Management
Dixie Grimmett, Chair
Dep't of Kinesiology & Physical
Education
(310) 985-4051

Fresno Pacific College — U
Fresno, CA 93702
Sport Management
William Cockerham, Program
Director
Dep't of Physical Education
(209) 453-2294

**San Jose State University
— U, G**
San Jose, CA 95192
Sport Management
Dick Montgomery
Dep't of Human Performance
(408) 924-3054

**University of the Pacific
— U, G**
Stockton, CA 95211
Sport Management
Linda Koehler, Program
Coordinator
Dep't of Sport Sciences
(209) 946-2531

**University of San Francisco
— U, G**
San Francisco, CA 94117
Undergraduate: Sports Administration
George H. McGlynn, Chair
Graduate: Sports & Fitness Management
Lawrence Wenner, Program
Director
Dep't of Exercise & Sport Science
(415) 666-6615

COLORADO

University of Denver — G
Denver, CO 80208
Sport Management
Gordon E. VonStroh, Chair
Daniels College of Business
(800) 622-4723

**University of Northern
Colorado — U, G**
Greeley, CO 80639
Sport Administration
David K. Stotlar, Program Director
School of Kinesiology & Physical
Education
(970) 351-1722

**Western State College of
Colorado — U**
Gunnison, CO 81230
*Special program: Ski Resort
Management*
Barbara Klingman
Dep't of Kinesiology & Recreation
(970) 943-2010

CONNECTICUT

**Southern Connecticut State
University**
New Haven, CT 06515
*Several undergraduate courses in Sports
Management; not a degree program*
Joan Barbarich, Chair
Dep't of Exercise Science
(203) 392-6080

**University of Connecticut
— U, G**
Storrs, CT 06269
Sport Management
William M. Servedio, Head
Dep't of Sport, Leisure & Exercise
Sciences
(860) 486-3625

**University of New Haven
— U, G**
West Haven, CT 06516
Sports Management
Allen L. Sack, Program Coordinator
Dep't of Management
(203) 932-7090

DISTRICT OF COLUMBIA

**George Washington University
— U, G**
Washington, DC 20052
Sports Management
Lisa Delpy, Program Director
School of Business & Public
Management
(202) 994-6281

FLORIDA

Barry University — U, G
Miami Shores, FL 33161
Sports Management
Leta Hicks, Chair
Dep't of Sport & Exercise Sciences
(305) 899-3490

**Florida International University
— U, G**
Miami, FL 33199
Undergraduate: Sports Management
Graduate: Sport Management
Robert Wolff, Chair
Dep't of Health, Physical Education
& Recreation
(305) 348-3486

**Florida State University
— U, G**
Tallahassee, FL 32306
Undergraduate: Sport Administration
Graduate: Sport Management
Dewayne Johnson, Chair
Dep't of Physical Education
(904) 644-4813

Jacksonville University — U
Jacksonville, FL 32211
Sports Administration
Peggy A. Phillips
Dep't of Physical Education
(904) 744-3950

Saint Leo College — U
Saint Leo, FL 33574-2098
Sport & Recreation Management
Tom Phillips, Chair
Div. of Professional Studies
(904) 588-8272

St. Thomas University — U, G
Miami, FL 33054
Sport Administration
Jan Bell
Dep't of Professional Management
(305) 628-6634

**University of Florida
— U, G**
Gainesville, FL 32611
Sport Administration
Robert N. Singer, Chair
Dep't of Exercise & Sport Sciences
(352) 392-0584

University of Miami — G
Coral Gables, FL 33124
Sports Administration
Harry C. Mallios, Chair
Dep't of Exercise & Sport Sciences
(305) 284-3011

University of Tampa — U
Tampa, FL 33606
Sports Management
Eric Vlahov, Chair
Dep't of Exercise Science & Sport
   Studies
(813) 253-3333

GEORGIA

**Georgia Institute of Technology
(Georgia Tech) — G**
Atlanta, GA 30332-0525
*Special program: International
   Sports Business & Economics*
Malcolm J. MacKenzie
Ivan Allen College
(404) 894-1039

**Georgia Southern University
— U, G**
Statesboro, GA 30460-8076
Sport Management
Undergraduate program: Ming Li,
   Coordinator
Graduate program: Larry McCarthy,
   Coordinator
Dep't of Sport Science & Physical
   Education
(912) 681-0200

Georgia State University — G
Atlanta, GA 30302
Sport Management
R. Cooter, Program Director
Dep't of Kinesiology & Health
(404) 651-4813

Kennesaw State College — U
Kennesaw, GA 30144-5591
Sport Management
Bernie Goldfine
Dep't of Health & Physical
   Education
(770) 423-6216

University of Georgia — G
Athens, GA 30602
Sport Management
Stan Brassie, Program Director
Dep't of Physical Education &
   Sports Studies
(706) 542-4379

IDAHO

Boise State University — G
Boise, ID 83725
Exercise & Sport Studies
Ross Vaughn, Chair
Dep't of Health, Physical Education
   & Recreation
(208) 385-1798

University of Idaho — G
Moscow, ID 83844-2401
Sport & Recreation Management
Cal Lathen
Dep't of Health, Physical
   Education, Recreation & Dance
(208) 885-7921

ILLINOIS

Eastern Illinois University
Charleston, IL 61920
*Several undergraduate and graduate
   courses in Sport Management; not a
   degree program*
Phoebe Church, Chair
Dep't of Physical Education
(217) 581-2215

Greenville College — U
Greenville, IL 62246
Sports Management
Phyllis Holmes, Program Director
Dep't of Health, Physical Education
   & Recreation
(618) 664-1748

Illinois State University — G
Normal, IL 61790
Sports Management
L. Marlene Mawson, Chair
Dep't of Health, Physical Education
   & Recreation
(309) 438-8661

MacMurray College — U
Jacksonville, IL 62650
Sports Management
Donald Mulhern, Chair
Dep't of Physical Education
(217) 479-7143

North Central College — U
Naperville, IL 60566
Sport Management
Gerald Gems, Chair
Dep't of Health & Physical
   Education
(708) 420-3470

**Northern Illinois University
— G**
DeKalb, IL 60115
Sport Management
Judith A. Bischoff, Chair
Dep't of Physical Education
(815) 753-1409

Quincy College — U
Quincy, IL 62301
Sports Management
John Ortwerth, Program Director
Dep't of Physical Education
(217) 228-5475

Southern Illinois University — U
Carbondale, IL 62901
Sports Management
Ronald G. Knowlton, Chair
Dep't of Physical Education
(618) 536-2431

**University of Illinois at Chicago
— G**
Chicago, IL 60680
Sports Management
Warren K. Palmer, Program
   Director
Dep't of Kinesiology
(312) 996-4810

**University of Illinois at
Urbana-Champaign — G**
Urbana, IL 61801
Sport Management
Jim Misner, Head
Dep't of Kinesiology
(217) 333-1083

Western Illinois University — G
Macomb, IL 61455
Sport Management
Charles Spencer, Graduate Advisor
Dep't of Physical Education
(309) 298-1981

Wheaton College — G
Wheaton, IL 60187-5593
Special program: Sport Ministry
Tony Ladd, Chair, Physical
   Education/Athletics
Dep't of Kinesiology
(630) 752-5079

INDIANA

Ball State University — U, G
Muncie, IN 47306
*Undergraduate: Sport Administration
Graduate: Sport Management*
John E. Reno
School of Physical Education
(317) 285-1451

**Indiana State University
— U, G**
Terre Haute, IN 47809
Sport Management
Tom Sawyer, Coordinator of
   Sport Management Programs
Dep't of Recreation & Sport
   Management
(812) 237-2186

Indiana University — U
Bloomington, IN 47405
Sport Management
Craig Ross
Dep't of Recreation & Park
   Administration
(812) 855-4711

Indiana Wesleyan University — U
Marion, IN 46953
*Athletic Training & Recreation
   Management*
Michael Fratzke, Director of Athletics
Dep't of Health, Physical Education,
   Recreation & Athletics
(317) 677-2318

University of Evansville — U
Evansville, IN 47722
Sports Management
Paul Jensen, Chair
Dep't of Physical Education
(812) 479-2848

Valparaiso University — U
Valparaiso, IN 46383
Sports Management
Jerome Stieger, Chair
Dep't of Physical Education
(219) 464-5235

IOWA

Iowa State University — G
Ames, IA 50011
Sports Management
Dean F. Anderson, Chair
Dep't of Health & Human
   Performance
(515) 294-8009

Loras College — U, G
Dubuque, IA 52004
Sports Management & Administration
Eric Johnson
Dep't of Physical Education
(319) 588-7165

Luther College — U
Decorah, IA 52101
Sports Management
Joe Thompson, Chair
Dep't of Health & Physical Education
(319) 387-1245

KANSAS

University of Kansas — U, G
Lawrence, KS 66045
Sport Administration
James D. LaPoint, Graduate
   Coordinator
Dep't of Health, Physical Education
   & Recreation
(913) 864-3371

Washburn University — U
Topeka, KS 66621
*Special program: Sports Facilities
   Management*
James H. McCormick, Chair
Dep't of Health & Physical Education
(913) 231-1010, ext. 1461

Wichita State University — U, G
Wichita, KS 67260
Undergraduate: Sport Business
Graduate: Sport Administration
Susan K. Kovar, Chair
Dep't of Health & Physical
    Education
(316) 978-3340

KENTUCKY

Eastern Kentucky University — U, G
Richmond, KY 40475
Undergraduate: Sport Supervision
Graduate: Sports Administration
Robert J. Baugh, Dean
College of Health, Physical
    Education, Recreation &
    Athletics
(606) 622-1682

University of Kentucky — G
Lexington, KY 40506
Sports Management
John Hall, Chair
Dep't of Kinesiology & Health
    Promotion
(606) 257-5826

University of Louisville
Louisville, KY 40292
School of Education:
Sport Administration — **U, G**
Richard Fee, Chair
Sport Administration Div.
Dep't of Health Promotion,
    Physical Education & Sport Studies
(502) 852-6642
School of Business:
Equine Industry Program — **U**
Robert Lawrence, Chair
School of Economics & Public
    Affairs
(502) 852-7617

LOUISIANA

Grambling State University — G
Grambling, LA 71245
Sports Administration
Willie Daniel
Dep't of Health, Physical Education
    & Recreation
(318) 274-2294

Northwestern State University of Louisiana — G
Natchitoches, LA 71497
Sport Management
Newton Wilkes, Chair
Dep't of Health & Human
    Performance
(318) 357-5126

Southeastern Louisiana University — U
Hammond, LA 70402
Sport Management
Betty Baker, Head of Program
Dep't of Kinesiology & Health
    Studies
(504) 549-2129

Tulane University — U
New Orleans, LA 70118
Sport Management
Peter J. Titlebaum, Program Director
Dep't of Exercise & Sport Sciences
(504) 865-5301

University of New Orleans — G
New Orleans, LA 70148
Sport & Athletic Administration
Bobby L. Eason, Chair
Dep't of Human Performance &
    Health Promotion
(504) 286-6361

MAINE

Husson College — U
Bangor, ME 04401
Sport Management
Tim Kilroy
Dep't of Business Administration
(207) 947-1121

MARYLAND

Towson State University — U
Baltimore, MD 21204
Sport Management
Maggie Faulkner
Dep't of Physical Education
(410) 830-3168

University of Maryland — G
College Park, MD 20742
Sport Management
David H. Clarke, Chair
Dep't of Kinesiology
(301) 405-2455

MASSACHUSETTS

Becker College — A
Leicester, MA 01524
Sports Administration
Ginger Daly
Dep't of Athletics
(508) 791-9241

Dean Junior College — A
Franklin, MA 02038
Sports Management
Karen M. Sykes, Chair
Dep't of Sport & Fitness Studies
(508) 528-9100

Salem State College — U
Salem, MA 01970
Sports Management
Joseph Lavacchia
Dep't of Sport, Fitness & Leisure
    Studies
(508) 741-6000

Springfield College — U, G
Springfield, MA 01109
Sports Management
Undergraduate program: Jack
    Costello
Graduate program: Betty L. Mann
Dep't of Physical Education
(413) 788-3000

University of Massachusetts — U, G
Amherst, MA 01003
Sport Management
Glenn M. Wong, Head
Dep't of Sport Studies
(413) 545-0441

MICHIGAN

Central Michigan University — G
Mount Pleasant, MI 48859
Sport Management
Walter R. Schneider
Dep't of Physical Education & Sport
(517) 774-6661

Concordia College — U
Ann Arbor, MI 48105
Sports Management
T. Alan Twietmeyer
Dep't of Physical Education
(313) 995-7300

Ferris State University — U
College of Business
Big Rapids, MI 49307
*Special program: Professional Golf
    Management*
Matthew Pinder
(616) 592-2380
*Special program: Professional
    Tennis Management*
Scott Schultz
(616) 592-2212

Michigan State University — G
East Lansing, MI 48824
Sports Administration
Deborah Feltz, Chair
Dep't of Physical Education &
    Exercise Science
(517) 355-4736

Spring Arbor College — U
Spring Arbor, MI 49283
Sports Administration
Craig Hayward
Dep't of Exercise & Sports Science
(517) 750-1200

University of Michigan — U, G
Ann Arbor, MI 48109
Sports Management
D. W. Edington, Program Director
Div. of Kinesiology
(313) 764-1817

Wayne State University — G
Detroit, MI 48202
Sports Administration
Todd Seidler
Div. of Health, Physical Education
    & Recreation
(313) 577-6218

Western Michigan University — G
Kalamazoo, MI 49008
Sports Administration
Roger Zabik, Chair
Dep't of Health, Physical Education
    & Recreation
(616) 387-2710

MINNESOTA

Bemidji State University — U
Bemidji, MN 56601
Sport Business & Management
Karl Salscheider, Chair
Dep't of Health, Physical Education
    & Recreation
(218) 755-2768

College of St. Scholastica — U
Duluth, MN 55811
Sport & Fitness Management
Jessica Jenner
Dep't of Management
(218) 723-6415

Mankato State University — G
Mankato, MN 56002
Sports Administration
Joe Walsh, Graduate Program
    Coordinator
Dep't of Human Performance
(507) 389-6313

Northwestern College — U
St. Paul, MN 55113
Sports Management
Wally Parish, Chair
Dep't of Physical Education
(612) 631-5100

COLLEGE PROGRAMS IN THE BUSINESS OF SPORTS

University of Minnesota
Minneapolis, MN 55455
Certificate program: Sport Management
Vickie Berg
School of Kinesiology & Leisure
  Studies
(612) 625-1007

MISSISSIPPI

Delta State University — U
Cleveland, MS 38733
Sport Management
Milton Wilder, Chair
Div. of Health, Physical Education
  & Recreation
(601) 846-4555

**Mississippi State University
— U, G**
Mississippi State, MS 39762
*Undergraduate: Professional Golf
  Management*
S. Roland Jones, Program Director
College of Business & Industry
(601) 325-3161
Graduate: Sport Administration
Robert Boling, Head
Dep't of Physical Education,
  Health & Recreation
(601) 325-2963

**University of Southern
  Mississippi — U, G**
Hattiesburg, MS 39406
Sport Administration
Sandra Gangstead, Program Director
School of Human Performance &
  Recreation
(601) 266-5386

MISSOURI

**Central Missouri State
  University — G**
Warrensburg, MO 64093
Sport Administration
James H. Conn, Chair
Dep't of Physical Education
(816) 543-8852

**Missouri Western State College
— U**
St. Joseph, MO 64507-2294
Sports Management
Brenda Blessing, Program Director
Dep't of Health, Physical Education
  & Recreation
(816) 271-4493

University of Missouri — G
Columbia, MO 65211
Sport Management
Richard H. Cox, Chair
Dep't of Health & Physical
  Education
(314) 882-7601

MONTANA

Carroll College — U
Helena, MT 59625
Sport Management
Lynette Zuroff, Chair
Dep't of Education & Physical
  Education
(406) 447-4353

NEBRASKA

Chadron State College — U, G
Chadron, NE 69337
Sports Management
Ann Smith, Chair
Dep't of Health, Physical Education
  & Recreation
(308) 432-6341

**Nebraska Wesleyan University
— U**
Lincoln, NE 68504
Sport Management
Pat Dotson Pettit, Chair
Dep't of Health & Physical
  Education
(402) 466-2371

**University of Nebraska at
  Kearney — U**
Kearney, NE 68849-3101
Sports Administration
Don Lackey, Chair
Dep't of Health, Physical Education,
  Recreation & Leisure Studies
(308) 865-8331

Wayne State College — U, G
Wayne, NE 68787
Sport Management
Ralph Barclay, Chair
Div. of Human Performance &
  Leisure Studies
(402) 375-7301

NEW HAMPSHIRE

Colby-Sawyer College — U
New London, NH 03257
Sport Management
Richard LaRue
Dep't of Sports Science
(603) 526-3615

Keene State College — U
Keene, NH 03431
Sports Management
Dorothy Watson
Dep't of Physical Education
(603) 352-1909

**University of New Hampshire
— U, G**
Durham, NH 03824
Sports Studies
Stephen Hardy, Coordinator
Dep't of Kinesiology
(603) 862-2076

NEW JERSEY

Jersey City State College — U
Jersey City, NJ 07305
Sport Management
Eugene Bacha, Chair
Dep't of Sport & Leisure Studies
(201) 200-3327

Montclair State University — G
Upper Montclair, NJ 07043
Sports Administration
Timothy Sullivan, Chair
Dep't of Health Professions,
  Physical Education, Recreation
  & Leisure Studies
(201) 655-5253

Rutgers University — U
New Brunswick, NJ 08903-0270
Sport Management
Edward J. Zambraski
Dep't of Exercise Science & Sport
  Studies
(908) 932-9525

Seton Hall University — U, G
South Orange, NJ 07079-2692
Sports Management
Ann Mayo, Director of Center for
  Sports Management
Stillman School of Business
(201) 761-9707

NEW MEXICO

**New Mexico State University
— U**
Las Cruces, NM 88003-8001
*Special program: Professional Golf
  Management*
Pat Gavin, Director, PGM Program
Dep't of Marketing & General
  Business
College of Business Administration
  & Economics
(505) 646-2814

University of New Mexico — G
Albuquerque, NM 87131-1251
Sports Management
Erick Kozlowski, Chair
Dep't of Physical Performance
  & Development
(505) 277-2783 or 5114

NEW YORK

Adelphi University — G
Garden City, NY 11530
Sports Management
Ronald S. Feingold
Dep't of Health Studies, Physical
  Education & Human
  Performance Studies
(516) 877-4270

Brooklyn College — M
Brooklyn, NY 11210-2889
Sports Management
Charles Tobey
Dep't of Physical Education
(718) 951-5514

Canisius College — G
Buffalo, NY 14208-1098
Sport Administration
James Riordan, Program Director
School of Education & Human
  Services
(716) 888-3179

Ithaca College — U
Ithaca, NY 14850
Sport Management
F. Wayne Blann, Program
  Coordinator
School of Health Sciences &
  Human Performance
(607) 274-3105

Medaille College — U
Buffalo, NY 14214
Sports Management
Jerry Kissel, Program Coordinator
Dep't of Business Management
(716) 884-3281

New York University
School of Continuing Education
New York, NY 10012
(212) 998-7171
*Evening, nondegree classes in Sports
  Marketing; two-week summer program*

St. John's University — U
Jamaica, NY 11439
Athletic Administration
Anthony Missere, Program Director
Dep't of Athletic Administration
(718) 990-6414

State University of New York at Brockport — U
Brockport, NY 14420
Sports Management
William F. Stier Jr.
Dep't of Physical Education & Sport
(716) 395-5331

State University of New York at Cortland — U
Cortland, NY 13045
Sport Management
Suzanne Wingate, Program Coordinator
Dep't of Physical Education
(607) 753-4947

State University of New York College of Agriculture & Technology — A, U
Cobleskill, NY 12043
Recreation & Sports Area Management
Douglas Goodale, Chair
Dep't of Plant Science
(518) 234-5321

Sullivan County Community College — A
Loch Sheldrake, NY 12759
Sports Management
Michael McGuire
Dep't of Athletics
(914) 434-5750

NORTH CAROLINA

Appalachian State University — G
Boone, NC 28608
Sports Administration
Vaughn Christian, Chair
Dep't of Health, Leisure & Exercise Science
(704) 262-3140

Barton College — U
Wilson, NC 27893
Sport Management
Claudia L. Duncan, Chair
Dep't of Physical Education & Sports Studies
(919) 399-6521

Belmont Abbey College — U
Belmont, NC 28012
Sports Management
Michael Reidy, Chair
Dep't of Recreational Studies
(704) 825-6801

Campbell University — U
Buies Creek, NC 27506
Sport Management
William Freeman, Chair
Dep't of Exercise Science
(910) 893-1360

Chowan College — U
Murfreesboro, NC 27855
Sport Management
Scott H. Colclough, Chair
Dep't of Health & Physical Education
(919) 318-6243

Elon College — U
Elon College, NC 27244
Sports Management
Mike Calhoun, Chair
Dep't of Health Education, Physical Education & Leisure/Sports Management
(910) 584-2321

Guilford College — U
Greensboro, NC 27410
Sport Management
Peter Farmer
Dep't of Sports Studies
(910) 316-2329

Lenoir-Rhyne College — U
Hickory, NC 28603
Sports Management
Jane Jenkins
Dep't of Physical Education
(704) 328-1741

Mars Hill College — U
Mars Hill, NC 28754
Sport Management
Thomas E. Coates
Dep't of Health, Physical Education & Recreation
(704) 689-1368

Methodist College — U
Fayetteville, NC 28311
Sports Management
Wenda Johnson, Chair
Dep't of Physical Education
(910) 630-7183

North Carolina State University — G
Raleigh, NC 27695
Sport Management
Phillip S. Rea, Chair
Dep't of Parks, Recreation & Tourism Management
(919) 515-3276

Pfeiffer University — U
Misenheimer, NC 28109
Sports Management
Edgar J. Ingram Jr.
Dep't of Sports Medicine & Management
(704) 463-1360

St. Andrews Presbyterian University — U
Laurinburg, NC 28352
Sport Management
Shelby French, Chair
Jim Lankford, Div. Head
Dep't of Mathematics, Natural & Health Sciences
(800) 763-0198

University of North Carolina — G
Chapel Hill, NC 27599
Sport Administration
John Billing
Dep't of Physical Education, Exercise & Sport Science
(919) 962-0017

Western Carolina University — U
Cullowhee, NC 28723
Sport Management
Susan Brown
Dep't of Health, Physical Education & Recreation
(704) 227-7211

Winston-Salem State University — U
Winston-Salem, NC 27110
Sport Management
Dennis Felder
Div. of Education
(910) 750-2583

OHIO

Baldwin-Wallace College — U
Berea, OH 44017
Sport Management
June Baughman, Chair
Dep't of Health & Physical Education
(216) 826-2306

Bowling Green State University — U, G
Bowling Green, OH 43403
Undergraduate: Sport Management
Graduate: Sport Administration
Joy Sidwell, Chair
Div. of Sport Management
(419) 372-7232

Capital University — U
Columbus, OH 43209
Fitness Management
Russ Hoff, Chair
Dep't of Health & Sport Sciences
(614) 236-6911

Cleveland State University — U, G
Cleveland, OH 44115
Sports Management
Richard Hurwitz
Dep't of Health, Physical Education, Recreation & Dance
(216) 687-2000

Defiance College — U
Defiance, OH 43512
Sports Management
Marvin Hohenberger
Dep't of Physical Education
(419) 784-4010

Kent State University — G
Kent, OH 44242
Sports Administration
Aaron Mulrooney
School of Exercise, Leisure & Sport
(216) 672-2012

Miami University — G
Oxford, OH 45056
Sport Management
Robert S. Weinberg
Dep't of Physical Education, Health & Sports Studies
(513) 529-2700

Mount Union College — U
Alliance, OH 44601
Sports Management
James Thoma, Chair
Dep't of Health, Physical Education, Sports Medicine & Sport Management
(216) 823-4772

Ohio Northern University — U
Ada, OH 45810
Sport Management
Gayle Lauth, Chair
Dep't of Health, Physical Education & Sport Studies
(419) 772-2440

Ohio State University — G
Columbus, OH 43210
Sport Management
Donna Pastone
School of Health, Physical Education & Recreation
(614) 292-7701

Ohio University — G
Athens, OH 45701-2979
Sports Administration
Charles Higgins, Program Coordinator
School of Health & Sport Sciences
(614) 593-4666

Tiffin University — U
Tiffin, OH 44883
Sports Management
Debra Israel, Dean, Academic
   Affairs
Div. of Business Administration
(419) 447-6442

University of Dayton — U
Dayton, OH 45469
Sport Management
John Schlepp
Dep't of Health & Sport Science
(513) 229-4225

Xavier University — U, G
Cincinnati, OH 45207-6311
Undergraduate: Sport Management
C. Charlie Song, Coordinator
Graduate: Sports Administration
Ronald W. Quinn, Coordinator
Dep't of Health, Physical Education
   & Sports Studies
(513) 745-3653

OKLAHOMA

**Oklahoma State University
— G**
Stillwater, OK 74078
Sports Administration
Lowell Caneday, Program
   Coordinator
Dep't of Health, Physical Education
   & Leisure
(405) 744-5493

Phillips University — U
Enid, OK 73701
Sports Management
Steve Hula, Chair
Dep't of Exercise & Sport Science
(405) 237-4433

University of Oklahoma — G
Norman, OK 73019-0615
Sport Management
Trent E. Gabert, Graduate Liaison
Dep't of Health & Sport Sciences
(405) 325-5211

OREGON

University of Oregon — U, G
Eugene, OR 97403-1208
Sports Marketing
Michael J. Ritchey, Program
   Director
Warsaw Sports Marketing Center
Lundquist College of Business
(541) 346-3495

PENNSYLVANIA

**Allentown College of St.
   Francis de Sales — U**
Center Valley, PA 18034
Sports Administration
Joy M. Richman, Program Director
Dep't of Sports Administration
(610) 282-1100

**East Stroudsburg University
— U, G**
East Stroudsburg, PA 18301
Sports Management
Robert Fleischman
Dep't of Movement Studies &
   Exercise Science
(717) 422-3316

Gettysburg College — U
Gettysburg, PA 17325-1486
Sport Management
Gareth Biser, Chair
Dep't of Health & Exercise Sciences
(717) 337-6441

**Indiana University of
   Pennsylvania — G**
Indiana, PA 15705
Sports Management
James C. Mill, Chair
Dep't of Health & Physical
   Education
(412) 357-2770

La Roche College — U
Pittsburgh, PA 15237
Sports Management
Harry Strickland, Chair
Dep't of Administration &
   Management
(412) 367-9300

**Pennsylvania State University
— U**
University Park, PA 16802
Professional Golf Management
Frank B. Guadagnolo, Professor-in-
   Charge
School of Hotel, Restaurant &
   Recreation Management
(814) 865-1851

Robert Morris College — U, G
Coraopolis, PA 15108
Sport Management
Susan Hofacre, Chair
Dep't of Sport Administration
(412) 262-8416

**Slippery Rock University
— U, G**
Slippery Rock, PA 16057
Sport Management
Katrina T. Higgs, Chair
Dep't of Physical Education
(412) 738-2072

Temple University — U, G
Philadelphia, PA 19122
Sport Management
Ira Shapiro, Chair
Dep't of Sport Management &
   Leisure Studies
(215) 204-8706

West Chester University — G
West Chester, PA 19383
Athletic Administration
Richard Yoder, Head
Dep't of Physical Education
(215) 436-2145

RHODE ISLAND

**Johnson & Wales University
— U**
Providence, RI 02903
Sports/Facilities Management
Kristina Knowles
(401) 598-1000

**University of Rhode Island
— G**
Kingston, RI 02881
Sports Management
Dan Doyle, Executive Director
Institute for International Sports
(401) 874-4503

SOUTH CAROLINA

College of Charleston — U
Charleston, SC 29424
Sport Management
Andrew H. Lewis, Chair
Dep't of Physical Education &
   Health
(803) 953-5558

Newberry College — U
Newberry, SC 29108
Sports Management
Dennis Obermeyer, Chair
Dep't of Physical Education
(803) 777-4690

**University of South Carolina
— U**
Columbia, SC 29208
Sport Administration
Guy Lewis, Chair
Dep't of Sport Administration
(803) 777-4690

TENNESSEE

University of Memphis — U, G
Memphis, TN 38152
Undergraduate: Urban Sport Studies
Graduate: Sport & Leisure Commerce
Ralph Wilcox, Chair
Dep't of Human Movement
   Sciences & Education
(901) 678-4410

University of Tennessee — U, G
Knoxville, TN 37996
Undergraduate: Sport Management
Graduate: Sport Administration
Dennie R. Kelly
Sport & Physical Activity Unit
(423) 974-8171
Ken Krick
Dep't of Health, Leisure & Safety
   Sciences
(423) 974-6045

**University of Tennessee at
   Martin — U**
Martin, TN 38238
Sports Management
George White, Chair
Dep't of Physical Education &
   Health
(901) 587-7310

TEXAS

**Abilene Christian University
— U**
Abilene, TX 79699
Sports Management
Cleddy Varner, Chair
Dep't of Exercise Science & Health
(915) 674-2327

Baylor University — G
Waco, TX 76798
Sports Management
Robert C. Cloud, Chair
Dep't of Health, Human
   Performance & Recreation
(817) 755-3505

LeTourneau University — U
Longview, TX 75607-7001
Sports Management
Dannie J. Tindle, Chair
Div. of Business Administration
(903) 753-0231

Rice University — U
Houston, TX 77005-1892
Sports Management
Simon Dalant
Dep't of Human Performance &
   Health Science
(713) 527-4808

Southwest Texas State University — G
San Marcos, TX 78666
Sport Management
Bobby Patton
Dep't of Health, Physical Education & Recreation
(512) 245-2938

Texas A&M University — U
College Station, TX 77843
Sports Management
Robert Armstrong, Chair
Dep't of Health & Kinesiology
(409) 845-3109

Texas Tech University — G
Lubbock, TX 79409
Sports Administration
Elizabeth Hall, Chair
Dep't of Health, Physical Education & Recreation
(806) 742-3371

Texas Wesleyan University — U
Fort Worth, TX 76105
Sport Management
Rosie Stallman
Dep't of Physical Education, Exercise & Sports Studies
(817) 531-4210

Tyler Junior College   A
Tyler, TX 75711
Special program: Tennis Teaching
Paul N. Soliz, Program Director
(903) 510-2473

University of Houston — U, G
Houston, TX 77204-5331
Sport Administration
Dale Pease, Chair
Dep't of Health & Human Performance
(713) 743-9840

University of North Texas — G
Denton, TX 76203
Sport, Fitness & Organization Management
Jim Morrow, Chair
Dep't of Kinesiology, Health Promotion & Recreation
(817) 565-3431

University of Texas — U, G
Austin, TX 78712
Undergraduate: Sport Management
Graduate: Sports Administration
Dorothy Lovett, Chair
Dep't of Kinesiology & Health Education
(512) 471-1273

West Texas A&M University — U, G
Canyon, TX 79016-0001
Sport Science/Management
Charles Chase, Head
Dep't of Sports & Exercise Sciences
(806) 656-2370

Western Texas College — A
Snyder, TX 79549
Special program: Golf Course Technology
James Eby or Don Buckland, GCT Office
(915) 573-8511

VERMONT

Lyndon State College — U
Lyndonville, VT 05851
Sports Management
Martha Wood
Dep't of Physical Education
Special program: Ski Resort Management
Catherine DeLeo
Dep't of Recreation
(802) 626-9371

VIRGINIA

Averett College — U
Danville, VA 24541
Sport Management
Tommy Foster, Program Director
Dep't of Physical Education
(804) 791-5660

Hampton University — U
Hampton, VA 23668
Special program: Professional Tennis Management
Robert Screen, Program Director
Dep't of Marketing
(804) 727-5435

James Madison University — U
Harrisonburg, VA 22807
Sport Management
Michael S. Goldberger, Chair
Dep't of Kinesiology
(703) 568-6211

Liberty University — U
Lynchburg, VA 24506
Sport Administration
Dale Gibson
Dep't of Sport Administration Studies
(804) 582-2000

Old Dominion University — U, G
Norfolk, VA 23529
Sports Management
Patrick Tow, Chair
Dep't of Health, Physical Education & Recreation
(804) 683-3000

University of Richmond — G
Richmond, VA 23173
Sport Management
Norris W. Eastman, Chair
Dep't of Health & Sport Science
(804) 289-8350

Virginia Tech — G
Blacksburg, VA 24061
Sport Management
Ronald R. Bos, Chair
Div. of Health & Physical Education
(703) 231-8286

WASHINGTON

Central Washington University — U
Ellensburg, WA 98926
Fitness & Sport Management
Jan Boyungs, Program Director
Dep't of Physical Education, Health & Leisure Studies
(509) 963-1911

Seattle Pacific University
Seattle, WA 98119
Courses in Sport Management; not a degree program
Daniel Tripps
Dep't of Physical Education
(206) 281-2896

Washington State University — U
Pullman, WA 99164-2136
Sport Management
Joanne Washburn
Dep't of Educational Leadership & Counseling Psychology
(509) 335-6363

WEST VIRGINIA

Davis & Elkins College — U
Elkins, WV 26241
Sport Management
A. Jean Minnick, Chair
Dep't of Health & Sport & Movement Sciences
(304) 637-1390

Marshall University — U
Huntington, WV 25755
Sports Management
C. Robert Barnett
Div. of Health, Physical Education & Recreation
(304) 696-6490

Salem-Teikyo College — U
Salem, WV 26426-0500
Sport Management
Janet Lozar, Chair
Dep't of Physical Education
(304) 782-5278

Shepherd College — U
Shepherdstown, WV 25443
Sport Management
Bev Holden, Chair
Dep't of Health, Physical Education, Recreation & Sport
(304) 876-5481

West Virginia University — U, G
Morgantown, WV 26506
Sport Management
Dallas Branch Jr.
School of Physical Education
(304) 293-0111

WISCONSIN

University of Wisconsin at LaCrosse — U, G
LaCrosse, WI 54601
Undergraduate: Sports Management
Graduate: Sport Administration
Sandra Price, Chair
Dep't of Exercise & Sport Science
(608) 785-8000

University of Wisconsin at Whitewater — U
Whitewater, WI 53190
Sports Management
Brenda Clayton, Chair
Dep't of Health, Physical Education, Recreation & Coaching
(414) 472-1140

WYOMING

University of Wyoming
Laramie, WY 82071
Several courses in Sport Administration; not a degree program
Ward K. Gates
School of Physical & Health Education
(307) 766-5449

Everything you need to know about

INTERNSHIPS

An applicant for even the most modest of jobs in the sports industry inevitably runs into this question: Do you have any work experience in this industry?

An internship helps you clear that hurdle.

The internship is a temporary placement with a sports organization for the purpose of getting on-the-job training. Though you may work 40 hours a week, the job pays little or no money, usually the latter, but it gets you into the work world of sports and gives you the experience you need to get your career in motion. It also gives you an opportunity to make useful contacts.

What's more, if you make a good impression on your host organization (the people you are working for), there's a good chance you'll be invited to join its permanent staff at full salary. It happens often.

Who's eligible for an internship? Anybody. College students are the principal users of the internship system, and they have an advantage in getting many of the better appointments, but you do not need to be college-connected to apply for an internship. With a little effort, you can arrange for an internship independently. See "Doing It on Your Own," below.

The College Set-Up

Placing students in internships is an integral part of college programs in sports management, on both the undergraduate and the graduate level. It is, in fact, an activity of high priority, and there are now thousands of sports organizations that cooperate with colleges on a fairly regular basis as employers of interns.

The watchful eye. Internships are supervised by a faculty advisor who apprises students of the placements available to them, or investi-gates other possible placements to meet a student's particular interest. The advisor also maintains a liaison with host organizations (the employers) to make sure the objectives of the internship are understood and are being met. If it turns out—and it occasionally does—that a host organization is really interested in cheap labor and uses an intern to stuff envelopes day after day, the advisor will, of course, end the relationship with that host.

The range of placements. Because professional sports has a special lure for students, most sports management programs make a particular effort to recruit pro franchises as hosts. The program at Bowling Green State University, for example, has placed interns with the Washington Capitals, Los Angeles Kings, Cleveland Cavaliers, Detroit Lions, Pittsburgh Penguins, Texas Rangers, and a dozen other big league and minor league clubs. But interns are also placed in all other areas of the sports industry, including facility management, television operations, sports resorts, and the sports marketing business.

Academic credit. Undergraduates and graduate students receive academic credits on completion of an internship. The number of credits varies from campus to campus. The general range is from 8 to 12 credits.

Length of internships. There are variations here too. The period of an internship can be as short as three months, or as long as a year. In some cases, the length is dictated by the host organization; more often, it's based on what's best or most convenient for both the student and the host.

Graduate students generally enter internships after their classroom courses are completed. Undergraduates usually do their internships before beginning their senior year, often during the summer.

Grading. An internship is regarded as a course and hence is graded. At some campuses, grading is on a pass/fail basis; at others, regular grades are given based on an evaluation by the student's host organization and, usually, a report submitted by the student.

Doing It on Your Own

There's nothing in the Constitution that says you can't scout for an internship spot on your own, without a college connection. But you may run into some roadblocks. Here's the picture: many sports organizations, especially the big ones, are more comfortable dealing with applicants who are sponsored by a college and tend to discourage independent applicants. At Turner Broadcasting, for example, the internship coordinator will tell you up front that "our internships are available *only* to college juniors, seniors, and graduate students." To press the point, she requires a letter from a faculty advisor, plus a college transcript. Some of the large organizations are less rigid, but your best targets are smaller operations (local radio stations, minor league clubs, sports marketing firms with small staffs, etc.), where your enthusiasm—and willingness to work for no pay—will get you a warmer reception. And who's to say you won't be better off in a small organization?

In the chapters ahead you'll find listings of all kinds of sports operations that offer opportunities for internships. Select the ones that interest you—presumably they'll be organizations within commuting distance—and get on the phone. Ask for the person who handles requests for internships (you may have that person's name already, from the listing). Make it clear you're eager to get into the sports industry, you're willing to work for no pay for three months or whatever it takes to

get some experience under your belt, and you're willing to do any kind of work, however lowly it may be.

A tip: A number of organizations in our listings are not identified as having interns. In many cases, it's because nobody has asked them for an internship. So don't pass them by; they may be happy to hear from you.

Compensation. Many host organizations have a flat no-pay policy. Their rationale: (1) they're giving students a valuable opportunity to learn the business, and (2) they're permitting their regular employees to take time from their work to provide training.

Interns who have the best chance of earning some money are those who sign on with large organizations (major league clubs, big sports marketing firms, broadcasting networks, etc.). The stipend may run from $600 to $1,000 or more a month, with the amount determined by the work assigned.

Small organizations occasionally offer stipends too, though the amounts may barely cover lunch and carfare. But it's the thought that counts.

Incidentally, a number of companies that have employee cafeterias offer free lunches as compensation. How do you feel about meatloaf?

A student who has an exciting internship opportunity that happens to be a long way from home faces the expense of transportation and lodging. Some hosts will pick up part of the costs, but it's rare.

Hosts: Big vs. small. There are advantages to both. An intern who joins a small sports marketing firm that specializes, for example, in handling professional tennis tournaments is often thrust into a cauldron of activity and gains immediate and valuable hands-on experience in special-event management. The training provided by large organizations is not likely to be so intense, but it usually gives the intern exposure to a wide array of operations and a better idea of career options.

HOW IMPORTANT IS AN INTERNSHIP?

"It's critical!!! In fact, it's all but impossible to get any job in sports without it. This is particularly true in intercollegiate and professional sports, but it's also true in all other sectors. To be competitive in the job market, you need all the experience and contacts you can get. The internship helps you get the experience and contacts."

—*Prof. Phillip S. Rea, North Carolina State University*

CHAPTER TWO

THE PROFESSIONAL LEAGUES

BASEBALL

BASKETBALL

FOOTBALL

HOCKEY

SOCCER

THEY GET LETTERS

The volume of letters that job seekers send to the professional leagues and their franchises each year far exceeds the number of jobs that actually exist.

In the words of one league official: "The reality is that there just aren't many job openings. If we do have an opening, we look for someone with related experience. Love of the game isn't enough to get you a job. Neither is a Harvard degree if it's not accompanied by experience. If you're just getting started in this business, try the minor leagues. Get experience."

*   *   *   *

Prospects are brighter when it comes to internships. League offices in all pro sports and on all levels hire interns. So do the individual clubs in those leagues.

*The best route to a job in the majors
is the one the players take—via the minors.
The next best: relying on a stroke of luck.*

BASEBALL

Sometimes, said Patrick Courtney, manager of public relations at Major League Baseball headquarters, it takes more than one internship to get started on a career in sports.

"I had two stints as an intern," he said. "I was an intern with the Philadelphia 76ers in the ticket department, and then became an intern for the New York Yankees in the media relations department. After a year with the Yankees, I was hired full-time as a staff researcher in the public relations department of the Commissioner's Office at Major League Baseball. And I've moved up to be the spokesperson and manager of public relations."

"An internship," he said, "is now very much a part of the scene—a very common way to start a career in baseball, both on the club level and within the central office."

Citing his own experience, Courtney said he found that an internship "gives you the opportunity to develop relationships with people in the business while gaining the experience that can help you secure a full-time position."

Luck, he said, can be an important factor too.

Luck describes how Phyllis Merhige found her way into baseball. Merhige was working as a secretary at the Singer Sewing Machine Company in New York. When the company announced it was moving to New Jersey, she decided not to go along. She sent a resume to the commissioner's office. Eight months later, she got a call. The American League was relocating too, moving from Boston to New York. Her resume had caught someone's eye and if she was still interested, a job was available.

"They said they rarely got resumes from secretaries and they were impressed by mine," she says. "I was just very lucky."

Merhige is now vice president for administration and media affairs for the American League and one of the highest-ranking women in baseball.

Katy Feeney is another MLB executive who started as a secretary. But it wasn't luck that got her that first job, it was whom she knew. Her father for many years was president of the National League. It was her talent, however, that moved her up the ladder. Feeney today is the highly regarded senior vice president of the National League.

Courtney, Merhige, and Feeney all work in Major League Baseball's headquarters at 350 Park Avenue, a large office building in Manhattan's high-rent district, but each is in a separate sphere of operations. Courtney is employed by the Office of the Commissioner, the top sphere; Merhige, as mentioned, works for the American League, and Feeney for the

National League. They occasionally run into each other in the elevator.

Courtney's precinct, the 17th-floor Office of the Commissioner, is more than a place where the commissioner hangs his hat. Occupying offices here are the chief financial officer, the controller, the general counsel, and departmental directors with responsibility for broadcasting, market development, security and facility management, public relations, baseball operations, government relations, special events, and minor league relations.

Also located here is Gregory B. Murphy, who in the summer of '96 took over as chief executive of the newly created Major League Baseball Enterprises, with the objective of finally bringing to baseball a coherent marketing plan. For years Major League Baseball has lagged far behind the National Football League and National Basketball Association in bestirring the kind of fan devotion that sells merchandise. The seven-month players' strike that began on August 12, 1994, made matters worse, producing a hostility you could cut with an axe. In 1995 the $1.6 billion in retail sales of licensed baseball goods was only half of what the NFL and NBA sold. What's more, attendance at games fell off and TV audiences declined, as did corporate sponsorships.

The job of MLB Enterprises is to regain for baseball its identity as America's favorite pastime through aggressive licensing, marketing, and publishing activities. For this purpose it has assembled a large staff of licensing managers, account supervisors, and administrative assistants, all engaged in the business of marketing the logos of MLB's 28—soon to be 30—clubs. In the past, when the division was known as MLB Properties, it put team logos on about 4,000 products, ranging from mugs to video games, and including, of course, apparel and accessories.

Gregory Murphy, a former General Foods Corp. executive, is expected to give Major League Baseball a strong marketing arm. A graduate of the Naval Academy, Murphy rose through the ranks of General Foods, becoming chief executive of the Kraft Bakeries Companies, where he made a big reputation with his successful development of fat-free cakes and cookies. Next, team logos.

Three blocks away, at 1301 Avenue of the Americas, is still another unit under the Office of the Commissioner. This one is called Major League Baseball International, and its functions are to promote baseball abroad, supervise the televising of games internationally, and organize foreign tours for players and teams. It, too, employs a large corps of managers and assistants.

In the offices of the American League and National League, the number of people employed takes a sharp drop. The roster of executives in each league consists mainly of the league president and directors of administration, media relations, finance, player records, and umpires. In addition, each league has a cadre of administrative assistants and is host to several interns.

Front-Office Jobs in the Bigs

If you're planning to have a shot at a job with one of the 28 franchises in the majors, it would probably be helpful if you mentioned your interest in a specific job or a particular department.

The following job areas pretty much apply to all clubs:

Administration. General counsel (that's a lawyer, of course), government affairs, broadcast coordinator, coordinator of special events, human resources (personnel), administrative assistant.

Accounting and finance. Controller, accounting manager, payroll/benefits administrator, accounts payable, assistant payroll administrator.

Baseball operations. Director of player development, director of scouting, director of minor league operations, director of travel, director of spring training operations, assistant to the general manager.

Stadium operations. Director of overall operations, director of event personnel, security manager, dining room manager, manager of home team clubhouse, manager of visiting team clubhouse.

Public relations. Director of media relations, director of publications, director of community services, director of communications, editor of publications, graphic artist, staff photographer.

Marketing and promotions. Director of marketing, promotions manager, advertising assistant.

Ticket sales. Director of ticket operations, director of ticket sales, telemarketing manager, customer service coordinator, luxury suites manager, group ticket coordinator.

Retailing. Director of retail operations, merchandise manager.

Broadcast production services. Director of productions, associate producer, editor.

Game broadcasts. Five announcers.

Up Through the Minors

There's no question about it: you need luck or personal contacts to move directly into the big leagues. If the fates deny you those privileges, you can do what the ballplayers do—you can try working your way up through the minors.

It's much easier to get an internship in the minor leagues, simply because there are so many clubs in the minors (see our listing). In fact, there's a good chance of getting an internship near your home. And—please note—you do not need a college connection to get it. Minor league clubs are inconsistent on that score. Some clubs require college auspices; some don't care and don't ask. And another thing: internships are open to both men and women (unless there's a Neanderthal in charge). Minor league experience can be valuable, even if you start with a bottom-rung Class A team. You'll be involved in every aspect of baseball operations—including after-

game cleanup—and if you give it your best, there's a good chance you'll be noticed by talent scouts higher up.

Jim Kelch, who is director of broadcasting for the Louisville Redbirds in the Triple-A American Association, came up by way of Peoria (Class A) and Chattanooga (Class AA).

"When I was doing play-by-play at Chattanooga, if we had a rain delay I'd throw the broadcast back to the station and go down on the field and help the grounds crew with the tarp," he says.

That's what minor league baseball can be like.

"I tell people interested in working in baseball it's mostly sales and marketing," Kelch says. "If they think they're going to spend their days figuring batting averages and earned run averages, they'll be disappointed. If they think they'd enjoy sales and marketing, there are opportunities. They'll be in a baseball setting, which is great for people who love the game, but they have to realize that 90 percent of the work is not involved directly with the team."

Kelch's club, Louisville, has 15 regular employees and hires three or four interns each year. Its sales manager and director of stadium operations both came there as interns.

Leanne Pagliai, general manager of the High Desert Mavericks in the Class A California League, operates the Mavericks with a staff of eight, plus interns. On this level, everybody has to be willing to do anything and everything, she says. A person might work in tickets one day, concessions the next, and media relations the day after that. For those who have a strong work ethic, she says, baseball offers many opportunities. For men *and* women. The old boys' network is a thing of the past, she says.

Pagliai, who is a general partner in the Mavericks as well as general manager, has been in baseball since 1986, when at the age of 28 she chucked a sales job at IBM and joined the Midland Angels in the Class AA

Texas League as sales manager. A sales background, she advises, gives a job applicant a big advantage, because the heart of the business is "ticket sales, promotions, and advertising."

At many of the minor league clubs, interns are paid. At some, they are not. The general range of pay is $500 to $700 a month. Regular employees make between $1,000 and $1,500 a month.

General managers usually make their selections of interns during the off-season. Incidentally, candidates gain an advantage if they can speak Spanish in addition to English.

Random Profiles

Ed Wade, assistant to the general manager, Philadelphia Phillies . . . Born in Carbondale, Pennsylvania, 1956 . . . Majored in journalism at Temple University . . . Began in baseball as an intern in Phillies' public relations department in 1977 . . . Appointed public relations assistant, Houston Astros, later that year . . . Became Astros' PR director in 1977 and moved to Pittsburgh Pirates as PR director in 1981 . . . Joined Tal Smith Enterprises, a base-

ball consulting company, in 1986 . . . Named assistant to the general manager, Philadelphia Phillies, in 1989 . . . Helps GM Lee Thomas with front-office details, handles waiver wire claims, negotiates contracts.

Ted Haracz, vice president/marketing, Houston Astros . . . Born in Chicago, 1942 . . . Majored in journalism, College of St. Thomas, in St. Paul . . . Spent 10 years in college sports information at the University of Illinois-Chicago, Notre Dame, and Purdue . . . Was director of public relations for NFL Chicago Bears for seven years and director of communications for the Ladies Professional Golf Association . . . Became vp, marketing, for the Astros in 1986 . . . Develops yearly marketing strategy and supervises broadcasting, communications, group and season sales, community services, advertising sales, and promotions. Member of the National League Schedule Committee and the Major League Corporate Marketing Advisory Committee.

John C. Blake, vice president for public relations, Texas Rangers . . . Born in Augusta, Maine, 1955 . . . Studied international politics at Georgetown University . . . Was sports information director at Georgetown from 1977 to 1979 . . . Assistant public relations director, Baltimore Orioles, 1979–84 . . . Director of media relations, Texas Rangers, 1984 . . . Appointed vp, public relations, in 1990 . . . Oversees all areas of media relations and community relations, player appearances, Rangers publications. Deals with the press daily.

Tom Cheek, play-by-play broadcaster, Toronto Blue Jays . . . Born 1940 in Pensacola, Florida . . . Attended Cambridge School of Broadcasting . . . Began radio career in Plattsburg, New York . . . Spent nine years as sales manager and sports director at three radio stations in Burlington and Rutland, both in Vermont . . . Did baseball, basketball, and hockey play-by-play for the University of Vermont . . . Worked on Montreal Expos broadcasts, 1974–76 . . . Broadcast college basketball for Mutual Radio Network . . .

HOW THEY GOT THERE

RANDY SMITH
GENERAL MANAGER, DETROIT TIGERS

It's a short story. Randy Smith got his first job in baseball early in 1984 as an administrative assistant with Beaumont of the Texas League, a farm club of the San Diego Padres. That September, when it looked as if the Padres would be making it to the National League playoffs, Smith was asked to join the Padres front-office staff to help with preparations for postseason play. A few months later, the Padres appointed him assistant director of scouting. After three years, he became director of scouting. In September 1991 the expansion Colorado  Rockies appointed him assistant general manager. In June 1993, at the age of 29, he returned to the Padres as vice president and general manager, the youngest GM in major league history. In 1995 he was named general manager of the Detroit Tigers.

Worked for ABC at 1980 Winter Olympics in Lake Placid and 1984 Winter Olympics in Sarajevo . . . Hired by the Blue Jays in 1977, their first season in MLB.

Baseball Promotions

In the minors, where baseball stadiums are close to their markets and small enough to permit a comfortable and congenial atmosphere, every home game is an occasion for a family night out. The fun is not only rooting for the home team but chatting with favorite players and enjoying the special entertainments that accompany the games—like old-time vaudeville acts, equestrian exhibitions, baton-twirling contests, polka concerts, and whatever else the club management can think up. Promotions like these are the lifeblood of baseball in the minors. For club interns, who participate in arranging the events, it's a lab course in marketing.

The atmosphere is different, of course, in the major leagues, where there has been a tendency to take for granted the public's undying devotion to the game. But the clubs are beginning to show interest in developing marketing strategies that go beyond fireworks displays, Old-Timers games, and giveaways. There may be opportunities for creative marketers here.

How to Be an Owner

Financial tip: If you have the wherewithal, investing in a minor league club would be a smart move because the minors are making money. (No multimillion-dollar salaries here for .240 hitters.) There are several publicly owned clubs you can buy a piece of. But don't be surprised if you find you have company. For example, the Rochester Red Wings in the Triple-A International League have 8,000 owners—Red Wings fans who bought into the team in 1956 for $10 a share.

Also publicly owned: the Batavia Clippers in the Single-A New York–Penn League and the Indianapolis Indians and Syracuse Chiefs in the International League.

The Chiefs have only 3,854 stockholders. Each season they get 10 free tickets to ball games and an invitation to "Shareholders' Night," a chance to mingle with the players before a game.

On second thought, maybe investing in a minor league club ought to be left to local fans.

A Good Calling: Umpiring

Under the terms of their 1995 deal, big league umpires get a base pay that ranges from $75,000 in their first year to $225,000 in their thirtieth year. Then come the extras. Working the All-Star Game, for example, is good for $5,000; in postseason, the new division series pays $12,500, the league championship series is worth $15,000, and the reward for calling the World Series is $17,500.

Interested?

You begin by applying to baseball's Umpire Development Program. To qualify for umpire training, you'll need a high school education, quick reflexes, good communication skills—and good eyesight.

But it's a long way to the majors. The training process begins with a five-week program at one of three independently operated umpire training schools. The top graduates of this program then undergo further testing by the Umpire Development Program's Evaluation Committee. Individuals who pass this scrutiny begin their careers with a job in a Class A minor league and are carefully monitored. Success in the job means moving up to Class AA, then Class AAA. It generally takes seven or eight years in the minors before an umpire is considered ready for the major leagues. Pay in the minors starts at $1,700 a month and rises to $3,100 a month in a Triple-A league.

The address of the Office for Umpire Development is P.O. Box A, 201 Bayshore Dr. SE, St. Petersburg, FL 33731. Phone: (813) 823-1286.

NATIONAL BASEBALL HALL OF FAME

Cooperstown, New York

Established in 1939, first of sports halls of fame. *Annual visitors:* 326,000. *Employees:* 75 full-time, another 75 added for peak season; several interns, paid and unpaid, engaged during the year. *Human resources director:* Patti Gulotta. *Address:* P.O. Box 590, Cooperstown, NY 13326. *Phone:* (607) 547-7200.

PROFESSIONAL BASEBALL LEAGUES

THE MAJOR LEAGUES

Office of the Commissioner
350 Park Ave., 17th Floor
New York, NY 10022
(212) 339-7800
Chairman, Executive Council: Allan
  H. "Bud" Selig
Occasional internships offered

AMERICAN LEAGUE

League office:
350 Park Ave., 18th Floor
New York, NY 10022
(212) 339-7600
League President: Gene Budig

Baltimore Orioles
333 W. Camden St.
Baltimore, MD 21201
(410) 685-9800
Gen Mgr: Pat Gillick
Ass't Gen Mgr: Kevin Malone
Internships: contact Martina Wylie
  Clinton

Boston Red Sox
Fenway Park
4 Yawkey Way
Boston, MA 02215
(617) 267-9440
Gen Mgr: Dan Duquette
Ass't Gen Mgrs: Mike Port, Elaine W.
  Steward
Internships: contact Debbie McIntyre

California Angels
Anaheim Stadium
2000 Gene Autry Way
Anaheim, CA 92806
(714) 937-7200
Gen Mgr: Bill Bavasi
Ass't Gen Mgr: Tim Mead
Internships: write to Disney Sport
  Enterprises, Human Resources Dep't
  DSE-MGT, 500 S. Buenavista St.
  Burbank, CA 91505

Chicago White Sox
333 W. 35th St.
Chicago, IL 60616
(312) 924-1000
Dir Baseball Opns: Dan Evans
Internships: contact Human Resources

Cleveland Indians
2401 Ontario St.
Cleveland, OH 44115
(216) 420-4200
Gen Mgr: John Hart
Ass't Gen Mgr: Dan O'Dowd
Internships: contact Gregg Olson

Detroit Tigers
Tiger Stadium
2121 Trumbull Ave.
Detroit, MI 48216
(313) 962-4000
Gen Mgr: Randy Smith
Ass't Gen Mgr: Steve Lubratich
Internships: contact David Glazier

Kansas City Royals
One Royal Way
Kansas City, MO 64129
(816) 921-2200
Gen Mgr: Herk Robinson
Ass't Gen Mgr: Jay Hinrichs
Internships: contact Lauris Hawthorne

Milwaukee Brewers
Milwaukee County Stadium
Milwaukee, WI 53214
(414) 933-4114
Sr. VP Baseball Opns: Sal Bando
Internships: contact Jon Greenberg

Minnesota Twins
501 Chicago Ave. S
Minneapolis, MN 55415
(612) 375-1366
Gen Mgr: Terry Ryan
Ass't Gen Mgr: Bill Smith
Internships: contact Human Resources

New York Yankees
Yankee Stadium
Bronx, NY 10451
(718) 293-4300
Gen Mgr: Bob Watson
Ass't Gen Mgr: Brian Cashman
Internships: contact Media Relations

Oakland Athletics
Oakland-Alameda County Coliseum
Oakland, CA 94621
(510) 638-4900
Gen Mgr: Sandy Alderson
Ass't Gen Mgr: Billy Beane
Internships: contact Ann Vargas

Seattle Mariners
83 S. King St.
Seattle, WA 98104
(206) 628-3555
VP Baseball Opns: Woody
  Woodward
Ass't to VP Baseball Opns:
  George Zuraw
Internships: contact Shirley Shreve

Texas Rangers
1000 Ballpark Way
Arlington, TX 76011
(817) 273-5222
Gen Mgr: Doug Melvin
Ass't Gen Mgr: Lee MacPhail
Internships: contact Kim Smith

Toronto Blue Jays
SkyDome
One Blue Jays Way, Suite 3200
Toronto, Ontario M5V 1J1, Canada
(416) 341-1000
Gen Mgr: Gordon Ash
Internships: contact Howard Starkman

NATIONAL LEAGUE

League office:
350 Park Ave., 18th Floor
New York, NY 10022
(212) 339-7700
League President: Leonard Coleman

Atlanta Braves
521 Capitol Ave. SW
Atlanta, GA 30312
(404) 522-7630
Gen Mgr: John Schuerholz
Ass't Gen Mgr: Dean Taylor
Internships: contact Lisa Stricklind

Chicago Cubs
Wrigley Field
1060 W. Addison St.
Chicago, IL 60613
(312) 404-2827
Gen Mgr: Ed Lynch
Internships: contact Deserae Brazelton

Cincinnati Reds
100 Riverfront Stadium
Cincinnati, OH 45202
(513) 421-4510
Gen Mgr: Jim Bowden
Internships: contact Brad Kullman

Colorado Rockies
2001 Blake St.
Denver, CO 80205
(303) 292-0200
Gen Mgr: Bob Gebhard
Internships: contact Mike Swanson,
  Liz Stecklein

Florida Marlins
2267 N.W. 199th St.
Miami, FL 33056
(305) 626-7400
Gen Mgr: David Dombrowski
Ass't Gen Mgr: Frank Wren
Internships: contact Jonathan Mariner

Houston Astros
8400 Kirby Dr.
Houston, TX 77054
(713) 799-9500
Gen Mgr: Gerry Hunsicker
Internships: write to Trey Wilkinson,
  Astros, P.O. Box 288, 77001-0288

Los Angeles Dodgers
1000 Elysian Park Ave.
Los Angeles, CA 90012
(213) 224-1500
Exec VP: Fred Claire
Admin Baseball Opns:
  Robert Schweppe
Internships: contact Irene Tanjy

Montreal Expos
4549 Pierre-de-Coubertin Ave.
Montreal, Quebec H1V 3N7, Canada
(514) 253-3434
Gen Mgr: Jim Beattie
VP Baseball Opns: Bill Stoneman
Internships: contact Human Resources

New York Mets
Shea Stadium
126th St. and Roosevelt Ave.
Flushing, NY 11368
(718) 507-6387
Exec VP Baseball Opns: Joe
  McIlvaine
Ass't VP Baseball Opns: Steve
  Phillips
Internships: contact Russ Richardson

Philadelphia Phillies
Veterans Stadium
Broad St. and Pattison Ave.
Philadelphia, PA 19148
(215) 463-6000
Gen Mgr: Lee Thomas
Ass't to the Gen Mgr: Ed Wade
Internships: contact David
  Montgomery

Pittsburgh Pirates
600 Stadium Circle
Pittsburgh, PA 15212
(412) 323-5000
Gen Mgr: Cam Bonifay
Dir of Baseball Operations: John
  Sirignano
Internships: contact Linda Zwergel

St. Louis Cardinals
250 Stadium Plaza
St. Louis, MO 63102
(314) 421-3060
Gen Mgr: Walt Jocketty
Admin Ass't: Judy Carpenter-Barada
Internships: contact Human Resources

San Diego Padres
Jack Murphy Stadium
9449 Friars Rd.
San Diego, CA 92108
(619) 283-4494
Gen Mgr: Randy Smith
Ass't Gen Mgr: Reggie Waller
Internships: contact Lucy Freeman

San Francisco Giants
Candlestick Park
San Francisco, CA 94124
(415) 468-3700
Gen Mgr: Bob Quinn
Ass't Gen Mgr: Brian Sabean
Internships: contact Joyce Thomas

The expansion teams:
The Arizona Diamondbacks and
Tampa Bay Devil Rays will join
Major League Baseball in 1998. Phone
numbers: for the Diamondbacks,
(602) 514-8500; for the Devil Rays,
(813) 825-3137.

THE MINOR
LEAGUES

AMERICAN ASSOCIATION

CLASS AAA

League office:
6801 Miami Ave., Suite 3
Cincinnati, OH 45243
(513) 271-4800
League President: Branch B. Rickey
Internships: contact Jennifer Garula

Buffalo Bisons
P.O. Box 450
Buffalo, NY 14205
(716) 846-2000
Gen Mgr: Mike Buczkowski
Stadium: North AmeriCare Park
  (20,900)
Affiliation: Cleveland Indians

Indianapolis Indians
501 W. Maryland St.
Indianapolis, IN 46225
(317) 269-3545
Pres/Gen Mgr: Max Schumacher
Stadium: Victory Field (15,500)
Affiliation: Cincinnati Reds

Iowa Cubs
350 S.W. First St.
Des Moines, IA 50309
(515) 243-6111
Gen Mgr: Sam Bernabe
Stadium: Sec Taylor (11,000)
Affiliation: Chicago Cubs

Louisville Redbirds
P.O. Box 36407
Louisville, KY 40233
(502) 367-9121
Gen Mgr: Dale Owens
Stadium: Cardinal (33,500)
Affiliation: St. Louis Cardinals

Nashville Sounds
P.O. Box 23290
Nashville, TN 37202
(615) 242-4371
Pres/Gen Mgr: Larry Schmittou
  (principal owner)
Stadium: Herschel Greer (17,000)
Affiliation: Chicago White Sox

New Orleans Zephyrs
P.O. Box 24672
New Orleans, LA 70184
(504) 282-6777
Gen Mgr: Jay Miller
Stadium: Privateer Park (4,700)
Affiliation: Milwaukee Brewers

Oklahoma City 89ers
P.O. Box 75089
Oklahoma City, OK 73147
(405) 946-8989
Pres: Clayton Bennett
Stadium: All-Sports (12,000)
Affiliation: Texas Rangers

Omaha Royals
P.O. Box 3665
Omaha, NE 68103
(402) 734-2550
Gen Mgr: Bill Gorman
Stadium: Johnny Rosenblatt (22,000)
Affiliation: Kansas City Royals

INTERNATIONAL LEAGUE

CLASS AAA

League office:
55 S. High St., Suite 202
Dublin, OH 43017
(614) 791-9300
League President: Randy Mobley
Internships: contact Randy Mobley

Charlotte Knights
P.O. Box 1207
Fort Mill, SC 29716
(803) 548-8050
Gen Mgr: Pete Moore
Stadium: Knights Castle (10,000)
Affiliation: Florida Marlins

Columbus Clippers
1155 W. Mound St.
Columbus, OH 43223
(614) 462-5250
Gen Mgr: Ken Schnacke
Stadium: Cooper (15,000)
Affiliation: New York Yankees

Norfolk Tides
150 Park Ave.
Norfolk, VA 23510
(804) 622-2222
Gen Mgr: Dave Rosenfield
Stadium: Harbor Park (12,067)
Affiliation: New York Mets

Ottawa Lynx
300 Coventry Rd
Ottawa, Ontario K1K 4P5, Canada
(613) 747-5969
Dir Baseball Opns: Joe Bohringer
Stadium: Ottawa (10,332)
Affiliation: Montreal Expos

Pawtucket Red Sox
P.O. Box 2365
Pawtucket, RI 02860
(401) 724-7300
Gen Mgr: Lou Schwechheimer
Stadium: McCoy (7,002)
Affiliation: Boston Red Sox

Richmond Braves
P.O. Box 6667
Richmond, VA 23230
(804) 359-4444
Gen Mgr: Bruce Baldwin
Stadium: The Diamond (12,500)
Affiliation: Atlanta Braves

Rochester Red Wings
333 N. Plymouth Ave.
Rochester, NY 14608
(716) 262-2009
Gen Mgr: Dan Mason
Stadium: Frontier Field (11,000)
Affiliation: Baltimore Orioles

**Scranton/Wilkes-Barre
  Red Barons**
P.O. Box 3449
Scranton, PA 18505
(717) 969-2255
Gen Mgr: Bill Terlecky
Stadium: Lackawanna County
  (10,400)
Affiliation: Philadelphia Phillies

Syracuse Chiefs
MacArthur Stadium
Syracuse, NY 13208
(315) 474-7833
Gen Mgr: Anthony Simone
Stadium: MacArthur (8,416)
Affiliation: Toronto Blue Jays

Toledo Mud Hens
2901 Key St.
Maumee, OH 43537
(419) 893-9483
Gen Mgr: Gene Cook
Stadium: Ned Skeldon (10,197)
Affiliation: Detroit Tigers

PACIFIC COAST LEAGUE

CLASS AAA

League office:
2345 S. Alma School Rd., Suite 110
Mesa, AZ 85210
(602) 838-2171
League President: Bill Cutler

Albuquerque Dukes
1601 Stadium Blvd. SE
Albuquerque, NM 87106
(505) 243-1791
Pres/Gen Mgr: Pat McKernan
Stadium: Albuquerque Sports (10,510)
Affiliation: Los Angeles Dodgers

Calgary Cannons
P.O. Box 3690, Station B
Calgary, Alberta T2M 4M4, Canada
(403) 284-1111
Gen Mgr: Tom Valcke
Stadium: Burns (7,500)
Affiliation: Pittsburgh Pirates

Colorado Springs Sky Sox
4385 Tutt Blvd.
Colorado Springs, CO 80922
(719) 597-1449
Pres/Gen Mgr: Bob Goughan
Stadium: Sky Sox (7,500)
Affiliation: Colorado Rockies

Edmonton Trappers
10233 96th Ave.
Edmonton, Alberta T5K 0A5, Canada
(403) 429-2934
Pres/Gen Mgr: Mel Kowalchuk
Stadium: Telus Field (9,200)
Affiliation: Oakland Athletics

Las Vegas Stars
850 Las Vegas Blvd. N
Las Vegas, NV 89101
(702) 386-7200
Gen Mgr: Don Logan
Stadium: Cashman Field (9,334)
Affiliation: San Diego Padres

Phoenix Firebirds
P.O. Box 8528
Scottsdale, AZ 85252
(602) 275-0500
Gen Mgr: Craig Pletenik
Stadium: Scottsdale (10,000)
Affiliation: San Francisco Giants

Salt Lake Buzz
P.O. Box 4108
Salt Lake City, UT 84110
(801) 485-3800
Owner/Gen Mgr: Joe Buzas
Stadium: Franklin-Quest Field
  (15,500)
Affiliation: Minnesota Twins

Tacoma Rainiers
P.O. Box 11087
Tacoma, WA 98411
(206) 752-7707
Owner/Pres: George Foster
Stadium: Cheney (10,000)
Affiliation: Seattle Mariners

Tucson Toros
P.O. Box 27045
Tucson, AZ 85726
(602) 325-2621
Gen Mgr: Mike Feder
Stadium: Hi Corbett Field (8,000)
Affiliation: Houston Astros

Vancouver Canadians
4601 Ontario St.
Vancouver, British Columbia V5V
3H4, Canada
(604) 872-5232
Gen Mgr: Brent Imlach
Stadium: Nat Bailey (6,500)
Affiliation: California Angels

EASTERN LEAGUE

CLASS AA

League office:
P.O. Box 60687
Harrisburg, PA 17106
(717) 233-4909
League President: John Levenda

Albany-Colonie Diamond Dogs
Heritage Park
Watervliet-Shaker Rd.
Albany, NY 12211
(518) 869-9234
Gen Mgr: Rip Rowan
Stadium: Heritage Park (6,000)
Affiliation: Independent
   Northeastern League

Binghamton Mets
P.O. Box 598
Binghamton, NY 13902
(607) 723-6387
Gen Mgr: R. C. Reuteman
Stadium: Binghamton Municipal
   (6,012)
Affiliation: New York Mets

Bowie Baysox
P.O. Box 1661
Bowie, MD 20717
(301) 805-6000
Gen Mgr: Jon Danos
Stadium: Prince George's (10,000)
Affiliation: Baltimore Orioles

Canton-Akron Indians
2501 Allen Ave. SE
Canton, OH 44707
(216) 456-5100
Gen Mgr: Jeff Auman
Stadium: Thurman Munson Memorial
   (5,700)
Affiliation: Cleveland Indians

Hardware City Rock Cats
P.O. Box 1718
New Britain, CT 06050
(203) 224-8383
Gen Mgr: Gerry Berthiaume
Stadium: New Britain (6,135)
Affiliation: Minnesota Twins

Harrisburg Senators
P.O. Box 15757
Harrisburg, PA 17105
(717) 231-4444
Gen Mgr: Todd Vander Woude
Stadium: RiverSide (6,300)
Affiliation: Montreal Expos

New Haven Ravens
63 Grove St.
New Haven, CT 06510
(203) 782-1666
Gen Mgr: Charles Dowd
Stadium: Yale Field (6,200)
Affiliation: Colorado Rockies

Portland Sea Dogs
P.O. Box 636
Portland, ME 04104
(207) 874-9300
Pres/Gen Mgr: Charles Eshbach
Stadium: Hadlock Field (6,500)
Affiliation: Florida Marlins

Reading Phillies
P.O. Box 15050
Reading, PA 19612
(610) 375-8469
Gen Mgr: Chuck Domino
Stadium: Municipal Memorial (8,000)
Affiliation: Philadelphia Phillies

Trenton Thunder
1 Thunder Rd.
Trenton, NJ 08611
(609) 394-8326
Gen Mgr: Wayne Hodes
Stadium: Mercer County Waterfront
   Park (6,500)
Affiliation: Boston Red Sox

SOUTHERN LEAGUE

CLASS AA

League office:
One Depot St., Suite 300
Marietta, GA 30060
(770) 428-4769
League President: Arnold Fielkow

Birmingham Barons
P.O. Box 360007
Birmingham, AL 35236
(205) 988-3200
Pres/Gen Mgr: Bill Hardekopf
Stadium: Hoover Metropolitan
   (10,800)
Affiliation: Chicago White Sox

Carolina Mudcats
P.O. Drawer 1218
Zebulon, NC 27597
(919) 269-2287
Gen Mgr: Joe Kremer
Stadium: Five County (6,000)
Affiliation: Pittsburgh Pirates

Chattanooga Lookouts
P.O. Box 11002
Chattanooga, TN 37401
(423) 267-2208
Gen Mgr: Frank Burke
Stadium: Engel (7,500)
Affiliation: Cincinnati Reds

Greenville Braves
P.O. Box 16683
Greenville, SC 29606
(864) 299-3456
Gen Mgr: Steve DeSalvo
Stadium: Greenville Municipal (7,027)
Affiliation: Atlanta Braves

Huntsville Stars
P.O. Box 2769
Huntsville, AL 35804
(205) 882-2562
Gen Mgr: Don Mincher
Stadium: Joe W. Davis (10,200)
Affiliation: Oakland Athletics

Jacksonville Suns
P.O. Box 4756
Jacksonville, FL 32201
(904) 358-2846
Gen Mgr: Peter Bragan Jr.
Stadium: Wolfson Park (8,200)
Affiliation: Detroit Tigers

Knoxville Smokies
633 Jessamine St.
Knoxville, TN 37917
(423) 637-9494
Gen Mgr: Dan Rajkowski
Stadium: Bill Meyer (6,412)
Affiliation: Toronto Blue Jays

Memphis Chicks
800 Home Run Lane
Memphis, TN 38104
(901) 272-1687
Gen Mgr: David Hersh
Stadium: Tim McCarver (9,841)
Affiliation: San Diego Padres

Orlando Cubs
287 Tampa Ave. S
Orlando, FL 32805
(407) 872-7593
Gen Mgr: Roger Wexelberg
Stadium: Tinker Field (5,104)
Affiliation: Chicago Cubs

TEXAS LEAGUE

CLASS AA

League office:
2442 Facet Oak
San Antonio, TX 78232
(210) 545-5297
League President: Tom Kayser
Internships: contact Tom Kayser

Arkansas Travelers
P.O. Box 5599
Little Rock, AR 72215
(501) 664-1555
Gen Mgr: Bill Valentine
Stadium: Ray Winder Field (6,183)
Affiliation: St. Louis Cardinals

El Paso Diablos
P.O. Drawer 4797
El Paso, TX 79914
(915) 755-2000
Gen Mgr: Rick Parr
Stadium: Cohen (10,000)
Affiliation: Milwaukee Brewers

Jackson Generals
P.O. Box 4209
Jackson, MS 39296
(601) 981-4664
Gen Mgr: Bill Blackwell
Stadium: Smith-Wills (5,000)
Affiliation: Houston Astros

Midland Angels
P.O. Box 51187
Midland, TX 79710
(915) 683-4251
Gen Mgr: Monty Hoppel
Stadium: Angels (5,000)
Affiliation: California Angels

San Antonio Missions
5757 Hwy 90 W
San Antonio, TX 78227
(210) 675-7275
Gen Mgr: Burl Yarbrough
Stadium: Nelson Wolff (6,000)
Affiliation: Los Angeles Dodgers

PROFESSIONAL BASEBALL LEAGUES

Shreveport Captains
P.O. Box 3448
Shreveport, LA 71133
(318) 636-5555
Pres: Taylor Moore (principal owner)
Gen Mgr: Gilbert Little
Stadium: Fair Grounds Field (6,200)
Affiliation: San Francisco Giants

Tulsa Drillers
P.O. Box 4448
Tulsa, OK 74159
(918) 744-5998
Gen Mgr: Chuck Lamson
Stadium: Drillers (10,811)
Affiliation: Texas Rangers

Wichita Wranglers
P.O. Box 1420
Wichita, KS 67201
(316) 267-3372
Gen Mgr: Steve Shaad
Stadium: Lawrence-Dumont (6,058)
Affiliation: Kansas City Royals

CALIFORNIA LEAGUE

CLASS A

League office:
2380 S. Bascon Ave., Suite 200
Campbell, CA 95008
(100) 369 0030
League President: Joe Gagliardi

Bakersfield Blaze
P.O. Box 10031
Bakersfield, CA 93389
(805) 322-1363
Gen Mgr: Rick Smith
Stadium: Sam Lynn Ballpark (4,300)
Affiliation: Co-op

High Desert Mavericks
12000 Stadium Way
Adelanto, CA 92301
(619) 246-6287
Gen Mgr: Steve Pastorino
Stadium: Maverick (3,500)
Affiliation: Baltimore Orioles

Lake Elsinore Storm
P.O. Box 535
Lake Elsinore, CA 92531
(909) 245-4487
Gen Mgr: Kevin Haughian
Stadium: The Diamond (8,066)
Affiliation: California Angels

Lancaster Jet Hogs
P.O. Box 56171
Riverside, CA 92517
(909) 784-4929
Gen Mgr: Jack Patton
Stadium: Sports Center (3,500)
Affiliation: Seattle Mariners

Modesto A's
P.O. Box 883
Modesto, CA 95353
(209) 529-7368
Gen Mgr: Tim Marting
Stadium: Thurman (2,500)
Affiliation: Oakland Athletics

Rancho Cucamonga Quakes
8408 Rochester Ave.
Rancho Cucamonga, CA 91730
(909) 481-5000
Pres/Gen Mgr: Hank Stickney
(principal owner)
Stadium: R.C. Sports Complex
(6,550)
Affiliation: San Diego Padres

San Bernardino Stampede
280 S. E St.
San Bernardino, CA 92401
(909) 881-1836
Gen Mgr: Jason Watson
Stadium: The Ranch (5,000+)
Affiliation: Los Angeles Dodgers

San Jose Giants
P.O. Box 21727
San Jose, CA 95151
(408) 297-1435
Gen Mgr: Mark Wilson
Stadium: Municipal (4,200)
Affiliation: San Francisco Giants

Stockton Ports
Sutter and Alpine Sts.
Stockton, CA 95204
(209) 944-5943
Gen Mgr: Dan Chapman
Stadium: Billy Hebert (3,500)
Affiliation: Milwaukee Brewers

Visalia Oaks
P.O. Box 48
Visalia, CA 93279
(209) 625-0480
Gen Mgr: Andrew Bettencourt
Stadium: Recreation Park (2,000)
Affiliation: Detroit Tigers

CAROLINA LEAGUE

CLASS A

League office:
P.O. Box 9503
Greensboro, NC 27429
Phone: (910) 691-9030
League President: John Hopkins

Durham Bulls
P.O. Box 507
Durham, NC 27702
(919) 688-8211
Gen Mgr: Peter Anlyan
Stadium: Durham Bulls Athletic Park
(9,033)
Affiliation: Atlanta Braves

Frederick Keys
P.O. Box 3169
Frederick, MD 21705
(301) 662-0013
Gen Mgr: Joe Preseren
Stadium: Grove (5,500)
Affiliation: Baltimore Orioles

Kinston Indians
P.O. Box 3542
Kinston, NC 28501
(919) 527-9111
Gen Mgr: North Johnson (principal
owner)
Stadium: Grainger (4,100)
Affiliation: Cleveland Indians

Lynchburg Hillcats
P.O. Box 10213
Lynchburg, VA 24506
(804) 528-1144
Gen Mgr: Paul Sunwall
Stadium: City (4,000)
Affiliation: Pittsburgh Pirates

Prince William Cannons
P.O. Box 2148
Woodbridge, VA 22193
(703) 590-2311
Gen Mgr: Pat Filippone
Stadium: County (6,000)
Affiliation: Chicago White Sox

Salem Avalanche
P.O. Box 842
Salem, VA 24153
(703) 389-3333
Gen Mgr: Dave Oster
Stadium: Salem Memorial (6,300)
Affiliation: Colorado Rockies

Wilmington Blue Rocks
801 S. Madison St.
Wilmington, DE 19807
(302) 888-2015
Gen Mgr: Chris Kemple
Stadium: Daniel S. Frawley (5,600)
Affiliation: Kansas City Royals

Winston-Salem Warthogs
P.O. Box 4488
Winston-Salem, NC 27115
(910) 759-2233
Gen Mgr: Peter Fisch
Stadium: Ernie Shore Field (6,280)
Affiliation: Cincinnati Reds

FLORIDA STATE LEAGUE

CLASS A

League office:
P.O. Box 349
Daytona Beach, FL 32115
(904) 252-7479
League President: Chuck Murphy

Brevard County Manatees
5800 Stadium Pkwy.
Melbourne, FL 32940
(407) 633-9200
Gen Mgr: Ken Lehner
Stadium: Space Coast (7,500)
Affiliation: Florida Marlins

Charlotte Rangers
P.O. Box 3609
Port Charlotte, FL 33949
(941) 625-9500
Gen Mgr: Tim Murphy
Stadium: Charlotte County (6,026)
Affiliation: Texas Rangers

Clearwater Phillies
P.O. Box 10336
Clearwater, FL 34617
(813) 441-8638
Gen Mgr: Jim Herlihy
Stadium: Jack Russell Memorial
(6,917)
Affiliation: Philadelphia Phillies

Daytona Cubs
P.O. Box 15080
Daytona Beach, FL 32115
(904) 257-3172
Gen Mgr: Debbie Berg
Stadium: Jackie Robinson Ballpark
(4,200)
Affiliation: Chicago Cubs

Dunedin Blue Jays
P.O. Box 957
Dunedin, FL 34697
(813) 733-9302
Gen Mgr: Gary Rigley
Stadium: Dunedin (6,218)
Affiliation: Toronto Blue Jays

Fort Myers Miracle
14400 Six Mile Cypress Pkwy.
Ft. Myers, FL 33912
(941) 768-4210
Gen Mgr: Mark Schuster
Stadium: Lee County Sports Complex
(7,500)
Affiliation: Minnesota Twins

PROFESSIONAL BASEBALL LEAGUES

Kissimmee Cobras
P.O. Box 422229
Kissimmee, FL 34742
(407) 933-5500
Gen Mgr: Jeff Mercer
Stadium: Osceola County (5,100)
Affiliation: Houston Astros

Lakeland Tigers
P.O. Box 90187
Lakeland, FL 33804
(813) 686-8075
Gen Mgr: Woody Hicks
Stadium: Joker Marchant (7,000)
Affiliation: Detroit Tigers

St. Lucie Mets
525 N.W. Peacock Blvd.
Port St. Lucie, FL 34986
(407) 871-2100
Gen Mgr: Ross Vecchio
Stadium: Thomas J. White (7,347)
Affiliation: New York Mets

St. Petersburg Cardinals
P.O. Box 12557
St. Petersburg, FL 33733
(813) 822-3384
Gen Mgr: Steve Cohen
Stadium: Al Lang (7,004)
Affiliation: St. Louis Cardinals

Sarasota Red Sox
2700 12th St.
Sarasota, FL 34237
(941) 365-4460
Gen Mgr: Kevin Cummings
Stadium: Ed Smith (7,500)
Affiliation: Boston Red Sox

Tampa Yankees
3802 W. Martin Luther King Blvd.
Tampa, FL 33614
(813) 875-7753
Gen Mgr: Scott Kelyman
Stadium: Legends Field (10,382)
Affiliation: New York Yankees

Vero Beach Dodgers
P.O. Box 2887
Vero Beach, FL 32961
(407) 569-4900
Gen Mgr: Tom Simmons
Stadium: Holman (6,484)
Affiliation: Los Angeles Dodgers

West Palm Beach Expos
P.O. Box 3566
West Palm Beach, FL 33402
(407) 684-6801
Gen Mgr: Chris Hammond
Stadium: Municipal (4,200)
Affiliation: Montreal Expos

MIDWEST LEAGUE

CLASS A

League office:
P.O. Box 936
Beloit, WI 53512
(608) 364-1188
League President: George Spelius
Internships: contact George Spelius

Beloit Snappers
P.O. Box 855
Beloit, WI 53512-0855
(608) 362-2272
Gen Mgr: Jeff Nelson
Stadium: Pohlman Field (3,500)
Affiliation: Milwaukee Brewers

Burlington Bees
P.O. Box 824
Burlington, IA 52601
(319) 754-5705
Gen Mgr: Chuck Heeman
Stadium: Community Field (4,000)
Affiliation: San Francisco Giants

Cedar Rapids Kernels
P.O. Box 2001
Cedar Rapids, IA 52406
(319) 363-3887
Gen Mgr: Jack Roeder
Stadium: Veterans Memorial (6,000)
Affiliation: California Angels

Clinton Lumber Kings
P.O. Box 1295
Clinton, IA 52733
(319) 242-0727
Gen Mgr: Lesa Brown
Stadium: Riverview (3,000)
Affiliation: San Diego Padres

Fort Wayne Wizards
4000 Parnell Ave.
Fort Wayne, IN 46805
(219) 482-6400
Gen Mgr: Bret Staehling
Stadium: Memorial (6,300)
Affiliation: Minnesota Twins

Kane County Cougars
34 W. 002 Cherry Lane
Geneva, IL 60134
(630) 232-8811
Gen Mgr: Bill Larsen
Stadium: Elfstrom (5,900+)
Affiliation: Florida Marlins

Lansing Lugnuts
505 E. Michigan Ave.
Lansing, MI 48933
(517) 485-4500
Gen Mgr: Jim Weigel
Stadium: Oldsmobile Park (10,000)
Affiliation: Kansas City Royals

Michigan Battle Cats
1392 Capital Ave. NE
Battle Creek, MI 49017
(616) 660-2287
Gen Mgr: Bill Davidson
Stadium: C.O. Brown (6,200)
Affiliation: Boston Red Sox

Peoria Chiefs
1524 W. Nebraska Ave.
Peoria, IL 61604
(309) 688-1622
Gen Mgr: Harold A. Vonachen III
Stadium: Pete Vonachen (6,200)
Affiliation: St. Louis Cardinals

Quad City River Bandits
P.O. Box 3496
Davenport, IA 52808
(319) 324-2032
Gen Mgr: Chris Holvoet
Stadium: John O'Donnell (5,500)
Affiliation: Houston Astros

Rockford Cubbies
P.O. Box 6748
Rockford, IL 61125
(815) 964-5400
Gen Mgr: Michael Holmes
Stadium: Marinelli Field (4,300)
Affiliation: Chicago Cubs

South Bend Silver Hawks
P.O. Box 4218
South Bend, IN 46634
(219) 235-9988
Pres/Gen Mgr: John Baxter
Stadium: Coveleski Regional (5,000)
Affiliation: Chicago White Sox

West Michigan Whitecaps
4500 W. River Dr.
Comstock Park, MI 49321
(616) 784-4131
Gen Mgr: Scott Lane
Stadium: Old Kent Park (10,000)
Affiliation: Oakland Athletics

Wisconsin Timber Rattlers
P.O. Box 464
Appleton, WI 54912
(414) 733-4152
Gen Mgr: Mike Birling
Stadium: Fox Cities (5,456)
Affiliation: Seattle Mariners

SOUTH ATLANTIC LEAGUE

CLASS A

League office:
P.O. Box 38
Kings Mountain, NC 28086
(704) 739-3466
League President: John Moss

Asheville Tourists
P.O. Box 1556
Asheville, NC 28802
(704) 258-0428
Gen Mgr: Ron McKee
Stadium: McCormick Field (3,500)
Affiliation: Colorado Rockies

Augusta Greenjackets
P.O. Box 3746
Hill Station
Augusta, GA 30904
(706) 736-7889
Gen Mgr: Chris Scheuer
Stadium: Lake Olmstead (4,500)
Affiliation: Pittsburgh Pirates

Capital City Bombers
P.O. Box 7845
Columbia, SC 29201
(803) 256-4110
Gen Mgr: Tim Swain
Stadium: Capital City (6,000)
Affiliation: New York Mets

Charleston Alley Cats
P.O. Box 4669
Charleston, WV 25304
(304) 925-8222
Gen Mgr: Tim Bordner
Stadium: Watt Powell Park (7,000)
Affiliation: Cincinnati Reds

Charleston Riverdogs
P.O. Box 20849
Charleston, SC 29413
(803) 723-7241
Gen Mgrs: Stan Hughes, Scott Skadan
Stadium: College Park (4,000)
Affiliation: Texas Rangers

Columbus Redstixx
P.O. Box 1886
Columbus, GA 31902
(706) 571-8866
Gen Mgr: John Dittrich
Stadium: Golden Park (5,000)
Affiliation: Cleveland Indians

Delmarva Shorebirds
1323 Mt. Hermon Rd.
Beaglin Park Plaza
Salisbury, MD 21801
(410) 219-3112
Gen Mgr: Keith Lupton
Stadium: Arthur W. Perdue (5,200)
Affiliation: Montreal Expos

Fayetteville Generals
P.O. Box 64939
Fayetteville, NC 28306
(910) 424-6500
Gen Mgr: Andy Berg
Stadium: J. P. Riddle (4,200)
Affiliation: Detroit Tigers

Greensboro Bats
510 Yanceyville St.
Greensboro, NC 27405
(910) 333-2287
Gen Mgr: John Frey
Stadium: War Memorial (7,500)
Affiliation: New York Yankees

Hagerstown Suns
P.O. Box 230
Hagerstown, MD 21741
(301) 791-6266
Gen Mgr: Winston Blenckstone
Stadium: Municipal (4,500)
Affiliation: Toronto Blue Jays

Hickory Crawdads
P.O. Box 1268
Hickory, NC 28603
(704) 322-3000
Gen Mgr: Marty Steele
Stadium: L. P. Frans (5,100)
Affiliation: Chicago White Sox

Macon Braves
P.O. Box 4525
Macon, GA 31208
(912) 745-8943
Gen Mgr: Mike Dunn
Stadium: Luther Williams Field
   (3,750)
Affiliation: Atlanta Braves

Piedmont Boll Weevils
P.O. Box 64
Kannapolis, NC 28082
(704) 932-3267
Gen Mgr: Mike Kardamis
Stadium: Fieldcrest Cannon (4,700)
Affiliation: Philadelphia Phillies

Savannah Sand Gnats
P.O. Box 3783
Savannah, GA 31414
(912) 351-9150
Gen Mgr: Richard Sisler
Stadium: Grayson (8,500)
Affiliation: Los Angeles Dodgers

NEW YORK—PENN LEAGUE

CLASS A

League office:
1629 Oneida St.
Utica, NY 13501
(315) 733-8036
League President: Robert Julian

Auburn Doubledays
108 N. Division St.
Auburn, NY 13021
(315) 255-2489
Gen Mgr: Mark Harrington
Stadium: Falcon Park (2,800)
Affiliation: Houston Astros

Batavia Clippers
P.O. Box 532
Batavia, NY 14021
(716) 343-5454
Gen Mgr: Shawn Smith
Stadium: Dwyer (3,000)
Affiliation: Philadelphia Phillies

Erie Sea Wolves
P.O. Box 1776
Erie, PA 16507
(814) 456-1300
Gen Mgr: Eric Haag
Stadium: Jerry Uht Park (6,000)
Affiliation: Pittsburgh Pirates

Hudson Valley Renegades
P.O. Box 661
Fishkill, NY 12524
(914) 838-0094
Pres/Gen Mgr: Skip Weisman
Stadium: Dutchess (4,320)
Affiliation: Texas Rangers

Jamestown Jammers
P.O. Box 638
Jamestown, NY 14702-0638
(716) 664-0915
Pres: Bob Rich Jr.
Stadium: College (3,324)
Affiliation: Detroit Tigers

Lowell Spinners
P.O. Box 778
Lowell, MA 01853
(508) 459-1702
Pres/Gen Mgr: Clyde Smoll (principal
   owner)
Stadium: Alumni Field (4,000)
Affiliation: Boston Red Sox

New Jersey Cardinals
94 Championship Pl.
Augusta, NJ 07822
(201) 579-7500
Gen Mgr: Tony Torre
Stadium: Skylands Park (4,400)
Affiliation: St. Louis Cardinals

Oneonta Yankees
95 River St.
Oneonta, NY 13820
(607) 432-6326
Gen Mgr: John Nader
Stadium: Damaschke Field (4,500)
Affiliation: New York Yankees

Pittsfield Mets
P.O. Box 328
Pittsfield, MA 01202
(413) 499-6387
Gen Mgr: Richard Murphy
Stadium: Wahconah Park (4,500)
Affiliation: New York Mets

St. Catharines Stompers
426 Merritt St.
St. Catharines, Ontario L2P 1P3, Canada
(905) 641-5297
Gen Mgr: Joan Belford
Stadium: Community Park (3,000)
Affiliation: Toronto Blue Jays

Utica Blue Sox
P.O. Box 751
Utica, NY 13503
(315) 738-0999
Gen Mgr: Rob Fowler
Stadium: Donovan (4,000)
Affiliation: Florida Marlins

Vermont Expos
Box 4, The Champlain Mill
Winooski, VT 05404
(802) 655-4200
Gen Mgr: Kyle Bostwick
Stadium: Centennial Field (4,000)
Affiliation: Montreal Expos

Watertown Indians
P.O. Box 802
Watertown, NY 13601
(315) 788-8747
Gen Mgr: Jack Tracz
Stadium: Duffy Fairgrounds (2,800)
Affiliation: Cleveland Indians

Williamsport Cubs
P.O. Box 3173
Williamsport, PA 17701
(717) 326-3389
Gen Mgr: Doug Estes
Stadium: Bowman Field (4,400)
Affiliation: Chicago Cubs

NORTHWEST LEAGUE

CLASS A

League office:
P.O. Box 4941
Scottsdale, AZ 85261
(602) 483-8224
League President: Bob Richmond

Bellingham Giants
1316 King St.
Bellingham, WA 98226
(360) 671-6347
Pres/Gen Mgr: Jerry Walker (principal
   owner)
Stadium: Joe Martin (2,200)
Affiliation: San Francisco Giants

Boise Hawks
5600 Glenwood St.
Boise, ID 83714
(208) 322-5000
Gen Mgr: John Cunningham
Stadium: Memorial (4,500)
Affiliation: California Angels

Eugene Emeralds
P.O. Box 5566
Eugene, OR 97405
(503) 342-5367
Pres/Gen Mgr: Bob Beban
Stadium: Civic (6,800)
Affiliation: Atlanta Braves

Everett Aquasox
P.O. Box 7893
Everett, WA 98201
(206) 258-3673
Pres: Bob Bavasi
Stadium: Everett Memorial (2,285)
Affiliation: Seattle Mariners

Portland Rockies
P.O. Box 998
Portland, OR 97207
(503) 223-2837
Gen Mgr: Mark Helminiak
Stadium: Civic (23,000)
Affiliation: Colorado Rockies

Southern Oregon Timberjacks
P.O. Box 1457
Medford, OR 97501
(503) 770-5364
Gen Mgr: Suzanne Daniel
Stadium: Miles Field (2,900)
Affiliation: Oakland Athletics

Spokane Indians
P.O. Box 4758
Spokane, WA 99202
(509) 535-2922
Gen Mgr: Andrew Billig
Stadium: Seafirst (7,101)
Affiliation: Kansas City Royals

Yakima Bears
P.O. Box 483
Yakima, WA 98907
(509) 457-5151
Gen Mgr: Bob Romero
Stadium: Yakima County (3,300)
Affiliation: Los Angeles Dodgers

---

*National Association of
Professional Baseball Leagues*

The National Association is
the top administrative
organization in minor league
baseball. Its mailing address:
P.O. Box A, St. Petersburg,
FL 33731. Phone: (813) 822-
6937. Officers: Mike Moore,
President; Stan Brand, Vice
President; Rob Dlugozima,
COO.

The NBA always had plenty of player talent.

But not until it learned to market the talent

was it able to rise to its current profitability.

BASKETBALL

In the early days the National Basketball Association shared an office and four secretaries with what was then the American Hockey League. "We were paid $35 a week," recalls Zelda Spoelstra, one of the former secretaries. "Half came from the NBA, half from the hockey league. We also got four tickets to each of the events at the old Madison Square Garden."

Today the NBA has 650 full-time and 30 part-time employees in its offices. Plus interns. League headquarters occupy four floors of the elegant Olympic Tower on Fifth Avenue in New York, opposite St. Patrick's Cathedral. There are additional offices and a television studio in Secaucus, New Jersey.

And still more offices in Geneva, Barcelona, and Hong Kong. Says Commissioner David J. Stern, "We don't speak of domestic and foreign operations. Global—that's the word for basketball."

Basketball has been marketed so well abroad that 115 networks around the world carry NBA games. In Melbourne, Australia, the NBA has a shop with a 50-foot window displaying larger-than-life images of NBA players, along with video screens showing NBA highlights and a ton of products for sale by NBA licensees. In Japan the league has a joint venture with the giant firm of C. Itoh, which sells NBA merchandise in more than 1,000 shops. Young people sporting apparel that announces their allegiance to a particular NBA team are a common sight throughout Europe .

According to NBA Properties, which handles licensing arrangements with manufactur-

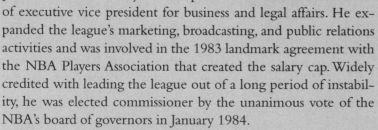

HOW   THEY   GOT   THERE

DAVID J. STERN
Commissioner, National Basketball Association

Even before his appointment as NBA commissioner, David Stern won recognition as one of the most innovative executives in sports.

A lawyer by profession, Stern began his association with the NBA over two decades ago, working on league cases as outside counsel. He joined the NBA officially in 1978 as general counsel, overseeing all litigation, negotiations, and government relations. In 1980 he was promoted to the newly created position of executive vice president for business and legal affairs. He expanded the league's marketing, broadcasting, and public relations activities and was involved in the 1983 landmark agreement with the NBA Players Association that created the salary cap. Widely credited with leading the league out of a long period of instability, he was elected commissioner by the unanimous vote of the NBA's board of governors in January 1984.

Stern is a native of New York and a graduate of Rutgers University and Columbia Law School.

ers, licensees in 1994–95 sold $3 billion worth of merchandise—all of it billboarding the NBA and its teams.

NBA Entertainment, based in Secaucus, is another major unit that oversees a broad range of activities including international television arrangements, the production of a weekly TV show, *Inside Stuff*, and the production of a line of videos made for retail.

The NBA also turns out books and various other publications including *Hoops*, a magazine circulated throughout the world in several languages.

And that only suggests the scope of the organization.

But the NBA's current success didn't come easily. In the early '80s, *Sports Illustrated* described the league as "a tattered army, marching out of step and casting worried glances at the sky for incoming missiles." At least half a dozen franchises were in financial trouble, and TV ratings ranged from disappointing to disappearing. Taking hold as commissioner in 1984, Stern gave professional basketball a new attitude. The NBA, he told franchise owners, should be thought of as an entertainment conglomerate. Market basketball as an entertainment. Sports fans want to focus on stars—so promote the stars. And hire people who can help you do that. It turned the NBA around.

The Job Picture

Gordon Frank, human resources consultant for the league, says that the league receives some 3,500 to 4,000 job inquiries each year. Many of the letters are poorly written, he says, and some are addressed to NBA executives with their names misspelled. Those inquiries get little consideration. So do letters that say "I am a hard worker" but offer no skills. Frank says that to get serious consideration, you must have an understanding of the job you're applying for and "you've got to bring some useful skills and work experience to the table."

Resumes that show skills appropriate to a particular department of the NBA are retained for openings in the future. "We keep tabs on good applicants," Frank says, "even if there are no immediate openings."

League Internships

The NBA has an internship program for undergraduate students that provides eight to 10 appointments in the winter-spring period and in the summer and fall. Each period is 12 weeks long. Interns are assigned to various departments, including public relations, team services, broadcasting, and NBA Photos. They put in a full workweek, Frank said, and receive a stipend. (The amount of the stipend was being reconsidered at this writing.) Out-of-towners are assisted in finding housing.

Team Internships

Most—not all—of the NBA franchises also employ interns. Some pay, some don't. Dave Senko, director of media services for the San Antonio Spurs, said that his club accepts eight to 10 students for the length of the basketball season. They work in media relations, ac-

HOW THEY GOT THERE

RICK WELTS
President, NBA Properties

Talk about modest beginnings— Rick Welts started out in pro basketball as a ball boy for the Seattle SuperSonics.

After his ball bag days, Welts became an assistant trainer for the Sonics, then a public relations assistant (while attending the University of Washington), and finally PR director. In 1979, after 10 years with the Sonics, he left the club to join a sports marketing and promotion firm in Seattle. In 1982 he went to New York to work for NBA Properties as director of national promotions, and later as vice president of marketing. In 1984 he was named NBA's vice president/communications, and four years later was appointed to his current post as president of NBA Properties.

counting, marketing, and community relations, and receive a stipend of as much as $600 a month. "Internships," said Senko, "are the only way to jobs."

The picture is different at the Los Angeles Clippers organization. The club employs 15

SUSAN O'MALLEY
President, Washington Wizards

Susan O'Malley is the first woman to head an NBA franchise. And the record shows she's doing a great job.

"We are in the entertainment business," O'Malley says, echoing Commissioner Stern. "It is our job to make sure that the people who purchase tickets to a game have an entertaining evening and are treated as guests in our building," she says. "If they are treated right, they will probably come back again."

Attendance jumped to new heights after her appointment in 1991, in part due to well-executed promotions. A favorite is tax night, a promotion in which the taxes of a lucky fan are paid by the Wizards (or as they used to be known, the Bullets).

The club's chief executive is a 1983 graduate of St. Mary's College in Emmitsburg, Maryland, where she got a bachelor's degree in business and finance. She worked for an advertising firm for three years, then joined the Bullets organization during the 1986–87 season as director of advertising. She moved up to director of marketing a year later and in 1988 was named executive vice president, with overall responsibility for marketing, sponsorships, ticket sales, advertising, accounting, public relations, and community relations.

Her appointment as president made her one of the highest-ranking women in professional sports—at the age of 29.

Says owner Abe Pollin, "I didn't realize that appointing a woman to run the team had not been done before. But she deserved it." He adds, "I can think of no better person in the league." O'Malley is in great demand as a speaker in the Washington-Baltimore area, and it keeps her busy almost every night of the week. She sees it as part of her job.

to 20 interns for the basketball season, according to Jill Wiggins, a member of the communications department, but only two or three work in front-office jobs. The rest work only on game nights. Chores include helping with the sale of Clipper merchandise and assisting the press with game stats. A couple of interns get a small stipend; the others are unpaid. Wiggins said a few interns have been hired for full-time jobs in recent years, mainly for PR work.

The Boston Celtics accommodate five interns in a summer program that draws a crush of applicants. It's a no-pay deal, but the club does pick up transportation expenses. Two of the five work in PR; the others are assigned to marketing, scouting, or tickets. The club also offers several internships during the playing season that are somewhat less competitive.

* * * *

What's the best club an intern can work for? It's got to be the Portland Trail Blazers.

There's a lot to be learned here. Even if you just stand by and watch.

The Blazers have developed a marketing program that's so smart and so well executed it makes other clubs look as though they're playing with a semi-inflated ball. The results: they hold the record for sold-out home games and lead the league in TV and radio ratings. And sponsors love them.

Most of their promotions are innovative and bright, some you wouldn't give two cents for, but everything seems to work. Would you believe a promotion built on an essay contest for schoolchildren? An essay contest? With a tour of the Blazers locker room as a prize? Never mind, more than 18,600 kids submitted essays.

(Raising this question: Who read all those essays?)

How about a promotional tie-in with a beer company where a certificate for free Blazers tickets is hidden in some of the company's 12-packs? Sales of Miller Genuine Draft 12-packs rose by 270 percent!

How do you sell bread and the Blazers at the same time? Easy. Each week you put a new, full-color trading card featuring a Blazers player into each loaf. And you back it up with a mix of radio, TV, and print advertising. Does it work? You bet.

Commissioner Stern says, "When it comes to sports marketing, I think the Portland Trail Blazers have taken it to an art form. They're really about as good as it gets in professional sports marketing."

It's a great training ground for an intern.

Worth Mining, the Minors

There are two minor leagues in men's professional basketball. They offer plenty of internships, and the training can be valuable.

The **Continental Basketball Association (CBA)** has been in operation for half a century and has a history of stability, but it is probably stronger now than ever because of a pact with the NBA that makes it the NBA's "official development league."

The affiliation gets Commissioner David Stern's full support. Says the commissioner: "As the official development league of the NBA, the CBA has a major impact on the NBA and professional basketball globally." He notes that the CBA elevates not only players and coaches, but also officials and executives. (In 1995–96, 46 of the 58 NBA referees had CBA experience.)

Not surprisingly, the NBA connection gives the CBA a cachet that attracts players of genuine talent, assuring ticket buyers and regional TV audiences a high level of entertainment. An indication of the CBA brand of basketball: in 1995–96, 30 players were called up to the NBA.

The CBA is composed of 11 clubs in a network that stretches from Connecticut to Washington State. (The directory of teams appears later in this section.) Slated to join the league for the 1997–98 season is a newly organized franchise in Boise, Idaho. The team will be known as the Idaho Stampede and its home venue will be the new 13,000-seat Idaho Center, the largest sports arena in the state.

League offices are in St. Louis. A staff of 15 is augmented by three or four interns. They're unpaid, but those who take an internship as part of a college program in sports management get academic credit.

Paul Thompson, head of the league's public relations office, says one of the main assignments given to interns at the league offices is helping in the preparation of the annual CBA media guide, a book of 350-plus pages with detailed accounts of each of the clubs, their stats, and their players, coaches, and executives. The job entails some heavy research. And proofreading.

Other assignments involve handling media and fan requests, maintaining files of newspaper clippings, assembling information for the all-star game program, and writing special pieces that the PR office might need from time to time.

As you might guess, Thompson is partial to candidates who can write. He also prefers candidates who are computer literate and who can sound intelligent on the phone.

Generally, the selection of interns is made three times a year, conforming to college semesters. But candidates do not have to be enrolled in college programs dealing with sports or any other college program.

Internships are also offered by the CBA franchises. Josh Tobin, media relations director for the Connecticut Pride, reports that his club selects about five interns over a year's time. Some are college students, some not. They're involved in many aspects of the team's operation, including PR, ticket sales, and game night duties.

Ken Koeller, PR director for the LaCrosse (Wisconsin) Bobcats, says that the club employs four interns on a regular basis (10 to 20 hours a week for three-month periods), but on game nights he might use as many as 10 interns (usually students) to help at the scorer's table, run stats, assist with contests and

---

NBA REFS DO NICELY

NBA referees, said Fred Slaughter, general counsel to the National Basketball Referees Association, come from "all walks of life." Meaning, one assumes, that candidates have worked high school and college games and games in lower leagues. Candidates who win the esteem of the association are passed on to the NBA's Rod Thorn, VP Operations, who makes the final judgment.

NBA referees have to put up with constant travel, intense game pressure, and the danger of colliding with a muscular giant in full throttle, but the pay is pretty good. A five-year deal signed in December 1995 will pay new officials about $80,000, with top-scale officials earning $261,000. In the fifth year, new officials will earn about $90,000 and top-scale officials will get $328,000.

The National Basketball Referees Association, which is composed only of NBA refs, can be reached by writing to P.O. Box 3522, Santa Monica, CA 90408. The phone number is (310) 393-3522.

BASKETBALL HALL OF FAME

Springfield, Massachusetts

An $11.5 million museum in the city where Dr. James Naismith invented basketball in 1891. *Annual visitors:* 70,000. *Employees:* 24 full-time, 20 to 25 part-time, 2 interns. *Director:* Joseph O'Brien. *Address:* 1150 W. Columbus Ave., Springfield, MA 01101-0179. *Phone:* (413) 781-6500.

promotions, and fill in where needed.

* * * *

It's called the **United States Basketball League**, and though its 11 franchises are all in the East and its season runs a bare eight weeks, it has found its niche in the crowded business of professional sports.

The USBL is a minor league circuit, a notch below the Continental Basketball Association but close enough to the NBA to permit its star players to make it to Broadway in one leap. Indeed, the league showcases an unending flow of NBA prospects, which makes its evenings of basketball a fine entertainment. In 1996, 62 USBL players were invited to NBA summer rookie camps.

The league was founded in 1985 by people who love the game. Its simple mission is to bring exciting basketball to places that big-time sports has passed by and to present it in a family environment at prices that are a fraction of what big arenas charge. The season runs from early May to early July, and games are played in arenas where an audience of 3,000 is a really big crowd. The home courts of several of the teams are on the campuses of local colleges.

The USBL has been known to try the un-

tried. In 1986 one of its athletes was Nancy Lieberman, the first woman to play in a men's professional basketball league. In 1991 the league hired Sandi Ortiz-Del Valle for its officiating staff, the first female referee in professional basketball.

On the subject of internships: the league usually has four interns for various lengths of time. The individual teams engage three to five interns. No pay, but it could be fun. If you're interested, get in touch with the league office at (203) 877-9508. The roster of teams is in the directory below (but call the league office). The '97 season may have a new team or two, possibly three. You might want to inquire about that.

Year of the Woman

The year 1996 was, of course, the Year of the Woman in Basketball, marked especially by the launching of not one but two professional leagues.

First to take the court was the eight-team American Basketball League, which got underway in October 1996. Formation of the second league, the Women's National Basketball Association, was announced in the summer of 1996, with the start of its inaugural season scheduled for June 1997.

* * * *

The ABL. The league seems to have all the ingredients for success. For one thing, it has the backing of Reebok and other prominent sponsors. It also has TV exposure, good timing, and most of the members of the U.S. Olympic team.

The ABL's eight teams are divided into two conferences. The Eastern Conference covers Atlanta, Columbus, Hartford/Springfield, and Richmond; teams from Denver, Portland, San Jose, and Seattle make up the Western Conference. The teams play a 40-game season. Salaries range from $40,000 to $70,000 a year, but the players also own 10 percent of the league.

Reebok, designated a "founding sponsor,"

has arranged to be the exclusive supplier of uniforms to four of the teams. The company also has endorsement contracts with a number of ABL players, including Olympic star Jennifer Azzi from Stanford, Saudia Roundtree from the University of Georgia, and All-Americans Sheri Sam from Vanderbilt and Shelley Sheetz from Colorado.

The league has a television contract with SportsChannel.

The WNBA. The new league, a creation of the NBA, is a logical step in Commissioner David Stern's fiendish plan to spread the influence of professional basketball over all of humankind.

"We think this is an idea whose time has come," said Stern, "because fans have come to appreciate the excellence of women's basketball." What's more, he said, the idea has elicited network and sponsor interest.

The decision to play a summer schedule was simply based on the greater availability of arenas and TV time, he said.

Like the American Basketball League, the WNBA will start with eight teams split into Eastern and Western Conferences. The cities chosen for the new teams all have NBA franchises. They include: Charlotte, Cleveland, Houston, New York, Los Angeles, Phoenix, Sacramento, and Salt Lake City.

The WNBA will conduct its first draft on April 28, 1997, and open training camps a month later. The 10-week season will begin June 21. Each team will play a 28-game regular season schedule, followed by playoffs and a championship game.

Television coverage over the season will be provided by NBC, ESPN, and Lifetime.

The first players to be signed by the league were Olympic gold medalists Rebecca Lobo and Sheryl Swoopes.

League president is Val Ackerman, who was vice president of business affairs for the NBA. Ackerman joined the NBA in 1988 as a staff attorney and two years later became special assistant to Commissioner Stern. She was named director of business affairs in 1992. She is a graduate of the University of Virginia, where she was twice an Academic All-American with the women's basketball team. She played a season of professional basketball in France before attending the UCLA law school, where she got her law degree in 1985.

PROFESSIONAL BASKETBALL LEAGUES

NATIONAL BASKETBALL ASSOCIATION

League office:
645 Fifth Ave.
New York, NY 10022
(212) 826-7000
Commissioner: David J. Stern
Internships offered

Atlanta Hawks
One CNN Center
S. Tower, Suite 405
Atlanta, GA 30303
(404) 827-3800
VP/Gen Mgr: Pete Babcock
Internships offered

Boston Celtics
151 Merrimac St.
Boston, MA 02114
(617) 523-6050
Exec VP/Gen Mgr: Jan Volk
Internships: contact Jeff Twiss

Charlotte Hornets
100 Hive Dr.
Charlotte, NC 28217
(704) 357-0252
Pres: Spencer Stolten
Internships: contact Harold Kaufman

Chicago Bulls
1901 W. Madison St.
Chicago, IL 60612
(312) 455-4000
VP Basketball Opns: Jerry Krause
Internships: contact Steve Schanwald

Cleveland Cavaliers
One Center Court
Cleveland, OH 44115
(216) 420-2000
VP/Gen Mgr: Wayne Embry
Internships: contact Ingrid Dasen

Dallas Mavericks
Reunion Arena
777 Sports St.
Dallas, TX 75207
(214) 748-1808
Gen Mgr: Norm Sonju
Internships: contact Kevin Sullivan

Denver Nuggets
1635 Clay St.
Denver, CO 80204
(303) 893-6700
Gen Mgr: Bernie Bickerstaff
Internships offered

Detroit Pistons
2 Championship Dr.
Auburn Hills, MI 48326-1752
(810) 377-0100
VP Basketball Opns: Bill McKinney
Internships: contact Human Resources

Golden State Warriors
1221 Broadway, 20th Floor
Oakland, CA 94621
(510) 986-2200
Gen Mgr: Ed Gregory
Internships offered

Houston Rockets
2 Greenway Plaza, Suite 400
Houston, TX 77046
(713) 627-3865
Gen Mgr: Bob Weinhauer
Internships: contact David Spangler

Indiana Pacers
300 E. Market St.
Indianapolis, IN 46204
(317) 263-2100
Pres: Donnie Walsh
Internships: contact Mark Andrew

Los Angeles Clippers
LA Memorial Sports Arena
3939 S. Figueroa St.
Los Angeles, CA 90037
(213) 745-0400
Exec VP: Elgin Baylor
Internships offered

Los Angeles Lakers
3900 W. Manchester Blvd.
Inglewood, CA 90306
(310) 419-3100
Gen Mgr: Mitch Kupchak
Internships: contact Bob Steiner

Miami Heat
1 S.E. Third Ave., Suite 2300
Miami, FL 33131
(305) 577-4328
VP Basketball Opns: Dave Wohl
Internships: contact Andy Elisburg

Milwaukee Bucks
1001 N. Fourth St.
Milwaukee, WI 53203
(414) 227-0500
Pres: Herb Kohl
Internships: contact John Steinmiller

Minnesota Timberwolves
600 First Ave. N
Minneapolis, MN 55403
(612) 673-1600
Gen Mgr: Jack McCloskey
Internships: contact Human Resources

New Jersey Nets
405 Murray Hill Pkwy.
East Rutherford, NJ 07073
(201) 935-8888
Exec VP/Gen Mgr: Willis Reed
Internships: contact Human Resources

New York Knickerbockers
2 Pennsylvania Plaza, 14th floor
New York, NY 10121
(212) 465-6000
Gen Mgr: Ernie Grunfeld
Internships: contact Human Resources

Orlando Magic
Orlando Arena
One Magic Pl.
Orlando, FL 32801
(407) 649-3200
Gen Mgr: John Gabriel
Internships: contact Tracy Blue

Philadelphia 76ers
CoreStates Center
One CoreStates Complex
Philadelphia, PA 19148
(215) 339-7600
Gen Mgr: John Lucas
Internships: contact Gerry Ryan

Phoenix Suns
201 E. Jefferson
Phoenix, AZ 85004
(602) 379-7900
Pres: Jerry Colangelo
Internships offered

Portland Trail Blazers
One Center Court, Suite 200
Portland, OR 97227
(503) 234-9291
Gen Mgr: Bob Whitsitt
Internships: contact Tracy Reandeau

Sacramento Kings
One Sports Pkwy.
Sacramento, CA 95834
(916) 928-0000
Gen Mgr: Geoff Petrie
Internships: contact Travis Stanley

San Antonio Spurs
100 Montana St.
San Antonio, TX 78203
(210) 554-7700
Gen Mgr: Gregg Popovich
Internships offered

Seattle SuperSonics
190 Queen Anne Ave. N, Suite 200
Seattle, WA 98109
(206) 281-5800
Gen Mgr: Wally Walker
Internships: contact Cheri White

Toronto Raptors
20 Bay St., Suite 1702
Toronto, Ontario M5J 2N8, Canada
(416) 214-2255
VP Basketball Opns: Isiah Thomas

Utah Jazz
301 W.S. Temple
Salt Lake City, UT 84101
(801) 325-2500
Gen Mgr: Tim Howells
Internships offered

Vancouver Grizzlies
800 Griffiths Way
Vancouver, British Columbia V6B
6G1, Canada
(604) 681-2226
Gen Mgr: Stu Jackson

Washington Bullets/Wizards
One Harry S Truman Dr.
Landover, MD 20785
(301) 773-2255
Gen Mgr: John Nash
Internships: contact Maureen Lewis

CONTINENTAL BASKETBALL ASSOCIATION

League office:
701 Market St.
St. Louis, MO 63101
(314) 621-7222
Commissioner: Steve Patterson
Internships: contact Human Resources

Connecticut Pride
21 Watervile Rd.
Avon, CT 06001
(860) 678-8456
Gen Mgr: Tyler Jones

Florida Beachdogs
1700 Palm Beach Lakes Blvd.
Suite 150
West Palm Beach, FL 33401
(561) 686-5266
Gen Mgr: Eric Musselman

Fort Wayne Fury
1010 Memorial Way, Suite 210
Fort Wayne, IN 46805
(219) 471-3879
Gen Mgr: Art Saltsberg
Internships offered

Grand Rapids Hoops
190 Monroe NW
Grand Rapids, MI 49503
(616) 458-7788
Gen Mgr: Bob Przybysz

LaCrosse Bobcats
200 Main St., Suite 200
LaCrosse, WI 54602-1717
(608) 796-2600
Gen Mgr: Jim Timm

with the league for at least 10 years, get a pension of $150 a month for each year of service.

Team Internships

Most of the clubs in the NFL employ interns, especially for the busy training-camp period. Check the team directory, page 50.

Best Chances for a Job: The Arena Football League

Arena football headed for its 11th season in the spring of 1997 with a roster of 14 franchises—all in good-sized markets—and a dis-

H O W T H E Y G O T T H E R E

PAUL TAGLIABUE
Commissioner, National Football League

Paul Tagliabue was elected commissioner of the NFL on October 26, 1989. He succeeded Pete Rozelle, who retired after serving as commissioner for 30 years.

Tagliabue was not an unknown to NFL owners. Like David Stern at the NBA, he had worked for the NFL for many years as an outside attorney. When he signed on as commissioner, he was a senior partner in Covington & Burling, one of Washington's top law firms.

In his high school days in Jersey City, he was an honor student, a state high-jump champion, and a highly recruited basketball player. He chose Georgetown University, where he was captain of the Hoyas, president of his senior class, and a Rhodes Scholar finalist. After Georgetown, he went to New York University Law School on a scholarship, was editor of the law review, and graduated with honors.

Tagliabue started his career in 1965 as a law clerk in Federal Court in Washington and the following year went to work for the U.S. Defense Department. When he left in 1969 to join Covington & Burling, he received the Secretary of Defense Meritorious Civilian Service Medal, the department's highest award.

tinct feeling of brio.

In 1996 total attendance for the 16-week season was 1,132,778, a new mark. Average number of fans per game was a healthy 10,788. What's more, said Nick Gandy, the league's PR director, the clubs were brimming with talent and prospects of even better figures in the years immediately ahead were keen indeed.

New to the league for the '97 season were two franchises that show an interesting trend in team ownership. The owner of one of the teams is the Meadowland Sports Complex in New Jersey. The owner of the other new team is Madison Square Garden.

The other franchises in the league, stretching from coast to coast, are in Albany (New York), Anaheim, Phoenix, Palm Beach, Des Moines, Milwaukee, Nashville, Orlando, Portland (Oregon), San Jose, Tampa, and Houston. *(For addresses and phone numbers, see the directory, page 51.)*

Eighteen games will be televised by ESPN and ESPN 2 on national and regional networks.

Arena football is played on an indoor padded Astroturf surface. The length of the field is 50 yards plus 8-yard end zones. The width, sideline to sideline, is 85 feet. Goalposts are 9 feet apart with a crossbar height of 15 feet. Players wear regulation football equipment. There are 8 players on offense and 8 on defense. Each team carries 20 players. Spectators are so close to the action they can feel the pops.

According to Gandy, with the likelihood of further expansion, the chances of getting an administrative job in the league—especially in marketing—have never been better. Beginning salaries range up from $25,000.

On the subject of internships: The league offices in Chicago use several interns. College students get academic credit for their stints; others get a small stipend. Almost all—if not all—of the clubs use interns too. If you're interested in working for a particular club, get

---

Oklahoma City Cavalry
100 W. Sheridan
Oklahoma City, OK 73102
(405) 232-3865
Pres/Gen Mgr: Kevin Leonard
Internships: contact David Klaassen

Omaha Racers
6800 Mercy Rd., Suite 201
Omaha, NE 68106-2137
(402) 551-5151
Gen Mgr: Rob Goodman
Internships: contact Greg Shea

Quad City Thunder
329 18th St.
Rock Island, IL 61201
(309) 788-2255
Gen Mgr: Mark Kimball
Internships offered

Rockford Lightning
3660 Publisher's Dr.
Rockford, IL 61109
(815) 874-8918
Gen Mgr: Mike Bohnstengel

Sioux Falls Skyforce
330 N. Main Ave., Suite 101
Sioux Falls, SD 57102
(605) 332-0605
Gen Mgr: Tommy Smith
Internships: contact John Hinz

Yakima Sun Kings
P.O. Box 2626
Yakima, WA 98907
(509) 248-1222
Gen Mgr: Kellie Connaughton

UNITED STATES BASKETBALL LEAGUE

League office:
46 Quirk Rd
Milford, CT 06460
(203) 877-9508
Commissioner: Daniel T.
  Meisenheimer III
Internships offered

Atlanta Trojans
P.O. Box 82915
Hapeville, GA 30354
(404) 763-3579
Gen Mgr: Al Outlaw

Atlantic City Seagulls
6 W. Lancaster Ave.
Ardmore, PA 19003
(610) 642-2900
Pres: Ken Gross

Carolina Cardinals
3516 Vest Mill Rd.
Winston-Salem, NC 27103
(910) 659-9077
Gen Mgr: John Aquino

Connecticut Skyhawks
P.O. Box 3156
Milford, CT 06460
(203) 874-2055
Pres: Terry Munk

Florida Sharks
P.O. Box 39042
Sarasota, FL 34238
(941) 927-DUNK
Pres: Andy Badolato

Jacksonville Barracudas
1243 Arlington Rd., Suite 218
Jacksonville, FL 32211
(904) 725-4800
Gen Mgr: Rex Morgan

Long Island Surf
Pro Hoops Long Island, Inc.
189 South St.
Oyster Bay, NY 11771
(516) 922-4421
Gen Mgr: Tauna Vandeweghe

New Hampshire Thunder Loons
1244 Hooksett Rd.
Hooksett, NH 03106
(603) 668-4973
Pres: Mike Cole

Portland Mountain Cats
P.O. Box 15034
Portland, ME 04101
(207) 874-2723
Pres: Mark McClure

Tampa Bay Windjammers
1325 Snell Isles Blvd NE, Suite 204A
St. Petersburg, FL 33704
(813) 894-3350
Gen Mgr: Jonard Solie

Treasure Coast Tropics
2440 S.E. Federal Hwy, Suite U
Stuart, FL 34994
(407) 288-7468
Gen Mgr: Trevor Clendenin

AMERICAN BASKETBALL LEAGUE

League office:
1900 Embarcadero Rd., Suite 110
Palo Alto, CA 94303
(415) 856-3ABL
COO: Steve Hams

Eastern Conference

Atlanta Glory
151 Ponce de Leon Ave. NE,
  Suite 200
Atlanta, GA 30308
(404) 872-7860
Gen Mgr: Debbie Miller-Palmore
Internships: contact Kelly Brown

Columbus Quest
7451 State Route 161
Dublin, OH 43016
(614) 873-6555
Gen Mgr: Brian Agler
Internships: contact Debbie Stocks

New England Blizzard
179 Allyn St., Suite 403
Hartford, CT 06103
(860) 522-4667
Gen Mgr: Pam Batalis
Internships: contact Lynne Liebhauser

Richmond Rage
7650 E. Parham Rd., Suite 260
Richmond, VA 23294
(804) 527-4373
Gen Mgr: Tammy Holder
Internships: contact Tanya Alleyne

Western Conference

Colorado Xplosion
800 Grant St., Suite 410
Denver, CO 80203
(303) 832-2225
Gen Mgr: Lark Birdsong
Internships: contact Jason Boothe

Portland Power
Memorial Coliseum
One Center Court
Portland, OR 97227
(503) 233-9559
Gen Mgr: Linda Weston
Internships: contact Linda Weston

San Jose Lasers
190 Park Center Plaza, Suite 210
San Jose, CA 95113
(408) 271-1500
Gen Mgr: Christine Forter
Internships: contact Christine Forter

Seattle Reign
400 Mercer St., Suite 408
Seattle, WA 98109
(206) 285-5225
Gen Mgr: Jim Weyermann
Internships: contact Jim Weyermann

WOMEN'S NATIONAL BASKETBALL ASSOCIATION

Organizational details, including team names, were not yet completed when this book went to press.

League office:
645 Fifth Ave.
New York, NY 10022
(212) 688-WNBA
President: Val Ackerman

Eastern Conference

Charlotte
100 Hive Dr.
Charlotte, NC 28217
(704) 357-0252

Cleveland
Gund Arena
One Center Court
Cleveland, OH 44115
(216) 420-2000

Houston
10 Greenway Plaza, Suite 400
Houston, TX 77046
(713) 627-3865

New York
Madison Square Garden
2 Pennsylvania Plaza
New York, NY 10121
(212) 465-6499

Western Conference

Los Angeles
Great Western Forum
3900 W. Manchester Blvd.
Inglewood, CA 90305
(310) 419-3100

Phoenix
Phoenix Suns Plaza
201 E. Jefferson
Phoenix, AZ 85004
(602) 379-7900

Sacramento
One Sports Pkwy.
Sacramento, CA 95834
(916) 928-0000

Salt Lake City
Delta Center
301 W.S. Temple
Salt Lake City, UT 84101
(801) 325-2500

The NFL went into the football business with the idea of selling seats. Unimagined was the fortune to be made selling clothes.

FOOTBALL

The business affairs of the National Football League are conducted with crisp, disciplined efficiency.

That's not the way it was in the beginning.

The beginning was in 1920, when representatives of four independent football teams got together in Canton, Ohio, with the idea of forming a professional league.

A league, they assured each other, would help win respect for the game.

To persuade the public that it was a serious undertaking, the organizers announced that every team wishing to join would have to pay an entry fee of $100.

Some months later, the American Professional Football Association, as the league was known then, opened its first season with a roster of 14 teams.

But none of the teams ever paid the $100 entry fee.

That offhand attitude would not be acceptable today. You can be sure that the Jacksonville Jaguars and the Charlotte Panthers, the latest teams to join the NFL, would not have been admitted without paying their entry fee, which now happens to be $140 million.

League Operations

The business of the league is conducted in a tall office building in the polished corporate environs of New York's Park Avenue—a far cry from the color and mayhem of the gridiron.

Encamped here are the commissioner, Paul Tagliabue, and the league president, Neil Austrian. Some of the other ranking officials located here: executive vice president and league counsel, Jay Moyer; executive vice president-labor relations, Harold Henderson; senior vice president-communications and government affairs, Joe Browne; senior vice president-league and football development, Roger Goodell; senior vice president-broadcast and network television, Val Pinchbeck Jr.; chief financial officer, Tom Spock.

An activity that gets a lot of attention at 280 Park is communications, a department replete with executives. Director of communications is Greg Aiello. Director of international public relations is Pete Abitante. Also on hand are: director of information-American Football Conference (AFC), Leslie Hammond; director of information-National Football Conference (NFC), Reggie Roberts; and director of corporate communications, Chris Widmaier.

Far down the list of league executives, after broadcasting, operations, officiating, and security, is the first female. She is Sue Robichek, director of special events planning.

Availability of jobs. Jobs at NFL headquarters are not usually available, but they do open up from time to time. The occasional openings are typically for secretaries, administrative assistants, and public relations assistants. Starting pay is about $20,000.

Internships. The league employs eight to 10 interns for a 10-week stretch each summer. Interns get a stipend; the amount varies, depending on the assignment.

Inquiries about jobs or internships can be directed to Janine Haunss or Alysse Sluka, who share the title of personnel coordinator. ("It's not easy to find an intern who is motivated, well organized, and has initiative," says Haunss. Can you make her job easier?)

The address of the NFL: 280 Park Ave., New York, NY 10022. Phone: (212) 758-1500.

Branches of the NFL

NFL Properties. This unit, the licensing, marketing, and publishing arm of the NFL, has a staff of 130. Its main activity is selling manufacturers the right to use team insignia on their products, and it's a big operation. Sales of licensed merchandise in 1994 totaled $3 billion.

Internships are available here.

NFL Properties is located at the league address, 280 Park Ave. Personnel manager is Bob Alacci, (212) 838-0660.

President of this multibillion-dollar company is Sara Levinson, former head of MTV (Music Television). She is probably the highest-ranking female executive in professional football.

Levinson is a native of Portsmouth, Virginia. She received a bachelor's degree from Cornell in 1972 and an MBA from Columbia in 1976. After two years as an account executive at Doyle Dane Bernbach, an advertising agency, she became advertising manager at Showtime, the cable TV network, and subsequently held a series of managerial jobs in the cable industry that led to her appointment in 1993 as president-business director of MTV. She took over as president of NFL Properties in September 1994.

NFL Films. A creative company that has won dozens of Emmys, NFL Films captures every play of every NFL game. It also turns out videos and documentaries for commercial sale and feeds action footage to broadcast and cable sports shows. It has a staff of 150 cinematographers, technicians, and writers.

Internships are available here too.

The address of NFL Films is 330 Fellowship Rd., Mt Laurel, NJ 08054. Phone: (609) 778-1600. President is Steve Sabol.

Game Officials

How does the NFL choose its gridiron officials? Very carefully, says Jerry Seeman, a former whistle-blower who is the NFL's director of officiating. A quick recall of game rules is important, of course; so is an agility of movement and keenness of wit when bodies go flying in all directions. But an official is worth nada if he doesn't have the courage to drop a flag on a fire-breathing, 300-pound behemoth guilty of holding for a second time.

The NFL employs 112 game officials. The search for new officials begins with a squad of 50 scouts who screen the thousands of refs working in Division I college conferences. About 150 prospects, each of whom is required to have at least five years of experience, get a closer look. Survivors are invited to NFL headquarters in New York for interviews with league executives, followed by a tough psychological exam. The next step is a background check on each candidate conducted by the NFL's 40-man investigation unit, which looks for any history of gambling, boozing, or associations with people of dubious reputation. Finally, the league usually selects six of the candidates to replace retiring officials or those who are fired.

The pay: For regular-season games, officials get $1,325 to $4,009 per game, depending on experience. For playoff games, the pay is $9,800; for the Super Bowl, it's $11,900. Travel and hotel accommodations are first-class, with per diems of $205 and $195 for the first and second nights away from regular weekday jobs. On retirement, officials who've been

in touch with that club directly.

The NFL Is Thinking Global

Having nailed down pro football's place as America's most popular team sport, the NFL has turned an eye to the rest of the world, with Europe as its immediate target.

Already underway is the NFL International program, a marketing strategy that aims at teaching millions of sports fans around the world the singular charms of pro football. What new jobs this will open up is not yet clear, but it wouldn't hurt if you brushed up on your language skills.

Heading the new division is Don Garber, formerly with NFL Properties.

The NFL's World League

Giving legs to the NFL International's European operation is the World League of American Football, a six-club league consisting of the Amsterdam Admirals, Barcelona Dragons, Frankfurt Galaxy, London Monarchs, Dusseldorf Rhein Fire, and Edinburgh Scottish Claymores. The teams play a 10-game spring schedule plus a championship game in the 11th week. In 1996 NFL teams allocated 72 players to World League teams. A sign of things to come: three Japanese players were selected by World League teams after tryouts in Tokyo.

The league is the creation of the NFL, but playing a big role in its development is Rupert Murdoch's Fox, Inc., now a major sports TV network. In the 1996 season, weekly telecasts reached 174 countries.

At World League headquarters in London, Oliver Luck, the league president, is assisted by a 17-member corps of administrators. Chipping in from offices in New York is Eric Tillman, director of football operations, and a staff of eight executives.

CFL: Back Over the Border

In 1994 the Canadian Football League made a bold move on the U.S. football mar-

ket, but it didn't take. When the curtain rose on the '95 season, the teams stateside were the Baltimore Stallions, Birmingham Barracudas, Memphis Mad Dogs, San Antonio Texans, and Shreveport Pirates. At the end of the season, they all disappeared, along with 150 administrative jobs and lots of internships.

The Canadian Football League is now wholly Canadian once more. (The roster of CFL teams appears in the directory, page 50.) However, there's talk that the NFL may be interested in working out some kind of relationship with the league, maybe on the order

H O W   T H E Y   G O T   T H E R E

PAT HANLON
Vice President, Public Relations, New York Giants

There's not much of a connection between Elizabethan sonnets and gridiron stats, but Pat Hanlon made his way from one to the other without dropping a line.

Hanlon, who grew up in Chambersburg, Pennsylvania, began a quest for a degree in English literature at Gettysburg College, meanwhile spending two summers steeped in American literature as an intern in the sports department of the Pittsburgh Press. His summer work led to an interview at the University of Pittsburgh for a job as a student assistant in the university's sports information office. He got the job, finished his studies in English lit at Pittsburgh, and was awarded a full-time position there as assistant sports information director. That was in 1985. In '86 he switched to the University of Oklahoma as assistant SID. In '87 he returned to Pittsburgh for a job with the NFL's Steelers as community relations coordinator and assistant director of public relations. Four years later he was appointed PR director for the New England Patriots. In April 1993, he arrived at the Meadowlands and settled in as director of PR for the Giants.

(Pat's comments on internships with the Giants: The club chooses three or four interns, all of whom are assigned to the summer camp. Later, one of the interns is selected to spend an entire season with the team. An internship, says Pat, "gives you a great look at the inner workings of a pro football franchise, but the situation is extremely competitive.")

of the joint-venture deal with Fox, which gave life to the World League of American Football in Europe.

Terry Bradway
Director of College Scouting, Kansas City Chiefs

A native of Trenton, New Jersey, Terry Bradway played football and got a phys ed degree at Trenton State and later studied for a master's. His track: graduate assistant in University of Cincinnati football program, assistant coach at the U.S. Merchant Marine Academy, assistant director of player personnel for the USFL's Philadelphia/Baltimore Stars, part-time scout for the New York Giants, full-time Giants scout for five years (was one of 10 scouts); got his current job in Kansas City Chiefs player personnel department in 1992.

Duties: Responsible for evaluating players in college draft and participates in club's final decisions . . . Supervises five area scouts and assigns colleges and players to each . . . Area scouts begin college visits in August, watching practice sessions, looking at tapes, interviewing players, talking to coaches . . . Bradway follows up with visits throughout the football season and covers postseason all-star games . . . In February he checks out 150 college prospects at the Indianapolis combine, commonly known as the meat market, where all prospects are poked and studied by the league's scouts and trainers . . . Predraft meetings with his staff follow, with daylong sessions devoted to one position at a time, leading to the crucial final evaluations of college players . . . Bradway also evaluates KC players in training camp.

What he likes best about the job: "The people in the business. I've never had a day when I came to work and didn't want to be there."

The downside: Having to be on the road 170 days or more and being away from his wife and three young children.

On interns: His most recent intern, a sports management major at the University of Kansas, was "outstanding." The intern was computer-wise, handled data input on prospects, and produced the "bible sheets" the office depended on. He also did some legwork in addition to office chores, got along well with people, and made himself indispensable. An intern like that, says Bradway, can't miss.

Pete Ward
Director of Operations, Indianapolis Colts

Whose job is it to see that the goalposts are up straight? At the RCA Dome, home of the Indianapolis Colts, it's one of a great number of responsibilities Pete Ward assigns to himself.

Pete Ward is the Colts' director of operations. It's a title that is given different interpretations around the league, but to Ward it has one simple meaning: make sure everything that affects the team, the game, and the fans is taken care of. It doesn't seem to leave much for others to do, but that's the way he likes it.

Take game staging. Ward not only checks out the field markings, advertising signage, game clock, goalposts, security, and public address system, he also oversees pregame events (including the choice of the anthem singer) and halftime shows. Plus scoreboard announcements.

When the team travels, he makes sure proper arrangements have been made for transportation and lodging. He goes along, of course, in case of mishaps.

When training camp opens, he's there to supervise all facilities and services, including meals.

He also oversees the club's sales and marketing activities. He is on call 24 hours a day.

During the season he works seven full days a week. During training camp, his days begin at 7 in the morning and often end at midnight. In the off-season, meaning February, he works an 8-to-5 day—"maybe."

What he likes best about the job: "Being involved in league competition and being part of the greatest sports entity in the world, the NFL!"

The downside: Time away from home.

Background: Born in California, grew up in the District of Columbia. Majored in sports management at the University of Virginia. In 1981, while still at the university, got an internship with the Colts. When he graduated the following year, the Colts offered him a job as an administrative assistant.

On internships: Ward uses one or two interns a year. The PR department, he said, employs five during training camp. It's the "best way" to break in, but getting a permanent job takes a lot of persistence. There's little turnover in this business. The Colts front office has had only five openings in the past 10 years.

Ed Carroll
Equipment Manager,
Baltimore Ravens

A football player with shoes that pinch or shoulder pads that shift with every bump is an unhappy and distracted player. On Ed Carroll's team there are no such complaints, because he personally fits each player with every item of clothing and protective device the player takes into battle.

As equipment manager, Carroll is responsible for the purchase, maintenance, and inventory of all the gear that players and coaches need, from socks to sleds. It sounds like a routine job; it isn't. Like all NFL equipment managers, Carroll feels his knowledge of football gear is only one element of the job. What makes Carroll and his counterparts truly essential in club operations is the intense, personal concern they bring to their work.

That means long hours. During the training period Carroll puts in 15-hour days, starting at 5:30 or 6 in the morning. Game days are almost as long. Two assistants help with laundering equipment every day and transporting equipment to away games and back

again, loading trucks to the airport, unpacking, and distributing gear to the individual lockers of players and coaches. Return flights from an away game sometimes get Carroll back to his home stadium in the early hours of the next day. To be ready for work at 6, he sleeps in his office. At the time of this interview, he hadn't taken a vacation in five years. He simply didn't want to take the time off, he said.

Carroll says that learning to become an equipment manager requires on-the-job training. He got his training as an assistant to the Cleveland Browns' equipment manager

HOW THEY GOT THERE

RON WOLF
Executive Vice President and General Manager,
Green Bay Packers

It's said that Ron Wolf's arrival in Green Bay in November 1991 made a greater impact on this section of Wisconsin than anyone since the advent of the legendary Vince Lombardi three decades ago. What impressed the citizenry were his quick and decisive moves in hiring a new head coach and executing a series of trades and acquisitions that in the course of a single year turned the Packers into a winning team after going 4 and 12. The *Sporting News* named him "NFL Executive of the Year."

Wolf was born in New Freedom, Pennsylvania, in 1938, and attended the University of Oklahoma, where he majored in history. His first job in football was with a Chicago-based publication, *Pro Football Illustrated*. In 1963, at the age of 25, he entered professional football when Al Davis invited him to join the then fledgling Oakland Raiders as a talent scout. What began as a distinctly minor job became, under Davis's tutelage, the key to his career. Working alongside Davis, he helped construct the Raiders' roster. In 1975 he took a job overseeing the formation of the newly franchised Tampa Bay Buccaneers, leaving after three years to rejoin the Raiders as head of player personnel operations. In 1990 he joined the New York Jets organization, and a year later he went to Green Bay as executive vice president and general manager.

in 1983. He left the Browns to work for an equipment manufacturer for several years and returned in 1990, when the manager's job opened up.

What he likes best about the job: The friendship and fun he has with the players, and being part of the team.

The downside: The hours.

His comments: There's not a lot of money to be made (the range is from $25,000 to $50,000), but it's a great job if you're not afraid of hard work. The best way to get started is by getting in touch with the Athletic Equipment Managers Association, which also covers high schools and colleges and has a job placement service.

The address of the association is 6224 Hester Rd., Oxford, OH 45056. Phone: (513) 933-2421.

SIDELINES

Picture This

Somebody gave Ed Sabol an 8mm movie camera as a wedding present, and look what happened.

In 1962 Ed Sabol was earning a living selling overcoats for his father-in-law's clothing company in Philadelphia. His hobby was using his gift camera to film his son Steve in local football games.

On a whim, he contacted NFL Commissioner Pete Rozelle and bid $3,000 for the rights to shoot the 1962 championship game between the New York Giants and the Green Bay Packers. Since no one topped that bid, he got the job. Pete Rozelle later called it the best football film he had ever seen. Ed Sabol's new company, Blair Motion Pictures, was off and running.

The next year, Blair Motion Pictures shot every NFL game, including the championship game between the Colts and the Browns. Sabol made highlight films from the footage and sent the films around the country. They stirred up tremendous interest in pro football.

In 1964, Sabol had only six filmmakers in his employ and he worried that his little company would not survive competition from larger, well-established filmmakers who were beginning to recognize the growing popularity of pro football. So Sabol persuaded Commissioner Rozelle that the NFL ought to have its own motion picture arm. Club owners agreed, and thus NFL Films was born. Beginning with the much-praised production "They Call It Pro Football," which featured the revolutionary use of ground-level slow motion, and a coach on the sidelines wired for sound, Sabol went on to introduce many innovative techniques that gave NFL Films a special stature in sports filmmaking.

President of NFL Films today is Ed Sabol's son Steve, himself a creative filmmaker of the first order. Steve Sabol's productions have won a third of the nearly 70 Emmys awarded to NFL Films. The volume of work hasn't slowed down. NFL Films turns out about 400 films annually for use on television and video.

The company now has a large, ultramodern studio complex in a campus setting of five acres in southern New Jersey. It is here that all the sports programming, syndicated television shows, sports marketing, and even film productions for business and industry are brought to life.

NFL Films not only is a big and profitable operation, it is also responsible in large measure for pro football's enormous popularity. And it all began with a gift camera in the hands of an amateur photographer.

PRO FOOTBALL HALL OF FAME

Canton, Ohio

Established in 1963 in the city where the NFL was born. *Annual visitors:* more than 225,000. *Employees:* 21 full-time, several summer part-timers, no interns. *Executive director:* John Bankert. *Address:* 2121 George Halas Dr. NW, Canton, OH 44708. *Phone:* (330) 456-8207.

MICHAEL L. HUYGHUE
Senior Vice President, Football Operations, Jacksonville Jaguars

Michael Huyghue (pronounced HEWG) got his first taste of pro football working as an intern for the NFL Players Association. It's a big jump from a nonpaying job as an intern to a top position with the Jacksonville Jaguars, but Huyghue made it in no time.

To begin at the beginning, Huyghue grew up in Windsor, Connecticut, in a neighborhood almost entirely white, and he found out early he was different from other kids. But he learned to deal with that. Excelling in sports helped. So did his involvement in Boys' Nation, which taught him confidence and spurred him to do well academically. He got a degree in communication arts at Cornell, where he starred in baseball and football. Later, he got a law degree at the University of Michigan.

After law school, he returned to the NFL, this time as labor relations counsel to the NFL's Management Council, where from 1987 to 1990 he advised the 28 member clubs on interpretation and enforcement of the provisions of the collective bargaining agreement between the league and the NFL Players Association. During his first year with the Management Council, he was also an integral member of the council staff that directed member clubs in the signing of replacement players during the 1987 players' strike. Rounding out his labor experience, Huyghue also served briefly in 1987 in the legal department of the NFL Players Association, based in Washington.

In 1991, Huyghue took a job as general manager of the Birmingham Fire in the World League of American Football and actually ran the league for some months before it was dissolved. On his return to the U.S., he got a position with the Detroit Lions as vice president of administration and general counsel. Two years later, Wayne Weaver, searching for a bright young executive who could help build the expansion Jacksonville Jaguars from the ground up, offered Huyghue the job. Huyghue joined the Jaguars in March 1994 at the age of 32. His job: directing all football operations with primary responsibility for negotiating player contracts, administering the salary cap, and overall administration and financial responsibility for the team.

Coach Tom Coughlin of the Jaguars is a fan of his. "Michael is great to work with," he says. He describes Huyghue as a hard worker who knows how to get things done. "And he has a great relationship with agents and players," he says.

How far will he go? The whole sports world is watching.

TO CLEVELAND BELONG THE BROWNS

Art Modell moved his NFL franchise from Cleveland to Baltimore in 1996, but at the insistence of the NFL the name of the team stayed behind.

The Cleveland Browns will reappear in 1999, either as an expansion franchise or as an existing club from another city.

The new Cleveland Browns will have a new 72,000-seat stadium, a consequence of an unusual public-private partnership. The stadium will be owned by the city of Cleveland, but the NFL will pick up a substantial part of construction costs.

NATIONAL FOOTBALL LEAGUE

League office:
280 Park Ave.
New York, NY 10022
(212) 758-1500
Commissioner: Paul Tagliabue
President: Neil R. Austrian
Internships: contact John Buzzeo

AMERICAN FOOTBALL CONFERENCE

Baltimore Ravens
11001 Owings Mills Blvd.
Owings Mills, MD 21117
(410) 654-6200
Pres: Arthur B. Modell
Internships offered

Buffalo Bills
One Bills Dr.
Orchard Park, NY 14127-2296
(716) 648-1800
Gen Mgr: John Butler
Internships: contact Denny Lynch

Cincinnati Bengals
One Bengals Dr.
Cincinnati, OH 45204
(513) 621-3550
Gen Mgr: Michael Brown

Denver Broncos
13655 Broncos Pkwy.
Englewood, CO 80112
(303) 649-9000
Gen Mgr: John Beake
Internships: contact Jim Saccomano

Houston Oilers
8030 El Rio
Houston, TX 77054
(713) 881-3500
Gen Mgr: Floyd Reese
Internships: contact Lewis Mangum

Indianapolis Colts
P.O. Box 535000
Indianapolis, IN 46253
(317) 297-2658
Gen Mgr: James Irsay
Internships: contact Craig Kelley

Jacksonville Jaguars
One Stadium Pl.
Jacksonville, FL 32202
(904) 633-6000
Pres/COO: David Seldin

Kansas City Chiefs
One Arrowhead Dr.
Kansas City, MO 64129
(816) 924-9300
Gen Mgr: Carl Peterson
Internships: contact Bob Moore

Miami Dolphins
7500 S.W. 30th St.
Davie, FL 33314
(954) 452-7000
Gen Mgr: Jimmy Johnson
Internships: contact Harvey Greene

New England Patriots
Foxboro Stadium
60 Washington St.
Foxboro, MA 02035
(508) 543-8200
Pres/CEO: Robert Kraft
Internships: contact Don Lowery

New York Jets
1000 Fulton Ave.
Hempstead, NY 11550
(516) 538-6600
Ass't Gen Mgr: James Harris
Internships offered

Oakland Raiders
1220 Harbor Bay Pkwy.
Alameda, CA 94502
(510) 864-5000
Pres: Al Davis
Internships: contact Mike Taylor

Pittsburgh Steelers
300 Stadium Circle
Pittsburgh, PA 15212
(412) 323-1200
Pres: Daniel M. Rooney
Internships: contact Joe Gordon

San Diego Chargers
P.O. Box 609609
San Diego, CA 92160-9609
(619) 280-2111
Gen Mgr: Bobby Beathard
Internships: contact Bill Johnston

Seattle Seahawks
11220 N.E. 53rd St.
Kirkland, WA 98033
(206) 827-9777
Pres/Gen Mgr: David Behring
Internships: contact Gary Wright

NATIONAL FOOTBALL CONFERENCE

Arizona Cardinals
P.O. Box 888
Phoenix, AZ 85001-0888
(602) 379-0101
Gen Mgr: Larry Wilson

Atlanta Falcons
One Falcon Pl.
Suwanee, GA 30174
(404) 945-1111
Pres: Taylor Smith
Internships: contact Charlie Taylor

Carolina Panthers
800 S. Mint St.
Charlotte, NC 28202-1502
(704) 358-7000
Gen Mgr: Bill Polian

Chicago Bears
Halas Hall
250 N. Washington Rd.
Lake Forest, IL 60045
(847) 295-6600
Pres: Michael B. McCaskey
Internships: contact Tim LeFevour

Dallas Cowboys
Cowboys Center
One Cowboys Pkwy.
Irving, TX 75063
(214) 556-9900
Pres/Gen Mgr: Jerry Jones
Internships: contact Rich Dalrymple

Detroit Lions
1200 Featherstone Rd.
Pontiac, MI 48342
(303) 335-4131
Exec VP/CEO: Chuck Schmidt
Internships: contact Mike Murray

Green Bay Packers
1265 Lombardi Ave.
Green Bay, WI 54304
(414) 496-5700
Gen Mgr: Ron Wolf
Internships: contact Lee Remmel

Minnesota Vikings
9520 Viking Dr.
Eden Prairie, MN 55344
(612) 828-6500
VP Admin/Ass't Gen Mgr:
  Jeff Diamond
Internships: contact Dave Pelletier

New Orleans Saints
5800 Airline Hwy.
Metairie, LA 70003
(504) 733-0255
VP/Gen Mgr: Bill Kuharich
Internships offered

New York Giants
Giants Stadium
East Rutherford, NJ 07073
(201) 935-8111
VP/Gen Mgr: George Young
Internships offered

Philadelphia Eagles
3501 S. Broad St.
Philadelphia, PA 19148
(215) 463-2500
Pres: Harry Gamble
Internships offered

St. Louis Rams
One Rams Way
St. Louis County, MO 63045
(314) 982-7267
Pres: John Shaw
Internships: contact Rick Smith

San Francisco 49ers
4949 Centennial Blvd.
Santa Clara, CA 95054-1229
(408) 562-4949
Pres: Carmen Policy
Internships: contact Rodney Knox

Tampa Bay Buccaneers
One Buccaneer Pl.
Tampa, FL 33607
(813) 870-2700
VP Admin: Richard McKay
Internships offered

Washington Redskins
Redskin Park
P.O. Box 17247
Washington, DC 20041
(703) 478-8900
Gen Mgr: Charley Casserly
Internships: contact John Autry

CANADIAN FOOTBALL LEAGUE

League office:
CFL Bldg., 5th Floor
110 Eglinton Ave. W
Toronto, Ontario M4R 1A3
Canada
(416) 322-9650
Commissioner: Larry W. Smith

B.C. Lions
10605 135th St.
Surrey, British Columbia V3T 4C8
Canada
(604) 930-5466
CEO: Mike McCarthy

Calgary Stampeders
McMahon Stadium
1817 Crowchild Trail NW
Calgary, Alberta T2M 4R6
Canada
(403) 289-0205
Gen Mgr: Wally Buono

PROFESSIONAL FOOTBALL LEAGUES

Edmonton Eskimos
9023 111th Ave.
Edmonton, Alberta T5B 0C3
Canada
(403) 448-1525
Gen Mgr: Hugh Campbell

Hamilton Tiger-Cats
Lloyd D. Jackson Sq.
2 King St. W
Hamilton, Ontario L8P 1A1
Canada
(905) 521-5666
Gen Mgr: Neil Lumsden

Montreal Alouettes
4545 Ave. Pierre de Coubertin
P.O. Box 65, Station M
Montreal, Ontario H1V 3L6
Canada
(514) 252-4666
Exec VP: Mitchell A. Garber

Ottawa Rough Riders
Coliseum Bldg., Landsdowne Park
1015 Bank St.
Ottawa, Ontario K1S 3W7
Canada
(613) 235-5554
CEO: Jim Durrell

Saskatchewan Roughriders
2940 10th Ave.
P.O. Box 1277
Regina, Saskatchewan S4P 3B8
Canada
(306) 569-2323
Gen Mgr: Alan Ford

Toronto Argonauts
P.O. Box 2005, Station B
Toronto, Ontario M5T 3H8
Canada
(416) 341-5151
CEO: Paul Beeston

Winnipeg Blue Bombers
1465 Maroons Rd.
Winnipeg, Manitoba R3G 0L6
Canada
(204) 784-2583
Dir Business Opns: Don Cozine

ARENA FOOTBALL LEAGUE

League office:
75 E. Wacker Dr., Suite 400
Chicago, IL 60601
(312) 332-5510
Commissioner: C. David Baker
Internships: contact Nick Gandy

Albany Firebirds
Knickerbocker Arena
51 S. Pearl St.
Albany, NY 12207
(518) 487-2222
Gen Mgr: Joe Hennessy
Internships offered

Anaheim Piranhas
2000 Gene Autry Way
Gate 6, Suite 202
Anaheim, CA 92806
(714) 940-2525
Pres: Roy Englebrecht

Arizona Rattlers
201 E. Jefferson
Phoenix, AZ 85004
(602) 514-8300
VP Admin: Gene Nudo
Internships: contact Cheryl Nauman

Florida Bobcats
139 Worth Ave.
Palm Beach, FL 33480
(407) 835-0224
Gen Mgr: Bruce Frey

Iowa Barnstormers
505 Fifth Ave., Suite 1001
Des Moines, IA 50309
(515) 282-3596
Gen Mgr: Jim Foster

Milwaukee Mustangs
740 N. Plankinton Ave., Suite 310
Milwaukee, WI 53203
(414) 272-3500
Gen Mgr: Chris Vallozzi
Internships offered

Nashville Kats
150 Second Ave. N, Suite 305
Nashville, TN 37201
(615) 254-5287
Gen Mgr: Billy McGehee

New Jersey Red Dogs
One Palmer Terrace
Carlstadt, NJ 07072
(201) 507-1303
Gen Mgr: Jim Leahy

New York CityHawks
Madison Square Garden
2 Pennsylvania Plaza
New York, NY 10021-0091
(212) 465-6482
Gen Mgr: Frank Murphy

Orlando Predators
20 N. Orange Ave., Suite 101
Orlando, FL 32801
(407) 648-4444
Gen Mgr: Alex Narushka
Internships: contact Robert Flynn

Portland Forest Dragons
7412 S.W. Beaverton-Hillsdale Hwy.,
   Suite 112
Portland, OR 97225
(503) 292-7210
Gen Mgr: TBA

San Jose Sabercats
40 N. First St.
San Jose, CA 95113
(408) 993-2287
Gen Mgr: Terry Malley
Internships offered

Tampa Bay Storm
401 Channelside Dr.
Tampa, FL 33602
(813) 276-7300
Gen Mgr: Tim Marcum
Internships offered

Texas Terror
10 Greenway Plaza E.
Houston, TX 77046
(713) 627-3865
Gen Mgr: Bill Reiss

WORLD LEAGUE OF AMERICAN FOOTBALL

League office:
410 Park Ave.
New York, NY 10022
(212) 758-1500
Dir Opns: Eric Tillman

Amsterdam Admirals
Museumplein
5A, 3rd Floor
1071 DJ Amsterdam
The Netherlands
Gen Mgr: Bill Peterson
Stadium: Olympic Stadium (38,000)
Phone: 31-20-6625-901

Barcelona Dragons
Estadi Olimpic de Montjuic
Passeig Olimpic 17-19
08038 Barcelona
Spain
Gen Mgr: Jordi Vila-Puig
Stadium: Estadi Olimpic de Montjuic
   (54,000)
Phone: 34-3-425-4949

Dusseldorf Rhein Fire
Tersteegenstrasse 63
407474 Dusseldorf
Germany
Gen Mgr: Alexander Leibkind
Stadium: Rheinstadion (32,000 seated)
Phone: 49-211-478-730

Edinburgh Scottish Claymores
23 Chester St.
Edinburgh EH3 7EN
Scotland
Gen Mgr: Michael Keller
Stadium: Murrayfield (67,000)
Phone: 44-131-220-1314

Frankfurt Galaxy
Eschersheimer Land Strasse 526
60433 Frankfurt 50
Germany
Gen Mgr: Chris Heyne
Stadium: Frankfurter Waldstadion
   (30,000 seated)
Phone: 49-69-530-9935

London Monarchs
Mellier House
26A Albemarle St.
London W1X 3FA
England
Gen Mgr: Gareth Moores
Stadium: White Hart Lane (30,000)
Phone: 44-171-629-1300

*Ardent and knowledgeable, patrons of ice hockey
are the coolest sports fans in North America.
The objective now is to increase their number.*

HOCKEY

Gary Bettman took over as commissioner at a favorable time, a time when the old perception of hockey as a regional sport—long an obstacle to network television coverage—had already been chipped away by expansion franchises in San Jose, Tampa Bay, Miami, and Anaheim. In the midsummer of 1994, the NHL got its best television deal, a five-year arrangement with Fox Sports for $155 million. ESPN got in on the deal for specific games. Nike and Anheuser-Busch came in early with heavy advertising commitments.

What drew everybody together was the prospect of reaching a big audience between the ages of 21 and 34, which is a choice grouping and one in which hockey fans may be found. But will their numbers increase? There are no fans in sportsdom more loyal and more fervid than hockey fans, yet when it comes to ticket sales and television viewership, hockey still ranks a rather distant fourth in professional team sports.

Hockey is fourth also in merchandise sales, but some of the newer clubs have been doing exceedingly well in this regard, a sign that the marketing of hockey is warming up. In 1991–92, their first year of operation, the San Jose Sharks sold a record $150 million worth of apparel and other items bearing their logo (despite a very unremarkable on-ice performance). The record was shattered in the 1993–94 season with the arrival of the Walt Disney Company's Mighty Ducks of Anaheim. The Mighty Ducks not only rang up the most sales in the NHL, they also outsold every professional team in every sport in North America.

Which was not altogether surprising given the awesomeness of the Disney marketing machinery. The club's objective, said Ken Wilson, vice president of sales and marketing, "is to get everybody in the country to wear Mighty Ducks merchandise."

Another powerful marketer newly arrived on the scene is the owner of the Florida Panthers, Wayne Huizenga, who is head of Blockbuster Entertainment, the movie rental empire. Huizenga also owns the Florida Marlins baseball team and part of the Miami Dolphins of the NFL. He is esteemed as a wise and farsighted businessman. When he first announced his plan to set up a hockey franchise in Miami, there were some who doubted the area had enough hockey fans to support it. Not to worry, he says. "Many Canadians come down to get away from the snow."

Tony Tavares, president of Disney Sports Enterprises, thinks the involvement of Blockbuster Entertainment and Disney brightens the future for professional hockey. The two companies, he believes, will bring new audiences to hockey.

The Job Picture

The league gets a heap of job inquiries from hockey fans every week, and so do the franchises, but employment opportunities are slim. Aside from the occasional appointment of a secretary or other office assistant, job placements—however few they are—go to people with appropriate experience, mainly in sales and marketing.

Internships. The league hires six to eight interns at its New York headquarters in the course of a year. Interns are generally assigned to public relations, special events (promotions), marketing, and administration. Competition for these internships is brisk.

Most of the U.S. clubs in the league also have internship programs.

The Mighty Ducks' internship program is especially interesting. Each year the club hires as many as 15 interns to work from May to June for college credit *plus* a stipend. Training is not limited to one or two aspects of club business but covers all of it. The catch: applicants must be enrolled in a college program in sports management.

Where to Start: The Minors

Executives at the NHL offer familiar advice to rookie job seekers—go to the minor leagues for experience. They point out that both the International Hockey League and the American Hockey League are in expansion moods and have increasing opportunities for jobs and internships.

International Hockey League

The 1996–97 season was the International Hockey League's 52nd consecutive season of operation.

The IHL started in 1945 with four teams, all based in Detroit or Windsor, Ontario. It is now one of North America's fastest-growing professional sports leagues, with 19 teams coast-to-coast, including two in Canada. (For locations and phone numbers, see the directory at the end of this section.)

The league plays its games in many of North America's best facilities, such as the Bradley Center in Milwaukee, the Palace of Auburn Hills, the Gund Arena in Cleveland, and the Delta Center in Salt Lake.

Total attendance has gone up every year for nine straight years. In 1996–97, total attendance (regular season and playoffs) was more than 6.2 million. Attributable are these factors: (1) a high quality of professional hockey, (2) lively family entertainment in a comfortable setting, and (3) a league requirement that a minimum of 5,000 seats are priced at $10 or less.

Also up, dramatically, are revenues from the sale of licensed merchandise bearing club logos. From $3 million in 1952–53, income from merchandise rose to $25 million in 1995–96, a real sign of fan identification with local clubs.

Internships. All teams in the league employ interns. At league headquarters, two interns provide full-time assistance for the 12 regular employees, and six additional interns are summoned when there's a need. According to Scott Woods in communications, the league has a good record of advancing interns to full-time jobs.

American Hockey League

The AHL, says marketing executive Maria D'Agostino, is in robust health and looking forward to further growth. Added for the 1996–97 season were three new franchises: the Hamilton Bulldogs, Kentucky Thoroughbreds, and Philadelphia Phantoms, bringing the total number of teams to 18, all affiliates of National Hockey League clubs.

The Kentucky team has already etched its name in American Hockey League history: it drew 17,503 fans to Rupp Arena in Lexington for its season opener, setting a new single-game attendance mark for the league.

The league's season attendance for 1995–96 was 3.7 million, the ninth straight record-breaking year.

Expected to join this happy group for the

1997–98 season is a new franchise in Palm Beach, Florida, and another in Lowell, Massachusetts.

Also increasing is television coverage of league games.

D'Agostino says that not only does the AHL entertain its customers throughout the league with hockey games of high quality, it also serves the valuable function of developing young players. She mentions with pride that 66 percent of the players in the National Hockey League came out of the AHL.

But, she adds, "as the premier professional development league for the NHL, the American Hockey League does more than develop players and coaches for the NHL—it also develops general managers, broadcasters, and other front-office personnel."

*　　*　　*　　*

For D'Agostino, a career in sports was exactly what she wanted, even if it took forever to get a job. It didn't take forever, but it did take three internships. After her first year in the sports management program at Springfield College in Massachusetts, she got a summer internship with the New York Rangers. She fielded phone calls from reporters, clipped newspaper articles and proofread copy for the media guide. The next summer she interned with Custom Event Marketing, a sports marketing firm. Again, much work on the phone. Her third internship was at the Basketball Hall of Fame in West Springfield, Massachusetts, where she wrote press releases.

In her final college year, she got a part-time job in the American Hockey League office in West Springfield compiling statistics. After graduation she was appointed assistant marketing director, handling public relations and the merchandising of products bearing the logos of the league's franchises. In 1993, at the age of 24, she became the league's marketing director.

D'Agostino says: "If you want a career in sports, you won't find it in the classified ads. Do as many internships as you are offered because it's a good way to meet people, and sooner or later one of those people is going to be helpful."

Internships. The league accepts as many as eight interns over the course of a year. The individual clubs also engage interns in various numbers.

HOW THEY GOT THERE

GARY B. BETTMAN
Commissioner, National Hockey League

Gary Bettman, a lawyer who was groomed in professional sports at the National Basketball Association, became the chief executive of the 77-year-old National Hockey League on February 1, 1993. The NHL consists of 26 franchises—18 in the U.S. and 8 in Canada. In 1967 it had six franchises.

The commissioner has a staff of 100 that's spread over three cities—New York, Montreal, and Toronto.

Bettman is a native of New York. He graduated from Cornell University in 1974 and from New York University's law school in 1977, and for four years he worked for a corporate law firm. In 1981, at the age of 29, he joined the NBA as assistant general counsel. He was with the NBA for 12 years, rising to the position of senior vice president and general counsel. He was a close associate of Commissioner David Stern and played a major role in shaping NBA operations.

His contract as NHL commissioner is for five years.

East Coast Hockey League

In only eight years, the ECHL has grown into the largest minor league hockey league with 23 teams in 13 states.

New to the league in 1996–97 were teams representing Peoria, Illinois, and Biloxi, Mississippi. Ready to join the league as soon as their new arenas are completed are teams from Greenville, South Carolina, and Trenton, New Jersey. What's more, league president and CEO Richard Adams has received inquiries from half a dozen other cities.

These are exciting times for the league. Adams thinks that in five years, the league will have 30 teams—and a more prominent role in developing players for the NHL.

Adams's confidence is based in part on the league's strong position in the South, which has helped double league attendance. Figures for the 1995–96 season showed an average of just under 5,000 fans for league games and a season league record of 3.6 million.

Along with the leadership of Richard Adams, accountability for the league's successes is shared by the league executives, all of whom, as it happens, are graduates of college programs in sports management. Scott Sabatino, director of business operations, studied for the graduate degree in sports management at the University of Massachusetts. Doug Price, director of hockey administration, got a bachelor's at Defiance College, Ohio, and Jana Spaulding, director of communications, attended the graduate program at Mankato State in Minnesota. The administrative assistant, Kathy Nee, studied sports management at both Dean Junior College in Massachusetts and Bowling Green State, Ohio.

Communications director Jana Spaulding came to the league as an intern. After several months of "really hard work," she was rewarded with the appointment she now holds. Her advice to others seeking internships is familiar: "Don't be picky. Take whatever you can get."

The Other Leagues

Both the Central Hockey League and the Colonial Hockey League anticipate good things ahead.

For the 1996–97 season, the Central Hockey League added teams representing Columbus and Macon, both in Georgia; Huntsville, Alabama, and Nashville, Tennessee. The four new franchises gave the league a total of 10 teams. A new franchise in St. Charles, Missouri, is expected to join the league.

Marilyn Cox, communications, said the league and its teams would welcome inquiries about internships. Interns are needed on both levels, she said.

In the Colonial Hockey League, the addition of Dayton, Ohio, for the 1996–97 season gave the league a membership of 10 also.

Katrina Simpson, media relations, said interns are not employed at the league's offices, but the teams rely on them.

(The rosters of all minor leagues follow the listing of NHL clubs.)

Game Officials

For NHL referees and linesmen of the future, the NHL officiating department scans amateur hockey, selects a small number of prospects it designates as trainees, and moves them into professional minor leagues under close supervision. After further training in the

That's Entertainment

Entertainment at East Coast Hockey League games includes live alligator wrestling on the ice.

H O W T H E Y G O T T H E R E

JACK FERREIRA
General Manager, Mighty Ducks of Anaheim

First general manager for the franchise … Born in Providence in 1944. Got a bachelor's degree in history at Boston University, where he won all-American honors as a goaltender on the hockey team … Served as assistant hockey coach at Princeton and Brown, and began his professional career in 1972 with the New England Whalers of the World Hockey Association as head scout and assistant general manager. From 1977 to 1986 was a scout for the NHL and Calgary Flames. Was director of player development for the New York Rangers until 1988, when he was named general manager of the Minnesota North Stars. In 1990 he helped start the San Jose Sharks franchise as executive vice president and general manager.

**U.S. HOCKEY
HALL OF FAME**

**Eveleth,
Minnesota**

Established in
1973 in a town
where hockey was
played as early as
1903. *Annual
visitors:* 10,000.
Employees: 2 full-
time, 3 part-time, 1
intern. *Director:* Ted
Brill. *Address:* 801
Hat Trick Ave.,
Eveleth, MN 55734.
Phone: (218) 744-
5167.

minors, the best of the prospects are given tentative NHL assignments for a final evaluation and then signed. The process may take from four to seven years.

In its negotiations with the NHL Officials Association on a new salary schedule, the NHL in late 1993 proposed the following: Base salaries for first-year referees would increase from $50,000 to $65,000 in the first year of the contract and to $80,000 by year four. For referees with 10 years' experience, salaries would rise from $80,000 to $125,000. For the most senior referees, the raise would be from $90,000 to $175,000. By the fourth year of the agreement, the salary scale would rise to a range of from $80,000 for first-year referees to $220,000 for the most senior referees. Salaries for linesmen begin at $52,000 and rise to $115,000 in 24 years.

The NHL's director of officiating is Bryan Lewis.

SIDELINES

• If you love hockey but you're being pressured to pursue a career in dentistry, here's news that will cheer you up: Every franchise in the NHL has a dentist on its club roster.

• One of the NHL's main objectives is to present hockey games in a wholesome, family atmosphere. That's no problem at Anaheim Arena, where employees set a fine example of decorum for hockey fans. If you work for the Walt Disney Company's Mighty Ducks of Anaheim, you see, there are strict rules of behavior and appearance. Some of the rules: For male workers, no beards or mustaches. Hair must not touch the collar. Sideburns cannot extend below the earlobes. For women, no eye liner or eye shadow, no frosting or streaking of hair. For both men and women, no visible tattoos, and only one ring is permitted per hand. "The look we want is natural, clean-cut, professional," said a Disney administrator.

• The National Hockey League now has 26 teams. That's 20 more than it had in 1967.

PROFESSIONAL HOCKEY LEAGUES

NATIONAL HOCKEY LEAGUE

League offices:
New York
1251 Ave. of the Americas, 47th Fl.
New York, NY 10020-1198
(212) 789-2000
Montreal
1800 McGill College Ave., Suite 2600
Montreal, Quebec H3A 3J6
Canada
(514) 288-9220
Toronto
75 International Blvd., Suite 300
Rexdale, Ontario, M9W 6LN
Canada
(416) 798-0809

Commissioner: Gary B. Bettman
Sr VP/COO: Stephen J. Solomon
Internships at New York headquarters:
    contact PR Dep't

Mighty Ducks of Anaheim
2695 Katella Ave.
P.O. Box 61077
Anaheim, CA 92803-6177
(714) 704-2700
Gen Mgr: Jack Ferreira
Internships offered

Boston Bruins
1 Fleet Center, Suite 250
Boston, MA 02114
(617) 624-1050
Gen Mgr: Harry J. Sinden
Internships: contact Heidi Holland

Buffalo Sabres
1 Seymour H. Knox III Plaza
Buffalo, NY 14203
(716) 855-4100
Gen Mgr: John Muckler
Internships: contact Steve Rossi

Calgary Flames
P.O. Box 1540, Station M
Calgary, Alberta T2P 3B9, Canada
(403) 777-2177
Gen Mgr: Doug Risebrough

Chicago Blackhawks
1901 W. Madison
Chicago, IL 60612
(312) 455-7000
Gen Mgr: Robert J. Pulford

Dallas Stars
211 Cowboy Pkwy.
Irving, TX 75063
(214) 868-2890
Gen Mgr: Bob Gainey
Internships: contact Larry Kelly

Detroit Red Wings
600 Civic Center Dr.
Detroit, MI 48226
(313) 396-7544
Gen Mgr: Scott Bowman
Internships: contact Bill Jamieson

Edmonton Oilers
11230 110th St.
Edmonton, Alberta T5G 3G8, Canada
(403) 474-8561
Pres/Gen Mgr: Glen Sather

Florida Panthers
100 N.E. Third Ave., 2nd Floor
Ft. Lauderdale, FL 33301
(305) 768-1900
Gen Mgr: Bryan Murray
Internships offered

Hartford Whalers
242 Trumbull St., 8th Floor
Hartford, CT 06103
(203) 728-3366
Gen Mgr: Jim Rutherford
Internships: contact Mark Mancini

Los Angeles Kings
The Forum
P.O. Box 17013
Inglewood, CA 90308
(310) 419-3160
Gen Mgr: Sam McMaster
Internships: contact Tami Cole

Montreal Canadiens
1260 de la Gauchetiere W
Montreal, Quebec H3H 5E8, Canada
(514) 932-2582
Gen Mgr: Serge Savard

New Jersey Devils
P.O. Box 504
East Rutherford, NJ 07073
(201) 935-6050
Gen Mgr: Lou Lamoriello
Internships: contact Peter McMullen

New York Islanders
Nassau Coliseum
Hempstead Tpke.
Uniondale, NY 11553
(516) 794-4100
Gen Mgr: Don Maloney
Internships: contact Ginger Killian

New York Rangers
2 Penn Plaza, 14th floor
New York, NY 10121
(212) 465-6485
Gen Mgr: Neil Smith
Internships: contact Pamela Marquis

Ottawa Senators
1000 Palladium Dr. 110
Kanata, Ontario K2V 1A5, Canada
(613) 721-0115
Gen Mgr: Randy J. Sexton

Philadelphia Flyers
The Spectrum
1 CoreStates Complex
Philadelphia, PA 19148
(215) 465-4500
Gen Mgr: Bob Clarke
Internships: contact Jill Vogel

Pittsburgh Penguins
Gate No. 9
Civic Arena
Pittsburgh, PA 15219
(412) 642-1300
Gen Mgr: Craig Patrick
Internships: contact Steve Swetoha

St. Louis Blues
1401 Clark Ave.
St. Louis, MO 63103
(314) 622-2500
Gen Mgr: Mike Keenan
Internships offered

San Jose Sharks
525 W. Santa Clara St.
San Jose, CA 95113
(408) 287-7070
Gen Mgr: Dean Lombardi
Internships offered

Tampa Bay Lightning
501 E. Kennedy Blvd., Suite 175
Tampa, FL 33602
(813) 229-2658
Gen Mgr: Phil Esposito
Internships: contact Gerry Helper

Toronto Maple Leafs
60 Carlton St.
Toronto, Ontario M5B 1L1, Canada
(416) 977-1641
Gen Mgr: Cliff Fletcher

Vancouver Canucks
800 Griffiths Way
Vancouver, British Columbia
V6B 6G1, Canada
(604) 899-4600
Gen Mgr: Pat Quinn

Washington Capitals
USAir Arena
1 Harry S Truman Dr.
Landover, MD 20785
(301) 386-7000
Gen Mgr: David Poile
Internships: contact Rosy Beauclair

INTERNATIONAL HOCKEY LEAGUE

League offices:
(Hockey Operations)
3850 Priority Way, Suite 110
Indianapolis, IN 46240
(810) 258-0580
Internships offered
(Business Office)
1577 N. Woodward, Suite 212
Bloomfield Hills, MI 48304
(810) 258-0580
Commissioner: Robert P. Ufer
Internships offered

Chicago Wolves
10550 Lunt Ave.
Rosemont, IL 60018
(847) 390-0404
Gen Mgr: Grant Mulvey
Affiliation: Independent
Internships: contact Shawn Hegan

Cincinnati Cyclones
2250 Seymour Ave.
Cincinnati, OH 45212
(513) 531-7825
Gen Mgr: Doug Kirchhofer
Affiliation: Florida Panthers
Internships: contact Terry Ficorelli

Cleveland Lumberjacks
One Center Ice, 200 Huron Rd.
Cleveland, OH 44115
(216) 420-0000
Gen Mgr: Larry Gordon
Affiliation: Pittsburgh Penguins
Internships: contact David Gordon

Detroit Vipers
2 Championship Dr.
Auburn Hills, MI 48326
(810) 377-8613
Gen Mgr: Rick Dudley
Affiliation: Independent

Fort Wayne Komets
1010 Memorial Way, Suite 100
Fort Wayne, IN 46805
(219) 483-0011
Gen Mgr: David Franke
Affiliation: Independent

Grand Rapids Griffins
190 Monroe Ave. NW, Suite 500
Grand Rapids, MI 49503
(616) 774-4585
Gen Mgr: Bob McNamara

Houston Aeros
P.O. Box 271469
Houston, TX 77277-1469
(713) 621-2842
Gen Mgr: Steve Patterson
Affiliation: Independent
Internships: contact Brad Ewing

Indianapolis Ice
222 E. Ohio St., Suite 810
Indianapolis, IN 46204
(317) 266-1234
Gen Mgr: Ray Compton
Affiliation: Chicago Blackhawks
Internships: contact Jeff Johnson

Kansas City Blades
1800 Genessee
Kansas City, MO 64102
(816) 842-5233
Gen Mgr: Doug Soetaert
Affiliation: Independent
Internships offered

Las Vegas Thunder
P.O. Box 70065
Las Vegas, NV 89170
(702) 798-7825
Gen Mgr: Bob Strumm
Affiliation: Phoenix Coyotes
Internships: contact Debbie Barrentine

Long Beach Ice Dogs
300 E. Ocean Blvd.
Long Beach, CA 90802
(310) 423-3647
Gen Mgr: John van Boxmeer

Manitoba Moose
1430 Maroons Rd.
Winnipeg, Manitoba Z3G 0L5
Canada
(204) 987-7825
Gen Mgr: Jean Perron

Michigan K-Wings
3620 Van Rick Dr.
Kalamazoo, MI 49002
(616) 349-9772
Dir of Operations: Ed O'Brien

Milwaukee Admirals
1001 N. Fourth St.
Milwaukee, WI 53203
(414) 227-0550
Gen Mgr: Pat Wittliff
Affiliation: Independent
Internships: contact Mike
   Wojciechowski

Orlando Solar Bears
P.O. Box 95
Orlando, FL 32802
(407) 428-6600
Gen Mgr: Don Waddell

Phoenix Roadrunners
1826 W. McDowell Rd.
Phoenix, AZ 85007
(602) 340-0001
Gen Mgr: Adam Keller
Affiliation: Los Angeles Kings
Internships: contact Bob Ohrablo

Quebec Rafales
2205 Ave Du Colisee
Quebec City, Quebec G17 4W7
Canada
(418) 522-3000
Gen Mgr: Joe Bucchino

Utah Grizzlies
301 S.W. Temple
Salt Lake City, UT 84101
(801) 325-7825
Gen Mgr: Butch Goring

AMERICAN HOCKEY LEAGUE

League office:
425 Union St.
West Springfield, MA 01089
(413) 781-2030
Pres: David Andrews
Internships: contact Maria D'Agostino

Adirondack Red Wings
One Civic Center Plaza
Glens Falls, NY 12801
(518) 798-0366
Gen Mgr: Ken Holland
Affiliation: Detroit Red Wings,
   Tampa Bay Lightning
Internships: contact Don Ostrom

Albany River Rats
51 S. Pearl St.
Albany, NY 12207
(518) 487-2244
Pres: Doug Burch
Affiliation: New Jersey Devils
Internships offered

Baltimore Bandits
201 W. Baltimore St., Suite 209
Baltimore, MD 21201
(410) 528-0200
Asst Gen Mgr: Mike Mudd
Affiliation: Mighty Ducks of Anaheim

Binghamton Rangers
One Stuart St.
Binghamton, NY 13901
(607) 723-8937
Managing Partner: Tom Mitchell
Affiliation: New York Rangers
Internships: contact Patrick Snyder

Carolina Monarchs
P.O. Box 5447
Greensboro, NC 27435
(910) 852-6170
Gen Mgr: Brian McKenna
Affiliation: Florida Panthers

Fredericton Canadiens
P.O. Box HABS
Fredericton, New Brunswick
E3B 4Y2, Canada
(506) 459-4227
Dir of Opns: Wayne Gamble
Affiliation: Montreal Canadiens

Hamilton Bulldogs
85 York Blvd.
Hamilton, Ontario L8R 3L4, Canada
(905) 529-8500
Gen Mgr: Scott Howson
Affiliation: Edmonton Oilers

Hershey Bears
P.O. Box 866
Hershey, PA 17033
(717) 534-3380
Gen Mgr: Jay Feaster
Affiliation: Philadelphia Flyers

Kentucky Thoroughbreds
410 W. Vine St.
Lexington, KY 40507
(606) 259-1996
Pres/CEO: Ron DeGregorio
Affiliation: San Jose Sharks
Internships: contact Jason Bitsoff

Philadelphia Phantoms
The Spectrum
1 CoreStates Complex
Philadelphia, PA 19148
(215) 465-4522
Pres/Gen Mgr: Bob Clarke
Affiliation: Philadelphia Flyers
Internships: contact Alice Marini

Portland Pirates
85 Free St.
Portland, ME 04101
(207) 828-4665
Gen Mgr: Dave Fisher
Affiliation: Washington Capitals

Providence Bruins
One LaSalle Sq.
Providence, RI 02903
(401) 273-5000
CEO: Ed Anderson
Affiliation: Boston Bruins
Internships: contact Lynn Skala

Rochester Americans
50 South Ave.
Rochester, NY 14614
(716) 454-5335
Gen Mgr: Joe Baumann
Affiliation: Buffalo Sabres
Internships: contact Peter Mancuso

Saint John Flames
P.O. Box 4040, Station B
Saint John, New Brunswick
E2M 5E6, Canada
(506) 635-2637
Dir of Opns: Allan Millar
Affiliation: Calgary Flames

St. John's Maple Leafs
6 Logy Bay Rd.
St. John's, Newfoundland A1A 1J3
Canada
(709) 726-1010
Gen Mgr: Glenn Stanford
Affiliation: Toronto Maple Leafs

Springfield Falcons
P.O. Box 3190
Springfield, MA 01110
(413) 739-3344
Pres: Bruce Landon
Affiliation: Hartford Whalers

Syracuse Crunch
800 S. State St.
Syracuse, NY 13202
(315) 473-4444
Gen Mgr: Vance Lederman
Affiliation: Vancouver Canucks

Worcester Icecats
303 Main St.
Worcester, MA 01608
(508) 798-5400
Gen Mgr: Jim Roberts
Affiliation pending
Internships: contact Peter Ricciardi

CENTRAL HOCKEY LEAGUE

League office:
5840 S. Memorial Dr., Suite 302
Tulsa, OK 74145
(918) 664-8881
Commissioner: Monte Miron
Internships: contact Jason Rothwell
Most franchises offer internships.

Fort Worth Fire
1300 S. University, Suite 515
Fort Worth, TX 76107
(817) 336-1992
Gen Mgr: Matt van Hala

Huntsville Channel Cats
Von Braun Civic Ctr.
700 Monroe St.
Huntsville, AL 35801
(205) 551-2383
Gen Mgr: John Stanley

Macon Whoopee
Macon Centreplex
Macon, GA 32101
(912) 741-1000
Gen Mgr: Pat Nugent

Memphis RiverKings
Mid-South Coliseum
Memphis, TN 38104
(901) 278-9009
Gen Mgr: Jim Riggs

Nashville Nighthawks
P.O. Box 198526
Nashville, TN 37219
(615) 259-7825
Owner: Barry Soskin

Oklahoma City Blazers
119 N. Robinson, Suite 230
Oklahoma City, OK 73102-9201
(405) 235-7825
Gen Mgr: Brad Lund

San Antonio Iguanas
110 Broadway, Suite 25
San Antonio, TX 78205
(210) 227-4449
Gen Mgr: Dan Heisserer

Tulsa Oilers
4528 S. Sheridan Rd., No. 212
Tulsa, OK 74145
(918) 663-5888
Gen Mgr: Jeff Lund

Wichita Thunder
4328 E. Kellogg
Wichita, KS 67218
(316) 264-4625
Gen Mgr: Bill Shuck

COLONIAL HOCKEY LEAGUE

League office:
34400 Utica Rd.
Fraser, MI 48026
(810) 296-5510
Commissioner: Michael D. Forbes
Internships: contact Doug Kennedy
Most franchises offer internships.

Dayton Ice Bandits
1001 Shiloh Springs Rd.
Dayton, OH 45415
(513) 279-1114
Gen Mgr: John Tull

Flint Generals
3501 Lapeer Rd.
Flint, MI 48503
(810) 742-9422
Gen Mgr: Robbie Nichols

Madison Monsters
1881 Expo Mall E
Madison, WI 53713
(608) 251-2884
Gen Mgr: Dan Wilhelm

Muskegon Fury
470 W. Western Ave.
Muskegon, MI 49440
(616) 726-5058
Gen Mgr: Tony Lisman

Port Huron Border Cats
3061 Commerce Dr., Suite 3
Fort Gratlot, MI 48059
(810) 385-8326
Gen Mgr: Costa Papista

Quad City Mallards
501 15th St., Suite 900
Moline, IL 61265
(309) 764-7825
Gen Mgr: Howard Cornfield

Saginaw Lumber Kings
4855 State St., Suite 3
Saginaw, MI 48603
(517) 790-3771
Gen Mgr: John Blum

Thunder Bay Senators
901 Miles St. E
Thunder Bay, Ontario P7C 1J9
Canada
(807) 623-7121
Gen Mgr: Gary Cook

Utica Blizzard
400 Oriskany St. W
Utica, NY 13502
(315) 793-1111
Pres/Gen Mgr: Jeff Croop

EAST COAST HOCKEY LEAGUE

League office:
125 Village Blvd., Suite 210
Princeton, NJ 08540
(609) 452-0770
Commissioner: Patrick J. Kelly
Internships: contact Rick Adams
Most franchises offer internships.

Baton Rouge Kingfish
P.O. Box 2142
Baton Rouge, LA 70821
(504) 336-4625
Gen Mgr: Ron Hansis

Birmingham Bulls
P.O. Box 1506
Birmingham, AL 35201
(205) 458-8833
Gen Mgr: Scott Myers

Charlotte Checkers
2700 E. Independence Blvd.
Charlotte, NC 28205
(704) 342-4423
Gen Mgr: Carl Scheer

Columbus Chill
7001 Dublin Park Dr.
Dublin, OH 43016
(614) 791-9999
Gen Mgr: David Paitson

Dayton Bombers
3640 Col. Glenn Hwy., Suite 417
Dayton, OH 45435
(513) 873-4747
Gen Mgr: Arnold Johnson

Hampton Roads Admirals
P.O. Box 299
Norfolk, VA 23501
(757) 640-1212
Gen Mgr: Allan MacIsaac

Huntington Blizzard
763 Third Ave.
Huntington, WV 25701
(304) 697-7825
Office Mgr: Alicia Dunwoody

Jacksonville Lizard Kings
5569-7 Bowden Rd.
Jacksonville, FL 32216
(904) 448-8800
Gen Mgr: Larry Lane

Johnstown Chiefs
326 Napoleon St.
Johnstown, PA 15901
(814) 539-1799
Gen Mgr: Toby O'Brien

Knoxville Cherokees
500 E. Church St.
Knoxville, TN 37915
(423) 546-7825
Dir Hockey Opns: Barry Smith

Louisiana IceGators
444 Cajundome Blvd.
Lafayette, LA 70506
(318) 234-4423
Gen Mgr: Dave Berryman

Louisville RiverFrogs
P.O. Box 36407
Louisville, KY 40233
(502) 367-9121
Gen Mgr: Dale Owens

Mississippi Sea Wolves
2350 Beach Blvd.
Biloxi, MS 39531
(601) 388-6151
Gen Mgr: Stephan Boutin

Mobile Mysticks
P.O. Box 263
Mobile, AL 36601-0263
(334) 434-7932
Gen Mgr: Steve Chapman

Pensacola Ice Pilots
201 E. Gregory St., Rear
Pensacola, FL 32501
(904) 432-7825
Gen Mgr: Joe Bucchino

Peoria Rivermen
201 S.W. Jefferson
Peoria, IL 61602
(309) 676-1040
Gen Mgr: Greg Griffith

Raleigh IceCaps
4000 W. Chase Blvd., Suite 110
Raleigh, NC 27607
(919) 755-1427
Gen Mgr: Larry Kish

Richmond Renegades
601 E. Leigh St.
Richmond, VA 23219
(804) 643-7825
Pres of Hockey Opns: Craig
Laughlin

Roanoke Express
4502 Starkey Rd. SW, Suite 211
Roanoke, VA 24014
(540) 989-4625
Gen Mgr: Pierre Paiement

South Carolina Stingrays
3107 Firestone Rd.
North Charleston, SC 29418
(803) 744-2248
Dir of Hockey Opns: Rick
Vaive

Tallahassee Tiger Sharks
505 W. Pensacola St., Suite 1
Tallahassee, FL 32303
(904) 224-7700
Gen Mgr: Tony Mancuso

Toledo Storm
One Main St.
Toledo, OH 43605
(419) 691-0200
Gen Mgr: Pat Pylypuik

Wheeling Thunderbirds
P.O. Box 6563
Wheeling, WV 26003-0815
(304) 234-4625
Gen Mgr: Marty Nash

There were many who said it would never catch on,
but solid ticket sales and quality performances
put a kick into America's top new soccer league.

SOCCER

History was on the side of the skeptics. Six times from 1960 to 1985 soccer boosters had tried to create a permanent, big-time soccer league, and each time the attempt flopped, affirming the standard notion that soccer could not compete within U.S. borders for the affection of sports fans already hooked on baseball, basketball, hockey, and American football.

Still, there were enough diehards around who clung to the belief that with proper entrepreneurship soccer could yet establish itself as America's fifth major professional sport. Thus it happened that on April 6, 1996, Major League Soccer, a new amalgam of 10 teams launched a seven-month season of play—this time to considerable success.

The inaugural season drew a surprising attendance: 2,786,673 in 160 regular-season games, an average of 17,416 per game. Playoffs drew 300,455 fans to 17 games, an average of 17,673.

"We've certainly exceeded expectations," MLS Commissioner Doug Logan told *Sports Illustrated* in the final week of the season. "We're 80 percent above our projections on attendance. Our TV partners are very happy, our sponsors are very happy, and we're all very pleased with the level of play."

A big factor in the league's future is its unusual structure. Unlike other professional sports leagues, which are confederations of independent franchises, MLS is owned in its entirety by investors. There are no individual franchise owners. Player contracts are owned by the league, not by individual teams, which means the league controls player salary limits. It also controls the number of international players on the 20-man team rosters. (In the opening season, each team was permitted four such players. The limit rose to five for the '97 season.)

In the first year of play, most of the players in the league made the minimum salary, $28,000. The maximum salary was $175,000. But several of the league's foreign stars were believed to have made close to $1 million, thanks to sponsor largess.

The '97 season runs from late March through late October and consists of 32 games plus playoffs, with the champions of the Western Conference meeting the champions of the Eastern Conference.

In the opening season, the Western Conference consisted of these teams: Dallas Burn (Cotton Bowl), Colorado Rapids (Mile High Stadium), Kansas City Wiz (Arrowhead Stadium), Los Angeles Galaxy (Rose Bowl), and San Jose Clash (San Jose State University's Spartan Stadium). In the Eastern Conference: New England Revolution (Foxboro Stadium), Columbus Crew (Ohio State University's Ohio Stadium), MetroStars (Giants Stadium), Tampa Bay Mutiny (Tampa Stadi-

Commissioner Logan

um), and Washington (D.C.) United (RFK Stadium).

For stability and growth, the league will be dependent, to a great extent, on television. TV connections at the start of play were encouraging. A three-year agreement provides for 10 games on ESPN, 25 games on ESPN2, and the championship game on ABC Sports. Univision, the Spanish-language network, broadcasts 26 Sunday afternoon matches, and, with ESPN, the MLS All-Star game. MLS has also arranged for TV broadcasts in local markets, a practice that puts 90 percent of league games on the screen.

Founder and chairman of the league is Alan I. Rothenberg, a Los Angeles lawyer who for several years has been the driving force behind this venture. Rothenberg has attracted some high-powered investors, including New York billionaire John Kluge, oilman Phillip Anschutz, and Lamar and Clark Hunt of the Texas oil family. Additional clout comes from an array of important corporate sponsors, among them AT&T, Nike, Kellogg, Pepsi, American Honda, Fujifilm, Anheuser-Busch, and MasterCard.

How good are the teams in the MLS? Good, say soccer experts. Not great, yet, but certainly worth the price of a ducat. A key objective is to retrieve top American players lured abroad by big money.

The quality of play is vital, because soccer fans know the game—especially the Latinos, who form a core fan base for the league. Just behind, of course, are the 13 million soccer-playing kids in the U.S. And their moms.

The Promise of Indoor Soccer

The **Continental Indoor Soccer League**, composed of 11 teams, mainly in the West, ended its 1996 season—the fourth of its existence—with attendance figures that exceeded 4 million for the third year in a row. Average attendance for all games was more than 6,000. The Houston Hotshots attracted a crowd of 15,000 for a championship series game with the Dallas Sidekicks, but Dallas topped that by drawing 16,000 to its park.

The season marked the league's fourth year with the Prime Sportschannel Network, which broadcast 15 games including the CISL All-Star Game. Some top corporate names are league sponsors, among them General Mills, Budweiser, McDonald's, Gatorade, and Southwest Airlines. Another sign of league stability: six of the clubs are owned by owners of NBA and NHL franchises.

Indoor soccer, designed as family entertainment, is played with six-man teams on a surface of artificial turf the size of a hockey rink. Scoring is more abundant than in outdoor soccer; there are more than a dozen goals in the average game. The league plays a 28-game regular schedule beginning in late June, with playoff games in October.

Internships: Just about all teams employ interns. Four interns, with stipends, work at league headquarters in Encino, California.

* * * *

A second indoor soccer league is the **National Professional Soccer League**, and it too is on steady legs. The circuit was begun in 1984-85, and in its first season drew an average attendance of 1,706. For 1993-94, attendance at games averaged 5,722.

There are 15 franchises, stretching from Baltimore to Wichita. The league office is in Canton, Ohio. Internships are available there and at most of the franchises.

A-League of USISL

The American Professional Soccer League, an outdoor minor league formed in 1990 by the merger of the Western Soccer League and the American Soccer League, in 1996 joined up with the United Systems of Independent Soccer Leagues to establish a new 24-team network known as the **A-League of the USISL.** It's a national showcase for players hoping to get the attention of Major League Soccer scouts. The season runs from April to late September.

UNITED STATES SOCCER FEDERATION

The USSF, the dominant soccer organization in America, is affiliated with FIFA, the international governing body in soccer. The USSF promotes the sport, sets the standard rules of play, sanctions tournaments, presents awards, compiles statistics, and maintains a hall of fame, museum, and library of films and videos. President and CEO is Alan I. Rothenberg. Executive director is Hank Steinbrecher. Offices are at 1801-1811 S. Prairie Ave., Chicago, IL 60616. Phone: (312) 808-1300.

Internships (at Chicago headquarters): Internships are offered in the areas of marketing, communications, and event management. Applicants do not need college sponsorship.

MAJOR LEAGUE SOCCER

Eastern Conference

Eastern Conference office:
110 E. 42nd St., Suite 1502
New York, NY 10017
(212) 687-1400
Internships: contact dep't head

Columbus Crew
77 E. Nationwide Blvd.
Columbus, OH 43215
(614) 221-2739
Gen Mgr: Jamey Rootes
Internships: contact Adam Low

New England Revolution
Foxboro Stadium, Route 1
Foxboro, MA 02035
(508) 543-0350
Gen Mgr: Brian O'Donovan
Internships: contact Peg Myers

New York/New Jersey MetroStars
One Harmon Plaza, 8th floor
Secaucus, NJ 07094
(201) 583-7000
Gen Mgr: Charlie Stillitano
Internships: contact Tim Kassel

Tampa Bay Mutiny
1408 N. Westshore Blvd., Suite 1004
Tampa, FL 33607
(813) 288-0096
Gen Mgr: Farrukh Quraishi
Internships: contact Ed Austin

Washington, D.C. United
13832 Redskin Dr.
Herndon, VA 22071
(703) 478-6600
Gen Mgr: Kevin Payne
Internships: contact office

Western Conference

Western Conference office:
2029 Century Park E, Suite 400
Los Angeles, CA 90067
(310) 772-2600
Internships: contact dep't head
Communications Dep't: Dan
  Courtemanche, Dir

Colorado Rapids
555 17th St., Suite 3350
Denver, CO 80202
(303) 299-1570
Pres: Robert Sanderman
Internships: contact office

Dallas Burn
2602 McKinney, Suite 200
Dallas, TX 75204
(214) 979-0303
Gen Mgr: Billy Hicks
Internships: contact Joe Bailey

Kansas City Wiz
706 Broadway St., Suite 100
Kansas City, MO 64105-2300
(816) 472-4625
Gen Mgr: Tim Latta
Internships: contact Evelyn Brey

Los Angeles Galaxy
1640 S. Sepulveda Blvd., Suite 114
Los Angeles, CA 90025
(310) 445-1260
Gen Mgr: Danny Villanueva Jr.
Internships: contact Veronica Avila

San Jose Clash
1265 El Camino Real, 2nd floor
Santa Clara, CA 95050
(408) 241-9922
Gen Mgr: Peter Bridgewater
Internships: contact David Ficklin

NATIONAL PROFESSIONAL SOCCER LEAGUE

League office:
115 DeWalt Ave. NW, 5th Floor
Canton, OH 44702
(330) 455-4625
Commissioner: Steve M. Paxos
Internships: The league office and
  most franchises employ interns.
  This is an indoor soccer league.

Baltimore Spirit
201 W. Baltimore St.
Baltimore, MD 21201
(410) 625-2320
Internships: contact Drew Forrester

Buffalo Blizzard
Marine Midland Arena
One Seymour Knox III Plaza
Buffalo, NY 14203
(716) 855-4400
VP/Gen Mgr: James L. May
Internships: contact Robin Lenhard

Cincinnati Silverbacks
2250 Seymour Ave.
Cincinnati, OH 45212
(513) 531-7825
Pres: Rich Neumann

Cleveland Crunch
34200 Solon Rd.
Solon, OH 44139
(216) 349-2090
Gen Mgr: Al Miller
Internships: contact Beth Ward

Columbus Invaders
6281 Busch Blvd.
Columbus, OH 43229
(614) 431-3732

Detroit Rockers
600 Civic Center Dr.
Detroit, MI 48226
(313) 396-7574
VP/Gen Mgr: Stu Mayer
Internships: contact Mike Zaretti

Edmonton Drillers
11230 110th St.
Edmonton, Alberta T5G 3G8, Canada
Gen Mgr: Mel Kowalchuk

Harrisburg Heat
P.O. Box 60123
Harrisburg, PA 17106
(717) 652-4328
Gen Mgr: Gregg Cook
Internships: contact Tom Harahan

Kansas City Attack
1800 Genessee, Suite 107
Kansas City, MO 64102
(816) 474-2255
Gen Mgr: Bob Wilber
Internships: contact Zoran Savic

Milwaukee Wave
12308 N. Corporate Pkwy., Suite 500
Mequon, WI 53092
(414) 243-4625
Exec VP: James W. Peters

Philadelphia Kixx
915 Montgomery Ave., Suite 300
Narberth, PA 19072
(610) 664-5499
Gen Mgr: Gerry Ryan

St. Louis Ambush
7547 Ravensridge
St. Louis, MO 63119
(314) 962-4625
Dir Opns: Daryl Doran

Tampa Bay Terror
400 First St. S
St. Petersburg, FL 33701
(813) 894-4625
Gen Mgr: Steven Powell
Internships: contact Rui Farias

Toronto Shooting Stars
123 Edward St., Suite 1508
Toronto, Ontario M5G 1E2, Canada
(416) 597-8277
Acting Gen Mgr: Hector Marinaro

Wichita Wings
500 S. Broadway
Wichita, KS 67202
(316) 262-3545
Gen Mgr: Dave Phillips

CONTINENTAL INDOOR SOCCER LEAGUE

League office:
16027 Ventura Blvd., Suite 605
Encino, CA 91436
(818) 906-7627
Commissioner: Ron Weinstein
Internships: The league office and
  most franchises employ interns.

Anaheim Splash
4100 Birch St., Suite 102
Newport Beach, CA 92660
(714) 752-9499
Gen Mgr: Don Ebert

Dallas Sidekicks
777 Sports St.
Dallas, TX 75207
(214) 653-0200
Dir Opns: Steve Letson
Internships: contact Public Relations

Detroit Neon
2 Championship Dr.
Auburn Hills, MI 48326
(810) 377-0100
Gen Mgr: Ron Campbell

Houston Hotshots
1400 Post Oak Blvd., Suite 1150
Houston, TX 77056
(713) 468-5100
Gen Mgr: Darrell Rogers
Internships: contact Darrell Rogers

Indianapolis Twisters
222 E. Ohio St., Suite 800
Indianapolis, IN 46204
(317) 231-2870
Gen Mgr: Bob Wilber

Monterrey La Raza
Vasconcelos 715-A Pte.
San Pedro Garza Garcia
Nuevo Leon, CP 66230
Mexico
(011) 528-338-5669
VP: Miguel Angel Garza

PROFESSIONAL SOCCER LEAGUES

Portland Pride
12064 S.W. Garden Place
Tigard, OR 97223
(503) 684-5425
Gen Mgr: Randy Nordlof
Internships: contact Rob Hawksford

Sacramento Knights
One Sports Pkwy.
Sacramento, CA 95834
(916) 928-0000
Gen Mgr: Hubert Rotteveel

San Diego Sockers
3500 Sports Arena Blvd.
San Diego, CA 92110
(619) 224-4625
Gen Mgr: Jeff Quinn
Internships: contact Steve Ferguson

Seattle SeaDogs
190 Queen Anne Ave. N, Suite 200
Seattle, WA 98109
(206) 281-5800
Pres: John Dresel
Internships: contact dep't head

Washington Warthogs
One Harry S Truman Dr.
Landover, MD 20785
(301) 499-6300
Gen Mgr: Mike Evans

A-LEAGUE OF THE UNITED SYSTEMS OF INDEPENDENT SOCCER LEAGUES

League office:
14497 N. Dale Mabry Hwy.,
Suite 211
Tampa, FL 33618
(813) 963-3909
Commissioner: Francisco Marcus
Internships: The league office and
  most franchises employ interns.

Atlantic Division

Carolina Dynamo
3517 W. Wendover Ave.
Greensboro, NC 27407
(910) 852-9969
Gen Mgr: Buckley Andrews

Charleston Battery
4401 Belle Oaks Dr., Suite 450
Charleston, SC 29405
(803) 740-7787
Gen Mgr: Nuno Piteira

Hershey Wildcats
100 W. HersheyPark Dr.
Hershey, PA 17033
(717) 534-8900
Gen Mgr: Todd Smith

Jacksonville Cyclones
9428 Bay Meadows Rd., Suite 175
Jacksonville, FL 32256
(904) 737-9800
Gen Mgr: Pete Petersen

Raleigh Flyers
130 Wind Chime Court
Raleigh, NC 27615
(919) 848-3063
VP Opns: Joseph Vartanesian Jr.

Richmond Kickers
2320 W. Main St.
Richmond, VA 23220
(804) 644-5425
Dir Opns: Charlie Morgan

Central Division

Atlanta Ruckus
1131 Alpharetta St.
Roswell, GA 30075
(770) 645-6655
Gen Mgr: Gabe Pascarella

Milwaukee Rampage
Uihlein Soccer Park
7101 W. Good Hope Rd.
Milwaukee, WI 53223
(414) 358-2655
Dir Opns: Jim Harwood

Minnesota Thunder
1700 105th Ave. NE
Blaine, MN 55449
(612) 785-3668
Gen Mgr: Peter Wilt

Nashville Metros
7115 S. Spring Dr.
Franklin, TN 37067-1616
(615) 771-8200
Gen Mgr: Steve Parker

New Orleans Riverboat Gamblers
5690 Eastover Dr.
New Orleans, LA 70128
(504) 241-4400
Gen Mgr: Henry Green

Orlando Sundogs
One Citrus Bowl Place
Orlando, FL 32805
(407) 872-0707
Gen Mgr: John W. Higgins

Northeast Division

Connecticut Wolves
P.O. Box 3196
Veterans Memorial Stadium
New Britain, CT 06050-3196
(860) 223-2759
Gen Mgr: Tom Jackson

Long Island Rough Riders
1670 Old Country Rd., Suite 227
Plainview, NY 11803
(516) 756-4625
Gen Mgr: Bill Manning

Montreal Impact
8000 Langelier, Suite 104
St. Leonard, Quebec H1P 3K2
Canada
(514) 328-3668
Gen Mgr: Joey Saputo

Rochester Raging Rhinos
333 N. Plymouth Ave.
Rochester, NY 14608
(716) 454-5425
Gen Mgr: Chris Economides

Toronto Lynx
55 University Ave., Suite 506
Toronto, Ontario M5J 2H7
Canada
(416) 360-4646
Gen Mgr: David Gee

Worcester Wildfire
500 Main St., Suite 515
Worcester, MA 01608
(508) 790-4782
Gen Mgr: Michael Jones

Pacific Division

California Jaguars
12 Clay St.
Salinas, CA 93901
(408) 757-7475
Dir Opns: Terry Fisher

Colorado Foxes
6200 Dahlia St.
Commerce City, CO 80022
(303) 893-6937
Gen Mgr: Rich Karlis

El Paso Patriots
6941 Industrial
El Paso, TX 79915
(915) 771-6620
Gen Mgr: Mitch Doblado

Orange County Zodiac
14210 Quail Ridge Dr.
Riverside, CA 92503
(714) 589-2698
Gen Mgr: Joe Supe

Seattle Sounders
1560 140th Ave. NE, Suite 200
Bellevue, WA 98005
(206) 622-3415
Gen Mgr: Tor Taylor

Vancouver 86ers
1126 Douglas Rd., Suite 102
Burnaby, British Columbia V5C 4Z6
Canada
(604) 273-0086
Gen Mgr: Carl Valentine

CHAPTER THREE

SPORTS FACILITIES MANAGEMENT

SECTIONS:

STADIUMS AND ARENAS

RACETRACKS

SPEEDWAYS

This is where sports business meets show business.
How would you feel about hosting a concert
by Nine Inch Nails? Couldn't be bad, right?

STADIUMS & ARENAS

The Nature of the Business

When the $186 million Alamodome was completed in May 1993, it was a dream come true for the citizens of San Antonio. At last they had what they had waited for so eagerly—a big-time sports facility—and an excited sellout crowd showed up for the opening event.

But it wasn't a San Antonio Spurs game that took place on that auspicious occasion. It was a Paul McCartney concert.

Nothing unusual about that. Today's sports palaces are too costly for the exclusive use of one tenant, however prized that tenant may be. The buildings can't sit in darkness waiting for the next basketball game; they've got to generate income—day by day, if possible. So whether they're owned by municipalities (as most of them are) or by private interests, there's constant pressure on facility managers to book revenue-producing attractions between the game dates of permanent tenants.

Often enough, the temporary attractions are sports events—a tennis tournament, for example, or a boxing card, a figure-skating competition, a horse show, a high school championship game, even a track meet.

But what facility managers really bank on are concerts by touring performers like Billy Joel or Garth Brooks or Pink Floyd or Smashing Pumpkins. The shows are easy to promote and relatively easy to set up and tear down, and they draw crowds. Concerts are so big a part of sports-venue operations, in fact, that facility staffers feel they're as deeply involved in show business as in sports business.

And that's not all of it. Many sports facilities also book such events as auto shows, boat shows, circuses, home-improvement shows, and trade conventions. In short, almost all sports facilities, from Madison Square Garden to the Alamodome, are really multipurpose venues.

If you're heading for an internship or a job with a sports facility, don't worry, you'll see plenty of sports events, but be prepared for anything.

* * * *

Scheduling events often requires the skill of a juggler. At the Bradley Center, a 20,000-seat Milwaukee arena, scheduling is especially tricky because the building has five regular tenants—the NBA Bucks, the Admirals of the International Hockey League, the National Professional Soccer League's Wave, the Arena Football League's Mustangs, and the Marquette University basketball team, all with overlapping seasons.

David Skiles, general manager of the Bradley Center, manages to keep them all happy, even while weaving a number of concerts into the schedule. In all, Skiles puts on about 200 events a year. "It's a challenge," he says, "but I relish it."

Skiles credits the competence of his staff for being able to handle as many as three events in a day, each with a different surface. One such day started with an indoor soccer game at one o'clock on Astroturf. After the game, the turf was removed and replaced by floorboards for a Lorrie Morgan concert. Following the concert, the floorboards were removed, and out came the Zamboni machine to set the scene for a hockey game.

* * * *

You'd think that setting up an indoor professional beach volleyball tournament wouldn't be much of a problem. Dump a few tons of sand on the arena floor and get the game going. But at Madison Square Garden, where the Evian Indoor Beach Volleyball Challenge was to be followed by an ice show, it *was* a problem. The sand had to be free of salt and other impurities that might ruin the ice underneath. After a search, the Garden crew found a deep pit out on Long Island with just enough of the right stuff.

The Key Jobs and What They Pay

The range of salaries takes into account the size and location of venues.

General Manager

Has overall responsibility for operations, revenues, expenditures, staffing, community relations, and development strategies. The GM is expected to have skills in business administration, risk management, contract negotiations, marketing, and public relations; a familiarity with the technical operations of the plant; a wide knowledge of sports and entertainment promoters to facilitate the acquisition of bookings; and the ability to deal diplomatically with public officials (or private owners of the facility). Salary: $70,000 to $100,000-plus.

Assistant Manager

Has direct supervision of day-to-day operations, with an eye on all functions, including security and crowd management; handles problems; purchases equipment. Salary: $60,000 to $85,000.

Business Manager

Responsible for accounting procedures, financial records, budgets, cash flow, payroll, expenditures. Salary: $50,000 to $70,000.

Operations Manager

In charge of all mechanical aspects and custodial operations, setup and teardown crews, maintenance of equipment and machinery. Salary: $40,000 to $50,000.

Box Office Manager

In charge of ticket systems and box office personnel. Salary: $35,000 to $45,000.

Events Manager

Responds to needs of tenants, coordinates schedules of events, makes sure everything is in readiness for individual events; also may assist in obtaining bookings. Salary: $30,000 to $40,000.

Beginning Jobs

The newcomer may be assigned to any one of a number of functions, including security and crowd control, marketing and sales, ticket operations, event coordinating, ushering, merchandise sales, and food and beverage sales (more and more facilities are dropping concessionaires and handling this business in-house). The pay for entry-level jobs: about $20,000.

Breaking Into the Business

Getting that first job with a stadium or arena is not easy. It takes persistence. But, say facility managers we talked to, once you're in, advancing to better-paying positions is a cinch.

When you're making job inquiries, it helps if you've received a degree in sports management and completed an internship. It means (a) you're serious about working in this business, and (b) you've picked up some experience.

That's not to say you *must* have a degree in sports management. A degree in some other discipline—say accounting, marketing, or public relations—can make a nice impression too, but the part of your resume that carries special weight is your experience as an intern.

If you haven't done an internship yet, and you'd like to, please know that internship opportunities are available at just about every sports facility in the country. (*Check the end of this section for places and people.*)

If you complete an internship and get a job offer, says Rick Nafe of the Tampa Sports Authority, don't turn it down because it sounds as though it comes with a mop and a bucket. "You must be willing to start at any level, do anything, work any hours," he says. "Later, when you've gotten some experience—and if you have the mobility to accept jobs in other locations—you can rise fast. Getting *into* the business is the hard part."

Brad Mayne, manager of Arrowhead Pond at Anaheim, stresses the importance of mobility in advancing to better jobs in bigger venues. Once you're in the business, he says, you'll hear of interesting job openings through the industry network, "but you will have to be willing to move around the country to take advantage of those opportunities."

Mayne's own career moves are pretty typical of what goes on. He got his start at the University of Utah sports complex with a job in the ticket office. He advanced later to event coordinator. That led to an invitation to become assistant director of the Tacoma Dome in Washington. Then came the big move to California as Arrowhead Pond's first general manager.

The Biggest Employers

A group of companies that offer facility owners an attractive service—complete management of their venues, with the promise of providing greater efficiency and profitabili-ty—is exerting a growing influence in the facility management business.

The companies make their pitch to all types of public-assembly facilities, including sports stadiums, multipurpose arenas (used for sports and nonsports activities), convention sites, and concert halls. The companies also target college stadiums and arenas and facilities abroad.

The companies are Ogden Entertainment Services (long prominent as food and beverage concessionaires), SMG (formed by the merger of Facilities Management Group and Spectacor Management), Centre Group (owners of USAir Arena and two sports franchises, the NBA Washington Bullets and NHL Washington Capitals), and Leisure Management International. Ogden and SMG are the biggest players.

The companies already have taken over the management of about 90 facilities (several are on college campuses, several abroad), and the number is sure to grow.

In each takeover, the companies bring in their own contingent of key personnel, which means they control a lot of jobs in the industry. *All have internship programs.*

Partial lists of the venues they're running appear below. The venues here are limited to sports stadiums, sports arenas, and multipurpose arenas, where sports events share the calendar with nonsports events.

Managed by Ogden Entertainment:
• Sullivan Arena, Anchorage, Alaska
• Arrowhead Pond of Anaheim, California
• The Great Western Forum, Inglewood, California
• Hartford Civic Center, Connecticut
• Pensacola Civic Center, Florida
• Rosemont Horizon, Illinois
• Roberts Stadium, Evansville, Indiana
• Hilton Coliseum, Ames, Iowa
• Five Seasons Center, Cedar Rapids, Iowa
• Mullins Center (University of Massachusetts at Amherst), Massachusetts

- Target Center, Minneapolis, Minnesota
- Fargodome, Fargo, North Dakota
- Ervin J. Nutter Center (Wright State University), Dayton, Ohio
- Recreation/Convocation Center (Temple University), Philadelphia, Pennsylvania
- North Charleston Coliseum, South Carolina
- Sioux Falls Arena, South Dakota

Headquarters: Ogden Entertainment Services, Two Pennsylvania Plaza, New York, NY 10121. Phone: (212) 868-6000. For information about internships here, contact Frank Russo or Robert Cavalieri.

For information about internships at a particular facility, contact that facility.

Managed by SMG:

- Mobile Civic Center, Alabama
- Long Beach Convention and Entertainment Center, California
- Los Angeles Memorial Coliseum, California
- Los Angeles Sports Arena, California
- Jacksonville Memorial Coliscum, Florida
- Gator Bowl, Jacksonville, Florida
- Wolfson Park, Jacksonville, Florida
- Peoria Civic Center, Illinois
- Kansas Expocentre, Topeka, Kansas
- Louisiana Superdome, New Orleans
- Centrum, Worcester, Massachusetts
- St. Louis Arena, Missouri
- Knickerbocker Arena, Albany, New York
- Nassau Memorial Coliseum, Long Island, New York
- Niagara Falls Civic Center, New York
- Spectrum, Philadelphia, Pennsylvania
- Philadelphia Civic Center, Pennsylvania
- Pittsburgh Civic Arena, Pennsylvania
- Three Rivers Stadium, Pittsburgh, Pennsylvania
- Richmond Coliseum, Virginia

Headquarters: SMG, 701 Market St., 4th Floor, Philadelphia, PA 19106. Phone: (215) 592-4100.

Internships are available at headquarters and at venues.

Managed by Centre Group:

- Baltimore Arena, Maryland
- Cleveland State University Convocation Center, Ohio
- Patriot Center (George Mason University), Fairfax, Virginia
- Springfield Civic Center, Massachusetts

Owned and managed by Centre Group:
- USAir Arena, Landover, Maryland

Headquarters: Centre Group, One Harry S Truman Dr., Landover, MD 20785. Phone: (301) 499-4500.

Internships at headquarters and venues.

Managed by Leisure Management International:

- Miami Arena, Florida
- Pontchartrain Center, Kenner, Louisiana
- The Pyramid Arena, Memphis, Tennessee
- The Summit, Houston, Texas

Headquarters: Leisure Management International, 11 Greenway Plaza, Suite 3106, Houston, TX 77046. Phone: (713) 623-4583.

Internships at headquarters and venues.

It's a Busy Time for Sports Architects

For the past few years expensive new stadiums and arenas have been rising across the nation at a faster rate than ever. Aging venues have been brought to life with elaborate remodeling. And more projects are in the works.

Venues Rising

Herewith, some of the sports facilities under construction:

Phoenix: A $187 million, 48,000-seat, retractable-roof baseball stadium that will be the home of the Arizona Diamondbacks, MLB expansion club. To be completed April '98. For information: (602) 379-2000.

San Francisco: The Giants will have a new stadium that occupies 13 acres and seats 42,000. No completion date at this writing.

Colorado Springs: A multipurpose building with special provisions for ice hock-

Lance W. Elder, general manager of the 18,000-seat Nassau Coliseum on Long Island, New York, has been at the arena since it opened in 1972, when he started with a job in security. He teaches "Stadium and Arena Management" at St. John's University.

ey. Completion in early '97.

Denver: A 19,000-seat arena to accommodate NBA and NHL teams. Completion in '98. For information: Gen. Mgr. Tim Romani, (303) 893-1997.

Washington, D.C.: A $150 million, 20,000-seat arena for NBA and NHL clubs. Plus a sports museum. To be completed October '97. For information: (407) 363-6100.

Sunrise, Fla.: A $172 million, 22,000-seat multipurpose arena that will be home for NHL's Panthers. Completion in '98. For in-

---

SIDELINES

Somebody get that elephant outta here!

"Facility managers," says Rick Nafe, president of the Stadium Managers Association, "live on the edge of crisis day after day—and yet they love the work."

———

What can possibly go wrong for a facility manager? Here's a sampling:

You open the basketball season in your domed stadium with a colorful fireworks display as the players come on the court, but it triggers the sprinkler system and everybody gets soaked.

You have a sellout crowd coming for a Streisand concert, and you get word that she's too ill to perform.

Two hours before a big hockey game, you learn that the ice-making apparatus isn't functioning.

Thousands of teenagers streaming in for an intracity basketball championship begin belting each other even before the game begins.

The concessionaire is selling warm beer, and angry fans in the upper deck are pouring it on the fans below.

The superexpensive electronic scoreboard suddenly goes dark in the middle of a baseball game.

You have an NBA playoff game scheduled to go on network television right after a circus clears out of your arena. There's just enough time for your crew to fit together the 200 coded pieces of basketball flooring. But a playful elephant being led out of the arena knocks over the carefully arranged stacks of flooring, scrambling the pieces every which way. And the clock is ticking.

Rival gangs show up for a rock concert looking for trouble.

A car backfires in the parking lot, and thousands of fans flee for the exits.

There's been a heavy snowstorm and just before the start of an NCAA Final Four game you're told the roof of your arena has begun to sag.

Your five-year-old artificial turf comes apart at the seams in the middle of your football field—early in the second quarter.

You arrange a five-year deal with a nonunion subcontractor who provides stagehands for concerts, then you announce a Barry Manilow concert and 50 members of the International Alliance of Theatrical Stage Employees show up with picket signs.

An Arena Manager Responds

The Bradley Center's David Skiles says that he, for one, does not "live on the edge of a crisis."

But he does admit that "when you have two million patrons in 200 days of events, you *will* see problems and you *will* experience stress." Especially during certain types of concerts.

There are things that all facility management teams are concerned about: injury to patrons, loss of services, crowd control problems, health problems—anything, in short, that results in harm to customers and employees or loss of business. At the Bradley Center, "we always pay attention to details," he says.

What that means is having paramedics on hand, security people at the ready, and the assurance of getting a quick response from the local constabulary.

In any case, it's true that despite the stresses and strains, facility managers do love their jobs. The reason: The work is never boring; every day is different. You meet famous people—in sports, show business, politics. You're where the action is. The pay is good. And you see a lot of games.

formation: (954) 627-5021.

Baltimore: A 68,000-seat stadium, adjacent to Oriole Park in the Camden Yards district, for the NFL's Baltimore Ravens. Completion in August '98.

Maryland's Prince George's County: A 78,000-seat Redskins football stadium. Completion in August '97.

Fayetteville, N.C.: A 13,000-seat arena for sports and entertainment. To be completed fall '97. For information: Gen. Mgr. Kendall Wall, Cumberland County Civic Center, (910) 323-5088.

Oklahoma City: A new multipurpose downtown arena that will provide about 18,000 seats for hockey. Completion in '99.

Greenville, S.C.: A 16,000-seat arena for hockey, other sports, and entertainment.

Orlando, Fla.: The Walt Disney World Sports Complex—a 200-acre site for more than 30 sports, with a baseball layout that includes a stadium for Atlanta Braves spring training, a nine-lane track and field facility, a tennis complex, and more. Completion March '97. Director of the overall facility is Mike Millay, (407) 627-5021.

Flushing Meadows, N.Y.: To be completed in '98 is the expanded USTA National Tennis Center, a complex of 23,000-, 10,000-, and 5,000-seat stadiums, along with accommodations for a variety of recreational events. Manager is David Meehan, (718) 592-9488.

For architectural companies that specialize in designing stadiums and arenas, business is brisk. But as far as jobs with architectural firms are concerned, there's really nothing available for the sports lover who wants to be part of the excitement of creating a great new stadium. We checked with half a dozen of the busiest companies and got the same answer from each: The only people being hired are applicants with architectural degrees. Even for low-level jobs, like carrying sample bricks to a client meeting.

"This is not a realistic job market for young people who are not formally trained as archi-

tects, landscape architects, or interior designers," said Jim Dunlap, an architect who handles staffing at HOK Sports Facilities Group, the most prominent outfit in the field.

Fred Coester, an architect who is director of human resources at Sink Combs Dethlefs, another leading firm, mentioned that clients who are building stadiums sometimes employ people to act as go-betweens with architects, but those jobs are likely to go to people with extensive experience in managing sports facilities.

Before you rush off to enroll in an architectural school, be advised that there are no schools that offer specialized training in designing sports facilities. That kind of skill is learned on the job—if you're lucky enough to connect with a firm that does business in this field.

Degrees in architecture. A bachelor's degree requires five years of study. A master's can be completed in two additional years. If you already have a bachelor's degree that's unrelated to architecture, you can get a master's in architecture in three years. A list of colleges offering accredited programs in architecture can be obtained from the National Architectural Accrediting Board, 1735 New York Ave. NW, Washington, DC 20006. (For more information about architecture as a career, write to the Director, Education Programs, The American Institute of Architects, at the same address.)

Earnings. Entry-level jobs as intern-architects generally pay between $23,000 and $25,000. With three years of experience, you can take a licensing exam, which establishes you as a professional. Licensed architects with more than eight years' experience usually earn between $35,000 and $38,000. If you can work your way up to a partnership in a successful firm, you can make real money—more than $100,000.

The Rent-a-Campus Business

There are roughly 4,000 arenas across the land that are of interest to promoters of sports contests, concerts, conventions, trade shows, circuses, rodeos, and other happenings known collectively as special events. A usable arena is one that is big enough (say, 3,500 seats) and has adequate parking, a surfeit of electrical power, and a house staff that knows how to accommodate a crowd.

About 90 percent of these venues are owned by municipal, county, or state governments. In other words, the public. A small number of the arenas are owned by private individuals and companies. The rest, several hundred, are owned by colleges and universities—institutions not averse to hawking the benefits of their athletic facilities to prospective renters.

The colleges bring a couple of distinct advantages to the marketplace. One is the handy presence of a large number of students, especially advantageous for concerts. Second is the fact that in most states, colleges have the biggest and best facilities.

In a few cases, a college's quest for outside bookings is handled by a private facility-management company. For example, the University of Massachusetts engaged Ogden Entertainment to manage UMass's Mullins Center, a job that includes finding outside renters. But on most campuses, rentals are handled by a member of the athletics department staff, usually an assistant athletics director, known sometimes as facilities director. Booking contracts are always cleared with the AD, of course.

How do you find renters? You advertise. To attract business for its new Aztec Bowl arena, San Diego State University's message in publications read by sports and entertainment promoters tells of "a 2.7 million population (in the San Diego area) with 28,000 students on the SDSU campus." Also, "A proven management team, a seating capacity of 12,000, a full-service box office/Ticketmaster outlet, individual dressing rooms for stars, work areas for the media, a 2,000-car garage, a VIP lounge," and more. The University of Florida advertises its O'Connell Center (12,500 seats) as the "largest facility in north central Florida." It's no match, though, for the University of North Carolina's Dean E. Smith Center, which offers 20,039 seats for concerts, 21,572 seats for basketball, and 22,000 seats for boxing. Or the University of Tennessee's 24,500-seat Thompson/Boling Arena, which offers "the finest in Southern hospitality." Or the ambiance of the University of Notre Dame's Joyce Center, which boasts of banquet facilities, meeting rooms, and exhibit space—all air-conditioned, mind you.

Industry Organizations

International Association of Assembly Managers (IAAM)

The IAAM is the primary trade association for managers of facilities for sports, concerts, and conventions.

H O W   T H E Y   G O T   T H E R E

KHALIL JOHNSON
General Manager, Georgia Dome

It turned out to be a lucky break. One day in 1977 Khalil Johnson walked in off the street and asked for a job—any job—at the Georgia World Congress Center in Atlanta. The only thing available was part-time grunt work in the operations department, setting up displays for trade shows and conventions. Johnson signed on, later became a full-time employee in operations, and in 1980 was elevated to event coordinator. He was good at it. After two years he was invited to join a start-up management team for the new Washington (D.C.) Convention Center as director of sales and event services. Then, in 1986, he was offered an opportunity he couldn't refuse. He returned "home" to Georgia World Congress Center as director of the venue's mega-events—in time to handle the Democratic National Convention.

He reached the top in September 1989, when he was named to his current position as general manager of the Georgia Dome, the 71,000-seat home of the Atlanta Falcons.

In the IAAM's own language, which tends to inflation, it is "the world's largest professional society devoted exclusively to the management of public assembly facilities, including amphitheaters, arenas, auditoriums, convention centers, performing arts theaters, and stadiums. IAAM provides management development resources and networking for its more than 2,500 members worldwide, standardizes practices and ethics of management, and maintains relationships with allied organizations."

Actually, members currently engaged in the business of facility management number 1,625. The rest, identified as "allied" members, "associate" members, etc., are mainly suppliers. Steps to encourage student membership have been disappointing. Only 28 students are members.

Still, for students interested in a career in the management of sports facilities—or facilities of any kind—the IAAM is an important networking medium. The organization's activities include regional meetings, an annual conference and trade show, seminars, and the dissemination of industry news through a semimonthly newsletter and a magazine that appears every other month.

The IAAM has lately begun an internship program in cooperation with a number of member facilities, and has established a fund for internship stipends. To be eligible for an internship, and stipend, applicants must be enrolled in a college program that includes at least one course focusing on facility management.

The IAAM also has a scholarship program that awards students $1,000 for each remaining year of college, to a maximum of $4,000. Preference is given to applicants pursuing a career in facility management or who are enrolled in a relevant degree program, such as sports management or hospitality management.

One of the IAAM's most popular programs is its "Public Assembly Facility Management School," a weeklong seminar held in June at Oglebay Park in Wheeling, West Virginia. Attendees sign up for two sessions, a year apart. Tuition and housing for each session cost $588 for a single and $792 for a double. Though it is advertised as a "basic course" in facility management, most of those who attend have been in the business for years.

For further information on any of the above, call the IAAM at (972) 255-8020. The address is 4425 W. Airport Freeway, Suite 590, Irving, Texas, 75062-5835. The executive director is John S. Swinburn.

Stadium Managers Association (SMA)

The SMA is an independent organization with a membership (as of June 1996) of 338 and growing. In addition to facilitating networking all year long, the organization rounds everybody up for an annual four-day seminar. A lively newsletter, *Score Board*, heightens the spirit of fraternity. Responding to an interest of its members in what's happening abroad, the SMA took an active role in the formation recently of the World Council for Venue Management. At home, it increased its recruitment of the managers of college and university stadiums. An immediate product of this collegiality was the establishment of a scholarship to Ohio University's esteemed graduate program in sports administration/facility management. Provisions of the scholarship include the waiver of tuition for two quarters and a grant of between $2,000 and $3,000 from the SMA for other campus expenses. Also part of the deal is an internship with the SMA. Candidates are required to have "an interest in the facility management sector of the sports industry." If you'd like more information, get in touch with Ohio University's School of Health & Sports Sciences, (614) 593-4666.

The SMA is developing additional scholarship plans, but these seem to be directed to individuals already employed in the business of facility management.

President of the Stadium Managers Association is Bill Wilson, who is manager of the San Diego Jack Murphy Stadium.

The address of the SMA is 875 Kings Highway, Suite 200, Woodbury, New Jersey, 08096-3172. Phone: (609) 384-6287.

Publications

Amusement Business

Weekly. Deep coverage of sports, entertainment, and convention venues by reporters who know the business. Address: 49 Music Square W, Nashville, TN 37203. Phone: (615) 321-4250.

Athletic Business

Monthly. A lively magazine that focuses on sports and fitness facilities and equipment. Address: 1846 Hoffman St., Madison, WI 53704. Phone: (608) 249-0186.

PART ONE

This section consists of stadiums and arenas that house major league teams or bowl games. Many of these facilities have regular internship programs, as noted.

ARIZONA

America West Arena
201 E. Jefferson St.
Phoenix, AZ 85004
(602) 379-2000
Owner: Phoenix Area Development
Mgr: Robert K. Machen
Seating: 20,000
Home of Phoenix Suns

Sun Devil Stadium
Fifth St,
Tempe, AZ 85287
(602) 965-5062
Owner: State of Arizona
Mgr: Charles Bethea
Seating: 73,273
Home of Arizona Cardinals

CALIFORNIA

Anaheim Stadium
2000 Gene Autry Way
Anaheim, CA 92806
(714) 254-3100
Owner: City of Anaheim
Dir: Greg Smith
Seating: 70,500
Home of California Angels

Arco Arena
One Sports Pkwy
Sacramento, CA 95834
(916) 928-0000
Owner: Kings Arco Arena, Ltd.
Mgr: Mike Duncan
Seating: 17,300
Home of Sacramento Kings
Internships offered

Arrowhead Pond of Anaheim
2695 E. Katella Ave.
Anaheim, CA 92806
(714) 704-2400
Owner: City of Anaheim
Dir: Brad Mayne
Seating: 19,400
Home of Mighty Ducks of Anaheim

Dodger Stadium
1000 Elysian Park Ave.
Los Angeles, CA 90012
(213) 224-1351
Owner: Peter O'Malley
Mgr: Robert Smith
Seating: 56,000
Home of Los Angeles Dodgers
Internships offered by dep't

Great Western Forum
3900 W. Manchester Blvd.
Inglewood, CA 90305
(310) 419-3100
Owner: Jerry Buss
Pres: Jeanie Buss
Seating: 18,679
Home of Los Angeles Lakers, Kings

**Los Angeles Memorial
Sports Arena**
3939 S. Figueroa St.
Los Angeles, CA 90037
(213) 748-6136
Owner: City of Los Angeles
Mgr: Pat Lynch
Seating: 16,500
Home of Los Angeles Clippers
Internships offered

**Oakland-Alameda County
Coliseum & Stadium**
7000 Coliseum Way
Oakland, CA 94621
(510) 615-4800
Owners: City and County
Mgr: Robert Quintella
Stadium seating: 62,500
Home of Oakland Raiders, Athletics
Arena seating: 25,000
Home of Golden State Warriors

Rose Bowl
1001 Rose Bowl Dr.
Pasadena, CA 91103
(818) 577-3100
Owner: City of Pasadena
Mgr: David Jacobs
Seating: 102,083
Home of Los Angeles Galaxy (MLS)

San Diego Jack Murphy Stadium
9449 Friars Rd.
San Diego, CA 92108
(619) 525-8266
Owner: City of San Diego
Mgr: Bill Wilson
Seating: 60,794
Home of San Diego Chargers, Padres
Internships: contact Sharon Wilkinson

San Jose Arena
525 W. Santa Clara St.
San Jose, CA 95113
(408) 287-7070
Owner: City of San Jose
Dir: Frank Jirik
Seating: 19,190
Home of San Jose Sharks
Internships: contact Carol Ross

3Com Park at Candlestick Point
P.O. Box 880232
San Francisco, CA 94188
(415) 467-1994
Owners: City and County of San
Francisco
Dir: Mike Gay
Seating: 70,270
Home of San Francisco Giants, 49ers
Baseball internships offered

COLORADO

Coors Field
1660 17th St.
Denver, CO 80202
(303) 825-0401
Owner: Jerry McMorris
Dir: Tom Gleason
Seating: 48,000
Home of Colorado Rockies

McNichols Sports Arena
1635 Bryant St.
Denver, CO 80204
(303) 640-7300
Owners: City and County of Denver
Dir: Gary Lane
Seating: 19,000
Home of Denver Nuggets, Colorado
Avalanche
Internships offered

Mile High Stadium
2755 W. 17th Ave.
Denver, CO 80204
(303) 458-4850
Owners: City and County of Denver
Mgr: Gary Jones
Seating: 76,123
Home of Denver Broncos, Colorado
Rapids (MLS)
Internships offered

CONNECTICUT

Hartford Coliseum
Hartford Civic Ctr.
One Civic Ctr. Plaza
Hartford, CT 06103
(860) 249-6333
Owner: City of Hartford
Dir: Harold Bannon
Arena seating: 16,500
Home of Hartford Whalers

DISTRICT OF COLUMBIA

**Robert F. Kennedy Memorial
Stadium**
2400 E. Capitol St. SE
Washington, DC 20003
(202) 547-9077
Owner: District of Columbia
Mgr: Tony Burnett
Seating: 56,454
Home of Washington Redskins,
United (MLS)
Internships offered

FLORIDA

Houlihan's Stadium
4201 N. Dale Mabry Hwy.
Tampa, FL 33607
(813) 673-4303
Owner: Tampa Sports Authority
Mgr: Mickey Farrell
Seating: 74,317
Home of Tampa Bay Buccaneers,
Mutiny (MLS)
Internships: contact Linda Black

Ice Palace
401 E. Channelside Dr.
Tampa, FL 33602
(813) 223-6100
Owner: Lightning Partners, Ltd.
Mgr: Jay Cooper
Seating: 21,500
Home of Tampa Bay Lightning

Jacksonville Municipal Stadium
One Stadium Place
Jacksonville, FL 32202
(904) 633-6100
Owner: City of Jacksonville
Mgr: Bob Downey
Seating: 73,000
Home of Jacksonville Jaguars
Internships offered

Pro Player Stadium
2269 N.W. 199th St.
Miami, FL 33056
(305) 623-6100
Owner: H. Wayne Huizenga
Dir: Bob Kramm
Seating: 74,916
Home of Miami Dolphins,
Florida Marlins
Internships offered

Miami Arena
701 Arena Blvd.
Miami, FL 33136
(305) 530-4400
Owner: City of Miami
Mgr: Robert Franklin
Seating: 16,640
Home of Miami Heat,
Florida Panthers

LEADING STADIUMS AND ARENAS IN THE U.S.

Orange Bowl Stadium
1501 N.W. Third St.
Miami, FL 33125
(305) 643-7100
Owner: City of Miami
Dir: Christina Abrams
Seating: 82,000

Orlando Centroplex
600 W. Amelia St.
Orlando, FL 32801
(407) 849-2000
Owner: City of Orlando
Dir: William Becker
Orlando Arena
Seating: 17,900
Home of Orlando Magic
Florida Citrus Bowl Stadium
Seating: 70,200

GEORGIA

Georgia Dome
One Georgia Dome Dr. NW
Atlanta, GA 30313
(404) 223-9200
Owner: State of Georgia
Mgr: Khalil Johnson
Stadium seating: 71,200
Home of Atlanta Falcons
Arena seating: 40,000

The Omni
100 Techwood Dr. NW
Atlanta, GA 30303
(404) 681-2100
Owner: City of Atlanta
Dir: Robert R. Williams
Arena seating: 17,200
Home of Atlanta Hawks

Turner Stadium
Atlanta, GA 30302
(404) 522-7630 (Braves office)
Owner: Atlanta Braves
Gen Mgr: John Schuerholz
Seating: 50,000
Home of Atlanta Braves

HAWAII

Aloha Stadium
P.O. Box 30666
Aiea, HI 96820
(808) 486-9555
Owner: State of Hawaii
Mgr: Edwin Hayashi
Seating: 50,419

ILLINOIS

Comiskey Park
333 W. 35th St.
Chicago, IL 60616
(312) 924-1000
Owner: State of Illinois
Sr VP Opns: Terry Savarise
Seating: 44,177
Home of Chicago White Sox
Internships offered

Soldier Field
425 E. McFetridge Dr.
Chicago, IL 60605
(312) 747-1285
Owner: Chicago Park District
Opns Dir: James M. Duggan
Seating: 66,950
Home of Chicago Bears

United Center Arena
1901 W. Madison St.
Chicago, IL 60612
(312) 455-4500
Owner: United Center Joint Venture
VP Opns: Terry Savarise
Seating: 23,000
Home of Chicago Bulls, Blackhawks

Wrigley Field
1060 W. Addison St.
Chicago, IL 60613
(312) 404-2827
Owner: Chicago Tribune
Gen Mgr: Ed Lynch
Seating: 39,012
Home of Chicago Cubs
Internships offered

INDIANA

Market Square Arena
300 E. Market St.
Indianapolis, IN 46204
(317) 639-6411
Owner: Marion County
Dir: Larry Taylor
Seating: 18,000
Home of Indiana Pacers

RCA Dome
100 S. Capitol Ave.
Indianapolis, IN 46225
(317) 262-3410
Owner: Capital Improvement Board
Dir: Barney Levengood
Seating: 60,500
Home of Indianapolis Colts
Internships offered

LOUISIANA

Louisiana Superdome
Sugar Bowl Dr.
New Orleans, LA 70122
(504) 587-3663
Owner: Louisiana Stadium
Mgr: Glen Mon
DomeArena seating: 19,000
Stadium seating: 72,704
Home of New Orleans Saints
Internships offered

MARYLAND

Memorial Stadium
1000 E. 33rd St.
Baltimore, MD 21218
(410) 396-7111
Owner: City of Baltimore
Mgr: Ralph Chase
Seating: 65,522
Home of Baltimore Ravens

Oriole Park at Camden Yards
333 W. Camden St., Suite 500
Baltimore, MD 21230
(410) 333-1560
Owner: Maryland Stadium Authority
Dir: Bruce Hoffman
Seating: 48,445
Home of Baltimore Orioles
Internships offered

USAir Arena
One Harry S Truman Dr.
Landover, MD 20785
(301) 350-3400
Owner: Abe Polin
Dir: Nancy Lacy
Seating: 19,500
Home of Washington Wizards, Capitals
Internships: contact Rosie Beauclair

MASSACHUSETTS

Fenway Park
4 Yawkey Way
Boston, MA 02215
(617) 267-9440
Owner: J.R.Y. Corp.
Facilities Mgr: Thomas Queenan Jr.
Seating: 34,142
Home of Boston Red Sox
Internships: contact Debbie McIntire

FleetCenter
One FleetCenter
Boston, MA 02114
(617) 624-1000
Owner: Delaware North Corp.
Mgr: Jason Beckett
Seating: 19,600
Home of Boston Celtics, Bruins
Internships offered

Foxboro Stadium
60 Washington St.
Foxboro, MA 02035
(508) 543-8200
Owner: Foxboro Stadium Associates
Mgr: Dan Murphy
Seating: 60,292
Home of New England Patriots,
   Revolution (MLS)
Internships offered

MICHIGAN

Joe Louis Arena
600 Civic Ctr. Dr.
Detroit, MI 48226
(313) 396-7444
Owner: City of Detroit
Dir: Atanas Illitch
Seating: 20,666
Home of Detroit Red Wings
Internships offered

The Palace at Auburn Hills
2 Championship Dr.
Auburn Hills, MI 48326
(810) 377-8222
Owner: Palace Sports &
   Entertainment, Inc.
Dir: Hugh Lombardi
Seating: 20,531
Home of Detroit Pistons
Internships: contact Hugh Lombardi

Pontiac Silverdome
12 Featherstone Rd.
Pontiac, MI 48342
(810) 858-7358
Owner: City of Pontiac
Dir: Eric Walker
Seating: 80,368
Home of Detroit Lions
Internships: contact Eric Walker

Tiger Stadium
2121 Trumbull Ave.
Detroit, MI 48216
(313) 962-4000
Owner: City of Detroit
Dir: John Pettit
Seating: 52,416
Home of Detroit Tigers
Internships: (313) 983-6000

MINNESOTA

Hubert H. Humphrey Metrodome
500 11th Ave. S
Minneapolis, MN 55415
(612) 332-0386
Owner: Metro Sports Commission
Dir: William Lester
Seating: 64,035
Home of Minnesota Twins, Vikings
Internships: contact William Lester

Target Center
600 First Ave. N.
Minneapolis, MN 55403
(612) 673-1300
Owner: City of Minneapolis
Dir: Dana Warg
Seating: 19,127
Home of Minnesota Timberwolves
Internships: contact Cathy Tryon

MISSOURI

Arrowhead Stadium
One Arrowhead Dr.
Kansas City, MO 64129
(816) 924-9300
Owner: Jackson County
Dir: Scott Indorf
Seating: 79,101
Home of Kansas City Chiefs,
    Wiz (MLS)
Internships: contact Bob Moore

Busch Stadium
200 Stadium Plaza
St. Louis, MO 63102
(314) 241-3900
Owner: Gateway Stadium Co.
Opns Mgr: Mike Bertani
Seating: 56,227
Home of St. Louis Cardinals
Internships: contact Marion Rhodes

Ewing M. Kauffman Stadium
One Royal Way
Kansas City, MO 64141
(816) 921-2200
Owner: Jackson County
Dir Stadium Opns: Rodney Lewellen
Seating: 40,625
Home of Kansas City Royals
Internships: contact Mike Behymer,
    Steve Fink

Kiel Center
1401 Clark Ave.
St. Louis, MO 63103
(314) 622-5400
Owner: Kiel Center Partners
VP Opns: Roger Dixon
Seating: 18,500
Home of St. Louis Blues
Internships: contact Kelly Leahy

**Transworld Dome at America's
    Center**
701 Convention Plaza
St. Louis, MO 63101
(314) 342-5036
Owner: City of St. Louis
Dir: Bruce T. Sommer
Seating: 66,000
Home of St. Louis Rams
Internships: contact Leo Ming

NEW JERSEY

Meadowlands Sports Complex
50 State Hwy. 120
East Rutherford, NJ 07073
(201) 935-8500
Owner: New Jersey Sports/Exposition
    Authority
Dir: Bob Castronova
Giants Stadium
Asst Mgr: Tim Hassett
Seating: 76,891
Home of New York Giants, Jets,
    MetroStars (MLS)
Continental Airlines Arena
Mgr: Bob Carney
Seating: 21,000
Home of New Jersey Nets, Devils
Internships: contact Gena Klein
*(Complex also consists of Meadowlands
Racetrack and Monmouth Park Racetrack)*

NEW YORK

Madison Square Garden
2 Penn Plaza, 14th Floor
New York, NY 10121
(212) 465-6000
Owner: ITT/Cablevision
Exec VP/Gen Mgr: Robert Russo
Seating: 20,650
Home of New York Knicks, Rangers
Internships offered

Marine Midland Arena
One Main St.
Buffalo, NY 14203
(716) 856-7300
Owners: City, State, Marine Midland
Dir Opns: Stan Makowski
Seating: 20,000
Home of Buffalo Sabres

Nassau Coliseum
1255 Hempstead Tpke.
Uniondale, NY 11553
(516) 794-9300
Owner: Nassau County
Gen Mgr: Lance Elder
Seating: 17,260
Home of New York Islanders
Internships offered

Rich Stadium
One Bills Dr.
Orchard Park, NY 14127
(716) 648-1800
Owner: Erie County
Dir: Jerry Foran
Seating: 80,290
Home of Buffalo Bills
Internships: contact Jerry Foran

Shea Stadium
126th St. & Roosevelt Ave.
Flushing, NY 11368
(718) 507-6387
Owner: City of New York
VP Stadium Opns: Bob Mandt
Seating: 55,601
Home of New York Mets
Internships: contact Russ Richardson

Yankee Stadium
161st St. & River Ave.
Bronx, NY 10451
(718) 293-4300
Owner: City of New York
Dir Stadium Opns: Sonny Hight
Seating: 57,545
Home of New York Yankees
Internships: contact Harvey Winston

NORTH CAROLINA

Charlotte Coliseum
P.O. Box 669247
Charlotte, NC 28266
(704) 357-4701
Owner: City of Charlotte
Dir: Steve Camp
Arena seating: 23,600
Home of Charlotte Hornets
Internships: contact Eric Scott

Ericsson Stadium
800 S. Mint St.
Charlotte, NC 28202
(704) 358-7000
Owner: City of Charlotte
Facilities Dir: Tom Fellows
Seating: 72,520

OHIO

Cleveland Municipal Stadium
1085 W. Third St.
Cleveland, OH 44114
(216) 696-2700
Dir: Larry Staverman
Seating: 80,032

Gund Arena
100 Gateway Plaza
Cleveland, OH 44115
(216) 420-2000
Owner: Gordon Gund
Gen Mgr: Roy Jones
Seating: 21,000
Home of Cleveland Cavaliers
Internships: contact Gail Creme

Jacobs Field
2401 Ontario St.
Cleveland, OH 44115
(216) 420-4200
Owner: Gateway Economic
    Development Corp.
Dir Ballpark Opns: Jim Folk
Seating: 42,800
Home of Cleveland Indians
Internships offered

Riverfront Stadium
201 E. Pete Rose Way
Cincinnati, OH 45202
(513) 352-5400
Owner: Hamilton County
Mgr: Willie Carden
Seating: 56,000
Home of Cincinnati Reds, Bengals
Internships: contact Willie Carden

OREGON

The Rose Garden
One Center Court
Portland, OR 97227
(503) 235-8771
Owner: Paul Allen
Mgr: Dave Hathaway
Seating: 20,000
Home of Portland Trail Blazers

PENNSYLVANIA

CoreStates Center
3601 S. Broad St.
Philadelphia, PA 19148
(215) 336-3600
Owner: Spectacor
CEO: Peter Luukko
Seating: 18,600
Home of Philadelphia 76ers, Flyers
Internships offered

Pittsburgh Civic Arena
300 Auditorium Pl.
Pittsburgh, PA 15219
(412) 642-1800
Owner: Public Auditorium Authority
Gen Mgr: Henry Abate
Seating: 19,000
Home of Pittsburgh Penguins
Internships: contact Cindi Warner

Three Rivers Stadium
400 Stadium Circle
Pittsburgh, PA 15212
(412) 321-0650
Owner: City of Pittsburgh
Gen Mgr: James Sacco
Seating: 59,600
Home of Pittsburgh Steelers, Pirates
Internships: contact Michelle
    Colaianni

LEADING STADIUMS AND ARENAS IN THE U.S.

Veterans Stadium
Broad St. & Pattison Ave.
Philadelphia, PA 19148
(215) 685-1500
Owner: City of Philadelphia
Dir: Greg Grillone
Seating: 66,000
Home of Philadelphia Phillies, Eagles
Internships: contact Greg Grillone
(graduate degrees only)

TEXAS

Alamodome
100 Montana St.
San Antonio, TX 78203
(210) 207-3663
Owner: City of San Antonio
Gen Mgr: Stephen Zito
Stadium seating: 65,000
Arena seating: 32,500
Home of San Antonio Spurs
Internships: contact Kent Meredith

Astrodome
P.O. Box 288
Houston, TX 77001
(713) 799-9500
Owner: Harris County
Pres/COO: Mike Puryear
Seating: 70,000
Home of Houston Astros, Oilers
Internships offered (with selected
colleges)

The Ballpark at Arlington
1000 Ballpark Way
Arlington, TX 76011
(817) 273-5100
Owner: Texas Rangers
Dir Opns: Mat Stolley
Seating: 49,292
Home of Texas Rangers
Internships offered

Cotton Bowl
P.O. Box 159090
Dallas, TX 75315
(214) 670-8400
Owner: City of Dallas
Mgr: Weldon Flanery
Seating: 72,000
Home of Dallas Burn (MLS)

Reunion Arena
777 Sports St.
Dallas, TX 75207
(214) 939-2770
Owner: City of Dallas
Mgr: Wil Caudell
Seating: 19,000
Home of Dallas Mavericks, Stars
Internships: (214) 748-1808

The Summit
10 Greenway Plaza
Houston, TX 77046
(713) 627-9470
Owner: City of Houston
Mgr: Gerald MacDonald
Arena seating: 17,064
Home of Houston Rockets
Internships: contact Gerald
MacDonald

Texas Stadium
2401 E. Airport Freeway
Irving, TX 75062
(214) 438-7676
Owner: Jerry Jones
VP/Dir: Bruce Hardy
Seating: 65,024
Home of Dallas Cowboys
Internships: contact Bruce Hardy

UTAH

Delta Center
301 W. S. Temple
Salt Lake City, UT 84101
(801) 325-2000
Owner: Larry H. Miller
Gen Mgr: Scott Williams
Arena seating: 20,000
Home of Utah Jazz
Internships: contact Kent Streuling

WASHINGTON

The Kingdome
201 S. King St.
Seattle, WA 98104
(206) 296-3663
Owner: King County
Acting Dir: Vern Wagner
Seating: 66,000
Home of Seattle Mariners, Seahawks
Internships: contact Carol Keaton

Seattle Center Key Arena
305 Harrison St.
Seattle, WA 98109
(206) 684-7202
Owner: City of Seattle
Mgr: Jyo Singh
Seating: 17,700
Home of Seattle SuperSonics
Internships offered

WISCONSIN

Bradley Center
1001 N. Fourth St.
Milwaukee, WI 53203
(414) 227-0400
Owner: State of Wisconsin
Mgr: David Skiles
Seating: 20,000
Home of Milwaukee Bucks

Lambeau Field
1265 Lombardi Ave.
Green Bay, WI 54304
(414) 496-5700
Owner: City of Green Bay
Dir: Jeff Cieply
Seating: 59,543
Home of Green Bay Packers
Internships: contact Lee Remmel

Milwaukee County Stadium
201 S. 46th St.
Milwaukee, WI 53214
(414) 933-4114
Owner: Milwaukee County
Dir Opns: Charles Ward
Seating: 55,000
Home of Milwaukee Brewers
Internships offered

PART TWO
The stadiums and arenas that
follow do not have major
league tenants, but all are large
venues with active programs.
Most, as noted, offer
internships.

ALABAMA

Crampton Bowl
Montgomery Civic Ctr.
P.O. Box 4037
Montgomery, AL 36103
(334) 241-2100
Dir: Hugh S. Austin Jr.
Stadium seating: 25,000

Ernest F. Ladd Stadium
P.O. Box 66721
Mobile, AL 36660
(334) 478-3344
Mgr: Paul Christopher
Seating: 41,000

Garrett Coliseum
P.O. Box 70026
Montgomery, AL 36107
(334) 242-5597
Dir: William H. Johnson III
Arena seating: 12,000

Legion Field Stadium
400 Graymount Ave. W
Birmingham, AL 35204
(205) 254-2556
Dir: Melvin Miller
Seating: 80,000

ALASKA

George M. Sullivan Sports Arena
1600 Gambell St.
Anchorage, AK 99501
(907) 279-0618
Mgr: Tom Anderson
Seating: 8,935

ARIZONA

Arizona Stadium
800 E. University Blvd.
Tucson, AZ 85719
(602) 621-2211
Dir: Kenneth Foster
Seating: 57,000

**Arizona Veterans Memorial
Coliseum & Exposition Center**
P.O. Box 6728
Phoenix, AZ 85005
(602) 252-6771
Dir: Bob Sigholtz
Coliseum seating: 15,681

Rawhide Pavilion & Rodeo Arena
23023 N. Scottsdale Rd.
Scottsdale, AZ 85255
(602) 502-5600
Mgr: Victor Ostrow
Arena seating: 12,000

ARKANSAS

Barton Coliseum
Arkansas State Fairgrounds
P.O. Box 166660
Little Rock, AR 72216
(501) 372-8341
Mgr: Jim Pledger
Seating: 10,219
Internships offered

Harper's Stadium
Kay Rodgers Park
P.O. Box 4145
Fort Smith, AR 72914
(501) 783-6176
Dir: Jim Berry
Seating: 13,000

War Memorial Stadium
P.O. Box 250222
Little Rock, AR 72225
(501) 663-6385
Mgr: Harold M. Steelman
Seating: 53,555
Internships offered

CALIFORNIA

Cow Palace
P.O. Box 34206
San Francisco, CA 94134
(415) 469-6000
Mgr: Michael J. Wegher
Seating: 16,500

Long Beach Arena
Long Beach Convention Ctr.
300 E. Ocean Blvd.
Long Beach, CA 90802
(310) 436-3636
Mgr: David Gordon
Seating: 13,609
Internships offered

San Diego Sports Arena
3500 Sports Arena Blvd.
San Diego, CA 92110
(619) 225-9813
Mgr: Jeff Quinn
Seating: 15,000
Internships: contact Jennifer Darnell

Selland Arena
Fresno Convention Ctr.
700 M St.
Fresno, CA 93721
(209) 498-1511
Dir: Ernest Valdez
Seating: 11,000
Internships: contact Greg Eisner

COLORADO

Colorado State Fair Arena
1001 Beulah Ave., Fairgrounds
Pueblo, CO 81004
(719) 561-8484
Dir: Jerry Robbe
Seating: 15,000
Internships offered

Denver Coliseum
4600 Humboldt St.
Denver, CO 80216
(303) 295-4444
Mgr: Fred Luetzen
Seating: 11,500

CONNECTICUT

New Haven Coliseum
275 S. Orange St.
New Haven, CT 06510
(203) 772-4200
Dir: James E. Perillo
Seating: 11,171
Internships: contact Laura Giammattei

FLORIDA

The Arena
Pensacola Civic Ctr.
201 E. Gregory St.
Pensacola, FL 32591
(904) 432-0800
Dir: Carol Pollock
Seating: 10,268
Internships: contact Kathleen Colley

Bayfront Center Arena
400 First St. S
St. Petersburg, FL 33701
(813) 892-5798
Mgr: Jeff Foreman
Seating: 10,000

Expo Hall
Florida State Fairgrounds
P.O. Box 11766
Tampa, FL 33680
(813) 621-7821
Dir: Rick Vymlatil
Seating: 12,000

George Jenkins Arena
Lakeland Civic Ctr.
P.O. Box 1810
Lakeland, FL 33802
(813) 499-8100
Dir: Allen Johnson
Seating: 10,000
Internships: contact Brenda Waldrop

Ocean Center Arena
101 N. Atlantic Ave.
Daytona Beach, FL 32118
(904) 254-4500
Dir: Rick Hamilton
Seating: 9,496

St. Petersburg ThunderDome
One Stadium Dr.
St. Petersburg, FL 33705
(813) 825-3120
Dir: Bob Leighton
Seating: 50,000
Internships offered

Tallahassee-Leon County Civic Center Arena
505 W. Pensacola St.
Tallahassee, FL 32302
(904) 487-1691
Dir: Ron Spencer
Seating: 14,000
Internships: contact Ron Spencer

Veterans Memorial Coliseum
1145 E. Adams St.
Jacksonville, FL 32202
(904) 630-3905
Mgr: Scott Indorf
Seating: 10,276
Internships offered

GEORGIA

Augusta-Richmond County Civic Center Arena
601 Seventh St.
Augusta, GA 30901
(706) 722-3521
Gen Mgr: Linda Roberts
Seating: 8,374
Internships: contact Linda Roberts

Columbus Memorial Stadium
400 Fourth St.
Columbus, GA 31901
(706) 571-5889
Mgr: Tony Ford
Seating: 20,000

Macon Coliseum
200 Coliseum Dr.
Macon, GA 31201
(912) 751-9152
Mgr: Gary Desjardins
Seating: 9,282
Internships offered

Martin Luther King Jr. Arena
Savannah Civic Ctr.
P.O. Box 726
Savannah, GA 31402
(912) 651-6550
Dir: Cynthia Brinson
Seating: 8,028

HAWAII

Blaisdell Center Arena
777 Ward Ave.
Honolulu, HI 96814
(808) 527-5400
Dir: Carla W. Coray
Seating: 8,733

ILLINOIS

International Amphitheatre
4220 S. Halsted St.
Chicago, IL 60609
(312) 254-6900
Mgr: Eugene Dibble
Seating: 10,500

The Mark of the Quad Cities
1201 River Dr.
Moline, IL 61265
(309) 764-2001
Exec Dir: Stephen R. Hyman
Seating: 12,000
Internships: contact Mary Beth Frecking

MetroCentre Arena
300 Elm St.
Rockford, IL 61101
(815) 968-5600
Mgr: Brad Walsh
Seating: 10,000
Internships: contact Jodi Foster Webber

Peoria Civic Center Arena
201 S.W. Jefferson St.
Peoria, IL 61602
(309) 673-8900
Mgr: Noel Brooks
Seating: 11,839
Internships: contact Debbie Ritschel

Rosemont Horizon
6920 N. Mannheim Rd.
Rosemont, IL 60018
(847) 635-6601
Dir: Harry Pappas
Arena seating: 18,000

INDIANA

The Arena
Genesis Convention Ctr.
One Genesis Ctr. Plaza
Gary, IN 46402
(219) 882-5505
Dir: Richard Henderson
Seating: 9,200
Internships: contact Debra Stevens

Memorial Coliseum
4000 Parnell Ave.
Fort Wayne, IN 46805
(219) 482-9502
Dir: Randy L. Brown
Seating: 9,500
Internships: contact Randy L. Brown

Pepsi Coliseum
Indiana State Fairgrounds
1202 E. 38th St.
Indianapolis, IN 46205
(317) 927-7500
Exec Dir: William Stinson
Arena seating: 9,900
Internships: contact Monica Brase

Roberts Stadium
2600 Division St.
Evansville, IN 47711
(812) 476-1383
Exec Dir: Sandie Aaron
Arena seating: 12,232
Internships: contact Sandie Aaron

IOWA

Five Seasons Center
370 First Ave. NE
Cedar Rapids, IA 52401
(319) 398-5211
Dir: Ann M. Larson
Seating: 10,000
Internships: contact Ann M. Larson

Veterans Memorial Auditorium
833 Fifth Ave.
Des Moines, IA 50309
(515) 242-2946
Dir: Mike Grimaldi
Arena seating: 11,700
Internships: contact Mike Grimaldi

KANSAS

Kansas Coliseum
P.O. Box 9112
Valley Center, KS 67277
(316) 755-1243
Dir: John Nath
Seating: 11,738

Landon Arena
Kansas Expocentre
One Expocentre Dr.
Topeka, KS 66612
(913) 235-1986
Mgr: Chris Carpenter
Seating: 10,000
Internships: contact Chris Carpenter

KENTUCKY

Cardinal Stadium/Freedom Hall
Kentucky Fair & Exposition Ctr.
P.O. Box 37130
Louisville, KY 40233
(502) 367-5000
Dir Opns: Larry Faue
Cardinal Stadium seating: 50,000
Freedom Hall (arena) seating: 19,800
Internships: contact personnel office

Rupp Arena
Lexington Ctr.
430 W. Vine St.
Lexington, KY 40507
(606) 233-4567
Mgr: Rick Reno
Seating: 23,500
Internships: contact Chester Maull

LOUISIANA

Cajundome
444 Cajundome Blvd.
Lafayette, LA 70506
(318) 265-2100
Dir: Greg Davis
Seating: 13,232

Hirsch Coliseum
Louisiana State Fairgrounds
P.O. Box 38327
Shreveport, LA 71133
(318) 635-1361
Gen Mgr: Sam Giordano
Seating: 10,330

Lakefront Arena
6801 Franklin Ave.
New Orleans, LA 70122
(504) 286-7171
Mgr: George Lewis
Seating: 10,000

Monroe Civic Center Arena
401 Lea Joyner Expwy.
Monroe, LA 71210
(318) 329-2225
Interim Mgr: Obie Webster
Seating: 9,000

Riverside Centroplex Arena
P.O. Box 4047
Baton Rouge, LA 70821
(504) 389-3030
Exec Dir: Will Wilton
Seating: 12,813

Tad Gormley Stadium
One Palm Dr.
New Orleans, LA 70124
(504) 482-4888
Mgr: Russell Doussan Jr.
Seating: 25,000

MAINE

George I. Lewis Auditorium
Cumberland County Civic Ctr.
One Civic Ctr. Sq.
Portland, ME 04101
(207) 775-3481
Gen Mgr: Steven Crane
Arena seating: 9,150

MARYLAND

Baltimore Arena
201 W. Baltimore St.
Baltimore, MD 21201
(410) 347-2020
Dir: Donna P. Julian
Seating: 14,096
Occasional home of Washington
   Bullets/Wizards
Internships: contact PR Dep't

MASSACHUSETTS

Centrum Arena
50 Foster St.
Worcester, MA 01608
(508) 755-6800
Gen Mgr: Sandy Dunn
Seating: 15,000
Internships: contact Amy Harwood

Civic Center Arena
1277 Main St.
Springfield, MA 01103
(413) 787-6610
Mgr: Kevin Barrett
Seating: 10,000
Internships: contact Kevin Barrett

MICHIGAN

Cobo Arena
600 Civic Ctr. Dr.
Detroit, MI 48226
(313) 396-7444
Mgr: John Pettit
Seating: 12,191
Internships offered

Van Andel Arena
245 Monroe NW
Grand Rapids, MI 49503
(616) 456-3995
Dir: Craig M. Liston
Seating: 12,100

MINNESOTA

St. Paul Civic Center
143 W. Fourth St.
St. Paul, MN 55102
(612) 224-7361
Dir: Chris Hansen
Managing Dir: Barbara Chandler
Seating: 16,000
Internships: contact Patrick Klinger

MISSISSIPPI

The Coliseum
Mississippi State Fairgrounds
P.O. Box 892
Jackson, MS 39205
(601) 961-4000
Dir: Billy Orr
Arena seating: 9,138

Mississippi Coast Coliseum
2350 Beach Blvd.
Biloxi, MS 39531
(601) 388-8010
Dir: Bill Holmes
Arena seating: 11,500
Internships: contact Bonnie Bishop

Tupelo Coliseum
P.O. Box 7288
Tupelo, MS 38801
(601) 841-6573
Dir: Michael Marion
Seating: 10,000

Veterans Memorial Stadium
2531 N. State St.
Jackson, MS 39296
(601) 354-6021
Mgr: Watt Watley
Seating: 60,942

MISSOURI

Kemper Arena
1800 Genessee
Kansas City, MO 64102
(816) 274-6222
Gen Mgr: Carolyn Foxworthy
Seating: 17,500

Municipal Auditorium Arena
301 W. 13th St., Suite 100
Kansas City, MO 64105
(816) 871-3700
Gen Mgr: Bill Langley
Seating: 10,537
Internships offered

MONTANA

MetraPark Arena
P.O. Box 2514
Billings, MT 59103
(406) 256-2400
Mgr: Bill Chiesa
Seating: 11,746
Internships: contact Sandra Hawke

NEBRASKA

Aksarben
6800 Mercy Rd.
Omaha, NE 68106
(402) 444-4000
CEO: Sharon Smith
Arena seating: 8,200

Civic Auditorium Complex
1804 Capital Ave.
Omaha, NE 68102
(402) 444-4750
Mgr: Larry Lahaie
Arena seating: 10,950
Rosenblatt Stadium seating: 20,100

NEVADA

Caesars Palace Sports Pavilion
3570 Las Vegas Blvd. S
Las Vegas, NV 89109
(702) 731-7110
Opns Mgr: Dan Reichartz
Seating: 15,000
Internships: contact HR Dep't

MGM Grand Garden
3799 Las Vegas Blvd. S
Las Vegas, NV 89109
(702) 891-7800
Opns Mgr: Terry Parsons
Seating: 15,200
Internships: contact HR Dep't

NEW MEXICO

Tingley Coliseum
P.O. Box 8546
Albuquerque, NM 87198
(505) 265-1791
Mgr: Dennis Campbell
Seating: 10,200

NEW YORK

Civic Center Arena
One Civic Ctr. Plaza
Glens Falls, NY 12801
(518) 798-0366
Dir: Don Ostrom
Seating: 8,000

Knickerbocker Arena
51 S. Pearl St.
Albany, NY 12207
(518) 487-2000
Mgr: Bob Belber
Seating: 17,500
Internships: contact Alicia Jacobs

Lake Placid Olympic Center
216 Main St.
Lake Placid, NY 12946
(518) 523-1655
Mgrs: Rich Cotton, Dennis Allen
Seating: 10,385
Internships: contact Don Krone

Niagara Falls Arena
Convention & Civic Ctr.
305 Fourth St.
Niagara Falls, NY 14303
(716) 286-4781
Dir: Harry Cann
Seating: 9,496

Oncenter Arena
800 S. State St.
Syracuse, NY 13202
(315) 435-8000
Dir: Jerry Gallagher
Seating: 9,200
Internships: contact Jerry Gallagher

Rochester Memorial Arena
100 Exchange Blvd.
Rochester, NY 14614
(716) 546-2030
Dir: Jeff Calkins
Seating: 14,000
Internships: contact Jeff Calkins

NORTH CAROLINA

Bowman Gray Stadium
Lawrence Joel Coliseum
P.O. Box 68
Winston-Salem, NC 27102
(919) 727-2976
Dir: Tex A. Leonard
Seating (Bowman Gray Stadium): 30,000
Seating (Lawrence Joel Coliseum): 14,400
Internships: contact Benjamin Dame

Greensboro Coliseum
1921 W. Lee St.
Greensboro, NC 27403
(910) 373-7400
Dir: Matthew G. Brown
Seating: 23,309
Internships: contact Robin Welborn

Independence Arena
2700 Independence Blvd.
Charlotte, NC 28205
(704) 372-3600
Mgr: George Hite
Seating: 11,000

NORTH DAKOTA

Bismarck Civic Center
601 E. Sweet Ave.
Bismarck, ND 58502
(701) 222-6487
Mgr: Richard L. Petersen
Seating: 10,100

Fargodome
1800 N. University Dr.
Fargo, ND 58102
(701) 241-9100
Dir: Paul Johnson
Seating: 28,310
Internships: contact John Gordon

OHIO

Cincinnati Gardens
2250 Seymour Ave.
Cincinnati, OH 45212
(513) 631-7793
Mgr: Joseph Jagoditz
Arena seating: 10,106

OKLAHOMA

Myriad Arena
One Myriad Gardens
Oklahoma City, OK 73102
(405) 232-8871
Dir: Wes Gray
Arena seating: 16,000

State Fair Arena
P.O. Box 74943
Oklahoma City, OK 73147
(405) 948-6700
Dir: Reba Jones
Seating: 12,000

Tulsa Convention Center Arena
100 Civic Ctr.
Tulsa, OK 74103
(918) 596-7177
Mgr: Bob Mayer
Seating: 8,992

PENNSYLVANIA

HersheyPark Arena & Stadium
100 W. HersheyPark Dr.
Hershey, PA 17033
(717) 534-3348
Gen Mgr: Dave Lavery
Arena seating: 9,062
Stadium seating: 25,000
Internships: contact Sharon Manton

RHODE ISLAND

Providence Civic Center
One LaSalle Sq.
Providence, RI 02903
(401) 331-0700
Dir: Stephen Lombardi
Arena seating: 14,572

SOUTH CAROLINA

Florence Civic Center
P.O. Box 6423
Florence, SC 29502
(803) 679-9417
Dir: A. C. Chapman
Seating: 10,000

North Charleston Coliseum
5001 Coliseum Dr.
North Charleston, SC 29418
(803) 529-5050
Dir: Dave Holscher
Arena seating: 14,500

SOUTH DAKOTA

Rushmore Plaza Civic Center
444 Mt. Rushmore Rd. N
Rapid City, SD 57701
(605) 394-4115
Mgr: Jerry Jasinski
Arena seating: 10,000
Internships: contact Jerry Jasinski

Sioux Falls Arena
1201 West Ave. N
Sioux Falls, SD 57104
(605) 367-7288
Dir: Rusty DeCurtins
Seating: 8,000
Internships offered

TENNESSEE

Mid-South Coliseum
996 Early Maxwell Blvd.
Memphis, TN 38104
(901) 274-3982
Mgr: Beth Wade
Seating: 12,035

LEADING STADIUMS AND ARENAS IN THE U.S.

Nashville Municipal Auditorium
417 Fourth Ave. N
Nashville, TN 37201
(615) 862-6390
Mgr: Robert Skoney
Arena seating: 9,475

Pyramid Arena
One Auction Ave.
Memphis, TN 38105
(901) 521-9675
Dir: Victor L. Cohen
Arena seating: 22,500
Internships: contact Terri Knight

TEXAS

Dallas Convention Center Arena
650 S. Griffin St.
Dallas, TX 75202
(214) 939-2750
Mgr: Oscar McGaskey Jr.
Arena seating: 9,816
Internships offered

Fort Worth/Tarrant County Convention Center
1111 Houston St.
Fort Worth, TX 76102
(817) 884-2222
Dir: Melvin Morgan
Arena seating: 13,956
Internships: contact Melvin Morgan

Freeman Coliseum
P.O. Box 200283
San Antonio, TX 78220
(210) 226-1177
Exec Dir: Hymie Gonzales
Arena seating: 13,000

Heart O' Texas Coliseum
4601 Bosque Blvd.
Waco, TX 76710
(817) 776-1660
Mgr: Mark Miller
Seating: 10,000

Lubbock Municipal Auditorium/Coliseum
1501 Sixth St.
Lubbock, TX 79401
(806) 767-2243
Mgr: Vicki Key
Arena seating: 9,324

Texas Exposition & Heritage Center
P.O. Box 9876
Austin, TX 78766
(512) 473-9200
Dir: John Emmons
Arena seating: 9,500

Will Rogers Coliseum
3401 W. Lancaster
Fort Worth, TX 76107
(817) 871-8150
Dir: B. Don Magness
Seating: 8,694

VIRGINIA

Hampton Coliseum
1000 Coliseum Dr.
Hampton, VA 23666
(804) 838-5650
Dir: Joe Tsao
Arena seating: 13,800
Internships

Norfolk Scope Arena
P.O. Box 1808
Norfolk, VA 23501
(804) 664-6464
Dir: William H. Luther
Seating: 13,500

Roanoke Civic Center
710 Williamson Rd.
Roanoke, VA 24016
(703) 981-2241
Mgr: Bob Chapman
Arena seating: 11,000
Stadium seating: 25,000

WASHINGTON

Spokane Arena
W. 720 Mallon Ave.
Spokane, WA 99201
(509) 324-7000
Mgr: Kevin Twohig
Seating: 12,500

Spokane Center
W. 334 Spokane Falls Blvd.
Spokane, WA 99201
(509) 353-6500
Dir: Michael Kobluk
Albi Stadium seating: 34,000

Tacoma Dome
2727 E. D St.
Tacoma, WA 98421
(206) 272-3663
Dir: John Croley
Arena seating: 23,000
Internships: contact Will Lofdahl

WEST VIRGINIA

Charleston Civic Center
200 Civic Ctr. Dr.
Charleston, WV 25301
(304) 345-1500
Dir: John Robertson
Arena seating: 13,500

Huntington Civic Arena
One Civic Ctr. Plaza
Huntington, WV 25727
(304) 696-5990
Dir Opns: Aaron Dillon
Arena seating: 11,000
Internships offered

WISCONSIN

Dane County Expo Center
1881 Expo Mall E
Madison, WI 53713
(608) 267-3976
Mgr: Ray Ritari
Seating: 10,250
Internships: contact Ted Ballweg

Wisconsin Center Arena
500 W. Kilbourn Ave.
Milwaukee, WI 53203
(414) 271-4000
Pres: Geoffrey Hurtado
Arena seating: 12,200
Internships: contact Sandra Lange

WYOMING

Casper Events Center
One Events Dr.
Casper, WY 82601
(307) 235-8441
Dir: Max Torbert
Arena seating: 10,452

ARCHITECTURAL FIRMS THAT SPECIALIZE IN SPORTS FACILITIES

Anderson DeBartolo Pan, Inc.
2480 N. Arcadia Ave.
Tucson, AZ 85712
(602) 795-4500

Angelo Francis Corva & Associates
1691 Northern Blvd.
Manhasset, NY 11030
(516) 794-9800

Aquatic Design Group
1901 Camino Vida Roble, Suite 125
Carlsbad, CA 92008
(619) 438-8400

Architectural Associates, Ltd.
5801 Washington Ave.
Racine, WI 53406
(414) 886-1700

Athletic Facilities Planning
1430 Massachusetts Ave., Suite 306
Cambridge, MA 02138
(617) 492-2677

Barker-Rinker-Seacat & Partners
2546 15th St.
Denver, CO 80211
(303) 455-1366

Bonestroo Rosene Anderlik & Associates
2335 W. Hwy. 36
St. Paul, MN 55113
(612) 636-4600

Braun & Steidl Architects, Inc.
1041 W. Market St.
Akron, OH 44313
(216) 864-7755

Brosso Wilhelm & McWilliams
8600 LaSalle Rd., Suite 503
Baltimore, MD 21286
(410) 321-6760

Browning Day Mullins Dierdorf
334 N. Senate Ave.
Indianapolis, IN 46204
(317) 635-5030

Cooke Douglass Farr Lemons
3780 I-55 N
Jackson, MS 39211
(601) 366-3110

Dahlin Group Architects
2671 Crow Canyon Rd.
San Ramon, CA 94583
(510) 837-8286

ARCHITECTURAL FIRMS THAT SPECIALIZE IN SPORTS FACILITIES

Daniel F. Tully Associates, Inc.
99 Essex St.
Melrose, MA 02176
(617) 665-0099

Di Geronimo Associates
598 Main St., P.O. Box 524
Sturbridge, MA 01566
(508) 347-5184

Edward Larrabee Barnes/
John M. Y. Lee & Partners
320 W. 13th St.
New York, NY 10014
(212) 929-3131

The Eggers Group, P.C.
440 Ninth Ave.
New York, NY 10001
(212) 629-4100

Ellerbe Becket, Inc.
800 LaSalle Ave.
Minneapolis, MN 55402
(612) 376-2312

Everett I. Brown Co.
950 N. Meridian St., Suite 200
Indianapolis, IN 46204
(317) 237-7000

Geiger Engineers
2 Executive Blvd., Suite 410
Suffern, NY 10901
(914) 368-3330

Giffels Hoyem Basso, Inc.
3150 Livernois, Suite 300
Troy, MI 48083-5028
(313) 680-0680

HNTB Sports Architecture
1201 Walnut, Suite 700
Kansas City, MO 64106
(816) 472-1201

HOK Sports Facilities Group
323 W. Eighth St., Suite 700
Kansas City, MO 64105
(816) 221-1576

Hansen/Murakami/Eshima, Inc.
100 Filbert St.
Oakland, CA 94607
(510) 444-7959

Hastings & Chivetta Architects,
Inc.
101 S. Hanley Rd., Suite 1700
St. Louis, MO 63105
(314) 863-5717

Heery International
999 Peachtree St., NE
Atlanta, GA 30367
(404) 881-9880

I. William Sizeler & Associates
300 Lafayette Mall, Suite 200
New Orleans, LA 70130
(504) 523-6472

John Williams & Associates
821 17th St., Suite 502
Denver, CO 80202
(303) 295-6190

KMR Architects, Ltd.
2501 Wayzata Blvd.
Minneapolis, MN 55405
(612) 377-8151

Kotz and Associates
130 E. Genesee St.
Syracuse, NY 13202
(315) 475-4157

Krummell & Associates
2712 Southern Blvd.
Virginia Beach, VA 23452
(804) 340-8336

LZT Associates, Inc.
124 S.W. Adams St., Suite 450
Peoria, IL 61602
(309) 673-3100

Linscott, Haylett, Wimmer &
Wheat Architects/Interiors
917 W. 43rd St.
Kansas City, MO 64111
(816) 531-8555

Magill Architects, Inc.
11615 Forest Central Dr., Suite 211
Dallas, TX 75243
(214) 343-1981

Maitland & Kuntz Architects
915 Duke St.
Alexandria, VA 22314
(703) 684-0680

Martinson Architects, Inc.
Old Fort Square
211 N. Broadway, Suite 205
Green Bay, WI 54303
(414) 432-2442

Michael Beattie Associates
P.O. Box 1010
Middletown Springs, VT 05757
(802) 235-2468

The ORB Organization, Inc.
607 S.W. Grady Way
Renton, WA 98055
(206) 226-3522

Odell Associates, Inc.
129 W. Trade St.
Charlotte, NC 28202-2143
(704) 377-5941

Osborn Architects & Engineers
668 Euclid Ave.
Cleveland, OH 44114
(216) 861-2020

The PWAE Group, Inc.
15 S. 10th St.
Columbia, MO 65201
(314) 449-2683

Prochaska & Associates
11317 Chicago Circle
Omaha, NE 68154-2633
(402) 334-0755

Richard Dattner Architect, P.C.
154 W. 57th St.
New York, NY 10019
(212) 247-2660

The Robinson Green Beretta
Corp.
50 Holden St.
Providence, RI 02908
(401) 272-1730

Roland/Miller/Associates
2421 Mendocino Ave., Suite 200
Santa Rosa, CA 95403
(707) 544-3920

Rosser International
524 W. Peachtree St. NW
Atlanta, GA 30308-0000
(404) 876-3800

Rossetti Associates Architects
280 N. Woodward Ave., Suite 300
Birmingham, MI 48009
(810) 644-0777

Rossman Schneider Gadbery Shay
Architects
8681 E. Via de Negocio
Scottsdale, AZ 85258-3330
(602) 991-0800

Sasaki Associates, Inc.
64 Pleasant St.
Watertown, MA 02172
(617) 926-3300

Scholer Corp., Architecture
& Engineering
P.O. Box 808
Lafayette, IN 47902
(317) 474-1478

Schrickel, Rollins and Associates
1161 Corporate Dr. W, Suite 200
Arlington, TX 76006
(817) 649-3216

Sink Combs Dethlefs
1900 Grant St., Suite 1250
Denver, CO 80203
(303) 830-1200

Stanmar, Inc.
130 Boston Post Rd.
Sudbury, MA 01776
(508) 443-9922

Sverdrup Facilities, Inc.
801 N. 11th St.
St. Louis, MO 63101
(314) 436-7600

Thomas, Miller & Partners
750 Old Hickory Blvd., Suite 222
Brentwood, TN 37027-4509
(615) 377-9773

Toltz, King, Duvall, Anderson &
Associates, Inc.
1500 Piper Jaffray Plaza
444 Cedar St.
St. Paul, MN 55101-2140
(612) 292-4400

Venable Architectural Group, Inc.
6073 Mt. Marian Extension, Suite 19
Memphis, TN 38115
(901) 797-9262

Ward Associates, P.C.
1500 Lakeland Ave.
Bohemia, NY 11716
(516) 563-4800

William Merci, Architect
1331 Sheridan Rd.
Wilmette, IL 60091
(708) 256-5658

Horse racing is the oldest organized sport in the world. Pageantry notwithstanding, its future will be influenced by technology.

RACETRACKS

NATIONAL MUSEUM OF RACING AND HALL OF FAME

Saratoga Springs, New York

After five years in temporary space, the museum moved to its current handsome setting in 1955 and was opened by Governor Averell Harriman. *Annual visitors:* 25,000. *Employees:* 15 full-time, 5 volunteers, 2 paid interns. *Director:* Peter Hammell. *Address:* 191 Union Ave., Saratoga Springs, NY 12866. *Phone:* (518) 584-0400.

How fares the sport of kings? At home, pretty well. Abroad, much better than that. Some U.S. tracks have had a dip in attendance. The actual number of races declined in 1995. But purses, a leading economic indicator of the health of racing, rose in the U.S. to a record $787,275,000, and the pari-mutuel handle was a record $10,428,822,300, according to Jockey Club figures.

Steven Crist, director of communications at the New York Racing Association, anticipated that some of the small tracks around the country would close if their business didn't improve enough to attract horses. But he saw the industry getting a boost from technological advances that will permit a greater use of television, simulcasting (interspersing a track's races with races from a distant track), and home betting. Simulcast activity more than doubled in 1995 over the previous year. Crist believes that advances like these will produce many new jobs in the industry.

John Walzak, associate coordinator of the University of Arizona's highly regarded Race Track Industry Program, agrees. "Three trends are reshaping the industry," he said. "First, betting is shifting to televised events, away from the traditional live, on-track event. Second, racetracks are looking to add other forms of gaming, especially slot machines and video lottery terminals, to their product offerings. And third, the industry is reengineering itself to incorporate up-to-date technology and management practices."

All this, he said, will open new opportunities "for innovative people with training in current management practices, marketing techniques, computer applications, and the regulatory and business structure of the industry."

The new opportunities, he said, "exist at racetracks, animal-related trade associations, regulatory agencies, technology suppliers, and trade publications."

* * * *

Meanwhile, elsewhere in the world, and especially in Asia, the sport is booming, and purses far exceed those in the U.S.

Tuned in to this development is the University of Louisville's excellent Equine Industry Program. The program, which is involved in several projects on the international scene, is headed by Robert G. Lawrence.

"One of the activities," he said, "is a six-month program to facilitate interaction between international trainers and officials and Kentucky's horses and horsemen. In 1996 we worked with trainers and stewards from Hong Kong, Japan, Singapore, and India. We are also initiating a program to give midlevel managers at international tracks a hands-on exposure to all segments of the industry in the United States, from the breeding farm to the mutuel window.

"We are also working with a university in Australia on plans to conduct an equine management specialty for its MBA program," he said.

Jobs in Management

The University of Arizona and the University of Louisville are recognized by the industry as having the best training programs for jobs in management. The programs are described on p. 8.

Some of the positions held by graduates of the University of Arizona program: chief operating officer, general manager, steward, racing secretary, executive director, editor, farm manager, off-track betting manager, trainer, marketing director, mutuel manager, director of racing, publicity director, intertrack wagering director, breed registry official, track handicapper, and track announcer.

Graduates of the University of Louisville program also are employed across the spectrum of the industry, from the TV simulcast director and broadcaster at Pimlico/Laurel to the director of equine special events for Disney World at Orlando and the director of the Quality Assurance Program for the Association of Racing Commissioners International.

At both the University of Arizona and the University of Louisville, students are placed in internships throughout the industry.

Jobs at the Track

In both thoroughbred racing and harness racing, job titles and salaries are similar, although the pay for a particular job may vary substantially from one track to another. Following are average salaries, with small tracks and big tracks taken into account. The salaries for some jobs at major tracks are actually twice as high as the average shown. At small tracks, salaries are considerably lower than what the averages indicate.

Management and Staff
- General manager: $83,000.
- Assistant general manager: $46,250.
- Mutuels director: $37,900.
- Assistant mutuels director: $22,600.
- Controller (determines purses, based on size of mutuel handles and attendance): $43,000.
- Assistant controller: $32,000.
- Admissions director: $24,700.
- Assistant admissions director: $13,900.
- Secretary: $23,600.

Officials
- Steward (enforces the rules of racing): $49,000.
- Timer: $20,500.
- Clerk of the course (records the weigh-ins before and after each race): $25,300.
- Judge (places the order of finish): $34,300.
- Patrol judge (watches for fouls): $16,300.
- Paddock judge (checks horses for proper equipment and gets them to the track): $21,600.
- Horse identifier (confirms identity of horses by checking tattooed markings): $15,700.
- Director of racing/racing secretary (sets up schedule of races, assigns stalls, etc.): $52,000.
- Starter: $50,000.
- Parade marshal: $17,000.

Marketing and Communications
- Director of marketing and promotions: $44,200.
- Director of public relations: $36,300.
- Publicity director: $32,400.
- Assistant publicity director: $23,700.
- Group sales director: $24,400.
- Director of TV and radio coverage: $32,000.
- Sound-system operator: $30,000.
- Track announcer: $30,000.
- Photo-finish camera operator: $41,600.

Others
- Medical services manager: $40,000.
- Track superintendent (responsible for track surface): $37,500.
- General superintendent: $38,000.
- Assistant superintendent: $29,000.
- Director of security: $34,000.
- Director of parking: $19,000.

INTERNSHIPS

Tracks throughout the country offer internships, as do many racing organizations and publications. (See the directory that follows for addresses and phone numbers of racetracks.)

T H O R O U G H B R E D   R A C I N G

ALABAMA

Birmingham Race Course
Jefferson County Racing Ass'n
1000 John Rogers Dr.
Birmingham, AL 35210
(205) 838-7500
Gen Mgr: Charles S. McIntosh

ARIZONA

Prescott Downs
Yavapai County Fair Ass'n
P.O. Box 346
Prescott, AZ 86302
(602) 445-7820
Gen Mgr: Dora Kittredge

ARKANSAS

Oaklawn Park
Oaklawn Jockey Club
P.O. Box 699
Hot Springs, AR 71902
(501) 623-4411
Gen Mgr: Eric Jackson

CALIFORNIA

Alameda County Fair
Alameda County Fair Ass'n
4501 Pleasanton Ave.
Pleasanton, CA 94566
(510) 426-7600
Gen Mgr: Peter Bailey

Bay Meadows
Bay Meadows Operating Co.
P.O. Box 5050
San Mateo, CA 94402
(415) 574-RACE
CEO: F. Jack Liebau

Cal Expo
California Exposition & State Fair
1600 Exposition Blvd.
Sacramento, CA 95815
(916) 924-2000
Gen Mgr: Joseph Barkett

Del Mar
Del Mar Thoroughbred Club
P.O. Box 700
Del Mar, CA 92014
(619) 755-1141
Pres/Gen Mgr: Joseph W. Harper

Fairplex Park
Los Angeles County Fair Ass'n
P.O. Box 2250
Pomona, CA 91769
(714) 623-3111
Pres: Ralph Hinds

Golden Gate Fields
Pacific Racing Ass'n
P.O. Box 6027
Albany, CA 94706-0027
(510) 559-7300
VP/Gen Mgr: Peter W. Tunney

Hollywood Park
Hollywood Park, Inc.
P.O. Box 369
Inglewood, CA 90306-0369
(310) 419-1500
Pres: Donald M. Robbins

Oak Tree
Oak Tree Racing Ass'n
285 W. Huntington Dr.
Arcadia, CA 91007-3439
(818) 574-7223
Exec VP: Sherwood Chillingworth

Santa Anita Park
Los Angeles Turf Club
P.O. Box 808
Arcadia, CA 91066-0808
(818) 574-7223
Pres: Clifford C. Goodrich

COLORADO

Arapahoe Park
Racing Associates of Colorado
P.O. Box 460370
Aurora, CO 80046
(303) 690-2400
Gen Mgr: K. B. Seymore

DELAWARE

Delaware Park
Delaware Racing Ass'n
P.O. Box 6008
Wilmington, DE 19804
(302) 994-2521
Gen Mgr: John E. Mooney

FLORIDA

Calder Race Course
Calder Race Course, Inc.
P.O. Box 1808, Carol City Branch
Opa-Locka, FL 33055-0808
(305) 625-1311
Pres: C. Kenneth Dunn

Gulfstream Park
Gulfstream Park Racing Ass'n
901 S. Federal Hwy.
Hallandale, FL 33009
(305) 454-7000
Gen Mgr: Richard Relicke

Hialeah Park
Hialeah, Inc.
P.O. Box 158
Hialeah, FL 33011
(305) 885-8000
Pres: John J. Brunett Jr.

Tampa Bay Downs
Tampa Bay Downs, Inc.
P.O. Box 2007
Oldsmar, FL 34677
(813) 855-4401
Gen Mgr: Stephen Baker

IDAHO

Les Bois
Les Bois Race Track, Inc.
5610 Glenwood Rd.
Boise, ID 83714
(208) 376-3991
CEO: Chris Christian

ILLINOIS

Arlington International Racecourse
Arlington International Racecourse, Ltd.
P.O. Box 7
Arlington Heights, IL 60006
(708) 255-4300
VP/Gen Mgr: Robert L. Bork

Balmoral Park Race Track
Balmoral Racing Club, Inc.
26435 S. Dixie Hwy.
Crete, IL 60417
(708) 672-7544
Gen Mgr: Dan Nemeth

Fairmount Park
Ogden-Fairmount, Inc.
Route 40
Collinsville, IL 62234
(618) 345-4300
Gen Mgr: Brian Zander

Hawthorne Race Course
Hawthorne Race Course, Inc.
3501 S. Laramie Ave.
Stickney/Cicero, IL 60804
(708) 780-3700
Gen Mgr: Thomas F. Carey

Sportsman's Park
National Jockey Club
3301 S. Laramie Ave.
Cicero, IL 60650
(312) 242-1121
Pres: Charles W. Bidwill Jr.

Wyoming Downs
Wyoming Downs Horse Racing, Inc.
P.O. Box 1607
Evanston, IL 82931
(307) 789-0511
Gen Mgr: Joseph F. Joyce

IOWA

Prairie Meadows
Racing Ass'n of Central Iowa
P.O. Box 1000
Altoona, IA 50009-0901
(515) 967-1000
Pres: Tom Timmons

KANSAS

The Woodlands
Sunflower Racing, Inc.
P.O. Box 12036
Kansas City, KS 66112
(913) 299-9767
Gen Mgr: H. Rick Henson

KENTUCKY

Churchill Downs
Churchill Downs, Inc.
700 Central Ave.
Louisville, KY 40208-1200
(502) 636-4400
Gen Mgr: Dan Parkerson

Ellis Park
Ellis Park Race Course, Inc.
P.O. Box 33
Henderson, KY 42420-0033
(812) 425-1456
Ass't to Pres: G. Edgar Steffee

Keeneland
Keeneland Ass'n
P.O. Box 1690
Lexington, KY 40592-1690
(606) 254-3412
Pres/Gen Mgr: William C. Greely

Turfway Park
Turfway Park Racing Ass'n
P.O. Box 8
Florence, KY 41022
(606) 371-0200
Gen Mgr: Gary L. Wilfert

LOUISIANA

Delta Downs
Delta Downs Racing Ass'n
P.O. Box 175
Vinton, LA 70668
(318) 589-7441
Gen Mgr: Ray Farrar

THOROUGHBRED RACING

Evangeline Downs
First Statewide Racing Co.
P.O. Box 90270
Lafayette, LA 70509-0270
(318) 896-7223
Pres: Charles B. Ashy Sr.

Fair Grounds Race Course
Fair Grounds Corp.
P.O. Box 52529
New Orleans, LA 70152
(504) 944-5515
Pres/Gen Mgr: Bryan G. Krantz

Jefferson Downs
Jefferson Downs Corp.
P.O. Box 640459
Kenner, LA 70064
(504) 466-8521
Gen Mgr: Gordon Robertson

Louisiana Downs
Louisiana Downs, Inc.
P.O. Box 5519
Bossier City, LA 71171-5519
(318) 742-5555
Exec VP: Thomas S. Sweeney

MARYLAND

Laurel Race Course
Laurel Racing Ass'n
P.O. Box 130
Laurel, MD 20725
(301) 725-0400
Gen Mgr: James P. Mango

Pimlico
Maryland Jockey Club of Baltimore
City
Pimlico Race Course
Baltimore, MD 21215
(410) 542-9400
Sr VP/Gen Mgr: James P. Mango

MASSACHUSETTS

Suffolk Downs
Sterling Suffolk Racecourse, LP
111 Waldemar Ave.
East Boston, MA 02128
(617) 567-3900
Gen Mgr: Louis J. Raffetto Jr.

MICHIGAN

Detroit Race Course
Ladbroke Racing Michigan, Inc.
28001 Schoolcraft
Livonia, MI 48150-2288
(313) 525-7300
VP/Gen Mgr: Richard T. Schnaars

MINNESOTA

Canterbury Downs
P.O. Box 508
Shakopee, MN 55379
(612) 445-7223
Gen Mgr: Terence McWilliams

MONTANA

MetraPark
P.O. Box 2514
Billings, MT 59103
(406) 256-2400
Gen Mgr: Bill Chiesa

Montana State Fair Race Meet
City of Great Falls
P.O. Box 1888
Great Falls, MT 59403
(406) 727-8900
Gen Mgr: Bill Ogg

NEBRASKA

Aksarben Field
Douglas Racing Corp.
P.O. Box 6069
Omaha, NE 68106-0069
(402) 444-4000
CEO: Sharon Smith

Columbus Races
Platte County Agricultural Society
P.O. Box 1335
Columbus, NE 68601
(402) 564-0133
Gen Mgr: Adrian Ewert

Fonner Park
Hall County Livestock Improvement
Ass'n
P.O. Box 490
Grand Island, NE 68802
(308) 382-4515
Gen Mgr: Hugh M. Miner Jr.

State Fair Park
Nebraska State Board of Agriculture
P.O. Box 81223
Lincoln, NE 68501-1223
(402) 473-4110
Gen Mgr: John Skold

NEW HAMPSHIRE

Rockingham Park
Rockingham Venture, Inc.
P.O. Box 47
Salem, NH 03079
(603) 898-2311
Gen Mgr: Edward Callahan

NEW JERSEY

Atlantic City
Atlantic City Racing Ass'n
P.O. Box 719
Atlantic City, NJ 08404
(609) 641-2190
Pres/Gen Mgr: James J. Murphy

Garden State Park
Garden State Race Track, Inc.
P.O. Box 4274
Cherry Hill, NJ 08034-0649
(609) 488-8400
Gen Mgr: Richard E. Orbann

The Meadowlands
New Jersey Sports & Exposition
Authority
Meadowlands Racetrack
East Rutherford, NJ 07073
(201) 935-8500
Gen Mgr: Robert J. Kulina

Monmouth Park
New Jersey Sports & Exposition
Authority
Monmouth Park, Route 36 &
Oceanport Ave.
Oceanport, NJ 07757
(908) 222-5100
Gen Mgr: Robert J. Kulina

NEW MEXICO

The Downs at Albuquerque
Santa Fe Racing, Inc.
P.O. Box 8510
Albuquerque, NM 87198
(505) 262-1188
Gen Mgr: Peter Drypolcher

La Mesa Park
La Mesa Racing Corp.
P.O. Box 1147
Raton, NM 87740
(505) 445-2301
Gen Mgr: Norman Faulk

Sunland Park
Nuevo Sol Turf Club
P.O. Box 1
Sunland Park, NM 88063
(505) 580-1131
Gen Mgr: Harold Payne

NEW YORK

Aqueduct
New York Racing Ass'n
P.O. Box 90
Jamaica, NY 11417
(718) 641-4700
Exec VP: Gerald Lawrence

Belmont Park
New York Racing Ass'n
P.O. Box 90
Jamaica, NY 11417
(718) 641-4700
Sr. VP Opns: Martin Lieberman

Finger Lakes
Finger Lakes Racing Ass'n
P.O. Box 25250
Farmington, NY 14425
(716) 924-3232
Gen Mgr: Hayes Taylor

Saratoga
New York Racing Ass'n
Track: P.O. Box 564
Saratoga Springs, NY 12866
Office: P.O. Box 90
Jamaica, NY 11417
(718) 641-4700
Exec VP: Gerald Lawrence

OHIO

Beulah Park
Capital Racing Club
P.O. Box 850
Grove City, OH 43123
(614) 871-9600
Gen Mgr: Richard S. Wilson

Thistledown
Thistledown Racing Club, Inc.
P.O. Box 28280
Cleveland, OH 44128
(216) 475-1224
Gen Mgr: Steven P. Sexton

OKLAHOMA

Blue Ribbon Downs
Race Horses, Inc.
P.O. Box 788
Sallisaw, OK 74955-5805
(918) 775-7771
Gen Mgr: Dwayne Burrows

Remington Park
Remington Park, Inc.
One Remington Place
Oklahoma City, OK 73111
(405) 424-1000
Gen Mgr: David M. Vance

OREGON

Grants Pass Downs
Southern Oregon Horse Racing Ass'n
P.O. Box 282
Grants Pass, OR 97526
(503) 582-1384
Gen Mgr: Kenneth Olmstead

T H O R O U G H B R E D   R A C I N G

Lone Oak Race Track
Oregon State Fair & Exposition
  Center
2330 17th St. NE
Salem, OR 97310
(503) 378-3247
Gen Mgr: Don Hillman

Portland Meadows
New Portland Meadows, Inc.
1001 N. Schmeer Rd.
Portland, OR 97219
(503) 285-9144
Gen Mgr: Bill Taylor

PENNSYLVANIA

Penn National Race Course
Penn National Turf Club
P.O. Box 32
Grantville, PA 17028
(717) 469-2211
Pres: Herb Grayek Jr.

Philadelphia Park
Bensalem Racing Ass'n
P.O. Box 1000
Bensalem, PA 19020-2096
(215) 639-9000
Gen Mgr: Donald Johnson

TEXAS

Bandera Downs
Bandera Downs, Inc.
P.O. Box 1775
Bandera, TX 78003
(210) 796-7781
Gen Mgr: Billy Bowers

Trinity Meadows
Trinity Meadows Raceway, Inc.
P.O. Box 121789
Fort Worth, TX 76121
(817) 441-9240
Pres: Jack L. Johnson

WASHINGTON

Harbor Park
Harbor Park Ass'n
P.O. Box 1229
Elma, WA 98541
(206) 482-2651
Gen Mgr: Dan Sharp

Playfair Race Course
Playfair Racing, Inc.
P.O. Box 2625
Spokane, WA 99220-2625
(509) 534-0505
Gen Mgr: Dan Hillyard

Sun Downs
P.O. Box 6662
Kennewick, WA 99336
(509) 582-5434
Gen Mgr: Doug Ray

Yakima Meadows
Apple Tree Turf Ass'n
P.O. Box 213
Yakima, WA 98907
(509) 248-3920
Gen Mgr: Jim Vanderweele

WEST VIRGINIA

Charles Town Races
Charles Town Races, Inc.
P.O. Box 551
Charles Town, WV 25414
(304) 725-7001
Gen Mgr: Donald Hudson

H A R N E S S   R A C I N G

CALIFORNIA

Cal-Expo
1600 Exposition Way
Sacramento, CA 95852
(916) 263-6055
Gen Mgr: Fred Kuebler

Los Alamitos Harness
4961 Katella Ave.
Los Alamitos, CA 90720
(714) 995-1234
Gen Mgr: Fred Kuebler

DELAWARE

Dover Downs
1131 N. DuPont Hwy.
Dover, DE 19901
(302) 674-4600
Gen Mgr: Jerry Dunning

Harrington Raceway
P.O. Box 28
Harrington, DE 19952
(302) 398-3269
Gen Mgr: John Walls

FLORIDA

Pompano Park Harness
1800 S.W. Third St.
Pompano Beach, FL 33073
(305) 972-2000
Exec VP: Harold Duris

ILLINOIS

Balmoral Park
26435 S. Dixie Hwy.
Crete, IL 60417
(708) 672-7544
Gen Mgr: Dan Nemeth

Fairmount Park
Route 40
Collinsville, IL 62234
(618) 345-4300
Gen Mgr: Brian Zander

Hawthorne Race Course
3501 S. Laramie Ave.
Stickney/Cicero, IL 60804
(708) 780-3700
Gen Mgr: Thomas F. Carey

Maywood Park
8600 W. North Ave.
Maywood, IL 60153
(708) 343-4800
Gen Mgr: Bill Moore

Quad City Downs
P.O. Box 368
East Moline, IL 61244
(309) 792-0202
Gen Mgr: William Mosenfelder

Sportsman's Park
3301 S. Laramie Ave.
Cicero, IL 60650
(312) 242-1121
Gen Mgr: William H. Johnston Jr.

Springfield
Horce Racing Program
801 E. Sangamon Ave.
Springfield, IL 62794-9281
(217) 782-4231
Gen Mgr: Harry H. Hall

INDIANA

Indiana State Fair
1202 E. 38th St.
Indianapolis, IN 46205-2869
(317) 927-7589
Exec Dir: Donald W. Moreau Sr.

KENTUCKY

The Red Mile
1200 Red Mile Rd.
Lexington, KY 40504
(606) 255-0752
Gen Mgr: Jerry Monahan

Riverside Downs
P.O. Box 1549
Henderson, KY 42420
(502) 826-9746
Gen Mgr: Jack Myers

MAINE

Bangor Raceway
100 Dutton St.
Bangor, ME 04401
(207) 947-3313
Gen Mgr: Michael Dyer

Scarborough Downs
P.O. Box 468
Scarborough, ME 04074
(207) 883-4331
Pres: Joseph J. Ricci

MARYLAND

Delmarva Downs
P.O. Box 11
Berlin, MD 21811
(410) 641-0600
Gen Mgr: Ed Young

Rosecroft Raceway
6336 Rosecroft Dr.
Fort Washington, MD 20744-1999
(301) 567-4000
Gen Mgr: Tom Barry

MASSACHUSETTS

Foxboro Park
Route 1
Foxboro, MA 02035
(508) 543-3800
Gen Mgr: Dan Bucci

MICHIGAN

Hazel Park Harness
1650 E. Ten Mile Rd.
Hazel Park, MI 48030
(313) 398-1000
Pres: Herbert Tyner

H A R N E S S   R A C I N G

Jackson Raceway
P.O. Box 881
Jackson, MI 49201
(517) 788-4500
Gen Mgr: James A. Young

Muskegon Racecourse
P.O. Box 252
Fruitport, MI 49415
(616) 798-7123
Exec VP: Dominick L. Marotta

Northville Downs
301 S. Center St.
Northville, MI 48167
(313) 349-1000
Exec Mgr: Margaret J. Zayti

Saginaw Harness Raceway
2701 E. Genesee St.
Saginaw, MI 48601
(517) 755-3451
Gen Mgr: Eugene T. Budd

Sports Creek Raceway
4290 Morrish Rd.
Swartz Creek, MI 48473
(313) 635-3333
Gen Mgr: Thomas Chuckas Jr.

NEW JERSEY

Freehold Raceway
P.O. Box 6249
Routes 9 & 33
Freehold, NJ 07728
(908) 462-3800
Gen Mgr: Ed Ryan

Garden State Park
Route 70 & Haddonfield Rd.
Cherry Hill, NJ 08034-0649
(609) 488-8400
Pres: Arthur Winkler

The Meadowlands
50 State Hwy. 20
East Rutherford, NJ 07073
(201) 935-8500
Gen Mgr: Bruce Garland

NEW YORK

Batavia Downs
8315 Park Rd.
Batavia, NY 14020
(716) 343-3750
Gen Mgr: Barry Lefkowitz

Buffalo Raceway
5600 McKinley Pkwy.
Hamburg, NY 14075
(716) 649-1280
Gen Mgr: Jerry Schweibel

Historic Track – Goshen
P.O. Box 192
Goshen, NY 10924
(914) 294-5333
Pres: Vincent N. Brescia

Monticello Raceway
Raceway Road
Monticello, NY 12701
(914) 794-4100
Gen Mgr: William J. Sullivan

Saratoga Harness
P.O. Box 356
Saratoga Springs, NY 12866-0356
(518) 584-2110
Gen Mgr: Warren DeSantis

The Syracuse Mile
P.O. Box 38
Hamburg, NY 14075
(716) 649-1280
Gen Mgr: Mark Coloton

Vernon Downs
P.O. Box 860
Vernon, NY 13476-0860
(315) 829-2201
Pres: Frank White Sr.

Yonkers Raceway
810 Central Ave.
Yonkers, NY 10704
(914) 968-4200
Gen Mgr: Robert Galterio

OHIO

Delaware Fair
P.O. Box 100
Delaware, OH 43015
(614) 363-6000
Pres: Henry C. Thomson

Lebanon Raceway
P.O. Box 50
Lebanon, OH 45036
(513) 932-4936
Gen Mgr: Keith Nixon

Northfield Park
P.O. Box 374
Northfield, OH 44067
(216) 467-4101
Gen Mgr: Thomas Aldrich

Raceway Park
5700 Telegraph Rd.
Toledo, OH 43612
(419) 476-7751
Gen Mgr: Aimee Thoreson

Scioto Downs
6000 S. High St.
Columbus, OH 43207
(614) 491-2515
Gen Mgr: Robert Steele

PENNSYLVANIA

Ladbroke at the Meadows
P.O. Box 499
Meadow Lands, PA 15347
(412) 225-9300
Gen Mgr: Randy Edmonds

Pocono Downs
Route 315
Wilkes-Barre, PA 18702
(717) 825-6681
Pres: Joseph B. Banks

I N D U S T R Y   O R G A N I Z A T I O N S

Harness Horse Youth Foundation
14950 Greyhound Court, Suite 210
Carmen, IN 46032
(317) 848-5132
Exec Dir: Ellen Taylor

Harness Tracks of America
35 Airport Rd.
Morristown, NJ 07960
(201) 285-9090
Exec Dir: Stanley F. Bergstein

The Jockey Club
40 E. 52nd St.
New York, NY 10022
(212) 371-5970
Exec Dir: Hans J. Stahl

Thoroughbred Club of America
P.O. Box 8098
Lexington, KY 40533
(606) 254-4282
Exec Dir: Jenny Johnson

**Thoroughbred Owners and
Breeders Association**
P.O. Box 4367
Lexington, KY 40544
(606) 276-2291
Pres: Robert N. Clay

Thoroughbred Racing Associations
420 Fair Hill Dr., Suite 1
Eklton, MD 21921
(410) 392-9200
Exec VP: Christopher Scherf

**Thoroughbred Racing
Communications**
40 East 52nd St.
New York, NY 10022
(212) 371-5910
Exec Dir: Tom Merritt

U.S. Trotting Association
750 Michigan Ave.
Columbus, OH 43215
(614) 224-2291
Exec VP: Fred Knowy

**United Thoroughbred Trainers
of America**
19899 W. 9 Mile Rd.
Southfield, MI 48075
(313) 354-3232
Exec Dir: Thomas A. Dorsey

The sport keeps growing in popularity,

but prospects for speedway jobs are as cheerful as a flat tire.

Best idea: an internship with a motorsports sponsor.

SPEEDWAYS

Attendance Is Up, Jobs Aren't

Major auto racing attendance has risen to new heights. According to statistics compiled by the Goodyear Tire & Rubber Company for 1995 (the latest figures when we went to press), some 14,873,796 fans watched a new generation of drivers (and some old favorites) win championships in the 13 professional racing series Goodyear monitored. It was an increase of more than half a million spectators.

Some specific numbers:

NASCAR's premier series, the Winston Cup, drew an audience of 5,326,721, up 8.8 percent.

The PPG IndyCar World Series, including the USAC-sanctioned Indianapolis 500, had a record 3,438,071 fans.

NHRA's 19 events were witnessed by an estimated 1,852,972 drag racing fans.

Great news, all of it. But how does it relate to the availability of speedway jobs? Sad to say, despite record attendance figures the tracks offer few opportunities for year-round jobs.

Problem: Nobody's Leaving

Gary Kale, who was auto racing editor at United Press International for 17 years, offers these observations:

There are about 300 tracks around the country, but unless you know somebody connected with a track the chances of getting a job are pretty slim. The reason: there's very little turnover. People employed at tracks are such intense racing fans that it would take a stick of dynamite to dislodge them. If you do land a job, it's likely to be seasonal, and the pay low.

But John Mattioli, who runs Pocono International Raceway in Long Pond, Pennsylvania, takes a slightly more optimistic view. "Yes," he says, "job openings are limited, but openings do occur." He believes that college grads with a background in business administration, marketing, and communications have an edge.

Nationally, the racing season runs from February through November. Pocono, not unlike other local tracks, operates a shorter season, from April through October. Activities include two NASCAR events. During the season, the track has about 50 employees, with a core of eight to 10 administrators who supervise seasonal workers hired at $5 to $8 an hour. Off-season, the number of employees shrinks to about 25. A few are office and sales personnel; the others are year-round maintenance people who work at getting the track in shape.

Types of Jobs

Owners of speedways are freewheeling folk who, by natural inclination, run their operations with an independent spirit. The result is that there is no consistency in the way track personnel are organized or paid. Every speedway seems to operate on a system of its own, and while each uses job titles that have a familiar ring, the meanings of those titles vary widely.

In general, and without ascribing a pecking order, speedways have people for the following functions: facilities management, public relations, marketing, operations management, sales, emergency services, security, traffic control, ticket management. There are people who check the credentials of race participants, serve as track announcers, turn out publications, handle advertising, look after the comfort of luxury-suite occupants—and people who work in the office.

So there are plenty of positions that need to be filled, but they're already filled. And again, nobody's leaving—even though salaries are sometimes meager.

The big money in auto racing is reserved for nonadministrative people. The chief of a pit crew, for example, can make more than $200,000 a year. Top drivers—worldwide there are 80 to 90 in this classification—make millions. You might want to check out the schools that train racing drivers.

Track personnel and average pay for the season:

Track director. Oversees all operations. $60,000.

Track control director. Designates garage space for racing teams and coordinates procedures for getting racing cars to the starting line. $35,000.

Track operations director. Directs the operation of scoring tower, which lists positions of cars after each lap. Facilitates communication among track marshals. $35,000.

Maintenance manager. Responsible for the condition of the track. $35,000.

Security director. In charge of the protection of vehicles, drivers, facilities, and the safety of spectators. $30,000.

Emergency services director. Oversees emergency crews. $30,000.

Media services director. Provides accommodations and services for reporters and television crews. $30,000.

Marketing/sales manager. Develops promotional activities. $40,000.

Some Notes From All Over

Janice Butler, head of the public relations and marketing firm of **Butler Communi-** **cations** in Dallas, acknowledges that auto racing is a tough field to break into, but new tracks are planned for Dallas, Nashville, Chicago, Orlando, and elsewhere, and that might open things up a bit. According to Butler, getting an internship is still the key. As for her own firm, "I don't hire racing fans," she said. "If I do hire someone, it's someone who wants to work in this industry. There's a difference." . . . Bill O'Neil, at the **Championship Group** in Atlanta, one of the top promotion firms in motorsports, says if you can't get an internship, put yourself in circulation by working as a volunteer at special events, even those run by local charities. He got his start as a volunteer at a major tennis tournament. . . . **DIRT Motorsports**, which sanctions about 500 racing programs at 27 or more dirt tracks in the Northeast and Canada, recruits interns by sending out flyers to colleges announcing "Intern Positions Available" from May through August. An applicant "must be a college junior or senior, or graduate student in marketing or related fields." DIRT is located in the upstate New York metropolis of Weedsport (grassroots America?). If you're interested, get in touch with Cory Reed, DIRT Motorsports, One Speedway Dr., Weedsport, NY 13166. . . . North Carolina's **Elon College**, in the heart of NASCAR country, runs a three-week winter course called "The Business of NASCAR." Field trips to Winston Cup tracks and shops give students a behind-the-scenes look at the economics of stock-car racing. The class fills up early.

The Corporate Sponsors

With almost every inch of racing vehicles covered by company names and logos, it's abundantly evident that there's been a big surge of interest in motorsports on the part of corporate America. Retailing and restaurant chains and suppliers of all kinds of consumer products and services have bought into the racing industry as sponsors of teams and dri-

THE BIG RIDE

Corporate America spends more of its sponsorship money on motorsports than on any other area of sports. *IEG Sponsorship Report,* the sports industry newsletter, predicted that sponsors would spend $920 million in 1996 on auto racing. In second place, with projected sponsorships of $555 million, was golf.

vers and special events.

As in other sports, sponsorship in motorsports is part of a company's marketing plan, aimed at increasing the company's visibility and enhancing its image. Its involvement in this sport often includes product endorsements and personal appearances by racing stars, and the privilege of entertaining VIPs at the track in the exciting atmosphere that's special to auto racing. Judging by the increase of sponsors in the past few years, and the high rate of retention, the tie-in with this sport has proven to be good business.

Bill Dyer of Barnes Dyer Marketing, a leading consulting firm in the racing industry, points out that many companies are so firmly committed to auto racing that they have set up special motorsports marketing departments in their organizations, separate from marketing activities in other sports.

Young people eager to get into the racing industry, says Dyer, would be wise to look into this aspect of the industry. If you join one of these companies it probably will be a while before you're ready for marketing responsibilities, he says, but that's where the jobs are, and the pay is a lot better than jobs at the track.

A Chance for an Internship

Following is a list of the racing industry's corporate sponsors, many of which employ interns in their marketing departments. You'll find addresses and phone numbers of their marketing departments in the directory of corporate sports sponsors beginning on page 116.

Motorsport Sponsors

Agency Rent-a-Car
Amoco Oil Co.
Anheuser-Busch Companies
Armor All Products Corp.
Armour Food Co./Process Meat Division
Automotive Engine & Machine, Inc.
Bojangles' Restaurants, Inc.
Borg-Warner Automotive, Inc.

Braun, Inc.
Brown & Williamson Tobacco Corp.
Canon USA
Castrol, Inc.
Century 21
Champion Spark Plug Co.
Chevrolet Motor Car Division/General Motors Corp.
Chrysler Corp.
Citgo Petroleum Corp.
Coca-Cola Co.
Conoco, Inc.
Conseco, Inc.
Continental Airlines
Coors Brewing Co.
Denon America
DuPont Co./Refinish Division
Duracell, Inc.
Eagle Snacks, Inc.
Eastman Kodak Co.
Emerson Radio Corp.
Exxon Co. USA
The Family Channel
First Brands Corp—STP Products
Ford Motor Co./Ford Division
Ford Motor Service Division
General Motors Service Parts Operations, AC-Delco Division
General Rent-a-Car
General Tire, Inc.
Gillette Co./Personal Care Division
Goodyear Tire & Rubber Co.
Hardee's Food Systems, Inc.
Hasbro, Inc./G.I. Joe Brand
Hershey Chocolate U.S.A.
Hooters of America, Inc.
Isuzu Motors, Inc., American
J.C. Penney Co.
Jeep/Eagle Division of Chrysler Corp.
Johnson & Son, Inc.
K Mart Corp.
Kal-Gard
Kawasaki Motors Corp., USA
Kellogg Co.
Kendall Motor Oil
Kenwood USA Corp.

INDIANAPOLIS MOTOR SPEEDWAY HALL OF FAME

Indianapolis, Indiana

Annual visitors: 350,000. *Employees:* 25 full-time, 15 part-time, no interns. *Director:* Ralph Kramer. *Address:* 4790 W. 16th St., Indianapolis, IN 46222. *Phone:* (317) 484-6749.

INTERNATIONAL MOTOR SPORTS HALL OF FAME

Talladega, Alabama

Annual visitors: 100,000. *Employees:* 8 full-time, no interns. *Director:* Don Naiman. *Address:* P.O. Box 1018, Talladega, AL 35161. *Phone:* (205) 362-5002.

Leaf, Inc./Jolly Rancher Brand
Lorillard Tobacco Co.
Mattel, Inc./Hot Wheels Brand
Mayflower Transit, Inc.
Meineke Discount Muffler Shops, Inc.
Michelin North America
Miller Brewing Co.
Molson Breweries
NAPA
NGK Spark Plugs USA, Inc.
Nestle USA
Nissan Motor Corp. USA
Old World Automotive Products/Peak
    Anti-Freeze Brand
Oldsmobile Div./General Motors Corp.
Olivetti Office USA
Outboard Marine Corp./Aluminum Boat
    Group/Grumman Boats Brand
PPG Industries, Inc.
Panasonic Co.
Parts Inc./Parts Plus Stores
Pennzoil Co.
Penske Corp.
Pepsi-Cola Co.
Philip Morris USA
Phillips 66 Co.
Piggly Wiggly Corp.
Pioneer Electronics USA, Inc.
Polar Corp.
Polaroid Corp.
Pontiac Division/General Motors Corp.
Porsche Cars North America, Inc.
Procter & Gamble Co.
Purolator Products, Inc.
Quaker Oats Co./Gatorade Brand
Quaker State Corp.
R.J. Reynolds Tobacco Co.
Saab Cars USA
Samsung Electronics America, Inc.
Save Mart Supermarkets
Sears Roebuck & Company/Craftsman
    Tools, Diehard Battery Brands
Subaru of America, Inc.
Sun Co./Sunoco Brands
3M Co.
Target Stores

Teledyne Water Pik
Texaco, Inc.
Textron, Inc.
Thrifty Rent-a-Car System, Inc.
Toledo Scale Corp.
Toshiba America Electronic Components,
    Inc.
Toyota Motor Sales USA, Inc.
True Value Hardware
Tyson Holly Farms
Uniroyal Goodrich Tire Co./B.F. Goodrich
    Brand
USAir, Inc.
U.S. Tobacco Co.
Valvoline, Inc.
Winn-Dixie Stores, Inc.
Wynn Oil Co.
Yamaha Motor Corp. USA

**MOTORSPORTS
HALL OF FAME**

Novi, Michigan

Annual visitors:
30,000. *Employees:*
2 full-time, 70
volunteers, several
PR interns over the
year. *Director:* Ron
Watson. *Address:*
P.O. Box 194, Novi,
MI 48376. *Phone:*
(810) 349-7223.

S P E E D W A Y S

SANCTIONING ORGANIZATIONS

Shown here are the most active organizations in the motorsports industry. Six offer internships.

Automobile Racing Club of America (ARCA)
P.O. Box 5217
Toledo, OH 43611
(313) 847-6726
Ron Drager, President
Employees: 8
Internships offered;
  college credit

Championship Auto Racing Team (CART)
755 W. Big Beaver Rd.
Troy, MI 48084
(810) 362-8800
Andrew Craig, President
Employees: 42
Internships offered;
  college credit

International Hot Rod Association (IHRA)
Highway 11E
Bristol, TN 37620
(423) 764-1164
Hayne Dominick, President
Employees: 15

International Motor Sports Association (IMSA)
P.O. Box 10709
Tampa, FL 33679
(813) 877-4672
George Silbermann,
  President
Employees: 15
Internships offered;
  college credit

National Association for Stock Car Auto Racing (NASCAR)
1801 W. International
  Speedway Blvd.
Daytona Beach, FL 32114
(904) 253-0611
Bill France, President
Employees: 120
Internships offered;
  college credit

National Hot Rod Association (NHRA)
2035 Financial Way
Glendora, CA 91741
(818) 914-4761
Dallas Gardner, President
Employees: 200
Internships offered

Sports Car Club of America (SCCA)
9033 E. Easter Place
Englewood, CA 80112
(303) 694-7223
Nicholas Craw, President
Employees: 43
Internships offered;
  college credit

United States Auto Club (USAC)
4910 W. 16th St.
Speedway, IN 46224
(317) 247-5151
Richard King, President
Employees: 18

World of Outlaws (WOO)
624 Krona Dr., Suite 115
Plano, TX 75074
(214) 424-2202
Ted Johnson, President
Employees: 16

SPEEDWAYS

Almost all tracks listed here employ interns. A college affiliation is not usually required.

ALABAMA

Huntsville Dragway
Birmingham, AL 35204
(205) 251-7311
George Howard, Promoter

Huntsville Speedway
Huntsville, AL 35803
(205) 882-9191
Ron & Bruce Stone, Promoters

Talladega Superspeedway
P.O. Box 777
Talladega, AL 35160-0777
(205) 362-2261
Grant Lynch, President

ARIZONA

Firebird International Raceway
P.O. Box 5023
2000 Maricopa Rd.
Chandler, AZ 85226
(602) 268-0200
Charley Allen, President

Phoenix International Raceway
P.O. Box 13088
Phoenix, AZ 85002-3088
(602) 252-3833
Emmett "Buddy" Jobe, Promoter

Tucson Raceway Park
P.O. Box 18759
Tucson, AZ 85731-8759
(602) 762-9200
Lee Baumgarten, Promoter

CALIFORNIA

Antioch Speedway
P.O. Box 430
Antioch, CA 94509
(510) 754-0222
Brynda Bockover, Promoter

Cajon Speedway
P.O. Box 7
El Cajon, CA 92022-0007
(619) 448-8900
Steve Brucker, Promoter

Laguna Seca Raceway
P.O. Box 2078
Monterey, CA 93942
(408) 648-5111
Gen Mgr: Scott Atherton

Los Angeles County Fairplex
P.O. Box 5555
Glendora, CA 91740
(818) 914-4761
Gen Mgr: Wayne McMurtry

Orange Show Speedway
P.O. Box 5325
San Bernardino, CA 92412
(909) 888-5801
Lynda Steinbeck, Promoter

Redwood Acres Raceway
Eureka, CA 95503
(707) 442-3232
Richard Olson, Promoter

San Jose Speedway
P.O. Box 1239
Soquel, CA 95073-1239
(408) 462-6101
Rick Farren, Promoter

Sears Point International Raceway
Sonoma, CA 95476
(800) 870-7223
Steve Page, President

Shasta Speedway
P.O. Box 524
Redding, CA 96099-0524
(916) 243-2921, ext. 311
Gary Cressey, Promoter

Stockton 99 Speedway
P.O. Box 690546
Stockton, CA 95269-0546
(209) 477-9030
Mgr: Duane Borovec

Watsonville Speedway
P.O. Box 1239
Soquel, CA 95073-1239
(408) 462-6101
Rick Farren, Promoter

COLORADO

Bandimere Speedway
Morrison, CO 80465-9748
(303) 697-6001
John Bandimere Jr., Promoter

Colorado National Speedway
Denver, CO 80205
(303) 291-1900
George Schillinger, Dir. of Operations

CONNECTICUT

Lime Rock Park
P.O. Box 111
Lakeville, CT 06049
(860) 435-5000
Michael Rand, Promoter

Stafford Motor Speedway
P.O. Box 105
Stafford Springs, CT 06076
(860) 684-2783
Mark Arute, Promoter

Thompson International Speedway
P.O. Box 278
Thompson, CT 06277
(203) 923-9591
Don Hoenig, Promoter

DELAWARE

Dover Downs International Speedway
P.O. Box 843
Dover, DE 19903-0843
(302) 674-4600, ext. 212
Public Relations: Al Robinson

S P E E D W A Y S

FLORIDA

Daytona International Speedway
Daytona Beach, FL 32114
(904) 254-2700
John E. Graham Jr., President

Gainesville Raceway
Gainesville, FL 32609
(904) 377-0046
Bob Moore, Promoter

JAX Raceways
Jacksonville, FL 32205
(904) 757-5425
Roger Godbee and Larry Browning,
  Coowners

Lake City Speedway
Daytona Beach, FL 32118
(904) 752-8888
Dir: Ron Compani

Sebring International Dragway
Sebring, FL 33870
(941) 655-1442
Tres Stephenson, Promoter

Volusia County Speedway
De Leon Springs, FL 32130
(904) 985-4402
Steve & Ronda Ross, Promoters

GEORGIA

Atlanta Dragway
Commerce, GA 30529
(706) 335-2301
Jason Thomas, Promoter

Atlanta Motor Speedway
P.O. Box 500
Hampton, GA 30228
(770) 946-3920
Ed Clark, Promoter

Lanier National Speedway
One Raceway Dr.
Braselton, GA 30517
(770) 967-8600
Bud Lunsford, Promoter

Oglethorpe Speedway Park
Route 5, Box 605
Raymond Rd.
Savannah, GA 31408
(912) 964-7069
Andy Stone, Promoter

Road Atlanta Raceway
5300 Winder Hwy.
Braselton, GA 30517
(770) 967-7214
Gen Mgr: Greg Bloodworth

IDAHO

Magic Valley Speedway
Twin Falls, ID 83301
(208) 734-3700
Steve York, Promoter

ILLINOIS

Gateway International Raceway
Fairmont City, IL 62201-1639
(618) 482-5501
Rod G. Wolter, Promoter

Knox County Speedway
Galesburg, IL 61401
(309) 289-6475
Dirs: Rick and Sandy Benson

Peoria Speedway
3520 W. Farmington Rd.
Peoria, IL 61604
(309) 674-7022
Chuck Hamilton, Promoter

Quincy Raceways
R.R. 1, Box 236
Quincy, IL 62301
(217) 222-3868
Albert Scott, Copromoter

Rockford Speedway
P.O. Box 1000
Rockford, IL 61105-1000
(815) 633-0735
Jody Deery, Promoter

Santa Fe Speedway
Hinsdale, IL 60521-6497
(708) 839-1050
Mary Lou Tiedt, Promoter

INDIANA

Indianapolis Motor Speedway
P.O. Box 24152
Indianapolis, IN 46224
(317) 481-8500
Anton H. George, President

Indianapolis Raceway Park
P.O. Box 34300
Indianapolis, IN 46234
(317) 293-7223
Mike Lewis, Promoter

Winchester Speedway
P.O. Box 31
Winchester, IN 47394-0031
(317) 584-9701
Linda Holdeman, Promoter

IOWA

Adams County Speedway
P.O. Box 8
Nodaway, IA 50857-0008
(712) 785-3271
Gail Hampel, Promoter

Dubuque Fairgrounds Speedway
Dubuque, IA 52002-9642
(319) 588-1406
Paul Vaassen, Promoter

Farley Speedway
P.O. Box 229
Swisher, IA 52338
(319) 857-4647
Al & Judy Frieden, Promoters

Hamilton County Speedway
P.O. Box 58
Redcliffe, IA 50230
(515) 899-2222
W. Allan Uhrhammer, Promoter

Park Jefferson Speedway
P.O. Box 508
Sioux City, IA 51102
(515) 832-5382
Mgr: Evan Schoenfish

West Liberty Raceway
P.O. Box 229
Swisher, IA 52338
(319) 857-4647
Al & Judy Frieden, Promoters

KANSAS

Heartland Park Topeka
Topeka, KS 66619-1319
(913) 862-4781
Bill Kentling, Promoter

Lakeside Speedway
Kansas City, KS 66109
(913) 541-8692
Gen Mgr: Bob Baker

KENTUCKY

Louisville Speedway
P.O. Box 19678
Louisville, KY 40259-0678
(502) 966-2277
Andy Vertrees, Promoter

LOUISIANA

State Capitol Dragway
P.O. Box 159
Erwinville, LA 70729
(504) 627-4574
Gen Mgr: Alan R. Miller

MAINE

Oxford Plains Speedway
Route 26, Box 208
Oxford, ME 04270-0208
(207) 539-8865
Michael Liberty, Promoter

MASSACHUSETTS

Lee USA Speedway
Newbury, MA 01951
(603) 659-2719
Gen Mgr: Phil Rowe

Riverside Park Speedway
P.O. Box 307
Agawam, MA 01001
(413) 786-9300, ext. 3301
Benjamin Dodge, Promoter

Star Speedway
Topsfield, MA 01983
(603) 679-5306
Dir: Bob Webber

MICHIGAN

Detroit Grand Prix
300 River Place, Suite 4000
Detroit, MI 48207
(313) 259-5400
H. Kent Stanner, President

Kalamazoo Speedway
3053 108th Ave.
Allegan, MI 49010-9716
(616) 673-4478
Martin Jones, Promoter

Michigan International Speedway
12626 U.S. 12
Brooklyn, MI 49230-9068
(800) 354-1010
Gen Mgr: Gene Haskett

MINNESOTA

Brainerd International Raceway
17113 Minnetonka Blvd., Suite 214
Minnetonka, MN 55345
(612) 475-1500
Mgr: Dick Roe

Elko Speedway
P.O. Box 246
Elko, MN 55020
(612) 461-3395
Robert Fredrickson, Promoter

S P E E D W A Y S

Raceway Park
One Checkered Flag Blvd.
Shakopee, MN 55379
(612) 445-2257
John Hellendrung, Promoter

Viking Speedway
P.O. Box 462
Alexandria, MN 56308
(612) 834-2471
Stu Olson, Promoter

MISSOURI

Bolivar Speedway
Route 5, Box 274
Lebanon, MO 65636
(417) 326-3966
Bill Willard, Owner

Capital Speedway
307 Oak St.
Fulton, MO 65251
(314) 896-5500
Cecil Graves, Promoter

I-70 Speedway
5615 Wolcott Dr.
Kansas City, KS 66109
(913) 299-2040
Bob Baker, Promoter

Lebanon I-44 Speedway
P.O. Box 1183
Lebanon, MO 65536
(417) 532-2060
Bill Don Willard, Promoter

Moberly Speedway
1408 Sunset
Blue Springs, MO 64015
(816) 228-0415
Dennis Roberts, Promoter

NEBRASKA

Eagle Raceway
P.O. Box 30532
Lincoln, NE 68503-0532
(402) 464-8118
Marty Beecham, Copromoter

Sunset Speedway
P.O. Box 34487
Omaha, NE 68134-0134
(402) 391-4000
Craig Kelley, Promoter

NEVADA

Las Vegas Speedway Park
Las Vegas, NV 89115
(702) 643-3333
Bob Butte, Promoter

NEW HAMPSHIRE

**New Hampshire International
Speedway**
P.O. Box 7888
Loudon, NH 03301-0788
(603) 783-4744
Gary Bahre, Promoter

NEW JERSEY

Atco Raceway
Atco, NJ 08004
(609) 768-2167
Bob VanSciver, Promoter

**Old Bridge Township Raceway
Park**
Englishtown, NJ 07726-8408
(908) 446-7800
Vincent & Richard Napoliello,
Copromoters

NEW YORK

Holland International Speedway
Holland, NY 14080
(716) 537-2272
Timothy M. Bennett, Promoter

**New York International Raceway
Park**
P.O. Box 296, 2011 New Rd.
Leicester, NY 14481
(716) 382-9061
Bob Metcalfe, Promoter

Riverhead Raceway
P.O. Box 148
Lindenhurst, NY 11757
(516) 842-7223
Jim and Barbara Cromarty, Promoters

Spencer Speedway
Fairport, NY 14450
(315) 589-3018
Dirs: Delbert, Walter, Merle, and
Bryan Spencer

Tioga Speedway
P.O. Box 539
Binghamton, NY 13902
(607) 724-1315
Andrew Harpel, Promoter

Watkins Glen International
P.O. Box 500
Watkins Glen, NY 14891
(607) 535-2481
John Saunders, President

NORTH CAROLINA

Ace Speedway
Julian, NC 27406
(910) 449-0122
Jim & Fred Turner, Promoters

Asheville Motor Speedway
P.O. Box 7097
Asheville, NC 28802-7097
(704) 254-4627
J. Roger Gregg, Promoter

Bowman Gray Stadium
Winston-Salem, NC 27104
(910) 766-8875
Dale and Johnnie Pinilis, Promoters

Champion Raceway
Hollister, NC 27844
(919) 586-3300
Gen Mgr: Alston Warren

Charlotte Motor Speedway
Concord, NC 28026-0600
(704) 455-3200
H. A. "Humpy" Wheeler, Promoter

Concord Motor Speedway
Concord, NC 28025
(704) 782-5863
Yvonne & Harry Lee Furr, Promoters

Hickory Motor Speedway
P.O. Box 1749
Hickory, NC 28603-1749
(704) 328-1050
Benny Yount, Promoter

North Carolina Motor Speedway
P.O. Box 500
Rockingham, NC 28380
(910) 582-2861
Jo DeWitt Wilson, Promoter

North Wilkesboro Speedway
P.O. Box 337
North Wilkesboro, NC 28659-0337
(910) 667-6663
Mike Staley, President

Orange County Speedway
P.O. Box 30
Rougemont, NC 27572
(910) 364-1222
Mgr: Phillip Walker

Rockingham Dragway
P.O. Box 70
Marston, NC 28363
(910) 582-3400
Steve Earwood, Promoter

Tri-County Motor Speedway
P.O. Box 309
Hudson, NC 28638-0309
(910) 672-9000
Russell Hackett, Promoter

OHIO

Burke Lakefront Airport
1 Erie View Plaza, Suite 1300
Cleveland, OH 44114
(216) 522-1200
H. Kent Stanner, President

Columbus Motor Speedway
Columbus, OH 43207
(614) 491-9576
James Nuckles, Promoter

Kil-Kare Speedway
Xenia, OH 45385
(513) 426-2764
Richard Chrysler, Promoter

**Marion County International
Raceway**
2454 Richwood-LaRue Rd.
LaRue, OH 43332
(614) 499-2581
Bill Guthery, Promoter

Mid-Ohio Sports Car Course
94 North High St., Suite 50
Dublin, OH 43017
(614) 793-4600
Michelle Trueman-Gajoch, Promoter

National Trail Raceway
2650 National Rd. SW
Hebron, OH 43025-9798
(419) 281-9877
Aaron Polburn, Promoter

Norwalk Raceway Park
1300 Route 18
Norwalk, OH 44857-9548
(419) 668-5555
Bill Bader, Promoter

Sandusky Speedway
614 W. Perkins Ave.
Sandusky, OH 44870
(419) 734-6046
Junior Buchanon, Promoter

OREGON

Portland International Raceway
Kent, WA 98042
(206) 631-1550
Jim Rockstad, Promoter

SPORTS FACILITIES/SPEEDWAYS **97**

Portland Speedway
P.O. Box 17588
Portland, OR 97217
(503) 285-2883
Gen Mgr: Craig Armstrong

Yakima Speedway
Portland, OR 97214
(509) 248-0647
Gen Mgr: Krissy Schille

PENNSYLVANIA

Grandview Speedway
Bechtelsville, PA 19505
(610) 754-7688
Bruce Rogers, Promoter

Jennerstown Speedway
P.O. Box 230
Jennerstown, PA 15547-0230
(814) 629-6677
Gen Mgr: Bob Duvall

Maple Grove Raceway
R.D. 3, Box 3420
Mohnton, PA 19540-9202
(610) 856-7200
Gen Mgr: George Alan Case

Motordrome Speedway
R. R. 1, Box 88-A
Smithton, PA 15479
(412) 872-7555
Don Gamble, Promoter

Nazareth Speedway
P.O. Drawer F
Nazareth, PA 18064
(610) 759-8000
Gen Mgr: Mike Moorehead

Pocono International Raceway
P.O. Box 500
Long Pond, PA 18344-0500
(717) 646-2300
Joseph Mattioli, President

SOUTH CAROLINA

Carolina Dragway
P.O. Box 260
Elko, SC 29826-0260
(803) 471-2285
Herbert Jeff Mills, Promoter

Darlington Raceway
P.O. Box 500
Darlington, SC 29532
(803) 395-8900
Jim Hunter, President

Florence Motor Speedway
Timmonsville, SC 29505
(803) 669-5901
Tom Hewitt, Promoter

Greenville-Pickens Speedway
P.O. Box 5206
Greenville, SC 29606
(864) 288-3056
Pete Blackwell, Promoter

Myrtle Beach Speedway
Myrtle Beach, SC 29577
(803) 399-6400
Billy Hardee, Promoter

Summerville Speedway
Summerville, SC 29483
(803) 761-7988
Troy Baird, Promoter

TENNESSEE

Bristol International Raceway
P.O. Box 3966
Bristol, TN 37625
(615) 764-1161
Gen Mgr: Jeff Bird

Memphis Motorsports Park
Millington, TN 38053
(901) 358-7223
Bill Whitton, Promoter

TEXAS

Big H Speedway
P.O. Box 9028
The Woodlands, TX 77387
(713) 458-5040
Jim Simmons, Promoter

Cowtown Speedway
P.O. Box 173446
Arlington, TX 76003
(817) 446-7295
Andy Adamcik, Promoter

Heart O' Texas Speedway
Waco, TX 76712
(817) 776-1576
Gene Adamcik, Promoter

Houston Raceway Park
P.O. Box 1345
Baytown, TX 77522-1345
(713) 383-2666
Greg Angel, Promoter

San Antonio Speedway
Kerrville, TX 78028
(210) 896-8337
Scott Holland, Promoter

Texas Motorplex
P.O. Box 1439
Ennis, TX 75120
(214) 875-2641
Gen Mgr: Gary Cox

VIRGINIA

Langley Raceway
P.O. Box 9156
Richmond, VA 23227
(804) 865-1992
Gen Mgr: Joe Baldacci

**Lonesome Pine International
Raceway**
P.O. Box 299
Coeburn, VA 24230
(540) 395-3338
Morris Stephenson, Promoter

Martinsville Speedway
P.O. Box 3311
Martinsville, VA 24115-3311
(703) 956-3151
H. Clay Earles, Promoter

New River Valley Speedway
Radford, VA 24141
(703) 639-1700
Ronnie Snoddy, Promoter

Old Dominion Speedway
Manassas, VA 22111
(703) 361-7753
Richard Gore, Promoter

Richmond International Raceway
P.O. Box 9257
Richmond, VA 23227-9257
(804) 345-7223
Paul Sawyer, President

South Boston Speedway
P.O. Box 759
South Boston, VA 24592
(804) 572-1013
Kathy Rice, Promoter

Southside Speedway
P.O. Box 9156
Richmond, VA 23227
(804) 744-1275
Joe Baldacci, Promoter

WASHINGTON

Evergreen Speedway
P.O. Box 879
Monroe, WA 98272-0879
(206) 776-2802
Gen Mgr: Tom Glithero

Seattle International Raceway
Kent, WA 98042
(206) 631-1550
Jim Rockstad, President

South Sound Speedway
Rochester, WA 98579
(360) 273-6420
Butch Behn, Promoter

Tri-City Raceway
Kennewick, WA 99337-5171
(509) 582-5694
Wayne and Karolyn Walden,
 Promoters

Wenatchee Valley Raceway
825 11th St. NE
East Wenatchee, WA 98802-4505
(509) 884-8592
John and Bonnie Ball, Promoters

WISCONSIN

Lacrosse Fairgrounds Speedway
P.O. Box 853
West Salem, WI 54669-0853
(608) 768-1525
Gen Mgr: Gerald Deery

Road America
P.O. Box P
Elkhart Lake, WI 53020-0338
(800) 365-7223
Gen Mgr: Jim Haynes

Wisconsin State Fair Park
8100 P.O. Box 14990
West Allis, WI 53214-0990
(414) 266-7000
Dir: Rick Bjorklund

WYOMING

Sweetwater Speedway
3320 Yellowstone Rd.
Rock Springs, WY 82901
(307) 352-6791
Kent Porenta, Promoter

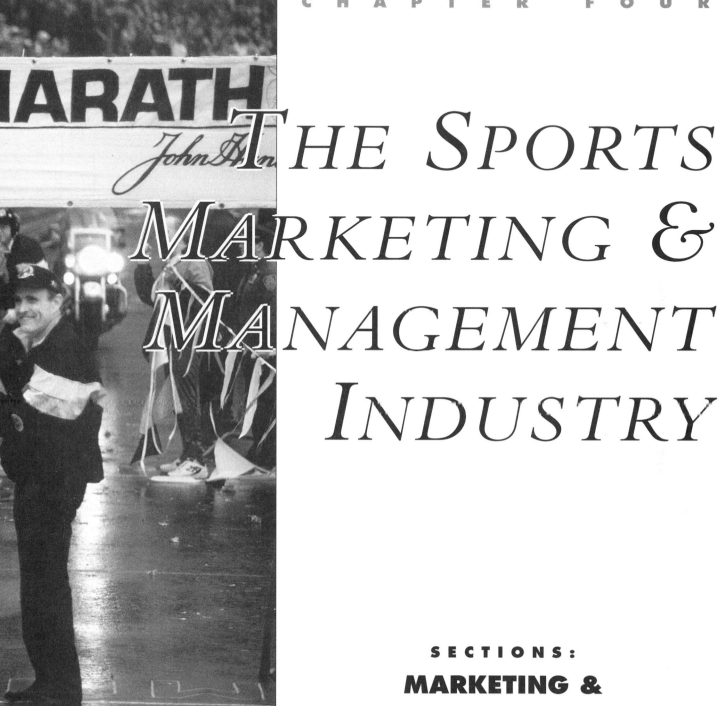

THE SPORTS MARKETING & MANAGEMENT INDUSTRY

SECTIONS:

MARKETING & MANAGEMENT AGENCIES

INDEPENDENT PLAYER AGENTS

The man who started this industry is said

to be the most powerful individual in sports.

Chances are you've never heard of him.

MARKETING & MANAGEMENT AGENCIES

THE RISE OF AN INDUSTRY

Twenty years ago you could have counted on one hand the number of agencies that identified themselves as being in the business of sports marketing and management. Two hands, at most.

Today there are more than a thousand companies in this line of work, and though most are small in terms of personnel, together they form a multibillion-dollar industry that reaches across the full landscape of competitive sports.

At the heart of the business are these three functions:

Athlete representation. It's the same work that independent player agents perform—handling all or part of a professional athlete's business affairs. The work usually includes contract negotiations, product endorsements, licensing arrangements, personal appearances, public relations, and financial counseling. It may also include counseling clients on their postathletic careers, after their knees go.

Creating a sports marketing plan. An agency's work consists of conceiving and executing, on behalf of a corporate client, a marketing program that utilizes sports and sports personalities.

The chief aims of such a program: to associate the client with the energy and excitement of sports, and to permit the client to target specific markets—local, national, or worldwide—at relatively low cost.

A corporate sports program can be com-posed of a variety of parts—projects as simple as printing and distributing a baseball schedule or a booklet on the rules of soccer. It can include giveaways at the ballpark, prizes at a horse show, or a tie-in with a community fund-raising marathon.

It can also include product endorsements by sports celebrities, regional cablecasts of college football, or renaming a prominent sports arena so that it thenceforth is known by the name of the corporation. There are a lot of things that can be done to give a company visibility.

Managing corporate-sponsored events. The sponsorship of a sports event is actually part of the package of activities that form a client's sports marketing program, but it is highlighted here because it is often a major undertaking by an agency, requiring considerable expertise on the part of the agency (and a sizable financial commitment by the client). In other words, there can be a lot riding on it.

To be clear about it, there are two types of sponsorships. In one case, the agency arranges for a client to affix its name to an existing, regularly scheduled event (a college bowl game, for example); in the other—and this really takes work—the agency creates a new event (example: a professional tennis tournament).

The work in implementing a special event includes budget preparation; negotiations with participants or their agents, sports facility managers, and public officialdom; merchandising tie-ins; production of promotion materials; advertising; publicity; ticket operations; arrangements for insurance and security; on-site hospitality arrangements for the client's guests (involving catering, decorating, celebrity hosts), and more. Here's how one agency, Pacific Sports of Monrovia, California, puts it: "We also handle the billing, the paying, the haggling. We hire the casual labor, hang the banners, write the scripts, send the tickets. We'll even pick up the laundry. Then, when the project is over, we'll do a post analysis."

* * * *

Athlete representation, corporate marketing, and event management—those are the basic activities in the sports marketing and management industry.

This is an industry that has grown rapidly in the past few years, attracting bold and creative entrepreneurs. But the new entrepreneurs have a long way to go to match the wizardry of the man who invented the industry in the early 1960s—and who is still showing how to capitalize on humankind's passion for sports.

The Man Who Started It All

His name is Mark Hume McCormack, and he has been called by *Sports Illustrated* "the most powerful man in sports."

McCormack is the sports impresario and superagent who founded and runs International Management Group, which employs nearly 2,000 people in 60 offices worldwide.

Now the largest sports marketing and management agency in the world, it started with a bit of luck.

The beginning. The practice of law was McCormack's original career goal. He graduated from Yale Law School, spent a couple of years with a Cleveland law firm, and in 1959 hung out his own shingle. And good fortune came through the door. The first client in his new, one-person office was a young professional golfer he had met when both were playing intercollegiate golf. The client's name: Arnold Palmer.

Before long, word got around the pro circuit that Arnold Palmer's lawyer was getting him fancy exhibition and endorsement deals. That brought two more young golfers to the office—Gary Player and Jack Nicklaus. Suddenly, McCormack's three clients were winning tournaments all over the country. McCormack dropped the idea of a general law practice and devoted himself fully to managing their careers, increasing their earnings through exhibitions, endorsements, advertising gigs, licensing arrangements, and, after a while, huge tournament appearance fees abroad. For the first time, the management of professional athletes, until then an uncertain occupation, became a stable and recognizable business, and, in McCormack's case, a lucrative one.

The IMG takes shape. Convinced that a sports boom lay ahead, and recognizing its infinite business possibilities, McCormack began signing up more golfers, moved into tennis with similar success, then penetrated Europe, recruiting many of its top players. Along the way, he set up International Management Group, staffing it with bright, well-paid associates. Now he was ready for an innovative plan of action: Instead of merely feeding his clients to U.S. and European tournament organizers, he began operating his own tournaments, an audacious move but an unstoppable one since IMG controlled so many of the big-name players.

It put McCormack in a unique and powerful position. He not only had the top players under contract, he owned the tournaments they played in. No one had ever accomplished that before. Or even thought of it.

With a prominence now that gave him entree into the world of big business, he took another unconventional step: He sold corporate leaders the idea of tying in with his golf and tennis activities as a means of promoting their products and enhancing their company

IMG's Big Names

Business at IMG includes the management of sports and entertainment personalities. The firm's best-known sports names follow:

Andre Agassi
Bob Costas
Chris Evert
Nick Faldo
Wayne Gretzky
Michael Johnson
Bernhard Langer
Nancy Lopez
John Madden
Joe Montana
Martina
     Navratilova
Arnold Palmer
Pete Sampras
Arantxa Sanchez
     Vicario
Jackie Stewart
Alberto Tomba
Herschel Walker
Chris Webber
Kristi Yamaguchi

image. It was the beginning of corporate sports marketing on a wide scale. In yet another innovation, he introduced the practice of on-site hospitality at major events, giving corporate sponsors the opportunity to entertain their own clients in a stylish setting made all the more glamorous by drop-in sports celebrities. As always, there was another move to make. In addition to marketing its own events, IMG took on the business of marketing other major events, beginning with the Wimbledon Championships. (IMG now handles such matters as licensing, corporate hospitality, broadcasting, and publishing for dozens of international sports competitions.)

Expansion continues. In 1966, anticipating the role television would play in the business of sports, IMG established a film and television division, Trans World International. It was another good call. The division is now one of the world's largest independent sources of televised sports, with production centers in Los Angeles, New York, and London. And since McCormack never does things by halves, the division also handles sales of broadcast rights for various other sports organizations, including the Olympic Committee.

In related ventures, IMG has produced sports videos and even went into the book-publishing business. (Good sellers were books by clients John Madden, Martina Navratilova, and Dennis Conner.)

Meanwhile, back at IMG's home base in Cleveland, headquarters of the company's worldwide operations, and at its handsome mansion in New York, IMG executives have continued to build the agency's client roster of sports personalities. Under contract now are some 300, for whom IMG makes available a menu of services ranging from personal appearances to complete financial management.

IMG's dominance has not endeared McCormack to his competitors. A few years ago a cry went up in the tennis industry when he bought the Nick Bollettieri Tennis Academy, a magnet for the world's most promising pubescent players. "You name it, IMG owns it," was the complaint. "It owns the tournaments, it owns the players, it owns the sponsors. And now it owns the academy and the next generation's players."

In the spring of '94, IMG launched still another enterprise, the Avanta Tour, a big-money senior tennis circuit starring John McEnroe, Jimmy Connors, Ivan Lendl, and other formerly top-ranked players.

The impact abroad. In the past few years, many of IMG's expansion moves have occurred outside the United States. In 1993 the opening of an office in Buenos Aires was followed by agreements to manage the South American Open Tennis Championships, the marketing of the Argentine Open Golf Championship, and a business affiliation with the Argentine Polo Association. Business activities in Mexico also increased, especially in the areas of golf and tennis. New offices in Moscow, Budapest, and Johannesburg generated additional activity.

The agency has been a force in the Far East sports market since 1969, when it opened an office in Tokyo. Since then it has established bases in Hong Kong, Singapore, Taipei, Bangkok, Jakarta, Bombay, and several places in New Zealand and Australia. In China, where in 1979 it was the first international company to promote sports events, IMG now represents the Chinese Football Association, the Chinese Basketball Association, and the Chinese Badminton Association, the three most popular sports in China.

Meanwhile, Trans World International, the agency's film and television division, continues to help spread IMG's influence around the world. During a single weekend in 1994, it handled live television coverage of six events in Asia: Marlboro League Soccer from China, Test Cricket from India, Test Cricket from Pakistan, the Singapore Open Golf Tournament, and the Phuket Triathlon and the Rugby World Cup Qualifying Matches from Kuala Lumpur.

At home or abroad, IMG is a tough act to follow.

IMG has an internship program. See the directory at the end of this section for contact information.

Teeing Up: Jack Nicklaus

In his early years as a professional golfer, Jack Nicklaus was part of the Palmer-Player-Nicklaus triumvirate that put Mark McCormack on the road to success. Now, after a 30-year career as the world's greatest golfer, Nicklaus is building his own global sports empire.

His company is Golden Bear International. Its activities encompass the following:

Marketing and management. Includes licensing trademarked Nicklaus and Golden Bear names (in use in 40 countries); organizing, marketing, and operating special sports events; managing affairs of professional sports figures, from contract negotiations to postcareer planning.

Television, film, and video productions. Includes telecasts of special events; video programs such as "The Bobby Jones Instructional Series" and "Golf My Way," featuring Jack Nicklaus; computer/video games, such as "Jack Nicklaus' Greatest 18 Holes of Major Championship Golf."

Publishing. Manages production and sale of books written and coauthored by Nicklaus. (Books appear in nine languages; more than 3.5 million sold.)

Design of golf courses. Already designed around the world are more than 100 courses, hosts of more than 185 professional tournaments; 15 courses are ranked among *Golf Digest's* Top 100.

Golf schools. Developed with Jim Flick, Nicklaus/Flick Golf Schools operate at golf resorts. Under way, development of licensed or franchised Jack Nicklaus Academies and Golf Centers, with facilities for practice and instruction. A worldwide operation.

Golf equipment. Cofounded with Nelson

Doubleday in 1992, Nicklaus Golf Equipment is turning out golf clubs and bags.

Jack Nicklaus

Other activities: The company is associated with Marriott Golf Management Services in a plan to develop new public courses and to acquire existing facilities. It has added Paragon Golf Construction, builders of courses, as an affiliate. And scheduled for '94 was the introduction by the Rockport Company of a Nicklaus golf shoe, which his company will help market.

As if all that isn't enough, Golden Bear International is negotiating with land developers for the creation of Jack Nicklaus/Golden Bear golf communities.

Company headquarters are in North Palm Beach, Florida. Additional offices are in New York, Chicago, Los Angeles, Columbus, Tokyo, and Hong Kong. At this writing, Golden Bear employed 130 to 140 people.

The North Palm Beach offices employ interns. See the directory listing at the end of this section.

A Sampling of Specializations

Most of the successful small and medium-size agencies are specialists of one kind or another. Some concentrate on a particular sport; others provide a service outside the range of big agencies. Here's a random selection of agencies that have found their niche in the industry.

Creative Sports Services (Peoria, Illinois). Advisor to colleges and universities on their sports programs. Audits overall performance of their departments of athletics, covering departmental organization and leadership, financial systems, marketing, fund-raising, NCAA compliance, strategic planning, and other operating procedures. It makes recommendations for change, if change is needed.

Barnes Dyer Marketing (Irvine, California). Formed by the merger in 1992 of Barnes Management and Dyer Group, the company holds a commanding position in its field—auto racing. Represents top drivers and racing teams and markets the sport for a long list of major corporate sponsors.

Sports Media Group (Mamaroneck, New York). Established by Andrea Kirby, a veteran broadcaster. Trains athletes, coaches, and managers to speak like Rex Harrison, face TV cameras with the élan of Ross Perot, and meet the press with the diplomacy of a State Department official.

Performance Research (Newport, Rhode Island). Conducts surveys for event sponsors to see if they're spending their money wisely. Fans are interviewed on-site or by phone to determine if sponsorship has paid off in increased product awareness or new feelings of friendship for the sponsor.

Acme Mascots (Brooklyn, New York). From the folks who brought you the endearingly funny Phillie Phanatic mascot comes a character named Sport, who will be roaming the entire sports circuit—bouncing belly and all—to bring merriment to patrons young and old. Sport has been given life by marketer Wayde Harrison, creator Bonnie Erickson, and inside man David Raymond, Phanatic's heart and soul for the first 16 years.

Pro Connection (Hermosa Beach, California). Kimbirly Orr's small agency concentrates on finding endorsement deals for women athletes. Clients include champions Karolyn Kirby (pro beach volleyball) and Patti Sherman (skiing), and professional race car driver Alice Ridpath.

Sports & Company (Stamford, Connecticut). The agency owns and produces professional bicycle races throughout the U.S., each bearing the name of a sponsor (Thrift Drug Classic of Pittsburgh, First Union Grand Prix of Atlanta, etc.).

Burns Sports Celebrity Service (Chicago). The business is matchmaking. An advertising agency seeking a specific type of sports figure for an ad campaign can almost always find that person in David Burns's

"Sport"

computer. Stored there are 3,500 names of past and current athletes and coaches, along with their height, weight, marital status, fee demands, agents, race, religion, personality traits, and anything else Burns thinks might one day help match sports star to product.

SkyBox Associates (Ambler, Pennsylvania). It's a new idea in the marketing of college sports, an extension of what the professional clubs have gone into in a big way—luxury suites. Recently established, SkyBox is in business to design, construct, finance, and operate luxury suites in campus stadiums and arenas.

SCA Promotions (Dallas). The company adds some fun to sports events by running contests for the customers. Typical, at football games, is "Kick for Kash." Fans are invited to try for field goals from the 15-yard line, 25-yard line, and 35-yard line. Winners get cash prizes. One of the contests at basketball games is "2 out of 3 from half-court." Fans who sink two win prizes; anyone who hits all three gets a double prize—and probably some phone calls from agents. The contests are a popular promotion around the country.

McClellan Sports Management Group (Santa Ana Heights, California). Its niche is representing athletes and promoting events in pro beach volleyball, triathlon, and snowboarding. Bob McClellan has signed up 10 top pros in beach volleyball, a fast-growing sport. His American Women's Snowboard Team appears throughout the U.S. in national competitions and exhibitions.

Equisport Marketing (Keswick, Virginia). Equisport handles all details on behalf of corporate sponsors of horse shows, including contract negotiations, promotions, hospitality activities, signage and displays, and postevent evaluation. Winnie Lee, the company's president, has attracted a distinguished list of clients. Lee came into the sports marketing business as an intern.

The Marquee Group (New York). New to the industry is this full-service marketing, management, and TV production company, the creation of Robert M. Gutkowski, former president of Madison Square Garden. The agency took over two firms that gave it immediate clout: Sports Marketing and Television International (SMTI), a sports event marketer, and Athletes and Artists, a sports and entertainment talent agency. Marquee's assets from SMTI include the Breeders' Cup, Tru-Value sponsorship of Major League Baseball, the College Football Association, the Isuzu Celebrity Golf Championship, the Senior Bowl, the Sun Bowl, and preseason games of the New York Giants and New England Patriots. Clients brought to Marquee by Athletes and Artists include Al Michaels and Dan Dierdorf of ABC Sports, ESPN's Chris Berman, Fred Hickman of CNN Sports, hockey players Brian Leech and Adam Oates, John Powers of the *Boston Globe*, author Dick Schaap, Christiane Amanpour of CNN News, and numerous other writers, sportscasters, and athletes. Gutkowski's singular mission: to overtake International Management Group.

Sponsorships. They Mean a Lot

In an earlier usage, the word *sponsor* was a Madison Avenue coinage for a company that bought advertising time on radio. As in "And now a word from our sponsor." Except for that, the word had little currency.

Today, the word is used all over the place, with all sorts of implications. Organizations can sponsor a poetry reading, a baking contest, a fund-raiser for a philharmonic orchestra, a charity raffle. Or, one can sponsor a person who wishes to come here from abroad, with the promise of a job for that person. (The last is closest to the true meaning of sponsor, which comes from the Latin *spondere*, to make a solemn pledge.)

But nowhere is the word so important as it is in the business of sports.

In sports, to sponsor means to spend a sum of money to affix a company's name to an 80,000-seat stadium, a college bowl, an international track meet, a golf tournament, a community marathon. It also means plastering a company's name on racing cars, sports shoes, arena walls, balloons, and blimps. Or buying the endorsements of famous athletes. It has *many* forms.

The sports industry would be half an industry without it.

Background. Sports marketing agencies began selling the idea of corporate-sponsored special events in the mid-1970s. By the mid-'80s, about 2,600 companies were in the game, spending close to a billion dollars. In 1994, according to the *IEG Sponsorship Report*, a Chicago-based newsletter that tracks sports marketing, corporate spending on sports sponsorships in North America amounted to $2.850 billion. In 1995 the figure rose to $3.050 billion, and it was expected to rise again in 1996 to $3.540 billion.

The sports areas that have drawn the most sponsorship dollars, said the *IEG Sponsorship Report*, are motorsports, golf, pro sports, Olympic teams, and tennis.

In 1995 motorsports had sponsorships amounting to $845 million, which was expected to increase to $920 million in 1996. Golf, in second place, attracted $520 million in sponsorships in 1995, with the anticipation of $555 million in '96.

A Trend Goes In-House

Anheuser-Busch, one of the paramount sponsors of sports events, is giving less business to sports marketing agencies, but only because more and more details of sponsorship are being handled in-house. Other big sponsors are doing that too, creating new departments to deal with many of the details previously executed by outside agencies. It's a definite trend.

Does that mean new job opportunities for college graduates? Not really, says Gary Ronberg, a public relations administrator in the

Anheuser-Busch sports marketing program. To qualify for a job in the sports marketing department of any corporation, a candidate has to have a thorough knowledge of the company, its products, and its goals. The suggestion, by Ronberg and others in the corporate world: take any job you can get in the company that interests you, work your way up the ladder, and keep an eye on the sports marketing department for a possible opening. It's easier to get into the department from inside the company. Especially if you make friends in the company.

On the Subject of Jobs

Dewey Blanton, who is vice president for communications at ProServ, describes his firm as a marketing company that happens to be in the business of sports.

That's about as plainly as it can be put. Being part of the business of sports has its advantages, of course. There's more glamour and fun in the sports industry than, say, the ball-bearings industry. But the essence of the business of sports marketing is marketing.

And it takes two forms: the first is selling corporations on the value of your agency's services; the second is coming up with a strategy that will help your client sell more of its products and enhance its public image. Both forms require skills—and experience.

"Rookies," says Don Dixon, head of Lifestyle Marketing Group and a leader in sports marketing, "do not work in my agency. Our business is consultation, and for that you need client-side experience."

Dixon, who is not alone in that view, says he looks for people who have worked in an industry other than sports and have an understanding of such things as brand management, marketing operations, and product planning. He also rates job applicants by their skills in writing and public speaking. Especially employable, he says, are people who can make clear and forceful presentations to clients. Anyone who has learned that skill, he says, "can get a job anywhere."

* * * *

Mike Stevens, president of Classic Sports, which operates professional golf and tennis tournaments, says he's turned off by applicants who say, "I really like sports and it would be neat to have a job in your company." The first, and usually last, question Stevens asks is, "What experience do you have?"

Basically, his job consists of sports marketing, sales promotion, and tournament operations. About 80 percent is marketing and sales; 20 percent is tournament details. Corporations put up big money for tournament sponsorships, and they expect the events to be marketed and promoted with a high degree of professionalism, Stevens says.

Stevens says that he looks with favor on applicants with degrees in sports management—if they've covered such subjects as marketing, accounting principles, and business logistics. For practical reasons, though, he hires only those who have been in the industry at least long enough to have gotten over their awe of TV cameras and the sports celebrities he works with.

Stevens himself prepared for a career in sports marketing at Penn State, where, he says, he was smart enough to take a core of advertising, marketing, and sales courses. Along with his courses, he took an internship on Hilton Head Island with the company that was operating the Heritage Classic golf tournament. When an opening in the tournament office came up, he leaped at it, even though the job was selling ads for the tournament guide. His advice to students: Get any kind of experience you can while you're still in college, even a menial job in the ticket office at the campus stadium.

* * * *

A fair number of interns are offered regular employment by their host organizations when suitable spots open up.

National Media Group, a sports marketing

THE BIG SPENDERS

In 1995, according to the IEG *Sponsorship Report, these were the top 10 spenders on corporate sponsorships:*

Philip Morris
Anheuser-Busch
Coca-Cola
General Motors
PepsiCo
Eastman Kodak
RJR Nabisco
AT&T
Chrysler
IBM

firm in New York, is one of the agencies that have a policy of hiring entry-level people from among their interns. "It's worked out very well for us," says Doug Drotman, vice president for public relations at NMG. "By hiring our former interns, we know exactly what we're getting. There's no risk of hiring a dud."

Entry-level personnel get a starting salary of between $15,000 and $20,000 and spend a year as "utility infielders," Drotman says. During that period, he explains, "they're likely to be working in more than one department and doing grunt work. In the second year, they settle in with a particular department."

The Industry Is Unconnected

For virtually every type of business under the sun there's an industry association, uniting companies with common interests. Unlinked, however, are the thousand-plus firms engaged in the business of sports marketing and management. No industry association here. No gatherings of sports marketers to discuss industry problems, no industry conventions to affirm their place in society and lift their spirits, no central apparatus for collecting and dispensing industry data, and no dependable source of information for job seekers. Despite its influential role in sports, it is still a fragmented industry—and a mystery to the public. It is so amorphous an industry, in fact, that the U.S. Department of Labor's comprehensive employment guide, *The Occupational Outlook Handbook,* makes no mention of it.

*　*　*　*

The industry is still young, of course, and one day it will unite itself. A first faint glimmer is the formation in New York City of a networking group called Women in Sports and Events (or WISE). It's composed of women working for sports marketing agencies and its main purpose is to exchange job information, but it also intends to lend a hand to women who want to enter the field. President of the group is Sue Rodin, who can be reached at WISE, 244 Fifth Ave., Suite 2087,

New York, NY 10001. Phone: (212) 726-8282.

A Magazine for Marketers

Serving "professionals in the business of marketing sport" is *Sport Marketing Quarterly,* an earnest journal that provides in-depth analyses of various aspects of the industry.

The editor is Stephen Hardy, coordinator of the sport studies program at the University of New Hampshire. An editorial board is composed equally of academics and sports marketing executives. The publication was founded in 1992 by Fitness Information Technology, P.O. Box 4425, Morgantown, WV 26504.

And books, too. Fitness Information Technology is the publisher of a new series of textbooks dealing with the business of sports. The titles and authors: *Sport Facility Planning and Management* (Peter J. Farmer, Aaron L. Mulrooney, Rob Ammon Jr.), *Fundamentals of Sport Marketing* (Brenda G. Pitts, David K. Stotlar), *Financing Sport* (Dennis R. Howard, John L. Crompton), *Sport Governance in the Global Community* (James E. Thoma, Laurence Chalip), *Ethics in Sport Management* (Joy T. DeSensi, Danny Rosenberg), *Sport Management Field Experiences* (Jacquelyn Cuneen, M. Joy Sidwell).

———

On the pages immediately following is a listing of sports marketing and management agencies and a listing of companies that sponsor athletic events. Both listings indicate the availability of internships.

A section on independent player agents begins on page 122. (A number of independent agents, however, are included in the listing of marketing and management agencies.)

SPORTS MARKETING AND MANAGEMENT AGENCIES AND RELATED BUSINESSES

The main role of *sports marketing and management agencies* is developing special events, or using existing events, for corporate clients interested in tapping into the citizenry's passion for sports. The work of the agencies involves selling clients on the wisdom of sponsoring a program of sports events and creating a marketing plan based on that sponsorship. In addition to handling such activities as public relations and merchandising tie-ins, large agencies frequently provide radio and TV production services.

If you're serious about working in the sports industry, you ought to get acquainted with this area. It's the fastest growing part of the industry, the work is interesting, and most agencies—large and small—offer internships (as we've indicated in the listing that follows).

A note of explanation: You will find some references in this directory to "athlete representatives," a refined term for player agents. There are a number of sports marketing and management services for professional athletes. In some cases, player agents have set up their own operations. A tip: player agents are not a likely target for internships.

Accord Cycle Group
P.O. Box 48464
Los Angeles, CA 90048
(213) 871-6959
Joe Kossack, President
Bicycle racing promotions

Acme Mascots
62 Pierrepont St.
Brooklyn, NY 11201-2442
(718) 722-7900
Wayde Harrison, President
Creation of mascot characters

The Action Group
26741 Portola Pkwy.
Foothill Ranch, CA 92610
(714) 699-0070
Charlie Hayes, President
Motorsports promotions

Action Sports of America
5351 Miller Rd.
Lilburn, GA 30087
(770) 564-3963
Carol McKown, Marketing Director
Event marketing
Internships: contact Public Relations,
(770) 469-6541

Advanced Promotional Concepts, Inc.
2802 N. Howard Ave.
Tampa, FL 33607
(813) 254-6600
Barbara Baker, President
Event promotions
Internships: contact Barbara Baker

Advantage International
1025 Thomas Jefferson St. NW,
    Suite 450 East
Washington, DC 20007
(202) 333-3838
Francis H. Craighill III, Managing
    Director
One of the largest sports marketing and management agencies; four offices in U.S., seven abroad
Internships: in Washington, contact
    Gina Ruby

Advantage Management
303 Church St., Suite 201
Nashville, TN 37201
(615) 255-5374
Steve Jones, President
Event management; athlete representation

Advantage Marketing Group
5215 N. O'Connor Blvd., Suite 770
Irving, TX 75039
(214) 869-2244
Werner Scott, President
Event management; athlete representation
Internships: contact Human Resources

Alan Taylor Communications
225 W. 34th St.
New York, NY 10122
(212) 714-1280
Alan Taylor, President
Publicity; event promotions
Internships: contact Alan Taylor

Allen Consulting
89 Middletown Rd.
Holmdel, NJ 07733
(908) 946-2711
Sylvia Allen, President
Public relations; event marketing

American Ski Racing Alliance
1431 N. Main Ave.
Scranton, PA 18508
(717) 344-2772
John Foy, President
Event management
Internships: contact John Foy

American Sports Marketing, Inc.
160 Fontaine Rd.
Mableton, GA 30059
(770) 941-9396
Sandra Tabler, President
Event management; licensing
Internships: contact Chris Hansard

Anthony M. Furman
250 W. 57th St.
New York, NY 10107
(212) 956-5666
Anthony Furman, President
Event management
Internships: contact Anthony Furman

Arocom Sports Marketing
1350 Euclid Ave.
Cleveland, OH 44115
(216) 696-9660
Steven Zweig, President
Event promotions
Internships: contact Kelly Class

Athlete Financial Management Service
8383 Wilshire Blvd., Suite 528
Beverly Hills, CA 90211
(213) 653-5934
Paul Sheehy, President

Athletic Associates, Inc.
15303 Dallas Pkwy., Suite 970
Dallas, TX 75248
(214) 702-7535
George A. Bass Jr., CFO
Athlete representation

Athletic Marketing Agency
528 Fayette St.
Conshohocken, PA 19428
(610) 941-0770
Brett W. Senior, Director
Event management; athlete representation
Internships offered

Athletic Resource Management
6075 Poplar Ave., Suite 920
Memphis, TN 38119
(901) 763-4900
Kyle Rote Jr., CEO
Athlete representation; corporate consulting
Internships: in Dallas, contact Brad
    Penman, (214) 404-0900

Barnes Dyer Marketing
15510 Rockfield Blvd., Suite C
Irvine, CA 92718
(714) 768-2942
Bill Dyer, Chairman/CEO
Bruce Barnes, President/COO
Full-service motorsports marketing

Battle Enterprises
320 Interstate N, Suite 102
Atlanta, GA 30339
(770) 956-0520
Bill Battle, President/CEO
Marketing and licensing activities, mainly motorsports
Internships: contact Derek Eiler

Beverly Hills Sports Council
9595 Wilshire Blvd., Suite 1010
Beverly Hills, CA 90212
(310) 858-1872
Dennis Gilbert, President
Player representation
Internships: contact Ken Gurnick

Bevilaqua International
1401 Peachtree St. NE, Suite 500
Atlanta, GA 30309
(404) 607-1999
John Bevilaqua, President
Full-service marketing, global scope
Internships: contact Paul Bourgeois

BEWI Productions
135 Second Ave.
Waltham, MA 02154
(617) 890-3234
Bernard Weichsel, President
Skiing promotions

Bien Internationale
9349 Melvin Ave., Suite 6
Northridge, CA 91324
(818) 709-9555
Nancy Bien, President/CEO
Athlete representation; event marketing, multilingual; Asian connections

Bill Michaels & Company
1666 Race St.
Denver, CO 80206
(303) 399-9005
Bill Michaels, President
Event management

Bird Special Events Group
113 N. Main St.
Elkhorn, NE 68022
(402) 289-3779
Fred Schweser, President
Event management

SPORTS MARKETING AND MANAGEMENT AGENCIES AND RELATED BUSINESSES

BKB Limited
P.O. Box 4184
Englewood, CO 80155
(303) 694-2030
Creigh Kelley, President
Production of about 40 sports events a
year, including running, walking,
cycling, cross-country skiing
Internships: contact Creigh Kelley

Bloks, USA
P.O. Box 38
Orinda, CA 94563
(800) 227-3323
Richard Cunningham, President
Event management, specializing in
equestrian events
Internships: contact Richard
Cunningham

Blumenfeld & Associates
130 W. 42nd St., 14th floor
New York, NY 10036
(212) 764-1690
Jeff Blumenfeld, President
Public relations
Internships offered

Bonham Communications
1625 Broadway, Suite 1530
Denver, CO 80202
(303) 592-4290
Dean Bonham, President
Event management; college sports
marketing
Internships: contact Rob Vogel

Brener Zwikel & Associates
6901 Canby Ave., Suite 105
Reseda, CA 91335
(818) 344-6195
Steve Brener, President
Event advertising and publicity; golf
tournaments; boxing
Internships: contact Steve Brener

Brian P. Hakan & Associates
10800 Farley, Suite 310
Oberlin Park, KS 66210
(913) 492-7900
Brian P. Hakan, President
Licensing specialists

Bruce Levy Associates
2 Penn Plaza, Suite 1500
New York, NY 10121
(212) 254-3222
Bruce Levy, President
Representation of players and coaches in
women's basketball; management of
clinics, tournaments

Burns Sports Celebrity Service
211 E. Chicago Ave., Suite 710
Chicago, IL 60601
(312) 951-5400
David Burns, President
Internships: contact Bob Williams

Butler Communications
13375 N. Stemmons Freeway
Suite 110
Dallas, TX 75234
(214) 247-3080
Janice S. Butler, President
Marketing, advertising, public relations,
specializing in motorsports
Internships offered

BW Sportswire
40 E. 52nd St., 19th Floor
New York, NY 10022
(212) 752-9600
Gregory M. Schmalz, National
Manager
Distribution of news releases electronically
to sports media across U.S. and beyond
Internships: contact Mike Maguire

Camp & Associates, Inc.
P.O. Box 3378
Concord, NC 28025
(704) 788-7979
Larry M. Camp, President
Marketing and public relations for racing
teams

Campbell & Company
15010 Commerce Dr. S, Suite 501
Dearborn, MI 48120
(313) 336-9655
R. M. Campbell, President
Public relations and promotions
Internships: contact Public Relations

Capital Sports, Inc.
Metro Center
One Station Place
Stamford, CT 06902
(203) 353-9900
John Arrix, Vice President
Event management; television packaging;
public relations
Internships: contact John Arrix

Cappy Productions
33 E. 68th St.
New York, NY 10021
(212) 249-1800
Bud Greenspan, President
Film company known especially for
Olympic Games coverage and
documentaries
Internships: contact Nancy Beffa

Career Sports Management
200 Galleria Pkwy., Suite 2060
Atlanta, GA 30339
(404) 955-1300
Beth Brandon, Marketing Director
Athlete representation
Internships: contact Angelo Pepper

Cargill Communications
461 Boston St., Suite A4-5
Topsfield, MA 01983
(508) 887-3600
Leslie Cargill, President
Event development and management

Carlson Marketing Group
P.O. Box 59159
Minneapolis, MN 55459
(612) 550-4069
Alan Thiry, Vice President
Event management
Internships: contact Public Relations

Catherine Miller & Associates
2171 India St., Suite E
San Diego, CA 92101
(619) 234-8791
Catherine Miller, President
Event development and management
Internships offered

Cato Johnson Sports Marketing
675 Avenue of the Americas
Suite 300
New York, NY 10010
(212) 941-3700
Steve Zammarchi, Vice President
Internships: contact Human Resources

Celtic Advertising
330 S. Executive Dr., Suite 206
Brookfield, WI 53005
(414) 789-7630
Martha Smith, President
Event management; licensing; radio and
TV production
Internships: contact Al Eickberg

The Championship Group
3690 N. Peachtree Rd.
Atlanta, GA 30341
(404) 457-5777
Ardy Arani, Founder and Partner
Full-service event management and
marketing
Internships: contact Chris Hayek

Charles J. Brotman
Communications
1120 Connecticut Ave. NW
Washington, DC 20036
(202) 296-7200
Charles J. Brotman, CEO
Public relations; marketing; advertising
Internships: contact Laurie Covets

Chester Gore Company
780 Third Ave., 10th Floor
New York, NY 10017
(212) 754-9111
Chester Gore, President
Event management

Cindrich & Company
552 Washington Ave.
Pittsburgh, PA 15106-2894
(412) 429-1250
Ralph E. Cindrich, President
Athlete representation

Classic Sports
79 Lighthouse Rd., Suite 414
Hilton Head Island, SC 29928
(803) 671-2448
Michael D. Stevens, President
Event management
Internships: contact Steve Wilmont

Cohn & Wolfe
225 Peachtree St. NE, Suite 2300
Atlanta, GA 30303
(404) 688-5900
Jim Overstreet, General Manager
Sports publicity; offices also in New York,
Chicago, Toronto, London, Milan;
190 employees
Internships: contact Angie Tranetham

College Prospects of America
P.O. Box 269
Logan, OH 43138-0269
(614) 385-6624
Recruiting service; maintains profiles of
high school athletes
Internships: contact Tom Starr

The Collegiate Licensing
Company
320 Interstate N, Suite 102
Atlanta, GA 30339
(404) 956-0520
Bill Battle, President
Representation of colleges and universities
in licensing activities; largest agency in
the field
Internships: contact Public Relations

Communications Diversified
440 Park Ave. S, 6th Floor
New York, NY 10016
(212) 213-3300
William Henneberry, President
Wide range of marketing activities
Internships offered

Cone Communications
90 Canal St.
Boston, MA 02114
(617) 227-2111
Carol L. Cone, President
Development of sponsored events; full-
service marketing
Internships: contact Carlyn Gaul

SPORTS MARKETING AND MANAGEMENT AGENCIES AND RELATED BUSINESSES

Conventures
250 Summer St.
Boston, MA 02210
(617) 439-7700
Dusty Rhodes, President
Event management
Internships: contact Andrea Mrusek

Cooksey & Associates
P.O. Box 497
Carmel, IN 46032
(317) 844-6221
Sally Cooksey, President
Event management
Internships offered

**Coordinated Sports
Management Group**
790 Frontage Rd.
Northfield, IL 60093
(708) 441-4315
Alan L. Nero, President
*Athlete representation (mainly pro baseball
and football)*
Internships offered

Cornerstone Sports
Chateau Plaza, Suite 940
2515 McKinney Ave.
Dallas, TX 75201
(214) 855-5150
Roscoe O. Hambric Jr., President
*Athlete representation (mainly pro golfers);
golf promotions*

Corporate Communications
Main St.
North Conway, NH 03860
(603) 356-7011
Kimberly Beals, President
Event development and management
Internships offered

Cotter Group
P.O. Box 900
Harrisburg, NC 28075
(704) 455-3500
Tom Cotter, President
Athlete representation; event marketing
Internships: contact Melanie Cannon

Cowen Media
1841 Broadway, 7th Floor
New York, NY 10023
(212) 582-4551
Robert Cowen, President
Packager of TV sports
Internships offered

Creamer Dickson Basford
1000 Turks Head Bldg.
Providence, RI 02903-2215
(617) 329-6400
Donald J. Goncalves, Vice President
Public relations services
Internships offered

Creative Sports Services
301 S.W. Adams, Suite 800
Peoria, IL 61602
(309) 671-4560
Lynn Snyder, Director
*Consulting services for intercollegiate
sports programs; financial planning for
pro athletes*
Internships offered

Curtis Management Group
1000 Waterway Blvd.
Indianapolis, IN 46202
(317) 633-2050
Mark Roesler, President & CEO
*Representation of pro athletes and sports
organizations*
Internships offered

Custom Event Marketing
666 Third Ave., 2nd Floor
New York, NY 10017
(212) 297-7150
Elizabeth Phillips, President
Marketing for major events
Internships: contact Elizabeth Phillips

Custom Sports/Promotions
1195 Niagara St.
Buffalo, NY 14213
(716) 878-8782
Michael Hurley, Executive Director
*Marketing campaigns for Buffalo's Bills,
Sabres, Bisons, and Blizzard*
Internships offered

**Dave McGillivray Sports
Enterprises**
21-H Olympia Ave.
Woburn, MA 01801
(617) 932-9393
David J. McGillivray, President
Event management
Internships offered

Dave Mona Sports Marketing
8400 Normandale Lake Blvd.
Bloomington, MN 55437
(612) 831-8515
Dave Mona, President
Event management
Internships offered

David Fishof Presents
252 W. 71st St.
New York, NY 10023
(212) 757-1605
David Fishof, President
Athlete representation
Internships offered

Davis Group
P.O. Box 1535
Thomasville, GA 31799
(912) 228-6030
Edward A. Davis, President
*Equestrian show production; corporate
sponsorship development*
Internships offered

DeAngelo, Minton & Associates
6090 Mahoning Ave.
Warren, OH 44481-9401
(216) 847-8900
Bill Korbus, Marketing Manager
Motorsports promotions

Del Wilber & Associates
1410 Springhill Rd., Suite 450
McLean, VA 22102
(703) 749-9300
Del Wilber, CEO
*Development and execution of wide range
of marketing programs, including special
events, for top North American
companies; offices in McLean, St.
Louis, Denver, Orlando, Toronto*
Internships: contact Angel Baker

D & F Group
5301 Wisconsin Ave. NW, Suite 325
Washington, DC 20015
(202) 364-8500
Allen S. Furst, Managing Director
Consultants to major corporations
Internships offered

DK Marketing
Camino del Rio S, Suite 215
San Diego, CA 92108
(619) 280-5200
Dale A. Kriebel, President
Event management and marketing

Dom Camera Associates
630 Third Ave.
New York, NY 10017
(212) 370-1130
Bill Lucano, President
Event management
Internships offered

Don King Productions
871 W. Oakland Park Blvd.
Ft. Lauderdale, FL 33311
(305) 568-3500
Don King, President
Boxing promotions
Internships offered

Don Smith Consultants
2 World Trade Ctr., Suite 2164
New York, NY 10048
(212) 912-0720
Donald G. Smith, President
*Public relations; marketing; event
management*
Internships offered

Donellen Public Relations
180 N. Michigan Ave., Suite 1505
Chicago, IL 60601
(312) 553-1240
Kevin Donellen, President
Athlete appearances; event management
Internships: contact Patty Morrison

DornaUSA
555 Madison Ave.
New York, NY 10022-3401
(212) 751-9191
Henry L. Usher, President
*International marketing firm best known for
AdTime, revolving signage system at
stadiums and arenas*
Internships offered

Driver Connection
106 Pierremount Ave.
New Britain, CT 06053
(203) 229-3970
Rick Raducha, President
Motorsports sponsor search; promotions
Internships

Eddie Elias Enterprises
1720 Merriman Rd.
Akron, OH 44334-0118
(216) 867-4388
*Athlete representation, mainly golf; founder
of television's longest-running sports
series, "The Professional Bowlers Tour"*
Internships: contact Marsha Wagner

Edelman Sports
211 E. Ontario, 13th Floor
Chicago, IL 60611
(312) 280-7087
Edward Manetta, Senior Vice
President
*Sports marketing branch of Daniel J.
Edelman Worldwide, public relations
firm*
Internships: contact Karen Ruwane

**E. J. Krause & Associates,
Sports Division**
7315 Wisconsin Ave., Suite 450 N
Bethesda, MD 20814
(301) 986-7800
Craig Tartasky, Executive Director
*Organizers of International Sport Summit,
annual conference and trade show for
sports marketers and managers of sports
facilities*
Internships offered

Equisport Marketing
P.O. Box 313
Keswick, VA 22947
(804) 977-0230
Winifred H. Lee, President
Equestrian sports promotions

SPORTS MARKETING AND MANAGEMENT AGENCIES AND RELATED BUSINESSES

Ernie Saxton Communications
1448 Hollywood Ave.
Langhorne, PA 19047-7417
(215) 752-7797
Ernie Saxton, President
*Motorsports promotions; publishes the
newsletter Motorsports Marketing News*
Internships offered

Evans Public Relations
2390 E. Camelback, Suite 325
Phoenix, AZ 85016
(602) 957-6636
Craig McKenzie, President
*Public relations and marketing services
focusing on golf*
Internships offered

**Event Marketing & Management
International**
1322 N. Mills Ave.
Orlando, FL 32803
(407) 896-1160
Natalie Williams Casey, Vice
President, Communications
Internships offered

The Eventors
1940 N. Lincoln Ave.
Chicago, IL 60614
(312) 944-6667
Jane E. Canepa, President
Special events coordinator
Internships offered

Executive Diversions
Rose Tree Corp. Center
1400 N. Providence Rd., Suite 107
Media, PA 19063
(215) 566-1171
Kevin M. Scanlon, President
Event development and management
Internships: contact Wes Waninger

Executive Sports
5300 W. Atlantic Ave., Suite 700
Delray Beach, FL 33484
(407) 499-3999
John D. Montgomery, President
*Management of major golf tournaments in
U.S. and abroad; consultants on
marketing*

Executive Sports Management
223 W. Jackson Blvd., Suite 405
Chicago, IL 60606
(312) 322-1870
David Goins, President
Event management and marketing
Internships: contact David Goins

Exsportise
410 Severn Ave., Suite 409
Annapolis, MD 21403
(410) 263-4412
Richard E. George, President
Sports consultant to business organizations

**Falk Associates Management
Enterprises (F.A.M.E.)**
5335 Wisconsin Ave. NW, Suite 850
Washington, DC 20015
(202) 686-2000
David Falk, Chairman/CEO
*Athlete representation: Michael Jordan;
'nuff said*
Internships: contact Brenda Dews

Fantastic Sports, Inc.
5925 Kearny Villa Rd.
San Diego, CA 92123
(619) 569-4101
Event management, hospitality
Internships: contact Chris Codington

Forbush & Associates
16322 Port Dickinson Dr.
Jupiter, FL 33477
(407) 747-4333
Robert B. Forbush, President
Marketing consultants, primarily golf

Foxhill Group
238 Oakland Ave.
Rock Hill, SC 29730
(803) 329-2600
Pete Davis, President
*Public relations; marketing; sponsor search;
specialty: motorsports*
Internships offered

Frankel & Company
111 E. Wacker Dr., 18th floor
Chicago, IL 60601
(312) 938-1900
Jim Mack, President
*Athlete appearances; licensing;
merchandising*
Internships: contact Pat Serfin

Freyer Management Associates
1 Essex Green Dr.
Peabody, MA 01960
(508) 977-9200
Stephen P. Freyer, CEO
Athlete representation

Front Runner, Inc.
P.O. Box 215
Lebanon, IL 62254
(618) 537-9500
Craig Virgin, President
Promotion of running and fitness events
Internships offered

Ganim Enterprises
374 Slate Run Dr.
Powell, OH 43065
(614) 548-4188
Doug Ganim, President
*Promotion of racquetball competitions;
representation of professional players*

GCI Group
777 Third Ave.
New York, NY 10017
(212) 546-2200
Jack Bergen, President
Event management and marketing
Internships offered

G & C Sports Management
1 Chase Manhattan Plaza, 46th Floor
New York, NY 10005
(212) 530-5442
Matthew D. Pace, President
Athlete representation (baseball)
Internships offered

George W. Campbell
2000 N. 15th St., Suite 507
Arlington, VA 22201
(703) 525-8500
George W. Campbell Jr., Director
Athlete representation (football)
Internships offered

GK SportsFlash
1376 W. Grand Ave.
Chicago, IL 60622
(312) 563-0777
Susan Wilsey, President
*Sports publicity firm specializing in
distribution of video news features to
media*
Internships offered

Global Television Sports
15 E. Ridge Pike, Suite 500
Conshohocken, PA 19428
(215) 825-4000
Jeff Ruday, President
*Production of sports telecasts for corporate
sponsors and sports organizations*
Internships: contact Vicki Zalcmann

GMR Marketing
16535 W. Bluemound Rd., Suite 230
Brookfield, WI 53005
(414) 786-5600
Gary Reynolds, President
Event management
Internships: contact Sharon Casey

Golden Bear International
11780 U.S. Highway One
North Palm Beach, FL 33408
(407) 626-3900
Jack Nicklaus, President
*A diverse, growing empire that owes as
much to Nicklaus's business acumen as
it does to his fame as golf's all-time
great; offices in North Palm Beach, New
York, Chicago, Los Angeles,
Columbus, Tokyo, and Hong Kong*
Internships at North Palm Beach
headquarters

Grand Slam III
401 Pennsylvania Pkwy., Suite 390
Indianapolis, IN 46280
(317) 575-5900
Milton O. Thompson, Partner
*Representation of athletes and coaches;
consultants on sports marketing*
Internships offered

Great Events
7833 Walker Dr., Suite 510
Greenbelt, MD 20770
(301) 513-0830
Jimena Ryan, President
Event development and management

Group Dynamics
1715 14th St.
Santa Monica, CA 90404
(310) 452-5056
Jack Butefish, President
*Event management and marketing; has an
office in Tokyo*
Internships offered

Half-Tyme Productions (H.T.P.)
3859 S. Cochrane Ave.
Los Angeles, CA 90008
(213) 938-9633
Ron Clark, CEO
Provides half-time variety acts

**Hampton Classic Horse
Show, Inc.**
P.O. Box 3013
Bridgehampton, NY 11932-3013
(516) 537-3177
Anthony F. Hitchcock, Jean Lindgren,
Executive Directors
*Producers of the Hampton Classic, the
prestigious hunter/jumper horse show*
Internships offered

Harold Curry & Associates
2242 S. Telegraph, Suite 200
Bloomfield Hills, MI 48302
(313) 335-9266
Harold Curry, President
Athlete representation
Internships offered

SPORTS MARKETING AND MANAGEMENT AGENCIES AND RELATED BUSINESSES

Horrow Sports Ventures
100 S.E. Second St., 36th Floor
Miami, FL 33131-2130
(305) 577-4045
Rick Horrow, President
Well-known sports specialist; provides
variety of services to sports businesses,
leagues, franchises, sports facilities,
and municipalities in developing their
projects and properties

Host Publications
546 E. Main St.
Lexington, KY 40596-3071
(606) 253-3230
College sports marketing; sports
publications
Internships: contact Jennifer Poage

Image Impact
348 E. 76th St.
New York, NY 10021
(212) 472-5200
Mickey Lawrence, President
Special-event marketing
Internships offered

Images USA
1718 Peachtree Rd., Suite 596
Atlanta, GA 30309
(404) 892-2931
Robert L. McNeil Jr., President
Public relations; event marketing;
sponsor search
Internships offered

Impact Sports & Entertainment
1900 Glades Rd., Suite 355
Boca Raton, FL 33431
(407) 393-1475
Mitch Frankel, President
Athlete representation

Inclyne Sports
410 W. Erie, Suite 410
Chicago, IL 60610
(312) 943-3444
Charles Graves, President
Athlete representation; event management
Internships offered

Integrated Sports International
One Meadowlands Plaza, Suite 1501
East Rutherford, NJ 07073
(201) 507-1122
Frank J. Vuono, President
Full-service marketing, all sports
Internships offered

Integrated Sports Marketing
64 Shoreham Village Dr.
Fairfield, CT 06430
(203) 255-8911
Richard D. Ryan, President
Event management; marketing; television
packaging
Internships offered

International Cycling Productions
1281 E. Main St.
Stamford, CT 06902
(203) 324-6800
Michael Halstead, President
Management and promotion of major
international races
Internships offered

International Events Group
213 W. Institute Place, Suite 303
Chicago, IL 60610-3175
(312) 944-1727
Lesa Ukman, President
Major source of sponsorship information;
publisher of IEG Sponsorship Report
(newsletter), Director of Sponsorship
Marketing, Legal Guide to
Sponsorship; conducts annual conference
for sponsor executives

International Management Group
World Headquarters:
One Erieview Plaza, Suite 1300
Cleveland, OH 44114-1782
(216) 522-1200
In New York:
22 E. 71st St.
New York, NY 10021
(212) 772-8900
Mark H. McCormack,
President/CEO
Largest sports marketing and management
company in the world; offices in 19
countries
Internships: in Cleveland, contact
Carroll Bronson

International Promotion
   Management
542 Hopmeadow St.
Simsbury, CT 06070
(860) 658-1100
Marian Melcher Hanson, Manager
Event management
Internships: contact Marian Melcher
Hanson

International Sports
   & Entertainment
   Representation Group
2000 L St. NW, Suite 403
Washington, DC 20036
(202) 833-3330
Dominick A. Pilli, President
Athlete representation
Internships offered

International Sports &
   Entertainment Strategies
230 Park Ave. S, 3rd Floor
New York, NY 10003
(212) 614-4962
Chip Campbell, Managing Director
Marketing services for corporate clients;
offices also in Atlanta, Los Angeles,
District of Columbia, London, Tokyo

International Sports Facilities
7 E. Skippack Pike, Suite 300
Ambler, PA 19002
(215) 885-7050
Louis C. Scheinfeld, Partner
Facilities management specialists, teamed
with Public Financial Management to
form SkyBox Associates, to construct,
finance, and operate luxury suites in
college stadiums and arenas
Internships offered

Jane Blalock Co.
66 Long Wharf
Boston, MA 02110
(617) 242-3100
Pamela Will, Vice President
Corporate marketing programs in golf,
tennis, and sailing
Internships offered

JED Sports Management
3711 Almaden Court
Cameron Park, CA 95682
(916) 677-7972
Jennifer Drury, President
Development of marketing plans for
sponsors and athletes
Internships: contact Jennifer Drury

Jewel Productions
555 Long Wharf Dr.
New Haven, CT 06511
(203) 776-7331
Charles Smith, Tournament Director
Promotion of international tennis
tournaments
Internships offered

John Iltis Associates
680 N. Lake Shore Dr., Suite 1328
Chicago, IL 60611
(312) 337-6012
John Iltis, President
Promotion of sponsored events
Internships offered

Joyce Julius & Associates
3785 Varsity Dr.
Ann Arbor, MI 48108
(313) 971-1900
Joyce Julius-Cotman, President
Analysis of exposure of events produced for
corporate sponsors; issues Sponsors
Report, a marketing research newsletter
Internships offered

J. Thomas Malatesta & Company
1000 Thomas Jefferson St. NW,
   Suite 600
Washington, DC 20007
(202) 965-2582
J. Thomas Malatesta, President
Event creation and management

Kazmaier Associates
676 Elm St.
Concord, MA 01742
(508) 371-1732
Richard W. Kazmaier, President
Sports business consultants with a wide
reach; activities include mergers and
acquisitions, joint ventures, new product
development, licensing programs
Internships offered

Kemper Sports Marketing
455 N. Cityfront Plaza Dr.
Chicago, IL 60611-5555
(312) 755-3500
Rick Singer, President
Event management and marketing;
involved in design, construction, and
management of golf facilities

The Kempton Group
1212 Sycamore St., Suite 21
Cincinnati, OH 45210
(513) 651-5556
Thomas E. Kempton, President
Marketing and special events

Keystone Marketing Co.
101 S. Stratford Rd., Suite 105
Winston-Salem, NC 27104
(910) 631-9375
Roger Bear, President
Public relations; promotions; marketing
services

Lapin East/West
200 N. Westlake Blvd.
Westlake Village, CA 91362
(805) 371-9797
Jackie Lapin, President
Full public relations services; New York
office at 386 Park Ave. S, Suite 501,
New York, NY 10016;
(212) 532-7673
Internships offered

Lazin Group
1333 N. Kingsbury, Suite 307
Chicago, IL 60622
(312) 642-5600
Terry Lazin, President
Promotions involving players in NFL,
NBA, MLB, and PGA
Internships: contact Nancy
Goldstucker

Licensing Resource Group
515 Kirkwood Ave.
Iowa City, IA 52244
(319) 351-1776
Richard L. Rademaker, CEO
Representation of colleges and universities
in licensing activities

SPORTS MARKETING AND MANAGEMENT AGENCIES AND RELATED BUSINESSES

Lifestyle Marketing Group
345 Park Ave. S
New York, NY 10010
(212) 779-6600
Donald R. Dixon II, Chairman
Creation of marketing programs, including sponsorship activities, for major companies
Internships: contact Donald Dixon

Mackey Marketing Group
12 Powder Springs St., Suite 220
Marietta, GA 30060
(404) 423-9593
Brian Mackey, President
Development of motorsports sponsorships

Main Event Productions, Inc.
811 Totowa Rd.
Totowa, NJ 07512
(201) 389-9000
Daniel S. Duva, President
Event management
Internships offered

Major Events
101 W. Grand Ave., Suite 504
Chicago, IL 60601
(312) 527-2200
Tom Cooney, President
Event management; handles Chicago Marathon
Internships (June–October): contact Susan Nicholl

Marathon Marketing & Promotions
1535 E. Broadway
Tucson, AZ 85719
(602) 623-4000
Diana Madaras, President
Packaging of sponsored events

The Marketing Arm
5757 Alpha Rd., Suite 625
Dallas, TX 75240
(214) 404-0900
Ray Clark, General Manager
Athlete representation; event management
Internships: contact Brad Penman

Marketing Associates International
2310 W. 75th St.
Prairie Village, KS 66208
(913) 384-8980
Mitch Wheeler, President
Event management from conception to production; consultant on sponsorship opportunities
Summer internships: contact Nancy

The Marquee Group
150 E. 58th St.
New York, NY 10155
(212) 977-0300
Robert Gutkowski, President
Comprehensive marketing, management, sales, and TV production services to sports businesses; Gutkowski is the former president and CEO of Madison Square Garden

Master Plan Management
125 S. Wacker Dr., Suite 300
Chicago, IL 60611
(312) 348-5828
Jane Wells May, President
Athlete representation

Matt Blair's Celebrity Promotions
200 W. Highway 13, Suite 210
Burnsville, MN 55337
(612) 895-5594
Matt A. Blair, President
Speakers' bureau, featuring motivational talks by Blair, former all-pro Minnesota Vikings linebacker
Internships offered

Maverick Marketing
1250 24th St. NW
Washington, DC 20037
(202) 466-0589
Mike Bovino, Partner
Marketing; public relations, sponsor search

McClellan Sports Management Group
20321 Birch St., Suite 203
Santa Ana Heights, CA 92707
(714) 752-6151
Bob McClennan, President
Representation of athletes in pro beach volleyball, snowboarding, and triathlon; event marketing
Internships offered

McCracken Brooks Sports & Sponsorship Group
717 Fifth Ave., 22nd Floor
New York, NY 10022
(212) 909-9876
Larry Sternbach, Director

Medalist Sports
3228-D W. Cary St.
Richmond, VA 23221
(804) 354-9934
Michael Plant, President
Event management
Internships offered

Millsport
750 Washington Blvd.
Stamford, CT 06901
(203) 977-0500
James R. Millman, Chairman
Consultant to corporations on sponsorships; public relations, tie-in sales promotions, television packaging

Monmar
513 Hanbury Lane
Foster City, IA 94404
(415) 349-9557
Martin Mulligan, President
Promotions and public relations

Morris International
301 East Blvd.
Charlotte, NC 28203
(704) 376-0736
Sid Morris, President
Promotions and publicity; specializing in motorsports and water sports
Internships offered

Muhleman Marketing
6000 Monroe Rd., Suite 300
Charlotte, NC 28212
(704) 568-2520
Max Muhleman, President & CEO
Multifaceted agency dealing with athlete representation, event management, promotions, and public relations; consultation on sports franchise acquisition
Internships offered

National Media Group
1790 Broadway
New York, NY 10019
(212) 307-5300
Peter Kaplan, President
Corporate sponsorships; event management; college sports marketing; talent representation; production of TV sports programming
Internships offered

Network International
701 Market St., Suite 4400
Philadelphia, PA 19106
(215) 922-7818
Richard H. Sherwood, General Manager
Event management and promotion; marketing services for stadiums and arenas
Internships offered

Nike Sports Management
One Bowerman Dr.
Beaverton, OR 97005
(503) 671-6453
Terdema Ussery, President
Nike has entered the field of athlete representation

NYT Event/Sports Marketing
5520 Park Ave.
Trumbull, CT 06611
(203) 373-7000
Anne Mullen, Director
Event management; marketing consultant to corporations
Internships offered

PACE Motor Sports
477 E. Butterfield Rd., Suite 400
Lombard, IL 60148
(630) 963-4810
Charles Becker, President
Event management; TV packaging
Internships: contact Marie LoIacono

Pacific Sports
106 W. Lime Ave.
Monrovia, CA 91016
(818) 357-9699
Bob Mendes, President
Athlete representation; event management and promotion
Internships offered

Paine Associates
535 Anton Blvd., Suite 450
Costa Mesa, CA 92626
(714) 755-0400
James H. Delulio, Executive Vice President
Public relations
Internships offered

People & Properties
345 Park Ave. South
New York, NY 10010
(212) 685-0615
Peter Chapman, Chairman
Television production and packaging of sports events
Internships offered

Performance Properties
340 Pemberwick Rd.
Greenwich, CT 06831
(203) 531-3600
Alex Nieroth, Executive Vice President
Development of marketing programs including sponsorships
Internships offered

Performance Research
25 Mill St.
Queen Anne Square
Newport, RI 02840
(401) 848-0111
Jed Pearsall, President
Market research for corporate sponsors
Internships: contact Doug Snell

Pilson Communications
516 Fifth Ave., 8th Floor
New York, NY 10036
(212) 382-2339
Neal Pilson, President
Former head of CBS has set up a TV packaging agency

Pinnacle Enterprises
1919 Gallows Rd., Suite 980
Vienna, VA 22182
(703) 761-4111
Robert C. Morris, President
Athlete representation; event management; marketing services for manufacturers of golf products
Internships offered

Pinnacle Marketing
2 Viking Park
14045 Petronella Dr.
Libertyville, IL 60048
(708) 816-6600
Jim Melvin and Dick Stahler, Co-directors
Event management

Polo Events
303 Cognewaugh Rd.
Cos Cob, CT 06807
(203) 625-0237
Luc Hardy, President
Polo events

Porter/Novelli
1633 Broadway
New York, NY 10019
(212) 872-8000
Bob Seltzer, General Manager
Public relations for sports products
Internships offered

Premier Sports Marketing
1212 N. Washington, Suite 301
Spokane, WA 99201
(509) 324-3365
Terry Pugh, President
Handles radio and TV production for sports venues throughout the US; maintains six offices

Pro Connection
1559-E Pacific Coast Hwy., Suite 618
Hermosa Beach, CA 90254
(310) 374-3154
Kimbirly Orr, President
Career management services for professional athletes, mainly women
Internships offered

Promo 1
450 Seventh Ave., Suite 933
New York, NY 10123
(212) 714-1914
Howard Freeman, President
Promotion of a variety of sports events (including cricket and ballooning)

ProServ
1101 Wilson Blvd.
Arlington, VA 22209
(703) 276-3030
Donald Dell, Chairman & CEO
One of the largest sports marketing and management agencies; six offices in U.S., four abroad
Strong internship program at Arlington headquarters (contact: Julie Kennedy)

PSP Sports Marketing
355 Lexington Ave.
New York, NY 10017
(212) 697-1460
Jared Metze, President/CEO
Turns out sports publications for corporate sponsors

RFTS
P.O. Box 414
Cuyahoga Falls, OH 44222-0414
(216) 928-3606
Thomas Amshay, President
Marketing consultant, auto racing
Internships offered

Riber Sports Marketing Group
7442 Jager Court
Cincinnati, OH 45230
(513) 624-2100
Burch Riber
Event management, mainly golf
Internships: contact Stephanie Tyler

Richard E. Madigan & Associates
248 Lorraine Ave.
Upper Montclair, NJ 07043
(201) 472-7227
Richard E. Madigan, President
Athlete representation

SCA Promotions
8300 Douglas Ave., Suite 625
Dallas, TX 75225
(214) 363-8744
Rob Harmon, Account Manager
Creation of contests for sports events promotions

Score International Sports
1900 Spring Rd., Suite 508
Hinsdale, IL 60521-1479
(708) 268-8000
Robert Koewler, Vice President
Marketing of LPGA
Internships offered

Scrutchfield Companies, Inc.
420 Lexington Ave., Suite 430
New York, NY 10170
(212) 599-0071
Fred Scrutchfield, President
Specialists in marketing golf events, with a particular interest in women's golf
Internships offered

Seena Hamilton & Associates
950 Third Ave., 26th Floor
New York, NY 10022
(212) 308-5368
Seena Hamilton, President
Marketing; public relations; event management
Internships: contact Jason Farrar

The Sherry Group
600 Parsippany Rd.
Parsippany, NJ 07054
(201) 884-8700
J. Greg Sherry, President
Event management; athlete management
Internships: contact Rosanne Ruggiero

SkyBox International
300 N. Duke St.
Durham, NC 27702
(919) 361-8100
Frank O'Connell, President
Manufacturing and marketing of trading cards; licensed by NBA, NFL, MLB
Internships offered

Soccer USA Partners
1633 Broadway, 27th Floor
New York, NY 10019
(212) 841-1580
Michael J. Forte, Chairman
Marketing for U.S. Soccer Federation
Internships offered

Sportcorp
P.O. Box 518
River Forest, IL 60305
(708) 771-2666
Molly Quinn, President
Event marketing and management
Internships offered

Sporting Image
P.O. Box 5204
Bear Valley, CA 95223
(702) 833-2500
Mark Phillips, President
Production of sponsored skiing and cycling events

Sports Advertising Network
1120 Ave. of the Americas, 4th Floor
New York, NY 10036
(212) 626-6530
Eugene McHale, President
Sales and marketing, exclusively for New York Yankees
Summer internships offered

Sports Communications
21041 S. Western Ave., Suite 220
Torrance, CA 90501
(310) 328-1089
Joseph Heitzler, President
Event management

Sports & Company
1281 E. Main St.
Stamford, CT 06902
(203) 324-6800
David M. Chauner, Chairman
Marketing firm specializing in arranging professional bicycle races throughout the U.S.
Internships offered

Sports Etcetera
2 Penn Plaza, Suite 1590
New York, NY 10121
(212) 465-6565
Ella Musolino-Alber, President
Event management
Internships offered

Sports Law Center
601 Montgomery St., Suite 1900
San Francisco, CA 94111-2603
(415) 362-4550
Gil B. Fried, Director
Consultants on contracts, financing, sponsorship negotiations, Title IX cases

SportsLink
441 Lexington Ave., Suite 1700
New York, NY 10017
(212) 605-0185
Rob Ingraham, Mark Brickley, Managing Directors
Event development and management, including television packaging

Sports Management & Marketing
707 Grant St.
Pittsburgh, PA 15219
(412) 281-7740
David J. Humphreys, President
Track and field specialists; management of events; promotion of athletes

Sports Media Group
629 N. Barry Ave.
Mamaroneck, NY 10543
(914) 381-3000
Andrea Kirby, President
Coaching of athletes in communications skills
Internships offered

Sports Mondial
408 W. 46th St.
New York, NY 10036
(212) 246-5050
George Taylor, President
Event management; marketing consultant to international organizations and corporations

Sports Stars International
18485 Mack Ave.
Detroit, MI 48236
(313) 886-9140
Peter J. Huthwaite, President
Athlete representation
Internships offered

SRO Communications
201 E. Jefferson St.
Phoenix, AZ 85004
(602) 379-7575
Ray Artigue, General Manager
Internships: contact Human Resources

SRO Motorsports
477 E. Butterfield Rd., Suite 400
Lombard, IL 60148
(708) 963-4810
Jim Kersten, Public Relations
Manager
*Major producer of monster truck racing,
truck and tractor pulling, mud racing,
and motorcycle racing; subsidiary of
Madison Square Garden Entertainment
Group*
Internships offered

Stadium Jumping
3104 Cherry Palm Dr., Suite 220
Tampa, FL 33619
(813) 623-5801
Eugene R. Mische, President
Horse jumping events

Stadium Promotions
Steven Buckthorne Lane
Greenwich, CT 06830
(312) 266-1561
Michael Freedman, President
Event promotion and advertising services

Starsports
4565 Hilton Pkwy., Suite 205
Colorado Springs, CO 80907-3541
(719) 531-0177
Steve Rempelos, President
Specializes in promotion of rodeos

Steinberg & Moorad
500 Newport Center Dr., Suite 820
Newport Beach, CA 92660
(714) 720-8700
Leigh Steinberg, Partner
Athlete representation

Steiner Sports Marketing
49 W. 27th St., 6th Floor
New York, NY 10001
(212) 689-9641
Brandon Steiner, President
*Public relations; endorsements; celebrity
service*

Stevenson & Brown International
P.O. Box 426, Main St.
Lakeville, CT 06039
(203) 435-0811
Fred Stevenson, President
*Public relations firm specializing in
motorsports*

Strategic Group
3350 Cumberland Cir., Suite 2000
Atlanta, GA 30339
(404) 980-0544
Rick Jones, President
Event management
Internships: contact Beth A. Allen

Strategic Marketing Associates
12 E. 41st St.
New York, NY 10017
(212) 481-5555
Rick White, CEO
*Licensing and consulting for professional
leagues and major colleges. White is the
former head of Major League Baseball
Properties.*

**Streetball Partners
International, Inc.**
4006 Beltline Rd., Suite 230
Dallas, TX 75244
(214) 991-1110
Doug Jarvie, President
*Runs NBA-sanctioned 3-on-3 Hoop-It-
Up basketball tournaments throughout
North America and Europe; sets up
local sports events sponsored by NFL,
MLB, and Association of Volleyball
Professionals*
Internships offered

Stringer Marketing Group
8251 Greensboro Dr., Suite 1150
McLean, VA 22102
(703) 506-0900
Ralph Stringer, President
*Marketing services for pro athletes; special-
event promotions*
Internships offered

Tabler Communications
304 W. Liberty St., Suite 301
Louisville, KY 40202
(502) 585-2299
Wm. Biggs Tabler, President
*Production and syndication of sports
programming for TV and cable*
Internships ("for those who can work
without monitoring")

Team Marketing Report
660 W. Grand Ave., Suite 100
Chicago, IL 60610
(312) 829-7060
Alan Friedman, Editor
Production of Team Marketing Report,
*monthly newsletter on successful sports
marketing activities,* Sports Sponsor
FactBook, *comprehensive annual
directory of sponsor personnel and sports
properties*
Internships offered

Theobald & Associates
15505 Bull Run Rd., Suite 271
Miami Lakes, FL 33014
(305) 437-2920
Karen Theobald, President
Marketing; public relations; sponsor search
Internships offered

Tom Villante Sports Marketing
1285 Ave. of the Americas
New York, NY 10019
(212) 459-6100
Tom Villante, President
*Marketing consultant for major league
clubs, broadcasting networks, ad agencies*

Tuxedo Brothers
4314 Matrea More Court
Indianapolis, IN 46254
(317) 328-1632
Donald E. Carr, Philip M. Carr,
Codirectors
Event management

United Sports of America
2310 W. 75th St.
Prairie Village, KS 66208
(913) 384-8930
Russ Cline, Managing Partner
Production of motorsports shows
Internships offered

Universal Marketing Associates
1870 The Exchange, Suite 100
Atlanta, GA 30339
(770) 951-7040
Scott Pederson, President
Event management; athlete promotions
Internships: contact Keith Johnson

USAthletes
705-M Lakeview Plaza Blvd.
Worthington, OH 43085
(614) 785-0066
Steve Luke, President
*Player agents; founded in '87 by Luke,
former defensive back for Green Bay
Packers*
Internships offered

Vantage Sports Management
174 W. Comstock Ave., Suite 220
Winter Park, FL 32789
(407) 628-3131
Scott Siegel, President
*Athlete representation, event management;
New York office: (212) 980-3991*

Weiner Sports Enterprises
One Westchester Tower, 10th Floor
Mt. Vernon, NY 10550
(914) 592-9333
Irwin Wiener, President
Player agents

Winchester Group
1771 Boston Post Rd. E
Westport, CT 06880
(203) 255-4114
Brien A. Engler, Senior Vice President
Event promotions; sponsor search
Internships offered

Wirz & Associates
16 Knight St.
Norwalk, CT 06851
(203) 866-9245
Robert A. Wirz, President
*Marketing services for Major League
Baseball*
Internships offered

Wishner Communications
440 Park Ave. South
New York, NY 10016
(212) 725-0006
Howard E. Wishner, President
*Public relations and marketing services for
corporations, sports organizations,
broadcasters, apparel retailers*
Internships offered

Witlin Professional Management
2800 Biscayne Blvd., Suite 900
Miami, FL 33137
(305) 576-4999
Barry E. Witlin, President
Player agents

The Works
303 E. Wacker Dr.
Chicago, IL 60601
(312) 552-2451
John Davidoff, Vice President
Event marketing
Internships: contact Tracy Zwirin

World Class, Inc.
2277 Dabney Rd.
Richmond, VA 23230
(804) 359-8147
Richard Peyton, President
Event management; television packaging

SPORTS MARKETING AND MANAGEMENT AGENCIES AND RELATED BUSINESSES

World Class Sports
9171 Wilshire Blvd., Suite 404
Beverly Hills, CA 90210
(310) 278-2010
Don Franken, President
Representation of athletes for commercials,
endorsements, personal appearances
Internships offered

World Premier Marketing
7700 Leesburg Pike, Suite 119
Falls Church, VA 22043
(703) 442-9883
Monica S. Baker, President
Consulting for sponsors of sports events
Internships offered

World Sports &
Entertainment Enterprises
500 Fifth Ave., Suite 1234
New York, NY 10110
(212) 221-3220
Bruce H. Lucker, President
Development of sports and entertainment
properties
Internships offered

Worldwide Tournaments
19 W. 44th St.
New York, NY 10036
(212) 302-5500
Yale Stogel, Partner
Advertising and promotions

Worldwide Tournaments, Inc.
11811 N. Tatum Blvd., Suite 3031
Phoenix, AZ 85028
(602) 953-6650
Brad Berko, Partner
Sponsor acquisition; event marketing
(focusing on golf)
Internships offered

WTS International
7200 Wisconsin Ave., Suite 713
Bethesda, MD 20814
(301) 654-3770
Gary J. Henkin, President
Planning of sports marketing programs for
corporate clients; consulting on
development of golf, tennis, and fitness
facilities
Internships offered

Zane Management
The Bellevue
Broad & Walnut Sts., Suite 600
Philadelphia, PA 19102
(215) 790-1155
Lloyd Zane Remick, President
Athlete representation; sponsor search
for events
Internships offered

Zucker Sports
Management Group
5 Revere Dr., Suite 201
Northbrook, IL 60062
(708) 205-1000
Steve Wade Zucker, President
Player and broadcaster representation

CORPORATE SPORTS SPONSORS

American corporations are spending about $3.5 billion a year in sponsoring sports events. Prominent among these companies are the 260-odd listed here. Many, as noted in this listing, employ interns in their in-house sports marketing activities (while also buying the services of outside sports marketing agencies). If you want to find out the availability of an internship or a job with a company for which no contact person or department is shown here, get in touch with the company's Human Resources Department. All the companies are quite large and all have personnel hiring departments. In a few places the old term Personnel Department is still used, but directing your inquiry to Human Resources will always get you the right office no matter what it may now be called.

Adidas America
541 N.E. 20th St., Suite 207
Portland, OR 97232
(503) 797-4416
Internships offered

Aetna Life & Casualty
151 Farmington Ave.
Hartford, CT 06156
(203) 273-0123
Internships offered

Alamo Rent-a-Car
110 S.E. Sixth St.
Ft. Lauderdale, FL 33301
(305) 522-0000

Alaska Airlines
4750 W. International Airport Rd.
Anchorage, AK 99502
(907) 266-7700

Alberto-Culver Co.
2525 Armitage Ave.
Melrose, IL 60160
(708) 450-3000

Allstate Insurance Co.
2775 Sanders Rd.
Northbrook, IL 60062
(708) 402-5000
Internships offered

America West Airlines
4000 E. Sky Harbor Blvd.
Phoenix, AZ 85034
(602) 693-0800
Internships offered

American Airlines
4333 Amon Carter Blvd.
Ft. Worth, TX 76155
(817) 963-1234

American Automobile
Association (AAA)
1000 AAA Dr.
Heathrow, FL 32746-5063
(407) 444-7000
Internships: contact Larry Argiro

American Express Co.
American Express Tower
3 World Financial Ctr.
New York, NY 10285
(212) 640-2000
Internships: contact Human Resources

American Greeting Corp.
One American Rd.
Cleveland, OH 44144
(216) 252-7300
Internships offered

Amoco Oil Co.
200 E. Randolph Dr.
Chicago, IL 60601
(312) 856-6111

Amtrak
60 Massachusetts Ave. NE
Washington, DC 20002
(202) 906-3000
Internships: contact Personnel Dep't

Amway Corp.
7575 Fulton St.
Ada, MI 49355
(616) 787-6000

Andrew Jergens Co.
2535 Spring Grove Ave.
Cincinnati, OH 45214
(513) 421-1400

Anheuser-Busch Companies
One Busch Place
St. Louis, MO 63118
(314) 577-2000

Arby's
1000 Corporate Dr.
Ft. Lauderdale, FL 33334
(954) 351-5100

Armor All Products Corp.
c/o Kennedy & Kennedy, Inc.
21161 Peppertree Lane
Mission Viejo, CA 92691
(714) 859-1235

Armour Food Co.
Div. of Conagra, Inc.
2001 Butterfield Rd.
Downers Grove, IL 60515
(708) 512-1840

AT&T
32 Ave. of the Americas
New York, NY 10013
(212) 389-5400

Atlantic Richfield Co.
515 S. Flower St.
Los Angeles, CA 90071
(213) 486-2562
Internships offered

Audi of America
3800 Hamlin Rd.
Auburn Hills, MI 48326
(810) 340-5000
Internships offered

Austin Nichols & Co.
156 E. 46th St.
New York, NY 10017
(212) 455-9403

Authentic Fitness Corp.
7911 Haskell Ave.
Van Nuys, CA 91410
(818) 376-0300

Automotive Engine &
Machine, Inc.
123 Clark St.
Waterloo, IA 50703
(319) 291-6569

Avis Rent-a-Car
900 Old Country Rd.
Garden City, NY 11530
(516) 222-3000

Bank of Boston Corp.
100 Federal St.
Boston, MA 02110
(617) 434-2200

BASF/Zerex Brand
100 Cherry Hill Rd.
Parsippany, NJ 07054
(201) 316-3255

Bausch & Lomb
42 East Ave.
Rochester, NY 14604
(716) 338-6000

Bell Atlantic Corp.
1717 Arch St., Suite 26 S
Philadelphia, PA 19103
(215) 963-4545
Internships offered

Bellsouth Mobility
5600 Glenridge Dr., Suite 600
Atlanta, GA 30342
(404) 847-4803

Benjamin Moore & Co.
51 Chestnut Ridge Rd.
Montvale, NJ 07645
(201) 573-9600

Black & Decker Corp.
701 E. Joppa Rd.
Towson, MD 21204
(410) 716-3900

Blockbuster Entertainment Corp.
One Blockbuster Plaza
Ft. Lauderdale, FL 33301-1860
(305) 524-8200

**Block Drug Co./Sensodyne, BC
  Powder Brands**
257 Cornelison Ave.
Jersey City, NJ 07302
(201) 434-3000
Internships: contact Human Resources

BMW of North America
300 Chestnut Ridge Rd.
Woodcliff Lake, NJ 07675
(201) 307-4000
Internships: contact Human Resources

Bob Evans Restaurants
3776 S. High St.
Columbus, OH 43207
(614) 491-2225

Bojangles' Restaurants, Inc.
9600-H Southern Pine Blvd.
Charlotte, NC 28273
(704) 527-2675

Borg-Warner Automotive, Inc.
200 S. Michigan
Chicago, IL 60604
(312) 322-8511

Bridgestone/Firestone
One Bridgestone Park
Nashville, TN 37214
(615) 391-0088

Bristol-Myers Squibb
345 Park Ave.
New York, NY 10054
(212) 546-4000

British Airways
75-20 Astoria Blvd.
Jackson Heights, NY 11370
(718) 397-4000

Brother International Corp.
200 Cottontail Lane
Somerset, NJ 08875-6714
(908) 356-8880

Brown & Williamson
1500 Brown & Williamson Tower
Louisville, KY 40202
(502) 568-7000

Budget Rent-a-Car Corp.
4225 Naperville Rd.
Lisle, IL 60532
(708) 955-1900

Buick Motor Car Div.
902 E. Hamilton Ave.
Flint, MI 48550
(810) 236-5000

Bulova Watch Co.
One Bulova Ave.
Woodside, NY 11377
(718) 204-3300

Bumble Bee Seafoods
8899 University Ctr. Lane
San Diego, CA 92122
(619) 550-4000

Burger King Corp.
17777 Old Cutler Rd.
Miami, FL 33157
(305) 378-7011
Internships: contact Human Resources

Burroughs Wellcome Co.
3030 Cornwallis Rd.
Research Triangle Park, NC 27709
(919) 248-3624

Cadillac Motor Car Div.
30009 Van Dyke
Warren, MI 48090
(810) 492-4245

Campbell Soup Co.
Campbell Place
Camden, NJ 08103-1799
(609) 342-4800
Internships: contact Human Resources

Canon USA
One Canon Plaza
Lake Success, NY 11042
(516) 488-6700

Carvel Corp.
20 Batterson Park Rd.
Farmington, CT 06032-2502
(203) 677-6811

Casio
570 Mt. Pleasant Ave.
Dover, NJ 07801
(201) 361-5400

Castrol, Inc.
1500 Valley Rd.
Wayne, NJ 07470
(201) 633-2200

Celestial Seasonings
4600 Sleepytime Dr.
Boulder, CO 80301-3292
(303) 530-5300
Internships offered

Century 21
6 Sylvan Way
Parsippany, NJ 07054
(201) 428-9700
Internships: contact Human Resources

Champion Spark Plug Co.
900 Upton Ave.
Toledo, OH 43661
(419) 535-2567
Internships offered

Chemical Bank
140 E. 45th St., 16th Floor
New York, NY 10017
(212) 622-8505
Internships offered

Chesebrough-Pond's, USA
33 Benedict Place
Greenwich, CT 06830
(203) 661-2000

**Chevrolet Motor Car Div./
  GM Corp.**
30007 Van Dyke Ave.
Warren, MI 48090
(313) 492-1816

Chevron USA Products Co.
575 Market St.
San Francisco, CA 94105
(415) 894-2888

Chock Full o' Nuts
370 Lexington Ave., 11th Floor
New York, NY 10017
(212) 532-0300

Chrysler Corp.
12000 Chrysler Dr.
Highland Park, MI 48288
(313) 956-5741

Cigna Co.
B 247
Hartford, CT 06152
(203) 726-5906

Citgo Petroleum Corp.
One Warren Place
Tulsa, OK 74136
(918) 495-4000

Citibank, N.A.
445 E. Illinois St.
Chicago, IL 60611
(312) 627-3000
Internships: contact Human Resources

Clairol
345 Park Ave.
New York, NY 10154
(212) 546-5000
Internships: contact Human Resources

Clorox Co.
1221 Broadway
Oakland, CA 94612
(510) 271-7595
Internships offered

Coca-Cola Co.
One Coca-Cola Plaza NW
Atlanta, GA 30301
(404) 676-2121
Internships offered

Columbia Sportswear Co.
6600 N. Baltimore
Portland, OR 97203
(503) 286-3676

Conoco, Inc.
600 N. Dairy Ashford
Houston, TX 77009
(713) 293-3987

Conseco, Inc.
11825 N. Pennsylvania
Carmel, IN 46032
(317) 573-6100

CORPORATE SPORTS SPONSORS

Continental Airlines
2929 Allen Pkwy., Suite 1288
Houston, TX 77019
(713) 834-5600
Internships offered

Coors Brewing Co.
311 Tenth St.
Golden, CO 80401-1295
(303) 277-2360

Corning
Houghton Park
Corning, NY 14831
(607) 974-9000
Internships offered

Danskin
111 W. 40th St.
New York, NY 10018-2506
(212) 930-9174
Internships offered

**Dean Witter Financial
   Services Group**
2 World Trade Ctr.
New York, NY 10048
(212) 392-4525
Internships offered

Delta Airlines
Dept 790, Adm. Bldg.
Hartsfield Atlanta Int'l Airport
Atlanta, GA 30320
(404) 715-2600

Denny's
203 E. Main St.
Spartanburg, SC 29319
(864) 597-8000

Denon America
222 New Rd.
Parsippany, NJ 07054
(201) 575-7810

Dial Corp.
Dial Tower 1750
Phoenix, AZ 85077
(602) 207-2800
Internships: contact Human Resources

Discover Card
2500 Lake Cook Rd.
Riverwoods, IL 60015
(708) 405-3368
Internships offered

**Dollar Systems/Dollar
   Rent-a-Car**
6141 W. Century Blvd.
Los Angeles, CA 90045
(310) 535-7500

Domino's Pizza
30 Frank Lloyd Wright Dr.
Ann Arbor, MI 48106
(313) 930-3030

Dr Pepper Co.
8144 Walnut Hill Lane
Dallas, TX 75231
(214) 360-7000
Internships offered

Dreyer's Ice Cream
5929 College Ave.
Oakland, CA 94618
(510) 652-8187

Dunkin' Donuts
Pacella Park Dr., Suite 14
Randolph, MA 02368
(617) 961-4000

DuPont
1007 Market St.
Wilmington, DE 19898
(302) 774-1000
Internships: contact Human Resources

Duracell, Inc.
Berkshire Industrial Park
Bethel, CT 06801
(203) 796-4000
Internships: contact Human Resources

Eagle Snacks, Inc.
8115 Preston Rd., Suite 300
Dallas, TX 75225
(214) 265-5101

Eastman Kodak Co.
343 State St.
Rochester, NY 14650
(716) 724-4000

Embassy Suites
850 Ridgelake Blvd., Suite 400
Memphis, TN 38120
(901) 680-7200

Emerson Radio Corp.
One Emerson Lane
North Bergen, NJ 07047
(201) 854-6600

**Equitable Life
   AssuranceCompanies**
135 W. 50th St.
New York, NY 10020
(212) 554-1234

Eveready Battery Co.
Checkerboard Sq.
St. Louis, MO 63164
(314) 982-1955

Evian Waters of France
500 W. Putnam Ave.
Greenwich, CT 06830
(203) 629-3642

Exxon Co. USA
800 Bell St.
Houston, TX 77002
(713) 656-8456

The Family Channel
Div. of International Family
   Entertainment, Inc.
1000 Centerville Tpke.
Virginia Beach, VA 23463
(804) 523-7301

Federal Express Corp.
2003 Corporate Ave.
Memphis, TN 38132
(901) 395-3502
Internships offered

Fila USA
11350 McCormick Rd., Suite 1200
Hunt Valley, MD 21031
(410) 785-7530
Internships offered

First Brands Corp.
426 Old Salem Rd., Suite A
Winston-Salem, NC 27107
(910) 725-2999

Fleet Financial Group
50 Kennedy Plaza
Providence, RI 02903
(401) 278-5800

Foodmaker/Jack-in-the-Box
9330 Balboa Ave.
San Diego, CA 92123
(619) 571-2130

Foot Locker
233 Broadway, Suite 10K
New York, NY 10279
(212) 720-3752

Ford Motor Co.
300 Renaissance Ctr.
Detroit, MI 48243
(313) 446-4450

Frito-Lay
7701 Legacy Dr.
Plano, TX 75024
(214) 334-7000

Fuji Photo Film USA
555 Taxter Rd.
Elmsford, NY 10523
(914) 789-8100

General Mills/Wheaties Brand
One General Mills Blvd.
Minneapolis, MN 55426
(612) 540-2311

**General Motors Service Parts
   Operations**
New Center One
3031 W. Grand Blvd.
Detroit, MI 48202
(313) 974-0134

General Rent-a-Car
2741 N. 29th Ave.
Hollywood, FL 33020
(305) 926-1700

General Tire, Inc.
One General St.
Akron, OH 44329
(216) 798-3000

Genessee Brewing Co.
445 St. Paul St.
Rochester, NY 14605
(716) 546-1030

**Gillette Co./Personal Care
   Shaving Div.**
One Gillette Park
Boston, MA 02127
(617) 421-7000

Goodyear Tire & Rubber Co.
1144 E. Market St.
Akron, OH 44316-0001
(216) 796-2121
Internships offered

GTE Telephone Operations
600 Hidden Ridge Dr.
Irving, TX 75038
(214) 718-6877

Hardee's Food Systems, Inc.
1233 N. Hardee's Blvd.
Rocky Mount, NC 27804
(919) 977-8943

Hasbro, Inc.
1027 Newport Ave.
Pawtucket, RI 02861
(401) 727-5807

Heineken USA
50 Main St.
White Plains, NY 10606
(914) 681-4100

Hershey Foods Corp.
P.O. Box 810
Hershey, PA 17033
(717) 534-7631

OFFICIAL SPORTS SPONSORS

Hertz Corp.
225 Brae Blvd.
Park Ridge, NJ 07656
(201) 307-2000

Hilton Hotels Corp.
9336 Civic Ctr. Dr.
Beverly Hills, CA 90210
(310) 278-4321

Hitachi America
50 Prospect Ave.
Tarrytown, NY 10591
(914) 332-5800
Internships offered

Honda Motor Co.
1919 Torrance Blvd.
Torrance, CA 90501
(310) 783-2000

Hooters of America, Inc.
4501 Circle 75 Pkwy., Suite E 5110
Atlanta, GA 30339
(404) 951-2040

Hunt-Wesson, Inc.
1645 W. Valencia Dr.
Fullerton, CA 92633
(714) 680-1000

Hygrade Food Products Corp.
40 Oak Hollow, Suite 355
Southfield, MI 48034
(810) 355-1100
Internships: contact Human Resources

**International Business
  Machines Corp.**
1133 Westchester Ave.
White Plains, NY 10604
(914) 642-3242

International Dairy Queen
5701 Green Valley Dr.
Minneapolis, MN 55437
(612) 830-0363

Isuzu Motors, Inc., American
13181 Crossroads Pkwy N
City of Industry, CA 91746
(310) 699-0500
Internships: contact Human Resources

ITT Corp.
1330 Ave. of the Americas
New York, NY 10019
(212) 258-1000

Jaguar Cars
555 MacArthur Blvd.
Mahwah, NJ 07430-2327
(201) 818-8500

J.C. Penney Co.
6501 Legacy Dr.
Plano, TX 75024
(214) 431-1000

Jeep/Eagle
Div. of Chrysler Corp.
12000 Chrysler Dr.
Highland Park, MI 48288
(313) 956-5741

John Hancock Financial Services
John Hancock Plaza
200 Clarendon St.
Boston, MA 02117
(617) 572-6000
Internships offered

Johnson & Son, Inc.
1525 Howe St.
Racine, WI 53403
(414) 631-2000

K Mart Corp.
3100 W. Big Beaver Rd
Troy, MI 48084-3163
(810) 643-1000

Kal-Gard
4476 DuPont Court
Ventura, CA 93003
(805) 642-4533

Kawasaki Motors Corp. USA
9950 Jeronimo Rd.
Irvine, CA 92718
(714) 770-0400

Kellogg Co.
One Kellogg Sq.
Battle Creek, MI 49016
(616) 961-2000

**Kemper National Insurance
  Companies**
1 Kemper Dr.
Long Grove, IL 60049
(708) 320-2000
Internships offered

Kendall Motor Oil
77 N. Kendall Ave.
Bradford, PA 16701
(814) 368-6111

Kenwood USA Corp.
2201 E. Dominguez St.
Long Beach, CA 90810
(310) 639-9000

Kimberly-Clark Corp.
2100 Winchester Rd.
Neenah, WI 54956
(414) 721-6888

Kraft General Foods
One Kraft Court
Glenview, IL 60025
(708) 646-2000
Internships offered

Leaf, Inc.
500 N. Field Dr.
Lake Forest, IL 60045
(708) 735-7500

Leica Camera
156 Ludlow Ave.
Northvale, NJ 07647
(201) 767-7500

Lever Brothers Co.
390 Park Ave.
New York, NY 10022
(212) 688-6000

Little Caesar Enterprises
2211 Woodward Ave.
Detroit, MI 48201-3400
(313) 983-6173
Internships offered

Longines Wittnauer Watch Co.
145 Huguenot St.
New Rochelle, NY 10802
(914) 576-1000

Lorillard Tobacco Co.
One Park Ave.
New York, NY 10016
(212) 545-3000

Lufthansa German Airlines
1640 Hempstead Tpke.
E. Meadow, NY 11554
(516) 296-9465
Internships: contact Personnel Dep't

M&M/Mars
High St.
Hackettstown, NJ 07840
(908) 852-1000
Internships offered

**Marathon Enterprises/
  Sabrett Brand**
66 E. Union Ave.
East Rutherford, NJ 07073
(201) 935-3330

Mattel, Inc.
333 Continental Blvd.
El Segundo, CA 90245
(310) 524-2000

Mayflower Transit, Inc.
9998 N. Michigan Rd.
Carmel, IN 46032
(317) 875-1749

Mazda Motor of America
7755 Irvine Ctr. Dr.
Irvine, CA 92718
(714) 727-1990

McDonald's Corp.
One McDonald's Plaza
Oak Brook, IL 60521
(708) 575-3000
Internships offered

MCI Communications Corp.
1801 Pennsylvania Ave. NW
Washington, DC 20006
(202) 887-2874

Meineke Discount Muffler Shops
128 S. Tryon St., Suite 900
Charlotte, NC 28202
(704) 377-8855

Mercedes-Benz of North America
One Mercedes Dr.
Montvale, NJ 07645
(201) 573-0600
Internships: contact Human Resources

Metropolitan Life Insurance Co.
One Madison Ave.
New York, NY 10010
(212) 578-2874
Internships offered

Michelin North America
One Parkway S
Greenville, SC 29615
(803) 458-5000
Internships: contact Human Resources

Miles/Alka Seltzer Div.
1127 Myrtle St.
Elkhart, IN 46514
(219) 264-8111
Internships offered

Miller Brewing Co.
3939 W. Highland Blvd.
Milwaukee, WI 53208
(414) 931-2000
Internships offered

Mobil Corporation
3225 Gallows Rd.
Fairfax, VA 22037
(703) 846-3000

Molson Breweries
175 Bloor St. E, 2nd Floor, N. Tower
Toronto, Ontario M4W 3S4, Canada
(416) 975-1786

Motorola, Inc.
1303 E. Algonquin Rd.
Schaumburg, IL 60196
(847) 523-8080

Mutual of New York/MONY
Glenpointe Central W
Teaneck, NJ 07666
(201) 907-6488
Internships: contact Human Resources

NAPA
2999 Circle 75 Pkwy.
Atlanta, GA 30339
(404) 956-2200

NGK Spark Plugs USA, Inc.
8 Whatney
Irving, CA 92718
(714) 855-8278

National Car Rental Systems
7700 France Ave. S
Minneapolis, MN 55435
(612) 830-2121

Nestle USA
800 N. Brand Blvd.
Glendale, CA 91203
(818) 549-6000

New England
501 Boylston St.
Boston, MA 02117
(617) 578-2000
Internships offered

Nike
One Bowerman Dr.
Beaverton, OR 97005
(503) 671-6453
Internships: contact Human Resources

Nissan Motor Corp. USA
18501 S. Figueroa St.
Carson, CA 90248
(310) 532-3111

Northwest Airlines
5101 Northwest Dr.
St. Paul, MN 55111-3034
(612) 726-2331

Ocean Spray Cranberries, Inc.
One Ocean Spray Dr.
Lakeville-Middleborough, MA 02349
(508) 946-1000

Old World Automotive Products
4065 Commercial Ave.
Northbrook, IL 60062
(708) 559-2000

Oldsmobile Div./GM Corp.
920 Townsend St.
Lansing, MI 48921
(517) 377-4472

Oscar Mayer Foods Corp.
2550 Golf Rd., 5th Floor
Rolling Meadows, IL 60008
(708) 734-2877
Internships: contact Human Resources

Outboard Marine Corp.
2900 Industrial Dr.
Lebanon, MO 65536
(417) 532-9101

Owens-Corning Fiberglas Corp.
Fiberglas Tower
Toledo, OH 43659
(419) 248-8000
Internships offered

PPG Industries, Inc.
19699 Progress Dr.
Strongville, OH 44136
(216) 572-2800

PaineWebber Group
The PaineWebber Bldg.
1285 Ave. of the Americas
New York, NY 10019
(212) 713-2000
Internships: contact Human Resources

Panasonic Co.
One Panasonic Way
Secaucus, NJ 07094
(201) 348-7000
Internships: contact External Affairs

Parts, Inc.
601 S. Dudley St.
Memphis, TN 38104
(901) 523-7711

Pennzoil Co.
P.O. Box 2967
Houston, TX 77052
(713) 546-4000

Penske Corp.
13400 Outer Dr. W
Detroit, MI 48239
(313) 592-7379

Pepsi-Cola Co.
One Pepsi Way
Somers, NY 10589
(914) 767-7106

Philip Morris USA
120 Park Ave.
New York, NY 10017
(212) 878-2778
Internships: contact Human Resources

Phillips 66 Co.
400 Credit Union Bldg.
Bartlesville, OK 74004
(918) 661-5700

Piggly Wiggly Corp.
1991 Corporate Ave.
Memphis, TN 38132
(901) 395-8215

Pioneer Electronics USA, Inc.
2265 E. 220th St.
Long Beach, CA 90810
(310) 835-6177

Pizza Hut
9111 E. Douglas
Wichita, KS 67207
(316) 681-9062

Planters
1100 Reynolds Blvd.
Winston-Salem, NC 27102
(910) 741-4879

Polar Corp.
40 Walcot St.
Worcester, MA 01603
(508) 753-4300

Polaroid Corp.
549 Technology Sq.
Cambridge, MA 02139
(617) 577-2000

Pontiac Div./GM Corp.
One Pontiac Plaza
Pontiac, MI 48053
(810) 857-1548

Porsche Cars North America, Inc.
100 W. Liberty St.
Reno, NV 89501
(702) 348-3000

PPG Industries
One PPG Place
Pittsburgh, PA 15272
(412) 434-3131

Procter & Gamble Co.
One Procter & Gamble Plaza
Cincinnati, OH 45202
(513) 983-1100

**Prudential Insurance Co.
of America**
751 Broad St.
Newark, NJ 07102
(201) 802-6000
Internships offered

Purolator Products, Inc.
6120 S. Yale Ave., Suite 1000
Tulsa, OK 74136
(918) 481-2300

Quaker Oats Co./Gatorade Brand
321 N. Clark, Suite 17-9
P.O. Box 9001
Chicago, IL 60604-9001
(312) 222-6057

Quaker State Corp.
255 Elm St.
Oil City, PA 16301
(312) 222-6057

Ralston Purina Co.
Checker Board Square
St. Louis, MO 63164
(314) 982-3400

Ramada Inn
339 Jefferson Rd.
Parsippany, NJ 07054
(201) 428-9700

Reebok International, Ltd.
100 Technology Ctr. Dr.
Stoughton, MA 02072
(617) 341-5000

RJR Nabisco
P.O. Box 311
Parsippany, NJ 07054
(201) 503-3363

R. J. Reynolds Tobacco Co.
401 N. Main St.
Winston-Salem, NC 27102
(910) 741-5000

Russell Athletic
272 Lee St.
Alexander City, AL 35010
(205) 329-4000
Internships offered

Saab Cars USA
4405-A Saab Dr.
Norcross, GA 30091
(404) 717-8160

**Samsung Electronics
America, Inc.**
105 Challenger Rd.
Ridgefield, NJ 07660
(201) 229-4000

Sara Lee Corp.
3 First National Plaza
Chicago, IL 60602
(312) 558-8718
Internships offered

Save Mart Supermarkets
1800 Standiford Ave.
Modesto, CA 95352
(209) 577-1600

Seagram, House of
375 Park Ave.
New York, NY 10152
(212) 572-7000
Internships offered

OFFICIAL SPORTS SPONSORS

Sears Roebuck & Co.
3333 Beverly Rd.
Hoffman Estates, IL 60179
(708) 286-2500

Seiko Corp. of America
1111 MacArthur Blvd.
Mahwah, NJ 07430
(201) 529-5730

Sharp Electronics
P.O. Box 650
Mahwah, NJ 07430
(201) 529-8200

Shell Oil Co.
One Shell Plaza
Houston, TX 77252
(713) 241-1156

State Farm Insurance Companies
One State Farm Plaza
Bloomington, IL 61710
(309) 766-2311
Internships: contact Personnel Dep't

Subaru of America, Inc.
2235 Route 70 W
Cherry Hill, NJ 08002
(609) 488-8500
Internships: contact Human Resources

Sun Co.
Second & Green Sts.
Markus Hook, PA 19061
(215) 447-1995

3M Co.
3M Center
St. Paul, MN 55144
(612) 733-1110

Target Stores
33 S. Sixth St.
Minneapolis, MN 55440
(612) 370-6073

Teledyne, Inc.
1730 E. Prospect Rd.
Ft. Collins, CO 80553
(303) 484-1352

Texaco, Inc.
1111 Rusk
Houston, TX 77002
(713) 752-6000
Internships: contact Human Resources

Textron, Inc.
40 Westminster St.
Providence, RI 02903
(401) 421-2800

Thrifty Rent-a-Car System
5330 E. 31st St.
Tulsa, OK 74135
(918) 665-3930
Internships: contact Human Resources

Tiffany & Co.
727 Fifth Ave.
New York, NY 10022
(212) 755-8000

Timberland Co.
11 Merrill Dr.
Hampton, NH 03842
(603) 926-1600
Internships offered

Toledo Scale Corp.
350 W. Wilson Bridge Rd.
Worthington, OH 43085
(614) 438-4511

**Toshiba America Electronic
    Components, Inc.**
9775 Toledo Way
Irvine, CA 92718
(714) 455-2000

Toyota Motor Sales USA, Inc.
19001 S. Western Ave.
Torrance, CA 90509
(310) 618-4000

Travelers Companies
One Tower Sq.
Hartford, CT 06183
(203) 277-3588

Tropicana Products, Inc.
1001 13th Ave. E
Bradenton, FL 34208
(813) 747-4461

True Value Hardware
2740 Clybourn Ave.
Chicago, IL 60614
(312) 975-8918

Tyson Holly Farms
2210 W. Oaklawn Dr.
Springdale, AR 72764
(501) 290-7017

Uniroyal Goodrich Tire Co.
600 S. Main St.
Akron, OH 44397
(216) 374-3000

United Airlines
1200 E. Algonquin Rd.
Elk Grove Village, IL 60007
(708) 956-2400
Internships offered

United Parcel Service of America
400 Perimeter Ctr.
Atlanta, GA 30346
(404) 913-6124

USAir, Inc.
Crystal Park Four
2345 Crystal Dr.
Arlington, VA 22227
(703) 418-7108

USF&G
100 Light St.
Baltimore, MD 21202
(410) 547-3000
Internships offered

U.S. Tobacco Co.
Highway 21 N, Westfield Dr.
Mooresville, NC 28115
(704) 664-1091

Valvoline, Inc.
3499 Dabney Dr.
Lexington, KY 40509
(606) 264-7777
Internships offered

VISA USA
P.O. Box 8999
San Francisco, CA 94128
(415) 432-3200

Volvo Cars of North America
P.O. Box 913
Rockleigh Industrial Park, Bldg. B
Rockleigh, NJ 07647
(201) 768-7300

**Warner-Lambert Co./American
    Chicle, Dentyne Brands**
201 Tabor Rd.
Morris Plains, NJ 07950
(201) 540-2000

Wendy's International
4288 W. Dublin-Granville Rd.
Dublin, OH 43017
(614) 764-6894

Whitehall Laboratories
685 Third Ave.
New York, NY 10017
(212) 878-5500

Wilson Sporting Goods
8700 W. Bryn Mawr
Chicago, IL 60631
(312) 714-6400

Winn-Dixie Stores, Inc.
550 Edgewood Court
Jacksonville, FL 32254
(904) 783-5000

Wrangler
335 Church Court
Greensboro, NC 27401
(910) 373-3413
Internships offered

Wynn Oil Co.
1050 W. Fifth St.
Azusa, CA 91702
(818) 334-0231

Xerox Corporation
P.O. Box 1600
Stamford, CT 06904
(203) 968-3000

Yamaha Motor Corp. USA
6555 Katella Ave.
Cypress, CA 90630
(714) 761-7300

Zenith Data Systems Corp.
2150 E. Lake Cook
Buffalo Grove, IL 60089
(708) 808-5000

"There are about 3,000 professional athletes in the United States, and what looks to me like 30,000 agents." —Bob Woolf

INDEPENDENT PLAYER AGENTS

The focus here is on player representatives who are independent operators, unrelated to large marketing organizations such as IMG or ProServ, where representation of athletes is one of several business activities.

Since there is no national system for registering agents, the actual number of people engaged in this business is unknown. A reasonable guess would put at one thousand the agents who have at least one client.

Unlike the client lists at the marketing agencies, which cover every sport under the sun, the clients of independent agents are mainly players in professional baseball, basketball, football, and hockey.

A growing number of independent agents are lawyers. Several of the successful ones now represent entertainment and media personalities as well as athletes.

So You Want to Be an Agent

If you're giving serious thought to becoming a player representative, there are a few things to be considered:

1. It's an overcrowded occupation.

2. You'll be competing against experienced agents with solid reputations.

3. It's okay to woo a prospective client with visions of great wealth and public adoration, but threatening to break his legs if he doesn't sign with you is not viewed as proper professional behavior.

The fact is, the matter of unethical and, at times, criminal conduct by persons cloaked as player agents has caused a shake-up in the business in recent years. Read on.

Not a Pretty History

For many years anybody who wanted to be an agent could be one. There were no requirements, no regulations, no questions, no dues. So assorted felons, con artists, and plain incompetents drifted into the business. Some stole money from their clients; some corrupted college athletes. There were even a few, reputedly mob-connected, who threatened players with bodily harm when they refused to sign up.

Several years ago, with the blessing of team owners in the NBA, MLB, NFL, and NHL, the players associations in those leagues finally set up standards of conduct for agents. At about the same time, a number of state legislatures around the country took similar action, stirred by reports that agents were luring college athletes into secret deals that violated NCAA rules.

The combined actions have had a cleansing effect, but not totally. The players associations in the NBA, MLB, and NFL have gone about as far as they can go, but most states, after the first flurry of interest, have not gotten around to adopting laws that would establish standards for agents.

Here's what you need to know about the steps taken by the players associations and by some state governments:

Action by the Players Associations

National Basketball Players Association: Agents must be certified by the association before they can represent NBA players.

Annual dues: $1,500. Certified agents in the association: 210. (Thirteen of 28 questions on the application form are intended to flush out miscreants.)

Major League Baseball Players Association: Agents must be certified by the association before they can represent MLB players. No registration fee, no dues. Certified agents in the association: more than 200. (A list of regulations governing agents runs to 18 pages. Single-spaced.)

National Football League Players Association: In 1989 the association ended its function as a union and became an independent professional organization. Because it does not have the right any longer to act as the collective bargaining agent for NFL players, "the competence with which an agent performs his or her job in representing an NFL player has gained increased importance." It invites agents who are willing to observe its code of conduct to join the association as "contract advisors." Application fee: $400. Annual membership fee: $300, which covers the cost of an annual agent seminar all agents are required to attend. Number of agents in the association: about 800.

National Hockey League Players Association: The association does not certify agents. It has what it calls a "voluntary agent registration program." Main purpose: "to facilitate the sharing of information between players and agents in a controlled manner." Annual fee: $900. Number of agents in the program: about 100.

Addresses of players associations on page 129.

Action by the States

Motivated mainly by a desire to protect student athletes (and the sports programs) at universities in their states, 20 state legislatures have taken some action—or at least considered some action—to control unethical agents. This is how far they've gone.

Alabama: Agents operating in the state must register. No fee (but that may change). No bond required (that may change too). Background checks are only sporadic, owing to shortage of personnel, but will be more consistent when office expands, says spokesperson.

Arkansas: Mandatory registration. Background check. $100 annual fee. Surety bond of $100,000 required.

California: Mandatory registration. $200 filing fee, $500 registration fee. $25,000 surety bond. Background check—including check of fingerprints. Department has privilege of examining applicant's place of business.

Florida: Mandatory registration, but only for agents interested in signing athletes at Florida colleges and universities. $500 registration fee. $440 renewal fee at two-year intervals.

Georgia: Mandatory registration. $200 fee. $200 renewal fee at two-year intervals. $10,000 surety bond. No background check.

Iowa: Mandatory registration. $300 registration fee, $150 annual renewal fee. $25,000 surety bond. No background check.

Kentucky: No registration of agents, but penal code prohibits soliciting student athletes before their playing eligibility is over.

Louisiana: Mandatory registration. $100 fee, $100 annual renewal. No bond. No background check.

Maryland: Mandatory registration. $1,000 annual fee.

Michigan: Proposed legislation to register agents is on hold.

Minnesota: Does not register agents but has a statute on code of conduct.

Mississippi: Mandatory registration. $50 annual fee. $100,000 surety bond—but only required of agents who handle their clients' finances; does not apply to contract negotia-

DAVID B. FALK

Michael Jordan's agent sets a new standard in the business

If Michael Jordan were his only client, David Falk would still be way ahead of most player agents. But Jordan isn't Falk's only client. Some of the others: Patrick Ewing, Alonzo Mourning, Juwan Howard, Dikembe Mutombo, Allen Iverson. That's big time.

A 1972 honors graduate of Syracuse University, where he received a degree in economics, Falk went on for a law degree at George Washington University in 1975. That year he joined ProServ, a big sports marketing firm that was more attuned to tennis pros than players in team sports. Falk was put in charge of the basketball division, which in time included a young Michael Jordan. In 1992 an impatient Falk arranged a buyout of the basketball division and set up his own shop, Falk Associates Management Enterprises. All his clients at ProServ, including Jordan, joined him. In charge, finally, as chairperson and chief executive officer of his own agency, Falk showed the full force of his personality and creativity. The high point came in a six-day period in July 1996, when he negotiated an unbelievable $400 million in contracts for NBA free-agent clients. The week's business included four of the five largest contracts in the history of team sports. Among those deals was a one-year, $30 million contract for Jordan, the biggest ever. In endorsement negotiations, Falk handled Nike, Reebok, and other power players with a toughness and effectiveness that brought everyone additional riches. With control over a large block of NBA players, he is considered the second most powerful person in the league, after Commissioner David Stern.

tions or other services. No background check.

Nevada: No registration, but agents must observe statute on conduct.

North Carolina: Mandatory registration. $200 annual fee. $100,000 bond required of agents who perform financial services. Background check.

Oklahoma: Mandatory registration. $1,000 annual fee. $100,000 bond.

Pennsylvania: Legislation pending.

South Carolina: Mandatory registration.

$300 fee every two years.

Tennessee: Requires agents to register and apply for permit from the secretary of state.

Texas: Mandatory registration. $1,000 annual fee. $100,000 bond if financial services are provided for clients.

Washington: Mandatory registration. $300 fee for individual agent or $500 if firm is registered.

Addresses of state agencies on page 129.

Well-Kept Secrets

The employment contract a professional athlete signs becomes a subject of public knowledge almost before the ink is dry, but the size of the agent's emolument is deemed too personal for public scrutiny.

In short, agents do not like to reveal the cut they get on a client's contract, which might be as high as 6 percent or as low as 1 percent (believe it).

Reasons for their reticence: It might suggest that they've taken advantage of a client's innocence or, conversely, that a 300-pound client with his own idea of what agents are worth forced them to their knees.

An agent's deal with a client might include special compensation for a variety of services performed for the client, like arrangements for product endorsements, which can produce a bundle for an agent.

Pay Agents by the Hour?

Dedicated to uplifting the business of player representation is SportSeminars, a nonprofit consulting group in Madison, Wisconsin, which is assisted in its mission by the University of Wisconsin Law School.

The organization runs seminars for lawyers on how to represent athletes competently and ethically. It also conducts on-campus seminars for college coaches and athletes, on the pitfalls of dealing with dishonest agents.

SportSeminars was founded in 1987 by Ed Garvey, a sports lawyer and former executive director of the NFL Players Association, and Frank Remington, a law professor at UW and former chair of the NCAA Infractions Committee.

One of their key objectives is to change the way agents are paid in negotiating player contracts.

They contend that the practice of giving agents a percentage of a player's salary, whether it's 3 percent or 6 percent, doesn't make sense. Commissions can produce a bonanza for an agent even though—as is often the case—a contract is predetermined by an athlete's draft position. In other words, an agent can get an enormous fee just for showing up at the signing.

In a more rational system, they say, agents would be entitled only to a percentage of the money they gain for their clients *above* initial club offers.

SportSeminars counsels athletes to select qualified attorneys who charge reasonable hourly fees and, unless they succeed in improving the salary offers, pay them only for hours spent working.

SportSeminars is located at 122 E. Dayton St., Madison, WI 53703. Phone: (608) 256-0025.

Happy With One Client

Agents like to say that they and their clients couldn't be closer. It's often an exaggeration. In the case of pitcher Jimmy Key and his agent, it's no exaggeration. Key's agent is his wife.

Cindy Key, who has a degree in business administration from Clemson University (where she met her husband), took over as agent in 1985, replacing an agent the Keys felt was too busy with other clients. Jimmy Key was then in his second year in the majors, a Toronto Blue Jays reliever with an uncertain future.

Eight years later, Cindy Key helped her husband get a four-year, $17 million contract from the Yankees.

One of the rare female representatives of professional athletes, she has never considered expanding her client list. It's a short list, she acknowledges, but a classy one.

A reporter once asked Jimmy Key how much of a commission his wife got on the Yankees contract. About 100 percent, he said.

Sports Law

Every sports team needs a lawyer—not

H O W   T H E Y   G O T   T H E R E

ELLEN M. ZAVIAN
Agent and Legal Representative

When U.S. women's teams took home gold medals in soccer and softball at the 1996 Olympics, they owed part of their success to Ellen Zavian. A lawyer and sports agent, Zavian stepped in before the Olympics to represent the U.S. Women's Soccer Team in a controversy with the sport's governing body, the U.S. Soccer Federation. She also helped the U.S. Women's Softball Team settle a conflict with the Amateur Softball Association. Without her involvement, the teams might never have taken the field.

Zavian's career in sports began when she was a student at the University of Maryland, where she worked in the university's intramural sports and recreation department. A plum summer internship at the National Football League Players Association led to a job as research assistant and a chance to learn about the NFL from the inside out. After earning a law degree at American University, Zavian worked in a sports law firm, but within a couple of years she opened up her own practice. Using her connections in pro football, Zavian became the first female agent to work with NFL players; she has represented 22 players since 1989. Today, though, she dedicates much of her time to women athletes, handling contracts and promotional deals for the U.S. women's soccer and softball teams, among others.

Ambitious and energetic, Zavian also works as a broadcaster at local and national all-sports radio stations and teaches courses in sports and entertainment law at the law schools of American University, George Washington University, and the University of Baltimore.

only to draw up player contracts, which can be very complicated, but also to handle such matters as taxes, insurance, and stadium leases. Also arising on occasion are questions of liability for damage or injury, which occur unforeseen and require the agility of the legal mind. (For example, is a club liable for the actions of a player who chooses to express his contempt for its customers by lobbing a firecracker into a group of fans in a stadium parking lot?)

HOW THEY GOT THERE

DENNIS GILBERT

After retiring as a baseball player, he began setting baseball records

After six years as an outfielder with minor league clubs, Dennis Gilbert threw his glove in a closet, took a job selling insurance—and made an interesting discovery: he was a helluva salesperson.

With a speed that earned him the baseball nickname "Go-Go," Gilbert developed a clientele of Hollywood celebrities (among them Sally Field and Liza Minnelli), selling as much as $200 million worth of insurance in a single year. But financial success couldn't shake baseball out of his bones.

So he joined with ex-Red Sox outfielder Tony Conigliaro to set up a sports agency, which became his when Conigliaro later died after a heart attack. Making good use of his minor league contacts, he soon had a sizable stable of young talent. And this time around, he got Major League Baseball's attention.

Three times in 30 months, from June 1990 through December 1992, Gilbert and the firm he cofounded, Beverly Hills Sports Council, negotiated contracts that broke baseball's salary record. First there was the $23.5 million for Jose Canseco, followed by a $29 million contract for Bobby Bonilla. Then came the astonishing $43.75 million deal the San Francisco Giants gave Barry Bonds (who said thanks by winning the MVP award).

Beverly Hills Sports Council handles only baseball players, which makes it a rarity among major sports reps. In addition to negotiating contracts, the agency arranges product endorsements, advises players on financial strategies, and prepares them for life after baseball. Some go into broadcasting. Some, not surprisingly, are steered into the insurance industry.

With the growth of the sports industry, the law profession has shown an increasing interest in sports law as a specialization, and a number of law schools have begun offering courses in that subject.

The Marquette University Law School, in Milwaukee, has established a National Sports Law Institute, which serves as a center of information on sports law. The institute was created with the financial support of the Green Bay Packers, Milwaukee Admirals, Milwaukee Brewers, Milwaukee Bucks, and the Miller Brewing Company.

Formed some years ago was the Sports Lawyers Association, a national organization that provides a forum for lawyers who represent athletes and lawyers for teams, leagues, athletic conferences, and other organizations in professional and amateur sports. The SLA sponsors an annual three-day Sports Law Conference and publishes a newsletter, *The Sports Lawyer*.

The association's address is 2017 Lathrop Ave., Racine, WI 53405. Phone: (414) 632-4040. President is A. Jackson Mills.

SIDELINES

You really want to be an agent?

Jonathan Gray would not recommend that idea. Gray is a 30-year-old Miami lawyer who became an agent in 1989. And all he had to show for it, he said the last time we talked, was a bruised ego and a bank balance he described as "extremely tentative."

The conversation with Gray revealed a man hip-deep in frustration.

"Look," he said, "ever since high school I had my heart set on being an agent. I loved sports and I wanted to be on the inside, where the action was. I took a master's degree in sports management because I thought that would prepare me for the business. Then I went to law school because it seemed as though every big-time agent was a lawyer. After I printed up my business cards, I learned some things no professor had ever mentioned.

"First, there are too many people in the business.

"Second, you can sign a promising young baseball player in the minors, but you lose him the minute he moves up to a Double-A or Triple-A team. Players have no loyalty. They look for a small agent when they're starting out, then sign with a big agent when they advance and begin making some money. It's a painful thing when that happens."

Trying to recruit college football and basketball players, he said, "can drive you out of your mind." He attributed part of the difficulty to unscrupulous agents who work in the shadows, offering "loans" of cash or cars to athletes with playing eligibility remaining. "Make no mistake," he said, "some of these creeps are still around."

When the NCAA announced a new policy that permits college head coaches to deal with agents on behalf of student athletes, Gray saw some hope. It was quickly dispelled. He told of a typical phone call to a coach.

Coach: "What did you say your name was? Yeah, okay, why don't you send me a letter."

Gray: "I already did."

Coach: "Well, I get a ton of letters from agents. Haven't got time to look at them all."

Gray: "I'd like to come and talk to you."

Coach: "Sorry, buddy, got no time for that."

Another brush-off.

What does the future hold for Gray? "I don't know," he said. "I'll cruise the minors again and sign up some more kids. And hope I can keep them."

Just before we went to press, a few months after the conversation above took place, we put in a call to Jonathan Gray to see how he was doing. We couldn't reach him. His phone had been disconnected.

HOW THEY GOT THERE

LEIGH STEINBERG
His career began with an unexpected phone call from a college buddy

At the age of 26, and just out of law school, Leigh Steinberg had yet to decide what to do with his life when he got an urgent phone call from his friend Steve Bartkowski, an all-American quarterback at the University of California at Berkeley.

Bartkowski had a problem. He'd been drafted by the Atlanta Falcons, but negotiations had broken down completely and he had just fired his lawyer. Would Leigh come and pick up the pieces?

"I didn't know much about negotiating," Steinberg admits now, but he researched the situation quickly and in his typically soft-spoken manner pulled off a small miracle—a four-year, $650,000 agreement. In 1975 it was the largest contract ever signed by an NFL rookie.

Probably the best-known agent in the United States, and widely respected by team owners for the brilliance of his presentations at the negotiating table, Steinberg doesn't need to recruit clients, he picks them. And the pickings have been pretty good. When Dan Wilkinson was first to be chosen in the 1994 NFL draft, it was the fifth time in six years that the number one draft selection was a Steinberg client.

A standout year for lucrative contracts was 1993. Top draft pick Drew Bledsoe signed a $14.5 million rookie contract; Steve Young got a $26.5 million contract, the biggest in NFL history; Thurman Thomas became the best-paid running back at the time with a deal worth $13.5 million. The year ended with Steinberg negotiating a seven-year, $50 million contract for Troy Aikman. These and other 1993 deals added up to $180 million worth of contracts.

A sampling of other players under contract with the firm of Steinberg and Moorad: NFL stars Warren Moon, Jeff George, Russell Maryland, Derrick Thomas; baseball's Will Clark, Gregg Olson, Eric Karros; and the New York Knicks' Greg Anthony and John Starks.

One of the things that distinguishes Steinberg from other agents is that he will represent only those athletes who are willing to share some of their earnings with their high schools and universities and with humanitarian organizations. The result is that his clients have parted with more than $50 million for scholarships and good causes. Steinberg, no pauper himself—his firm has about 150 clients—leads the way in charitable contributions and social involvement.

Steinberg and his partner, Jeffrey Moorad, have offices in Berkeley and Newport Beach, California.

A Conversation with Bob Woolf

Bob Woolf, one of the most respected agents in sports, died suddenly in December 1993. Commenting on his career, The New York Times *said he was well known "partly because he was one of the first sports agents, and partly because he brought to his profession both skill and a special sense of ethical responsibility." Shortly before Woolf died, he gave us this interview.*

Q. How long have you been in business?
A. I've been an attorney for 41 years, and I've been representing athletes for 30 years.

Q. How did you get started as an agent?
A. By total chance. In 1964 I was an attorney for a Red Sox pitcher named Earl Wilson, who had a no-hitter. He asked me to handle the requests he was getting for personal appearances. It worked out so well that other players became interested. By 1967 I was representing 14 Red Sox players. In those days, you understand, very few athletes used outside representation.

Q. How would you compare standards today with those of five years ago?
A. The standards are much better now, because the business is far more demanding. With salary caps and other financial complications, you really have to know what you're doing. It takes more than street smarts. Also, the various players associations are helping to improve standards through the certification of agents. It's becoming more of a lawyers' business. The American Bar Association has a sports law forum, many law schools now offer sports law courses, and there's a sports lawyer organization.

Q. How big is your company?
A. We have 65 employees in four offices— New York, Boston, San Francisco, and Madrid. We handle contract negotiations, appearances, books, financial management, wills, trusts, insurance. I have negotiated thousands of contracts over the years. We now have several hundred clients. We've worked for Larry Bird, Dr. J., John Havlicek, Joe Montana, Carl Yastrzemski—and we've just added Rocket Ismail and Florence Griffith Joyner. Like a lot of other firms in our business, we also have clients in the media and entertainment. For example, we represent Larry King and New Kids on the Block.

Q. What courses would you recommend for prospective agents?
A. Contract law, tax law, accounting, and, if it's offered, ethics.

Q. What advice do you have for young people interested in representing athletes?
A. There are approximately 3,000 professional athletes in the United States today, and what looks to me like 30,000 agents. So the market is very crowded. Anyway, the first step would be to contact the players associations for certification and possible leads. But I think there are better opportunities with the sports marketing firms, especially those involved in professional tennis and golf.

PROFESSIONAL PLAYERS ASSOCIATIONS

**National Basketball
Players Association**
1775 Broadway, Suite 2401
New York, NY 10019
Simon Gourdine, Exec Dir
(212) 333-7510

**Major League Baseball
Players Association**
12 E. 49th St.
New York, NY 10017
Donald M. Fehr, Exec Dir
(212) 826-0808

**National Football League
Players Association**
2021 L St. NW
Washington, DC 20036
Gene Upshaw, Exec Dir
(202) 463-2200

**National Hockey League
Players' Association**
One Dundas St. W, Suite 2406
Toronto, Ontario M5G 1Z3
Canada
Robert W. Goodenow, Exec Dir
(416) 408-4040

STATE OFFICES THAT REGULATE PLAYER AGENTS

ALABAMA
Alabama Athlete Agent Regulatory
  Commission
Alabama State House
11 S. Union
Montgomery, AL 36130
Pearl Maxwell
(205) 242-7844

ARKANSAS
W. J. Bill McCuen, Secretary of State
Room 026
Arkansas State Capital
Little Rock, AR 72201
Beverly Benjamin
(501) 682-5070

CALIFORNIA
California State Labor Commissioner's
  Office
Attn: Licensing
P.O. Box 603
San Francisco, CA 94102
Ignacio Rico
(415) 703-5530

FLORIDA
Department of Professional Regulation
Athlete Agent Registration Department
Northwood Centre
1940 N. Monroe St.
Tallahassee, FL 32399-0750
Betty Chester
(904) 488-9832

GEORGIA
Georgia Athletic Agent Regulatory
  Commission
166 Pryor St. SW
Atlanta, GA 30303
(404) 656-6719

IOWA
Iowa Secretary of State
Attn: Corporation Division
Hoover Bldg, 2nd Floor
Des Moines, IA 50319

LOUISIANA
Secretary of State's Office
Attn: Corporations Division
P.O. Box 94125
Baton Rouge, LA 70804-9125
(504) 925-4704

MARYLAND
State Athletic Commission
501 St. Paul Pl., 14th Floor
Baltimore, MD 21202-2272
(401) 333-6322

MISSISSIPPI
Secretary of State's Office
P.O. Box 136
Jackson, MS 39205
Ray Bailey
(601) 359-1633

NORTH CAROLINA
Secretary of State's Office
Securities Division
300 N. Salisbury St.
Raleigh, NC 27603-5909
(919) 733-3924

OKLAHOMA
Secretary of State's Office
Records Department
101 State Capitol
Oklahoma City, OK 73105
Ms. Julie Parrish
(405) 521-3911

SOUTH CAROLINA
Department of Consumer Affairs
P.O. Box 5757
Columbia, SC 29250
(803) 734-9452

TEXAS
Secretary of State's Office
Statutory Documents
P.O. Box 12887
Austin, TX 78711-2887
(512) 463-5558

WASHINGTON
Department of Licensing
Professional Licensing Services
Athlete Agents
P.O. Box 9649
Olympia, WA 98507-9649
(206) 753-2803

CHAPTER FIVE

COLLEGE SPORTS MANAGEMENT

The pressure to turn out

winning teams can take

the bloom off campus living.

CAMPUS OPERATIONS
INTERCOLLEGIATE ASSOCIATIONS
AND CONFERENCES

CAMPUS OPERATIONS

The Best of Jobs. Maybe.

Could anything be better than a job as director of athletics at a Division I-A school? Consider the benefits: good pay, prestige, a stimulating environment, lots of authority—everything you could hope for. Including a front row seat at every sports event.

But there's a drawback. The job doesn't seem to offer much security these days. Actually, the turnover rate is murder.

In an article in a fall 1996 issue of the *NCAA News*, Vincent J. Dooley, athletics director at the University of Georgia and an officer of the National Association of Collegiate Directors of Athletics, delivered a stunning observation on the tenure of ADs in the NCAA's elite category.

Of the 107 Division I-A ADs in 1990, he said, only 24 were still in their jobs in 1996, a turnover rate of 80 percent.

How come this precious job, once so comfortable and secure, is now so unsure? The answer is in the new and heavy load of responsibilities that now come with the title.

In years past, it was not uncommon to hand the job to a retired coach who was reluctant to leave the scene of his glory days. It's not a good idea anymore. The job now requires talents not related to coaching.

What's needed, especially, is a talent for business management. The athletics director is the CEO of a complex operation supported by a budget as high as $20 million or more (example: the athletics department's budget at the University of Alabama is $22 million). Management also means supervising a staff of assistants with widely different functions and hiring coaches for a score or more varsity sports.

Some of the responsibilities that come within the AD's purview: the athletics department budget; maintenance (and often con-

struction) of facilities; risk management (protecting the safety of athletes and spectators); television and other revenue-producing activities; compliance with federal, NCAA, and conference regulations; the academic development of student athletes; media relations; scheduling of all varsity sports; events marketing; corporate sponsorships of events; ticket sales; relations with the campus community and alumni, and with civic and business organizations; the development of women's sports; and fund-raising in all its forms.

And that's not all. The AD is also expected to supervise the campus's intramural, recreational, and club sports activities.

At most schools, the AD reports directly to the institution's president, especially in matters dealing with the hiring and firing of coaches, still another responsibility of the AD.

It must be said, however, that at some institutions an AD's relationship with a head coach can be a matter of rather extreme sensitivity. Can a director of athletics exercise authority over, say, Steve Spurrier, football coach at the University of Florida, whose income is a million dollars a year, more than four times the salary of the university president and a far greater multiple over the AD's? Not likely. But that's one of the things that makes the AD's job so interesting.

A fairly common intrusion on the pleasures of campus life is the pressure to turn out winning teams, a circumstance that can lead coaches and assistant coaches and team boosters into grievous lapses of honor.

The fact is, abuses of accepted codes of conduct occur with frequency in every part of the country. Here are some sample violations, taken from a long list published routinely by the NCAA. Each applies to a well-known college.

"Improper recruiting contacts and inducements in men's basketball; payment of excess wages to an athlete; cash given to an athlete by a booster."

"Cash payments to a football player by an

assistant coach, an athletics department official, and a booster; ineligible athletes permitted to compete; excess scholarships."

"Improper benefits to athletes, including free airline tickets; tuition money to an athlete ineligible for a scholarship."

"Payment for a prospective athlete to attend junior college."

"Coach helped falsify an athlete's test scores."

"Cash given to the girlfriend of a men's basketball player."

"An athlete who was not admitted to the school received meals and lodging and competed with the men's tennis team."

"Athletes on men's cross-country team competed under assumed names."

"Football players paid by boosters for work not performed."

"Extra benefits to men's basketball players and their families, including free apartments."

"Academically ineligible athletes allowed to compete in eight men's and women's teams."

"Interest-free loans to athletes; failure to have coaches properly report outside income, improper compensation to coaches."

"Ineligible athletes in men's and women's track; falsified participation lists."

"Improper benefits to athletes; too much influence by head coach over awarding of need-based financial aid."

. . . And so it goes.

Responsibility for keeping a college's sports operation tidy falls heavily on the athletics director. The responsibility goes beyond the violation of NCAA rules. It includes dealing with two other campus blights: (1) Criminal behavior by the school's athletes. Acts of criminality by athletes—rape, assault, burglary, drunk driving, gambling, domestic violence—are a national disgrace, touching campuses from coast to coast. (2) The rebarbative activities of player agents who prey on gullible (or greedy) athletes, exposing them to punitive measures by the NCAA.

In all, running the sports program of a Division I-A institution is a job and a half.

What Universities Look for in an AD

Here are some specific criteria posed by several universities that went shopping for new ADs:

The search committee at the University of Michigan said candidates were expected to have "superior interpersonal and verbal communication skills" and "an unswerving commitment to academic integrity and the further development of the women's athletic programs."

At Kansas State University, the search committee looked for candidates capable of hiring, supervising, and evaluating 75 coaches, and guiding the department's marketing and fund-raising activities.

Temple University stressed the importance of an AD's fund-raising activity. Yale University sought a candidate with "proven leadership and administrative experience." Central Michigan said its AD "must be dedicated to the academic success of student athletes." Alfred University covered most of the bases. "Responsibilities," it said, "include long-range planning; selecting and supervising coaches and department personnel; managing financial resources; administering facilities; developing and maintaining productive relationships with alumni, boosters, campus constituents, and community; and ensuring compliance with the rules of the university and NCAA."

A candidate with a frozen personality would not be suitable for the University of Alaska at Fairbanks. The search committee for the nation's northernmost university said it was looking for a director of athletics with "a good sense of humor."

About the Pay

The main factors that influence an AD's salary are (1) the size and stature of the athletics program, (2) the AD's enthusiasm for fund-raising, and (3) how well the school's football and basketball teams are faring.

In Divisions II and III, salaries range from

Vivian L. Fuller has headed the athletics program (Division I) at Northeastern Illinois University since 1992. Earlier, she was assistant AD at North Carolina A&T State and associate AD at Indiana University of Pennsylvania. She has a doctorate in education administration from Iowa State.

$35,000 to $60,000. In Division I the pay can rise to six figures. At least one athletics director (in the Southwest) makes $125,000.

In big-time programs, an AD's salary is often accompanied by a generous expense account, and if the school's football team gets to play in a postseason bowl game, or if the basketball team makes the NCAA tournament's Final Four, the AD can expect a bonus.

The AD's Assistants

About 900 of the nation's four-year colleges (the number fluctuates year to year) are members of the NCAA.

In the interest of fair competition, the NCAA divides its members into three classifications: Division I, the highest level of competition; Division II, where the number of athletics scholarships is scaled down; and Division III, where student athletes are walk-ons. (Division I is divided further into Division I-A, I-AA, and I-AAA.)

The full glamour and excitement of college sports, the biggest staffs, and the best-paying jobs are, of course, in Division I, which consists of about 300 schools. The material that follows deals with the responsibilities, qualifications, and earnings of the principal assistants to the directors of athletics in Division I.

The operation of a major sports program involves a complement of associate ADs, assistant ADs, and support personnel big enough to fill a lecture hall. But no two organizational charts of major programs are exactly alike, and definitions of roles vary, so what follows is a general picture of what an AD's executive assistants and their assistants cover.

Senior Woman Athletics Administrator (SWA)

The title, created by the NCAA in the continuing quest for gender equity, designates the top woman administrator after the director of athletics (who in some instances is female). The SWA's function is to oversee the department's adherence to Title IX, the law

Congress passed back in 1972 to bar sex discrimination. The SWA's regular, full-time position might be women's basketball coach, or director of sports facilities, or any one of a number of other jobs not necessarily related to women's sports.

Senior Associate AD

The title designates the second in command, who assists in policy making and directing the diverse operations of the program. Responsibilities may include supervision of nonrevenue sports and coaching staffs, scheduling the use of facilities by outside organizations, monitoring compliance requirements, and overseeing marketing and public relations activities. The job generally goes to someone in the organization. Salary: $40,000 and up.

Business Manager

The business manager supervises the overall fiscal operation of the athletics department, including budget preparation, personnel functions, purchasing, payroll, cash deposits, mail and telephone systems, and preparation of certain contracts. The business manager also oversees the ticket office. A degree in accounting or business is often required, but John Giannoni, president of the College Athletic Business Management Association, says many business managers are graduates of sports administration programs. Salary range: $30,000 to $65,000.

Coordinator of Women's Athletics

Responsibilities include scheduling women's intercollegiate events, supervising coaches, and developing and administering budgets. A candidate must have a bachelor's degree, preferably in sports management. A master's is better. Salary: $25,000 and up.

Director of Marketing

In Division I, where marketing is a high-priority activity, job candidates need substantial experience in marketing and sales, media

John Swofford, widely recognized as a top sports administrator, has been AD at the University of North Carolina since 1980. He is a former president of the National Association of College Directors of Athletics. He received a bachelor's degree from UNC in '71 and a master's from Ohio University in '73.

relations, and public relations. The job includes establishing radio/TV shows for coaches, licensing the team logo for use on commercial products, attracting corporate sponsorship of events, selling advertising for game programs, and dealing with TV sports packagers and cable systems. Salary range: $40,000 to $65,000.

Director of Development

The position has many names: "associate director of athletics for external operations," or "external affairs," or "athletic advancement," or "sports promotion." If you haven't guessed, the job is directing fund-raising activities designed to elicit the support of alumni and other prospective benefactors, usually to meet what seems to be an ever-pressing need to improve or expand sports facilities. In Division I, candidates for a job as head of a fund-raising program have to prove they've mastered the art by previous experience. Salary range: $45,000 to $80,000, occasionally higher.

Director of Sports Facilities

It's an executive-level job that requires real experience. Responsibilities include scheduling, personnel supervision, budget development and administration, supervision of maintenance and support services, and all aspects of event management. Professionalism is essential if the university makes its stadium and arena available for rentals by outside organizations (an important source of income). Renting facilities brings additional responsibilities that include contract negotiations, special staffing, traffic and security management, insurance coverage, accommodations for displays (trade shows), special lighting (concerts), not to mention advertising and promotions to attract renters. Salary range: $40,000 to $65,000 (and more, depending on how much business is done in rentals).

Sports Information Director

The SID handles media coverage of events;

develops feature stories and arranges interviews; produces media guides, promotional brochures, and events programs; maintains up-to-date stats for media and NCAA. Requirements: a journalism background and knowledge of sports; writing and publication skills; the freedom to travel and work all hours. Salary range: $25,000 to $45,000.

Ticket Manager

The ticket manager works with the AD and other athletics department executives in establishing ticket policies and ticket promotions. Responsibilities include management of computerized ticket systems, accounting and auditing controls, group sales, and training of assistants. Often required of job applicants is five years of experience with Paciolan Systems athletics software and proven abilities in customer relations. Salary range: $35,000 to $50,000. Assistants: $15,000 to $30,000.

Equipment Manager

Responsibilities often include equipment management for physical education and campus recreation activities as well as intercollegiate athletics. Primary duties: purchase, inventory, and maintenance of all equipment; supervision of assistants; and participation in determining budgets. Often required is a bachelor's degree in phys ed or sports management and at least three years of experience in equipment room procedures on the college level. Salary range: in Divisions II and III, $16,000 to $18,000; in Division I, $25,000 to $33,000.

Academic Counselor

Due to NCAA pressure, this position now is ranked as associate athletics director at many Division I institutions. The job involves the implementation of programs with a threefold objective: to help student athletes adjust to the college environment, to see that they make satisfactory progress toward graduation, and to assist them in planning their future careers.

Michael A. Wadsworth, who became director of athletics at the University of Notre Dame, his alma mater, in 1994, was a defensive tackle on Ara Parseghian's 1964 team. A native of Toronto, Wadsworth was in Canada's diplomatic corps and served as ambassador to Ireland before returning to UND.

Duties include academic counseling, coordinating the work of an army of student mentors or tutors, and maintaining contact with head coaches, faculty, and athletics department administrators. Generally required for appointment is a master's degree in counseling or education (a doctorate is preferred) and at least two years of counseling student athletes in smaller college programs. Salary range: $18,000 to $25,000 for full-time assistants, up to $50,000 for the program director.

Compliance Coordinator

It's the newest job category in major college sports programs, part of the reform movement making its way across the college landscape. The function of compliance coordinators is to keep their colleges out of trouble with the NCAA and their conferences by meeting the multitude of rules that now govern college sports, from recruiting restrictions to time limits for practice sessions. The responsibility of a compliance coordinator is to know all the rules (no easy task), investigate possible infractions, turn in reports required by the NCAA, and run workshops to teach the rules to athletes, coaches, and college officials. Candidates for the job are required to have at least a bachelor's degree and some experience in college sports administration. Salary range: $21,000 to $27,000.

Trainers

The salary range for head trainers is $22,000 to $80,000. For assistant trainers, the range is $15,000 to $40,000. For information about the training of trainers and job opportunities in college sports and pro sports, see page 205.

The colleges provide excellent opportunities for internships, often with pay. A fairly typical notice from an Ivy League school, appearing in the classified section of the *NCAA News*, announced the availability of a five-and-a-half-month internship that offered training in various phases of sports administration along with a stipend of $4,000.

Judith M. Sweet, director of athletics at the University of California at San Diego since 1975, was one of the first women to run a combined men's and women's intercollegiate program. In 1991 she was elected to a two-year term as president of the NCAA.

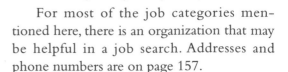

*   *   *   *

For most of the job categories mentioned here, there is an organization that may be helpful in a job search. Addresses and phone numbers are on page 157.

The Cry 'Gender Equity!' Is Heard in the Land

High on the list of things to do these days is building up women's sports. And there's some urgency about it, because more and more colleges are getting hit with lawsuits by women athletes and coaches demanding a fair share of money spent on sports.

The quest for equity has its roots in a federal law that bars sex discrimination by colleges and universities that receive any kind of government aid (which covers just about all institutions). The law, commonly referred to as Title IX, was passed by Congress in 1972, and at many campuses women's sports advocates are beginning to lose patience with the rate of progress.

Congress turned the screw in 1994 by passing the Equity in Athletics Disclosure Act, which requires ADs to assemble and make public all kinds of statistics on their men's and women's sports programs. Details include team sizes, operating and recruiting expenses, sex and annual salary of each coach, spending on athletics scholarships, the ratio of male to female recipients—plus the male-female breakdown of undergraduate enrollment.

Prominent among the institutions that have made substantial gains in women's sports is Stetson University in De Land, Florida. The AD at Stetson is Robert Jacoby. He has five daughters.

Publications

Take note, please. Openings for jobs and internships in college athletics departments are advertised in these two weekly newspapers:

The NCAA News

Address: National Collegiate Athletic Association, 6201 College Blvd., Overland Park,

KS 66211-2422. Phone (913) 339-1906 for subscription information.

The Chronicle of Higher Education

Address: 1255 23rd St. NW, Washington, DC 20037. Phone (202) 466-1000 for subscription information. (There's a good chance the publication is available in your public library.)

*   *   *   *

The following are annual publications that provide extensive information on colleges and organizations involved in intercollegiate sports:

The National Directory of College Athletics

Address: Collegiate Directories, Inc., P.O. Box 450640, Cleveland, OH 44145. For the price, phone toll-free (800) 426-2232. This is the official directory of the National Association of Collegiate Directors of Athletics.

Blue Book of College Athletics

Address: 2540 E. Fifth St., Montgomery, AL 36107. For the price, phone (205) 263-4436.

SIDELINES

Fashion Note

Any way you wear it—frontward, backward, or sideways—there's nothing more chic than a peaked cap bearing the name of the team that has just won the NCAA hoops title.

Merchandise with a collegiate touch is old hat, of course, but never have the nation's malls sold so much of it. Caps, T-shirts, jackets, blankets, mugs, and a hundred other products adorned with the names of colleges or team logos are a $2.5-billion business at retail, and insiders think it will go to $4 billion by the year 2000.

Never mind that some of the best customers are high school dropouts, the sale of this merchandise produces a bundle for higher education.

Manufacturers of the merchandise pay colleges an average royalty of 7 percent for the right to use their names, logos, mascots, and colors. The practice of selling rights is called trademark licensing, an activity that many colleges put in the hands of their sports marketing directors.

The institution that probably profits the most from licensing activities is the University of Michigan, which reports annual revenues of $6 million. In 1981, when Michigan began its licensing program, its royalties amounted to only $1,832. At least 20 other institutions make more than $1 million a year from trademark licensing.

School Ties

A goodly number of college sports administrators are employed by the colleges they attended as undergraduates. That includes athletics directors, who may have returned to the alma mater after working elsewhere, and not necessarily in sports administration.

*   *   *   *

M. Joe Roberson, athletics director at the University of Michigan, is a thrice-validated alumnus of that institution, having received the bachelor's, master's, and doctoral degrees there (in education administration). Dr. Roberson got the appointment as AD after serving the university as a development officer. Before settling down as a member of the maize & blue community, he pitched for five years in the minor leagues, a farmhand of the Brooklyn Dodgers.

*   *   *   *

Paul Hoolahan is athletics director at Vanderbilt University, but alumni mail comes from the University of North Carolina, which not only gave him a degree in English but also his first job in sports administration.

Hoolahan graduated from UNC (where he was an All-ACC offensive tackle) in 1971, went to Columbia University for a master's in psychology, then returned to UNC to work in the athletics department in various capacities. When he rose to associate AD, Vanderbilt made him an offer he couldn't refuse.

*   *   *   *

Barbara Hedges has been director of athletics at the University of Washington since 1991. In 1996 she took on the added responsibilities of president of the National Association of Collegiate Directors of Athletics, becoming the first woman ever to hold that post. A former gymnastics coach and phys ed teacher at the University of Arizona, Hedges first moved into sports administration in 1973 at the University of Southern California.

Bob Frederick, who got his bachelor's, master's, and doctoral degrees at the University of Kansas, has been athletics director there since 1987. Earlier, he worked as a fund-raiser in the KU athletics department.

*   *   *   *

Peter T. Dalis has been associated with UCLA, first as a student and later as an employee, since 1955. Before his appointment in 1983 as UCLA's director of athletics, Dalis showed his mettle by managing a university-wide recreation/sports program that included intramural sports, club sports, activity instruction, recreation clubs, and cultural activities. He was also in charge of the university athletics facilities, including the athletics fields, men's and women's gymnasiums, swimming pools, golf areas, tennis courts, Pauley Pavilion, Drake Stadium, the Sunset Canyon Recreation Center, and the John R. Wooden Sports Center. As AD, he has continued the Bruin tradition of competing for conference championships and national titles.

*   *   *   *

A 1973 graduate of Boston College, **Chet Gladchuk** didn't get back to the Chestnut Hill campus until his appointment there as athletics director in 1990. After graduating from BC, he got a master's in sports administration from the University of Massachusetts-Amherst, then spent four years as director of athletics and football coach at a New England prep school. In 1978 he returned to UMass as assistant director of athletics; in 1985 he was at Syracuse University as associate athletics director, and in 1988 he was hired as AD by Tulane University. In two and a half years at Tulane, he revived its Division I basketball program, started construction of a new baseball stadium, and directed a $25 million fund-raising campaign for the athletics program. He's having a similar effect at BC.

*   *   *   *

A graduate of Kansas State, where he had drawn attention as a track star, **DeLoss Dodds** got his chance to show he could handle a big

sports program when State named him its AD. In 1981 the University of Texas at Austin lured him away, and since that time his success in directing the Texas program (and especially in steering it through some of the Southwest Conference's most tumultuous years) has made him one of the most highly regarded administrators in college athletics. But it was his alma mater that gave him his break.

New: A Legal Specialty

NCAA crackdowns on recruitment violations have given rise to a new specialty for lawyers, tentatively called compliance law. Clients are Division I schools needing advice on (1) how to deal with the NCAA's numerous and complex rules, and (2) how to escape a violation of rules with the least possible damage. For practitioners of the new specialty, business has been brisk.

New: Skyboxes

Skyboxes, a status symbol in professional sports, are now found in dozens of college stadiums and arenas. The luxury boxes are used, of course, to entice corporate support. Clemson University has gone in for it in a big way, building 102 skyboxes in its football stadium. The boxes accommodate eight to 12 spectators and are sold for the season at prices ranging from $8,000 to $20,000. The University of Florida has 46 stadium boxes with 16 seats that sell for $26,000 to $33,000. The University of Nevada-Las Vegas has built 30 boxes in its basketball arena. They seat 10 to 20 and are priced at $42,000 to $80,000.

The directory of athletics directors in NCAA Division I and II starts on page 140. Information about college associations and conferences begins on page 153.

Deborah Yow, AD at the University of Maryland, was a highly successful coach of women's basketball when she switched to sports administration. In 1987 she became assistant AD at the University of North Carolina's Greensboro campus, and in 1990 she took over management of the St. Louis University athletic program. She left for Maryland in 1994.

Women ADs

By 1996, 17 women held the position of director of athletics at Division I institutions. In Division II the number had grown to 24.

DIVISION I

Eve Atkinson, Lafayette College
Sandy Barbour, Tulane University
Kathy D. Clark, University of Idaho
Judith A. Davidson, California State University, Sacramento
Vivian L. Fuller, Northeastern Illinois University
Cary Groth, Northern Illinois University
E. Kaye Hart, Austin Peay State University
Barbara A. Hedges, University of Washington
Judy MacLeod, University of Tulsa
Marilyn A. McNeil, Monmouth University
Patricia Meiser-McKnett, University of Hartford
Judith L. Ray, University of New Hampshire
Judy Rose, North Carolina University, Charlotte
Andrea Seger, Ball State University
Helen Smiley, Western Illinois University
Suzanne J. Tyler, University of Maine, Orono
Deborah A. Yow, University of Maryland

DIVISION II

Elizabeth A. Alden, San Francisco State University
Virginia Babel, College of Notre Dame
Linda Bennett, University of Charleston (WV)
Rita M. Castagna, Assumption College
G. Jean Cerra, Barry University
Deborah Chin, University of New Haven
Patricia A. Dolan, University of Missouri, St. Louis
Carol M. Dunn, California State University, Los Angeles
Mary Gardner, Bloomsburg University
Linda C. Hackett, Bryant College
Linda Lowery, Concordia University
Jane Meier, Northern Kentucky University
Pat Merrier, University of Minnesota, Duluth
Karen L. Miller, California State Poly University
Jody E. Mooradian, Edinboro University
Doreen Powell, Christian Brothers University
Shirley G. Reese, Albany State College (GA)
Barbara J. Schroeder, Regis University (CO)
Nancy P. Simpson, California State University, San Bernardino
Ronnie Spry, Paine College
Sharon E. Taylor, Lock Haven University
Mary E. Topping, Southampton College, Long Island University
E. D. Wilkens, Le Moyne-Owen College
Katy Wilson, Moorhead State University (MN)

(This information was provided by the NCAA.)

ATHLETICS DIRECTORS IN NCAA DIVISION I & DIVISION II

DIVISION I

Sports programs in Division I are an excellent source of internships. Get in touch with the office of the athletics director.

ALABAMA

Alabama State University
Montgomery, AL 36101-0271
AD: Curtis Williams
(334) 293-4507

Auburn University
Auburn, AL 36831-0351
AD: David Housel
(334) 844-4750

Jacksonville State University
Jacksonville, AL 36265-1602
AD: Jerry N. Cole
(205) 782-5365

Samford University
Birmingham, AL 35229
AD: Stephen C. Allgood
(205) 870-2966

Troy State University
Troy, AL 36082
AD: Johnny Williams
(334) 670-3480

**University of Alabama
at Birmingham**
Birmingham, AL 35294
AD: B. Gene Bartow
(205) 934-7252

**University of Alabama
at Tuscaloosa**
Tuscaloosa, AL 35487
AD: Robert L. Bockrath
(205) 348-3697

University of South Alabama
Mobile, AL 36688
AD: Joe Gottfried
(334) 460-7121

ARIZONA

Arizona State University
Tempe, AZ 85287-2505
AD: Kevin M. White
(602) 965-3482

Northern Arizona University
Flagstaff, AZ 86011
AD: Steven P. Holton
(520) 523-5353

University of Arizona
Tucson, AZ 85721
AD: Jim Livengood
(520) 621-2200

ARKANSAS

Arkansas State University
State University, AR 72467
AD: Barry Dowd
(501) 972-3880

**University of Arkansas
at Fayetteville**
Fayetteville, AR 72701
AD (Men): J. Frank Broyles
(501) 575-2755
AD (Women): Beverly R. Lewis
(501) 575-4959

**University of Arkansas
at Little Rock**
Little Rock, AR 72204-1099
AD: Rick Mello
(501) 569-3306

CALIFORNIA

California Poly State University
San Luis, CA 93407
AD: John F. McCutcheon
(805) 756-2923

**California State University
at Fresno**
Fresno, CA 93740-0048
Interim AD: Benjamin F. Quillian Jr.
(209) 278-3178

**California State University
at Fullerton**
Fullerton, CA 92834-6810
AD: John Easterbrook
(714) 773-3058

**California State University
at Long Beach**
Long Beach, CA 90840-0118
AD: David P. O'Brien
(310) 985-7976

**California State University
at Northridge**
Northridge, CA 91330
AD: Paul Bubb
(818) 677-3208

**California State University
at Sacramento**
Sacramento, CA 95819
AD: Judith Davidson
(916) 278-6481

Fresno State University
Fresno, CA 93740-0027
AD: Allen Bohl
(209) 278-2643

Long Beach State University
Long Beach, CA 90840
Interim AD: Bill Shumard
(310) 985-7976

Loyola Marymount University
Los Angeles, CA 90045-2699
AD: Brian Quinn
(310) 338-2765

Pepperdine University
Malibu, CA 90263
AD: Wayne Wright
(310) 456-4150

St. Mary's College
Moraga, CA 94575
AD: Richard Mazzuto,
(510) 631-4383

San Diego State University
San Diego, CA 92182
AD: Rick Bay
(619) 594-5163

San Jose State University
San Jose, CA 95192
AD: Thomas M. Brennan
(408) 924-1200

Santa Clara University
Santa Clara, CA 95053
AD: Carroll M. Williams
(408) 554-4063

Stanford University
Stanford, CA 94305
AD: Ted Leland
(415) 723-4591

**University of California
at Berkeley**
Berkeley, CA 94720
AD: John V. Kasser
(510) 642-0580

University of California at Irvine
Irvine, CA 92697
AD: Daniel G. Guerrero
(714) 824-6931

**University of California
at Los Angeles**
Los Angeles, CA 90095-1639
AD: Peter T. Dalis
(310) 825-8699

**University of California
at Santa Barbara**
Santa Barbara, CA 93106
AD: Gary A. Cunningham
(805) 893-3400

University of the Pacific
Stockton, CA 95211
AD: Robert M. Lee
(209) 946-2472

University of San Diego
San Diego, CA 92110-2492
AD: Thomas Iannacone
(619) 260-2930

University of San Francisco
San Francisco, CA 94117-1080
AD: Bill Hogan
(415) 422-6891

University of Southern California
Los Angeles, CA 90089
AD: Michael Garrett
(213) 740-3843

COLORADO

Colorado State University
Fort Collins, CO 80523
AD: Tom Jurich
(970) 491-5300

U.S. Air Force Academy
USAF Academy, CO 80840-5461
AD: Col. Randall W. Spetman
(719) 472-4008

University of Colorado
Boulder, CO 80309
AD: William C. Marolt
(303) 492-7931

CONNECTICUT

**Central Connecticut State
University**
New Britain, CT 06050-4010
AD: Charles Jones
(860) 832-3040

Fairfield University
Fairfield, CT 06430-7524
AD: Eugene Doris
(203) 254-4000, ext. 2208

University of Connecticut
Storrs, CT 06269
AD: Lewis Perkins
(860) 486-2725

University of Hartford
West Hartford, CT 06117-1599
AD: Patricia Meiser-McKnett
(860) 768-4658

Yale University
New Haven, CT 06520-7398
AD: Tom Beckett
(203) 432-4747

ATHLETICS DIRECTORS IN NCAA DIVISION I & DIVISION II

DELAWARE

Delaware State University
Dover, DE 19901
AD: John C. Martin
(302) 739-4928

University of Delaware
Newark, DE 19716
AD: Edgar N. Johnson
(302) 831-4006

DISTRICT OF COLUMBIA

American University
Washington, DC 20016
AD: Lee McElroy Jr.
(202) 885-3000

Georgetown University
Washington, DC 20057
AD: Joseph C. Lang
(202) 687-2435

George Washington University
Washington, DC 20052
AD: Jack E. Kvancz
(202) 994-6650

Howard University
Washington, DC 20059
AD: Henry Ford
(202) 806-7110

FLORIDA

Bethune-Cookman College
Daytona Beach, FL 32114-3099
AD: Lynn W. Thompson
(904) 255-1401, ext. 319

Florida A & M University
Tallahassee, FL 32307
AD: Ken Riley
(904) 599-3868

Florida Atlantic University
Boca Raton, FL 33431-0991
Interim AD: Tom Cargill
(407) 367-3710

Florida International University
Miami, FL 33199
AD: Theodore A. Aceto
(305) 348-2756

Florida State University
Tallahassee, FL 32306
AD: Dave Hart Jr.
(904) 644-1079

Jacksonville University
Jacksonville, FL 32211
AD: Thomas M. Seitz
(904) 745-7400

Stetson University
De Land, FL 32720
AD: Jim Kuebler
(904) 822-8100

University of Central Florida
Orlando, FL 32816-0002
AD: Steve Sloan
(407) 823-2256

University of Florida
Gainesville, FL 32604
AD: Jeremy Foley
(352) 375-4683

University of Miami
Coral Gables, FL 33124
AD: Paul T. Dee
(305) 284-3822

University of South Florida
Tampa, FL 33620
AD: Paul S. Griffin
(813) 974-2125

GEORGIA

Georgia Institute of Technology
Atlanta, GA 30332
AD: Homer C. Rice
(404) 894-5400

Georgia Southern University
Statesboro, GA 30460-8033
AD: Sam Baker
(912) 681-5376

Georgia State University
Atlanta, GA 30303
AD: Orby Moss Jr.
(404) 651-2772

Mercer University
Macon, GA 31207
AD: Bobby Pope
(912) 752-2994

University of Georgia
Athens, GA 30613
AD: Vincent J. Dooley
(706) 542-9036

HAWAII

University of Hawaii
Honolulu, HI 96822-2370
AD: Hugh Yoshida
(808) 956-7301

IDAHO

Boise State University
Boise, ID 83725
AD: Gene Bleymaier
(208) 385-1288

Idaho State University
Pocatello, ID 83209
AD: Irv Cross
(208) 236-2771

University of Idaho
Moscow, ID 83843
AD: Oval Jaynes
(208) 885-0200

ILLINOIS

Bradley University
Peoria, IL 61625
AD: Ken Kavanagh
(309) 677-2670

Chicago State University
Chicago, IL 60628
AD: Charles N. Smith
(312) 995-3661

DePaul University
Chicago, IL 60614
AD: Bill Bradshaw
(312) 325-7526

Eastern Illinois University
Charleston, IL 61920
AD: Open
(217) 581-2319

Illinois State University
Normal, IL 61761
AD: Richard Greenspan
(309) 438-3633

Loyola University
Chicago, IL 60626
AD: Charles T. Schwarz
(312) 508-2560

Northeastern Illinois University
Chicago, IL 60625
AD: Vivian L. Fuller
(312) 794-3081

Northern Illinois University
DeKalb, IL 60115-2854
Interim AD: Cary Groth
(815) 753-1295

Northwestern University
Evanston, IL 60208
AD: Rick Taylor
(847) 491-3205

Southern Illinois University
Carbondale, IL 62901
AD: Jim Hart
(618) 453-5311

**University of Illinois
at Champaign**
Champaign, IL 61820
AD: Ronald E. Guenther
(217) 333-3631

University of Illinois at Chicago
Chicago, IL 60680
AD: James Schmidt
(312) 996-2772

Western Illinois University
Macomb, IL 61455
AD: Helen Smiley
(309) 298-1106

INDIANA

Ball State University
Muncie, IN 47306
AD: Andrea Seger
(317) 285-1671

Butler University
Indianapolis, IN 46208
AD: John C. Parry
(317) 940-9375

Indiana State University
Terre Haute, IN 47809
AD: Larry Gallo Jr.
(812) 237-4040

Indiana University
Bloomington, IN 47405
AD: Clarence Doninger
(812) 855-2794

Purdue University
West Lafayette, IN 47907
AD: Morgan J. Burke
(317) 494-5236

University of Evansville
Evansville, IN 47722
AD: James A. Byers
(812) 479-2238

University of Notre Dame
Notre Dame, IN 46556
AD: Michael A. Wadsworth
(219) 631-6107

Valparaiso University
Valparaiso, IN 46383-6493
AD: William L. Steinbrecher
(219) 464-5230

IOWA

Drake University
Des Moines, IA 50311-4505
AD: Lynn King
(515) 271-2102

Iowa State University
Ames, IA 50011
AD: Eugene D. Smith
(515) 294-3662

University of Iowa
Iowa City, IA 52242
AD (Men): Robert A. Bowlsby
(319) 335-9435
AD (Women): Christine Grant
(319) 335-9247

University of Northern Iowa
Cedar Falls, IA 50614
AD: Christopher Ritrievi
(319) 273-3100

KANSAS

Kansas State University
Manhattan, KS 66506
AD: Max Urick
(913) 532-6910

University of Kansas
Lawrence, KS 66045
AD: Robert E. Frederick
(913) 864-3143

Wichita State University
Wichita, KS 67260
AD: Willard S. Belknap
(316) 689-3250

KENTUCKY

Eastern Kentucky University
Richmond, KY 40475-3101
AD: Robert Baugh
(606) 622-3654

Morehead State University
Morehead, KY 40351-1689
AD: Steve Hamilton
(606) 783-2088

Murray State University
Murray, KY 42071
AD: Michael D. Strickland
(502) 762-6184

University of Kentucky
Lexington, KY 40506-0032
AD: C. M. Newton
(606) 257-8000

University of Louisville
Louisville, KY 40292
AD: William C. Olsen
(502) 588-5732

Western Kentucky University
Bowling Green, KY 42101
Interim AD: Lewis Mills
(502) 745-3542

LOUISIANA

Centenary College
Shreveport, LA 71134-1188
AD: Russ Sharp
(318) 869-5275

Grambling State University
Grambling, LA 71245
AD: Fred C. Hobdy
(318) 274-2634

Louisiana State University
Baton Rouge, LA 70803
AD: Joe Dean
(504) 388-6606

Louisiana Tech University
Ruston, LA 71272
AD: James Oakes
(318) 257-4111

McNeese State University
Lake Charles, LA 70609
AD: Bobby Keasler
(318) 475-5200

Nicholls State University
Thibodaux, LA 70310
AD: Mike Knight
(504) 448-4806

Northeast Louisiana University
Monroe, LA 71209-3000
AD: Richard C. Giannini
(318) 342-5365

Northwestern State University
Nachitoches, LA 71497-0003
Interim AD: Donnie Cox
(318) 357-5251

Southeastern Louisiana University
Hammond, LA 70402
AD: Tom Douple
(504) 549-2253

Southern University and A & M
Baton Rouge, LA 70813
AD: Marino H. Casem
(504) 771-3170

Tulane University
New Orleans, LA 70118
AD: Sandy Barbour
(504) 865-5500

University of New Orleans
New Orleans, LA 70148
AD: Ronald J. Maestri
(504) 286-6239

University of Southwestern Louisiana
Lafayette, LA 70504-1008
AD: Nelson Schexnayder
(318) 48CAJUNS

MAINE

University of Maine
Orono, ME 04469
AD: Suzanne Tyler
(207) 581-1058

MARYLAND

Coppin State College
Baltimore, MD 21216
AD: Ron Mitchell
(410) 383-5688

Loyola College
Baltimore, MD 21210
AD: Joseph Boylan
(410) 617-5014

Morgan State University
Baltimore, MD 21239
AD: Garnett Purnell
(410) 319-3050

Mount St. Mary's College
Emmitsburg, MD 21727
AD: Harold P. Menninger
(301) 447-5296

Towson State University
Towson, MD 21204
AD: Wayne Edwards
(410) 830-2759

U.S. Naval Academy
Annapolis, MD 21402
AD: Jack Lengyel
(410) 268-6220

University of Maryland, Baltimore County
Baltimore, MD 21228-5398
AD: Charles R. Brown
(410) 455-2126

University of Maryland, College Park
College Park, MD 20740
AD: Deborah Yow
(301) 314-7075

University of Maryland, Eastern Anne
Princess Anne, MD 21853-1299
AD: Hallie E. Gregory
(410) 651-6496

MASSACHUSETTS

Boston College
Chestnut Hill, MA 02167-3934
AD: Chester S. Gladchuk
(617) 552-8520

Boston University
Boston, MA 02215
AD: Gary Strickler
(617) 353-4630

College of the Holy Cross
Worcester, MA 01610-2395
AD: Ronald S. Perry
(508) 793-2571

Harvard University
Cambridge, MA 02138-3800
AD: William J. Cleary Jr.
(617) 495-2204

Northeastern University
Boston, MA 02115-5096
AD: Barry C. Gallup
(617) 373-2672

University of Massachusetts
Amherst, MA 01003
AD: Robert K. Marcum
(413) 545-2342

MICHIGAN

Central Michigan University
Mount Pleasant, MI 48859
AD: Herb Deromedi
(517) 774-3041

Eastern Michigan University
Ypsilanti, MI 48197
AD: Tim Weiser
(313) 487-1050

Michigan State University
East Lansing, MI 48824
AD: Merritt J. Norvell
(517) 355-1623

University of Detroit Mercy
Detroit, MI 48219-0900
AD: Bradford E. Kinsman
(313) 993-1700

University of Michigan
Ann Arbor, MI 48109-1340
AD: Joe Roberson
(313) 747-2583

Western Michigan University
Kalamazoo, MI 49008-5134
AD: Charles W. Elliott
(616) 387-8650

MINNESOTA

University of Minnesota
Minneapolis, MN 55455
AD (Men): Mark Dienhart
(612) 625-9579
AD (Women): Chris Voelz
(612) 624-4044

MISSISSIPPI

Alcorn State University
Lorman, MS 39096-9402
AD: Lloyd Hill
(601) 877-6500

Jackson State University
Jackson, MS 39217
AD: Paul Covington
(601) 968-2291

Mississippi State University
Mississippi State, MS 39762-5509
AD: Larry Templeton
(601) 325-2532

Mississippi Valley State University
Itta Bena, MS 38941
AD: Charles Prophet
(601) 254-3550

University of Mississippi
University, MS 38677
AD: James T. Boone
(601) 232-7241

University of Southern Mississippi
Hattiesburg, MS 39406-5001
AD: Bill McLellan
(601) 266-5017

MISSOURI

St. Louis University
St. Louis, MO 63108
AD: Doug Woolard
(314) 977-3177

Southeast Missouri State University
Cape Girardeau, MO 63701-4799
AD: Richard A. McDuffie
(573) 651-2227

Southwest Missouri State University
Springfield, MO 65804
AD: Bill Rowe Jr.
(417) 836-5244

University of Missouri at Columbia
Columbia, MO 65211
AD: Joseph R. Castiglione
(573) 882-6501

University of Missouri at Kansas City
Kansas City, MO 64110
AD: Lee Hunt
(816) 235-1048

MONTANA

Montana State University
Bozeman, MT 59717
AD: Douglas B. Fullerton
(406) 994-4221

University of Montana
Missoula, MT 59812-1291
AD: Wayne Hogan
(406) 243-5331

NEBRASKA

Creighton University
Omaha, NE 68178-0001
AD: Bruce Rasmussen
(402) 280-2720

University of Nebraska
Lincoln, NE 68588
AD: C. William Byrne Jr.
(402) 472-4224

NEVADA

University of Nevada at Las Vegas
Las Vegas, NV 89154
AD: Charles Cavagnaro
(702) 895-4729

University of Nevada at Reno
Reno, NV 89557
AD: Chris Ault
(702) 784-6900

NEW HAMPSHIRE

Dartmouth College
Hanover, NH 03755
AD: Richard Jaeger
(603) 646-2465

University of New Hampshire
Durham, NH 03824
AD (Men): Gilbert Chapman
(603) 862-1850
AD (Women): Judith L. Ray
(603) 862-1822

NEW JERSEY

Fairleigh Dickinson University
Teaneck, NJ 07666
AD: Gerald Oswald
(201) 692-2254

Monmouth College
West Long Branch, NJ 07764
AD: Marilyn McNeil
(908) 571-3415

Princeton University
Princeton, NJ 08544
AD: Gary D. Walters
(609) 258-3535

Rider College
Lawrenceville, NJ 08648-3099
AD: Curtis W. Blake
(609) 896-5054

Rutgers University
New Brunswick, NJ 08903
AD: Frederick E. Gruninger
(908) 932-8610

St. Peter's College
Jersey City, NJ 07306
AD: William A. Stein
(201) 915-9100

Seton Hall University
South Orange, NJ 07079
AD: Laurence C. Keating Jr.
(201) 761-9497

NEW MEXICO

New Mexico State University
Las Cruces, NM 88003
AD: Albert Gonzales
(505) 646-4126

University of New Mexico
Albuquerque, NM 87131
AD: Rudy Davalos
(505) 925-5500

NEW YORK

Canisius College
Buffalo, NY 14208-1098
AD: Daniel P. Starr
(716) 888-2970

Colgate University
Hamilton, NY 13346-1304
AD: Mark H. Murphy
(315) 824-7611

Columbia University —Barnard College
New York, NY 10027
AD: John A. Reeves
(212) 854-2537

Cornell University
Ithaca, NY 14853
AD: Charles H. Moore
(607) 255-5220

Fordham University
Bronx, NY 10458
AD: Francis X. McLaughlin
(718) 817-4300

Hofstra University
Hempstead, NY 11550
AD: Jim Garvey
(516) 463-6750

Iona College
New Rochelle, NY 10801
AD: Rich Petriccione
(914) 633-2304

Long Island University, Brooklyn Campus
Brooklyn, NY 11201
AD: James Martin
(718) 488-1030

Manhattan College
Riverdale, NY 10471
AD: Robert J. Byrnes
(718) 862-7227

Marist College
Poughkeepsie, NY 12601-1387
AD: Timothy S. Murray
(914) 575-3699, ext. 2328

Niagara University
Niagara University, NY 14109
AD: Michael L. Jankowski
(716) 286-8601

St. Bonaventure University
St. Bonaventure, NY 14778
AD: David L. Diles
(716) 375-2282

St. Francis College
Brooklyn Heights, NY 11201-4398
AD: Tom Thompson
(718) 522-2300, ext. 365

St. John's University
Jamaica, NY 11439
AD: Edward J. Manetta Jr.
(718) 990-6224

Siena College
Loudonville, NY 12211-1462
AD: John M. D'Argenio
(518) 783-2551

State University of New York at Buffalo
Buffalo, NY 14260
AD: Nelson E. Townsend
(716) 645-3141

Syracuse University
Syracuse, NY 13244
AD: Jake Crouthamel
(315) 443-2385

U.S. Military Academy
West Point, NY 10996
AD: Col. (Ret.) Albert Vanderbush
(914) 938-2973

Wagner College
Staten Island, NY 10301
AD: Walt Hameline
(718) 390-3433

NORTH CAROLINA

Appalachian State University
Boone, NC 28608
AD: Roachel Laney
(704) 262-4010

Campbell University
Buies Creek, NC 27506
AD: Tom Collins
(919) 893-1325

Davidson College
Davidson, NC 28036
AD: Jim Murphy
(704) 892-2800

Duke University
Durham, NC 27708
AD: Tom Butters
(919) 684-2120

East Carolina University
Greenville, NC 27858-4353
AD: Mike Hamrick
(919) 328-4600

North Carolina A & T State University
Greensboro, NC 27411
AD: Willie J. Burden
(910) 334-7687

North Carolina State University
Raleigh, NC 27695-7001
AD: Open
(919) 515-2101

University of North Carolina at Asheville
Asheville, NC 28804-3299
AD: Tom Hunnicutt
(704) 251-6459

University of North Carolina at Chapel Hill
Chapel Hill, NC 27514
AD: John D. Swofford
(919) 962-6000

University of North Carolina at Charlotte
Charlotte, NC 28223
AD: Judy Rose
(704) 547-4920

University of North Carolina at Greensboro
Greensboro, NC 27412-5001
AD: Nelson E. Bobb
(919) 334-5213

University of North Carolina at Wilmington
Wilmington, NC 28403-3297
AD: Paul A. Miller
(919) 962-3232

Wake Forest University
Winston-Salem, NC 27109
AD: Ronald D. Wellman
(919) 759-5616

Western Carolina University
Cullowhee, NC 28723
AD: Larry L. Travis
(704) 227-7132

OHIO

Bowling Green State University
Bowling Green, OH 43403
AD: Ron Zwierlein
(419) 372-2401

Cleveland State University
Cleveland, OH 44115
AD: John Konstantinos
(216) 687-4808

Kent State University
Kent, OH 44242
AD: Laing E. Kennedy
(330) 672-5974

Miami University
Oxford, OH 45056
Interim AD: Eric Hyman
(513) 529-3113

Ohio State University
Columbus, OH 43210
AD: Andy Geiger
(614) 292-7572

Ohio University
Athens, OH 45701
AD: Tom Boeh
(614) 593-1000

University of Akron
Akron, OH 44325
AD: Michael Bobinski
(330) 972-7080

University of Cincinnati
Cincinnati, OH 45221
AD: Gerald O'Dell
(513) 556-4603

University of Dayton
Dayton, OH 45469-1220
AD: Ted Kissell
(513) 229-2100

University of Toledo
Toledo, OH 43606
AD: Pete Liske
(419) 530-4184

Wright State University
Dayton, OH 45435-0001
AD: Michael J. Cusack
(513) 873-2771

Xavier University
Cincinnati, OH 45207
AD: Jeffrey H. Fogelson
(513) 745-3414

Youngstown State University
Youngstown, OH 44555-0001
AD: Jim Tressel
(330) 742-3739

OKLAHOMA

Oklahoma State University
Stillwater, OK 74078
AD: Terry D. Phillips
(405) 744-7740

Oral Roberts University
Tulsa, OK 74171
AD: Mike Carter
(918) 495-7100

University of Oklahoma
Norman, OK 73019
AD: Steve Owens
(405) 325-8200

University of Tulsa
Tulsa, OK 74104
AD: Judy MacLeod
(918) 631-2381

OREGON

Oregon State University
Corvallis, OR 97331
AD: Dutch Baughman
(541) 737-2547

University of Oregon
Eugene, OR 97403-1226
AD: Bill Moos
(541) 346-5464

University of Portland
Portland, OR 97203-5798
AD: Joseph A. Etzel
(503) 283-7117

PENNSYLVANIA

Bucknell University
Lewisburg, PA 17837
AD: Rick R. Hartzell
(717) 524-1232

Drexel University
Philadelphia, PA 19104
AD: Lou Marciani
(215) 590-8943

Duquesne University
Pittsburgh, PA 15282
AD: Brian Colleary
(412) 396-6565

Lafayette College
Easton, PA 18042
AD: Eve Atkinson
(610) 250-5470

LaSalle University
Philadelphia, PA 19141-1199
AD: Robert W. Mullen
(215) 951-1516

Lehigh University
Bethlehem, PA 18015
AD: Joseph D. Sterrett
(215) 758-4320

Pennsylvania State University
University Park, PA 16802
AD: Tim Curley
(814) 863-1000

Robert Morris College
Coraopolis, PA 15108-1189
AD: Bruce Corrie
(412) 262-8302

St. Francis College
Loretto, PA 15940-0600
AD: Frank S. Pergolizzi
(814) 472-3276

St. Joseph's University
Philadelphia, PA 19131
AD: Don J. DiJulia
(610) 660-1707

Temple University
Philadelphia, PA 19122
AD: David P. O'Brien
(215) 204-7447

ATHLETICS DIRECTORS IN NCAA DIVISION I & DIVISION II

University of Pennsylvania
Philadelphia, PA 19104-6380
AD: Steve Bilsky
(215) 898-6121

University of Pittsburgh
Pittsburgh, PA 15260
AD: Steve Pederson
(412) 648-8200

Villanova University
Villanova, PA 19085
AD: Gene DeFilippo
(610) 519-4130

RHODE ISLAND

Brown University
Providence, RI 02912
AD: David T. Roach
(401) 863-2211

Providence College
Providence, RI 02918
AD: John M. Marinatto
(401) 865-2265

University of Rhode Island
Kingston, RI 02881
AD: Ronald J. Petro
(401) 874-5245

SOUTH CAROLINA

Charleston Southern University
Charleston, SC 29423-8087
AD: W. Howard Bagwell
(803) 863-7679

The Citadel
Charleston, SC 29409
AD: Walt Nadzak
(803) 953-5030

Clemson University
Clemson, SC 29633
AD: Robert W. Robinson
(803) 656-1935

Coastal Carolina University
Conway, SC 29526
AD: Buddy Sasser
(803) 349-2820

College of Charleston
Charleston, SC 29424
AD: Jerry I. Baker
(803) 953-5556

Furman University
Greenville, SC 29613
AD: John Block
(803) 294-2150

South Carolina State University
Orangeburg, SC 29117-0001
AD: Timothy Autry
(803) 536-7242

University of South Carolina
Columbia, SC 29208
AD: Mike McGee
(803) 777-4202

Winthrop University
Rock Hill, SC 29733
Interim AD: Thomas Hickman
(803) 323-2129

Wofford College
Spartanburg, SC 29303
AD: Danny Morrison
(864) 597-4090

TENNESSEE

Austin Peay State University
Clarksville, TN 37044-4576
AD: Kaye Hart
(615) 648-7903

East Tennessee State University
Johnson City, TN 37614
AD: H. Keener Fry Jr.
(423) 439-4343

Middle Tennessee State University
Murfreesboro, TN 37132
AD: Lee Fowler
(615) 898-2450

Tennessee State University
Nashville, TN 37209-1561
AD: Howard Gentry Jr.
(615) 963-5861

Tennessee Technological University
Cookeville, TN 38505-0001
AD: David Larimore
(615) 372-3940

University of Memphis
Memphis, TN 38152
AD: R. C. Johnson
(901) 678-2331

University of Tennessee at Chattanooga
Chattanooga, TN 37403-2598
AD: Edward G. Farrell
(615) 755-4495

University of Tennessee at Knoxville
Knoxville, TN 37996
AD (Men): Douglas A. Dickey
(423) 974-1212
AD (Women): Joan C. Cronan
(423) 974-4275

University of Tennessee at Martin
Martin, TN 38238-5021
AD: Benny Hollis
(901) 587-7660

Vanderbilt University
Nashville, TN 37212
AD: Todd Turner
(615) 322-4727

TEXAS

Baylor University
Waco, TX 76711
AD: Tom Stanton
(817) 755-1234

Lamar University
Beaumont, TX 77710
AD: Michael E. O'Brien
(409) 880-2248

Prairie View A & M University
Prairie View, TX 77446
Interim AD: Hensley W. Sapenter
(409) 857-2236

Rice University
Houston, TX 77251
AD: John R. May
(713) 527-4077

Sam Houston State University
Huntsville, TX 77341
AD: Ronnie Choate
(409) 294-1726

Southern Methodist University
Dallas, TX 75275
AD: Jim Copeland
(214) 768-2864

Southwest Texas State University
San Marcos, TX 78666-4615
AD: Richard Hannan
(512) 245-2114

Stephen F. Austin State University
Nacogdoches, TX 75962
AD: Steve McCarty
(409) 568-3502

Texas A & M University
College Station, TX 77843
AD: Wally Groff
(409) 845-5129

Texas Christian University
Fort Worth, TX 76129-0001
AD: Frank Windegger
(817) 921-7965

Texas Southern University
Houston, TX 77004
AD: Bill Thomas
(713) 313-7271

Texas Tech University
Lubbock, TX 79409
Interim AD: Gerald Myers
(806) 742-3355

University of Houston
Houston, TX 77204
AD: William C. Carr III
(713) 743-9370

University of North Texas
Denton, TX 76203-6737
AD: Craig Helwig
(817) 565-3646

University of Texas at Arlington
Arlington, TX 76019
AD: Peter Carlon
(817) 273-2261

University of Texas at Austin
Austin, TX 78712
AD (Men): DeLoss Dodds
(512) 471-4602
AD (Women): Jody Conradt
(512) 471-7693

University of Texas at El Paso
El Paso, TX 79968
AD: John K. Thompson
(915) 747-5347

University of Texas —Pan American
Edinburg, TX 78539-2999
AD: Gary Gallup
(210) 381-2221

University of Texas at San Antonio
San Antonio, TX 78249
AD: Bobby Thompson
(210) 458-4161

UTAH

Brigham Young University
Provo, UT 84602-2240
AD: Rondo Fehlberg
(801) 378-6164

Southern Utah University
Cedar City, UT 84720
AD: Jack Bishop
(801) 586-1937

University of Utah
Salt Lake City, UT 84112
AD: Christopher Hill
(801) 581-8171

Utah State University
Logan, UT 84322-7400
AD: Charles Bell
(801) 797-1850

Weber State University
Ogden, UT 84408-2701
AD: Dutch Belnap
(801) 626-6500

VERMONT

University of Vermont
Burlington, VT 05405
AD: Richard A. Farnham
(802) 656-3074

VIRGINIA

College of William and Mary
Williamsburg, VA 23187
AD: Terry Driscoll
(757) 221-3400

George Mason University
Fairfax, VA 22030
AD: Tom O'Connor
(703) 993-3200

Hampton University
Hampton, VA 23668
AD: Dennis E. Thomas
(804) 727-5641

James Madison University
Harrisonburg, VA 22807
AD: Donald L. Lemish
(703) 568-6164

Liberty University
Lynchburg, VA 24506
AD: Chuck Burch
(804) 582-2100

Old Dominion University
Norfolk, VA 23529
AD: James Jarrett
(804) 683-3375

Radford University
Radford, VA 24142
AD: Greig Denny
(540) 831-5228

University of Richmond
Richmond, VA 23173-1903
AD: Charles S. Boone
(804) 289-8371

University of Virginia
Charlottesville, VA 22903
AD: Terry Holland
(804) 982-5000

Virginia Commonwealth University
Richmond, VA 23284-2003
AD: Richard L. Sander
(804) 828-4000

Virginia Military Institute
Lexington, VA 24450
AD: Davis C. Babb
(540) 464-7251

Virginia Polytechnic Institute
Blacksburg, VA 24061
AD: David T. Braine
(540) 231-6796

WASHINGTON

Eastern Washington University
Cheney, WA 99004-2499
AD: John W. Johnson
(509) 359-2463

Gonzaga University
Spokane, WA 99258
AD: Dan Fitzgerald
(509) 328-4220, ext. 4203

University of Washington
Seattle, WA 98195
AD: Barbara A. Hedges
(206) 543-2212

Washington State University
Pullman, WA 99164
AD: Rick Dickson
(509) 335-0311

WEST VIRGINIA

Marshall University
Huntington, WV 25715
AD: Lance West
(304) 696-5408

West Virginia University
Morgantown, WV 26506
AD: Ed Pastilong
(304) 293-5621

WISCONSIN

Marquette University
Milwaukee, WI 53233
AD: William L. Cords
(414) 288-6303

University of Wisconsin at Green Bay
Green Bay, WI 54311-7001
Acting AD: Dennis (Otis) Chambers
(414) 465-2145

University of Wisconsin at Madison
Madison, WI 53706
AD: Pat Richter
(608) 262-5068

University of Wisconsin at Milwaukee
Milwaukee, WI 53201
AD: Bud K. Haidet
(414) 229-5669

WYOMING

University of Wyoming
Laramie, WY 82071
AD: Lee Moon
(307) 766-2292

DIVISION II

The programs are not so big as those in Division I, but internships are available and it's a good place to start.

ALABAMA

Alabama A & M University
Normal, AL 35762
AD: Jerome Fitch
(205) 851-5365

Jacksonville State University
Jacksonville, AL 36265-9982
AD: Jerry N. Cole
(205) 782-5365

Livingston University
Livingston, AL 35470
AD: Dee Outlaw
(205) 652-9661, ext. 558

Miles College
Fairfield, AL 35064
AD: Augustus James
(205) 923-2771

Tuskegee University
Tuskegee Institute, AL 36088
AD: Rick Comegy
(334) 727-8849

University of Alabama, Huntsville
Huntsville, AL 35899
AD: Jim Harris
(205) 895-6144

University of Montevallo
Montevallo, AL 35115
AD: Bob Reisener
(205) 665-6600

University of North Alabama
Florence, AL 35632
AD: Dan Summy
(205) 760-4397

University of West Alabama
Livingston, AL 35470
AD: Dee Outlaw
(205) 652-3784

ALASKA

University of Alaska, Anchorage
Anchorage, AK 99508
AD: Timothy Dillon
(907) 786-1230

University of Alaska, Fairbanks
Fairbanks, AK 99775-7440
AD: Kelly Higgins
(907) 474-7205

ARIZONA

Grand Canyon University
Phoenix, AZ 85017
AD: Keith Baker
(602) 589-2806

ARKANSAS

Arkansas Tech University
Russellville, AR 72801
AD: Dean Lee
(501) 968-0345

Harding University
Searcy, AR 72149
AD: Ted Altman
(501) 279-4305

Henderson State University
Arkadelphia, AR 71999-0001
AD: Ken Turner
(501) 230-5161

Southern Arkansas University
Magnolia, AR 71753
AD: W. T. Watson
(501) 235-4102

University of Arkansas, Monticello
Monticello, AR 71656
AD: Lawrence Smithmier
(501) 460-1058

University of Central Arkansas
Conway, AR 72035-0001
AD: Bill Stephens
(501) 450-3150

ATHLETICS DIRECTORS IN NCAA DIVISION I & DIVISION II

CALIFORNIA

California Poly State University
San Luis Obispo, CA 93407
AD: John F. McCutcheon
(805) 756-2923

California State Poly University
Pomona, CA 91768
AD: Karen L. Miller
(909) 869-2810

California State University, Bakersfield
Bakersfield, CA 93311-1099
AD: Rudy Carvajal
(805) 664-2188

California State University, Chico
Chico, CA 95929-0300
AD: Don W. Batie
(916) 898-6470

California State University, Dominguez Hills
Carson, CA 90747
AD: Ron Prettyman
(310) 516-3893

California State University, Hayward
Hayward, CA 94542
AD: Douglas Weiss
(510) 885-3038

California State University, Los Angeles
Los Angeles, CA 90032-8240
AD: Carol M. Dunn
(213) 343-3080

California State University, San Bernardino
San Bernardino, CA 92407
AD: Nancy P. Simpson
(909) 880-5011

California State University, Stanislaus
Turlock, CA 95382
AD: Joseph T. Donahue
(209) 667-3566

Chapman University
Orange, CA 92666
AD: David Currey
(714) 997-6691

College of Notre Dame
Belmont, CA 94002
AD: Virginia Babel
(415) 508-3590

Humboldt State University
Arcata, CA 95521
AD: Scott Nelson
(707) 826-3666

San Francisco State University
San Francisco, CA 94132
AD: Betsy Alden
(415) 338-2218

Sonoma State University
Rohner Park, CA 94928
AD: Ralph Barkey
(707) 664-2521

University of California, Davis
Davis, CA 95616
AD: Greg Warzecka
(916) 752-1111

University of California, Riverside
Riverside, CA 92521
AD: John Masi
(909) 787-5432

COLORADO

Adams State College
Alamosa, CO 81102
AD: Roger Jehlicka
(719) 587-7401

Colorado Christian University
Lakewood, CO 80226
AD: Michael Sumpter
(303) 238-5386, ext. 164

Colorado School of Mines
Golden, CO 80401
AD: Marvin L. Kay
(303) 273-3363

Fort Lewis College
Durango, CO 81301-3999
AD: Daryl Leonard
(303) 247-7571

Mesa State College
Grand Junction, CO 81501
AD: James Paronto
(970) 248-1635

Metropolitan State College of Denver
Denver, CO 80217-3362
AD: William M. Helman
(303) 556-8300

Regis University
Denver, CO 80221
AD: Barbara Schroeder
(303) 458-4070

University of Colorado, Colorado Springs
Colorado Springs, CO 80933
AD: Theophilus D. Gregory
(719) 593-3575

University of Denver
Denver, CO 80208-0320
AD: Joel Maturi
(303) 871-2275

University of Northern Colorado
Greeley, CO 80639
AD: Jim Fallis
(970) 351-2534

University of Southern Colorado
Pueblo, CO 81001-4601
AD: Tony Taibi
(719) 549-2711

Western State College
Gunnison, CO 81231
AD: Greg Waggoner
(970) 943-2079

CONNECTICUT

Quinnipiac College
Hamden, CT 06518
AD: Jack McDonald
(203) 281-8620

Sacred Heart University
Fairfield, CT 06432-1000
AD: C. Donald Cook
(203) 371-7827

Southern Connecticut State University
New Haven, CT 06515
AD: Darryl Rogers
(203) 392-6000

University of Bridgeport
Bridgeport, CT 06601
AD: Robert Baird
(203) 576-4059

University of New Haven
West Haven, CT 06516
AD: Deborah Chin
(203) 932-7017

DISTRICT OF COLUMBIA

University of the District of Columbia
Washington, DC 20008
AD: Dwight F. Datcher
(202) 274-5024

FLORIDA

Barry University
Miami Shores, FL 33161
AD: G. Jean Cerra
(305) 899-3550

Eckerd College
St. Petersburg, FL 33711
AD: James R. Harley
(813) 864-8251

Florida Institute of Technology
Melbourne, FL 32901-6988
AD: William K. Jurgens
(407) 768-8000

Florida Southern College
Lakeland, FL 33801-5698
AD: Hal Smeltzly
(941) 680-4244

Lynn University
Boca Raton, FL 33431
AD: Dick Young
(407) 994-0770, ext. 116

Rollins College
Winter Park, FL 32789-4499
AD: J. Phillip Roach
(407) 646-2366

St. Leo College
St. Leo, FL 33574
AD: Ted Owens
(352) 588-8221

University of North Florida
Jacksonville, FL 32224-2645
AD: Richard E. Gropper
(904) 646-2833

University of Tampa
Tampa, FL 33606
AD: Hindman Wall
(813) 253-6240

GEORGIA

Albany State College
Albany, GA 31705
AD: Shirley Reese
(912) 430-4754

Armstrong State College
Savannah, GA 31419-1997
AD: Eddie Aenchbacher
(912) 927-5336

Augusta College
Augusta, GA 30910
AD: Clint Bryant
(706) 737-1626

Clark Atlanta University
Atlanta, GA 30314
AD: Richard Cosby
(404) 880-8126

Columbus College
Columbus, GA 31907-5645
AD: Herbert Greene
(404) 568-2204

Fort Valley State College
Fort Valley, GA 31030
AD: Douglas T. Porter
(912) 825-6209

Georgia College
Milledgeville, GA 31061
AD: Stan Aldridge
(912) 453-6341

Georgia Southern University
Statesboro, GA 30460
AD: Sam Baker
(912) 681-5376

Kennesaw State College
Marietta, GA 30061
AD: Dave Waples
(770) 423-6284

Morehouse College
Atlanta, GA 30314
AD: Arthur J. McAfee Jr.
(404) 215-2669

Morris Brown College
Atlanta, GA 30314
AD: Gene Bright
(404) 220-3615

Paine College
Augusta, GA 30910
AD: Ron Spry
(706) 821-8353

Savannah State College
Savannah, GA 31404
Interim AD: Hornsby Howell
(912) 356-2228

State University of West Georgia
Statesboro, GA 30118
AD: Ed Murphy
(770) 836-6533

Valdosta State University
Valdosta, GA 31698-0500
AD: Herb F. Reinhard III
(912) 333-5890

West Georgia College
Carrolton, GA 30118
AD: Ed Murphy
(404) 836-6533

HAWAII

Chaminade University
Honolulu, HI 96816
AD: Al Walker
(808) 735-4790

University of Hawaii, Hilo
Hilo, HI 96720-4091
AD: Bill Trumbo
(808) 933-3520

ILLINOIS

Augustana College
Rock Island, IL 61201
AD (Men): John Farwell
AD (Women): Diane Schumacher
(309) 794-7521

College of St. Francis
Joliet, IL 60435
AD: Pat Sullivan
(815) 740-3464

Lewis University
Romeoville, IL 60441
AD: Paul Ruddy
(815) 838-0500, ext. 5247

Quincy University
Quincy, IL 62301
AD: Jim Naumovich
(217) 228-5290

Southern Illinois University
Edwardsville, IL 62026
AD: Cindy Jones
(618) 692-2871

INDIANA

**Indiana University/Purdue
University, Fort Wayne**
Fort Wayne, IN 46805
AD: Butch Perchan
(219) 481-6643

**Indiana University/Purdue
University, Indianapolis**
Indianapolis, IN 46202-5193
AD: Mike Moore
(317) 274-0622

Oakland City University
Oakland City, IN 47660
AD: Mike Sandifar
(812) 749-1264

St. Joseph's College
Rensselaer, IN 47978
AD: Lyn Plett
(219) 866-6386

University of Indianapolis
Indianapolis, IN 46227
AD: David Huffman
(317) 788-3246

University of Southern Indiana
Evansville, IN 47712
AD: Steve Newton
(812) 464-1846

IOWA

Morningside College
Sioux City, IA 51106
AD: Bill Goldring
(712) 274-5192

KANSAS

Emporia State University
Emporia, KS 66801
AD: William W. Quayle
(316) 341-5354

Fort Hays State University
Hays, KS 67601-4099
AD: Tom Spicer
(913) 628-4050

Pittsburg State University
Pittsburg, KS 66762
AD: Bill Samuels
(316) 235-4389

Washburn University
Topeka, KS 66621
Interim AD: Janet Degginger
(913) 231-1134

KENTUCKY

Bellarmine College
Louisville, KY 40205
AD: Jay Gardiner
(502) 452-8381

Kentucky State University
Frankfort, KY 40601
AD: Donald W. Lyons
(502) 227-6014

Kentucky Wesleyan College
Owensboro, KY 42302-1039
AD: Bill Meadors
(502) 683-4795

Northern Kentucky University
Highland Heights, KY 41099-7500
AD: Jane Meier
(606) 572-5193

MARYLAND

Bowie State University
Bowie, MD 20715
AD: Charles A. Guilford
(301) 464-6683

MASSACHUSETTS

American International College
Springfield, MA 01109
AD: Robert E. Burke
(413) 747-6540

Assumption College
Worcester, MA 01615-0005
AD: Rita Castagna
(508) 767-7279

Bentley College
Waltham, MA 02154-4705
AD: Robert A. DeFelice
(617) 891-2256

Merrimack College
North Andover, MA 01845
AD: Robert M. DeGregorio Jr.
(508) 837-5341

Springfield College
Springfield, MA 01109
AD: Edward Bilik
(413) 748-3332

Stonehill College
North Easton, MA 02357
AD: Paula Sullivan
(508) 230-1384

**University of Massachusetts,
Lowell**
Lowell, MA 01854
AD: Dana Skinner
(508) 934-2310

MICHIGAN

Ferris State University
Big Rapids, MI 49307-2741
AD: Larry Marfise
(616) 592-2860

Grand Valley State University
Allendale, MI 49401
AD: Tim W. Selgo
(616) 895-3259

Hillsdale College
Hillsdale, MI 49242
AD: Mike Kovalchik
(517) 437-7341

ATHLETICS DIRECTORS IN NCAA DIVISION I & DIVISION II

Lake Superior State University
Sault St. Marie, MI 49783
AD: William Crawford
(906) 635-2627

Michigan Technological University
Houghton, MI 49931-1295
AD: J. Richard Yeo
(906) 487-3070

Northern Michigan University
Marquette, MI 49855-5349
AD: Rick Comley
(906) 227-2105

Northwood University
Midland, MI 48640-2398
AD: Dave Coffey
(517) 837-4381

Oakland University
Rochester, MI 48309
AD: Jack G. Mehl
(810) 370-3190

Saginaw Valley State University
University Center, MI 48710-0001
AD: Robert T. Becker
(517) 791-7306

Wayne State University
Detroit, MI 48202-3489
AD: Bob Brennan
(313) 577-4280

MINNESOTA

Bemidji State University
Bemidji, MN 56601
AD (Men): R. R. "Bob" Peters
AD (Women): Doreen Zierer
(218) 755-2941

Mankato State University
Mankato, MN 56002
AD (Men): Donald Amiot
AD (Women): Georgene Brock
(507) 389-6111

Moorhead State University
Moorhead, MN 56560
AD: Katey Wilson
(218) 299-5824

St. Cloud State University
St. Cloud, MN 56301-4498
AD (Men): Morris Kurtz
AD (Women): Gladys Ziemer
(612) 255-3102

Southwest State University
Marshall, MN 56258
AD: Ron Flowers
(507) 537-7271

University of Minnesota, Duluth
Duluth, MN 55812
AD: Bruce McLeod
(218) 726-8168

University of Minnesota, Morris
Morris, MN 56267
AD: Mark Fohl
(612) 589-6425

Winona State University
Winona, MN 55987-5838
AD: Open
(507) 457-5210

MISSISSIPPI

Delta State University
Cleveland, MS 38733
AD: James H. Jordan
(601) 846-4300

Mississippi College
Clinton, MS 39058
AD: Terry McMillan
(601) 925-3341

Mississippi University for Women
Columbus, MS 39701
AD: Jo Spearman
(601) 329-7225

MISSOURI

Central Missouri State University
Warrensburg, MO 64093
AD: Jerry Hughes
(816) 543-4250

Drury College
Springfield, MO 65802
AD: Bruce Harger
(417) 873-7265

Lincoln University (Missouri)
Jefferson City, MO 65102-0029
AD: Ron Coleman
(573) 681-5342

Missouri Southern State College
Joplin, MO 64801-1595
AD: Jim Frazier
(417) 625-9317

Missouri Western State
St. Joseph, MO 64507
AD: Don Kaverman
(816) 271-4481

Northwest Missouri State University
Maryville, MO 64468
AD: James C. Redd
(816) 562-1713

Southwest Baptist University
Bolivar, MO 65613
AD: Rex Brown
(417) 326-1746

Truman State University
Kirksville, MO 63501
AD: Walter H. Ryle IV
(816) 785-4235

University of Missouri, Rolla
Rolla, MO 65401
AD: Mark Mullin
(314) 341-4175

University of Missouri, St. Louis
St. Louis, MO 63121
AD: Patricia Dolan
(314) 553-5661

MONTANA

Montana State University, Billings
Billings, MT 59101-0298
AD: Gary Gray
(406) 657-2369

Montana State University —Bozeman
Bozeman, MT 59717
AD: Chuck Lindemann
(406) 994-4221

NEBRASKA

Chadron State College
Chadron, NE 69337
AD: Bradley Roy Smith
(308) 432-6345

University of Nebraska, Kearney
Kearney, NE 68849
AD: Richard M. Dull
(308) 865-8514

University of Nebraska, Omaha
Omaha, NE 68182
AD: Don Leahy
(402) 554-2305

Wayne State College
Wayne, NE 68787
AD: Pete Chapman
(402) 375-7520

NEW HAMPSHIRE

Franklin Pierce College
Rindge, NH 03461
AD: Bruce Kirsh
(603) 899-4087

Keene State College
Keene, NH 03435-2301
AD: John Ratliff
(603) 358-2813

New Hampshire College
Manchester, NH 03106-1045
AD: Joseph Polak
(603) 645-9604

St. Anselm College
Manchester, NH 03102-1310
AD: Theodore S. Paulauskas
(603) 641-7800

NEW MEXICO

Eastern New Mexico University
Portales, NM 88130
AD: Chris Gage
(505) 562-2153

New Mexico Highlands University
Las Vegas, NM 87701
AD: Robert N. Evers
(505) 425-7511

Western New Mexico University
Silver City, NM 88061
AD: Dick Drangmeister
(505) 538-6235

NEW YORK

Adelphi University
Garden City, NY 11530
AD: Robert E. Hartwell
(516) 877-4240

College of St. Rose
Albany, NY 12203
AD: Catherine Haker
(518) 454-5282

Concordia College
Bronxville, NY 10708
AD: Lou Kern
(914) 337-9300, ext. 2450

Dowling College
Oakdale, NY 11769
AD: Robert Dranoff
(516) 244-3019

Le Moyne College
Syracuse, NY 13214
AD: Richard Rockwell
(315) 445-4450

Long Island University/ C. W. Post
Brookville, NY 11548
AD: Vincent Salamone
(516) 299-2289

ATHLETICS DIRECTORS IN NCAA DIVISION I & DIVISION II

Long Island University,
Southampton
Southampton, NY 11968
AD: Mary E. Topping
(516) 287-8387

Mercy College
Dobbs Ferry, NY 10522
AD: Neil D. Judge
(914) 674-7220

Molloy College
Rockville Center, NY 11570
AD: Bob Houlihan
(516) 678-5000

New York Institute
of Technology
Westbury, NY 11568-8000
AD: Clyde Doughty Jr.
(516) 686-7626

Pace University
Pleasantville, NY 10570
AD: TBA
(914) 773-3411

Queens College (New York)
Flushing, NY 11367
AD: Richard Wettan
(718) 997-2770

State University of New York,
Albany
Albany, NY 12222
AD: Milton E. Richards
(907) 786-1230

State University of New York,
Stony Brook
Stony Brook, NY 11794
AD: Sandy Weeden
(516) 632-7205

NORTH CAROLINA

Barton College
Wilson, NC 27893
AD: Gary Hall
(919) 399-6514

Belmont Abbey College
Belmont, NC 28012
AD: Michael Reidy
(704) 825-6801

Catawba College
Salisbury, NC 28144-2488
AD: Dennis Davidson
(704) 637-4474

Elizabeth City State University
Elizabeth City, NC 27909
AD: Edward McLean
(919) 335-3385

Elon College
Elon College, NC 27244-2010
AD: Alan J. White
(910) 584-2443

Fayetteville State University
Fayetteville, NC 28301-4298
AD: Horace T. Small
(910) 486-1314

Gardner-Webb University
Boiling Springs, NC 28017
AD: F. Osborne McFarland
(704) 434-4340

High Point University
High Point, NC 27262-3598
AD: Jerry Steele
(910) 841-9000

Johnson C. Smith University
Charlotte, NC 28216
AD: Stephen Wayne Joyner
(704) 378-1072

Lenoir-Rhyne College
Hickory, NC 28603
AD: Keith Ochs
(704) 328-7115

Livingstone College
Salisbury, NC 28144
AD: Clifton Huff
(704) 638-5714

Mars Hill College
Mars Hill, NC 28754
AD: Ed Hoffmeyer
(704) 689-1219

Mount Olive College
Mount Olive, NC 28365
AD: Allen Cassell
(919) 658-5056

North Carolina Central University
Durham, NC 27707
AD: William E. Lide
(919) 560-5427

Pembroke State University
Pembroke, NC 28372
AD: Ray Pennington
(910) 521-6227

Pfeiffer College
Missenheimer, NC 28109
AD: T. J. Kostecky
(704) 463-1360, ext. 2407

Queens College (North Carolina)
Charlotte, NC 28274
AD: Dale Layer
(704) 337-2509

St. Andrews Presbyterian
Laurinburg, NC 28352
AD: Carl Ullrich
(910) 277-5274

St. Augustine's College
Raleigh, NC 27811
AD: Open
(919) 516-4171

Shaw University
Raleigh, NC 27601
AD: Keith Smith
(919) 546-8281

Wingate College
Wingate, NC 28174
AD: Beth Lawrence
(704) 233-8193

Winston-Salem State University
Winston-Salem, NC 27102
AD: Albert Roseboro
(910) 750-2141

NORTH DAKOTA

North Dakota State University
Fargo, ND 58105
AD: Robert Entzion
(701) 231-8982

University of North Dakota
Grand Forks, ND 58202
AD: Terry Wanless
(701) 777-2234

OHIO

Ashland College
Ashland, OH 44805
AD: William J. Weidner
(419) 289-5441

University of Findlay
Findlay, OH 45840
AD: Ron Neikamp
(419) 424-4663

OKLAHOMA

Cameron University
Lawton, OK 73505
AD: Sam Carroll
(405) 581-2460

University of Central Oklahoma
Edmond, OK 73034
AD: John Wagnon
(405) 341-2980

OREGON

Portland State University
Portland, OR 97207
AD: Jim Sterk
(503) 725-4000

Southern Oregon State College
Ashland, OR 97520
AD: Monty Cartwright
(541) 552-6789

PENNSYLVANIA

Bloomsburg University
of Pennsylvania
Bloomsburg, PA 17815
AD: Mary Gardner
(717) 389-4050

California University
of Pennsylvania
California, PA 15419
AD: Thomas Pucci
(412) 938-4351

Cheyney University
Cheyney, PA 19319
AD: Andy Hinson
(610) 399-2287

Clarion University
Clarion, PA 16214
AD: Bob Carlson
(814) 226-1997

East Stroudsburg University
East Stroudsburg, PA 18301
AD: Earl W. Edwards
(717) 422-3642

Edinboro University
Edinboro, PA 16444
AD: Jody Mooradian
(814) 732-2776

Gannon University
Erie, PA 16541
AD: Richard Dunford
(814) 871-7416

Indiana University
of Pennsylvania
Indiana, PA 15705-1077
AD: Frank J. Cignetti
(412) 357-2751

Kutztown University
Kutztown, PA 19530
AD: Clark Yeager
(610) 683-4094

Lehigh University
Bethlehem, PA 18015
AD: Joe Sterrett
(610) 758-4300

Lock Haven University
Lock Haven, PA 17745
AD: Sharon E. Taylor
(717) 893-2102

Mansfield University
Mansfield, PA 16933
AD: Roger Maisner
(717) 662-4860

Mercyhurst College
Erie, PA 16546
AD: Pete Russo
(814) 824-2228

Millersville University
Millersville, PA 17551
AD (Men): Gene A. Carpenter
AD (Women): Marjorie Trout
(717) 872-3361

**Philadelphia College of
Textiles & Science**
Philadelphia, PA 19144-5497
AD: Thomas R. Shirley Jr.
(215) 951-2720

Shippensburg University
Shippensburg, PA 17257
AD: James Pribula
(717) 532-1711

Slippery Rock University
Slippery Rock, PA 16057
AD: Paul Lueken
(412) 738-2021

**University of Pittsburgh,
Johnstown**
Johnstown, PA 15904
AD: C. Edward Sherlock
(814) 269-2000

West Chester University
West Chester, PA 19383
AD: Edward M. Matejkovic
(610) 436-3555

RHODE ISLAND

Bryant College
Smithfield, RI 02917
AD: Linda C. Hackett
(401) 232-6070

SOUTH CAROLINA

Coker College
Hartsville, SC 29550
AD: Tim Griggs
(803) 383-8073

Converse College
Spartanburg, SC 29302-0006
AD: Margaret S. Moore
(803) 596-9150

Erskine College
Due West, SC 29639
AD: Bill Lesesne
(803) 379-8850

Francis Marion University
Florence, SC 29501-0547
AD: Gerald Griffin
(803) 661-1240

Lander University
Greenwood, SC 29649
AD: Jeff May
(864) 388-8316

Limestone College
Gaffney, SC 29340
AD: Dennis Bloomer
(803) 489-7151, ext. 568

Newberry College
Newberry College, SC 29108
AD: William Grafton Young Jr.
(803) 321-5155

Presbyterian College
Clinton, SC 29325
AD: Allen Morris
(803) 833-8240

**University of South Carolina,
Aiken**
Aiken, SC 29801
AD: Randy Warrick
(803) 648-6851

**University of South Carolina,
Spartanburg**
Spartanburg, SC 29303
AD: Mike Hall
(864) 503-5141

Wofford College
Spartanburg, SC 29303
AD: Daniel B. Morrison Jr.
(803) 597-4090

SOUTH DAKOTA

Augustana College
Sioux Falls, SD 57197
AD: Bill Gross
(605) 336-4311

Northern State University
Aberdeen, SD 57401
AD: James Kretchman
(605) 626-2488

South Dakota State University
Brookings, SD 57007
AD: Fred M. Oien
(605) 688-5625

University of South Dakota
Vermillion, SD 57069-2390
AD: Jack Doyle
(605) 677-5309

TENNESSEE

Carson-Newman College
Jefferson City, TN 37760
AD: David Barger
(423) 471-3360

Christian Brothers University
Memphis, TN 38104
AD: Doreen Powell
(901) 321-3374

Lane College
Jackson, TN 38301
AD: J. L. Perry
(901) 426-7568

Le Moyne-Owen College
Memphis, TN 38126
AD: E. D. Wilkens
(901) 942-7323

Lincoln Memorial University
Harrogate, TN 37752
AD: Jack Bondurant
(423) 869-6285

TEXAS

Abilene Christian University
Abilene, TX 79699
AD: Stan Lambert
(915) 674-2440

Angelo State University
San Angelo, TX 76909
AD (Men): Jerry Vandergriff
AD (Women): Kathleen Brasfield
(915) 942-2091

East Texas State University
Commerce, TX 75429
AD: Margaret Harbison
(903) 886-5549

Hardin-Simmons University
Abilene, TX 79698
AD: Merlin Morrow
(915) 670-1473

Jarvis Christian College
Hawkins, TX 75765
AD: Open
(903) 769-5883

Midwestern State University
Wichita Falls, TX 76308-2099
AD: Stephen Holland
(817) 689-4767

Tarleton State University
Stephenville, TX 76402
AD: Lonn Reisman
(817) 968-9178

**Texas A & M University,
Kingsville**
Kingsville, TX 78363
AD: Ron Harms
(512) 593-2411

West Texas A & M University
Canyon, TX 79016
AD: Ed B. Harris
(806) 656-2069

VERMONT

St. Michael's College
Colchester, VT 05439
AD: Edward P. Markey
(802) 654-2000

VIRGINIA

Hampton University
Hampton, VA 23668
AD: Dennis E. Thomas
(804) 727-5641

Longwood College
Farmville, VA 23909
AD: Jack Williams
(804) 395-2057

Norfolk State University
Norfolk, VA 23504
AD: William Price
(757) 683-8152

St. Paul's College
Lawrenceville, VA 23868
AD: Harold Williams
(804) 848-2001

Virginia State University
Petersburg, VA 23803
AD: Alfreeda Goff
(804) 524-5030

Virginia Union University
Richmond, VA 23220
AD: James Battle
(804) 342-7376

ATHLETICS DIRECTORS IN NCAA DIVISION I & DIVISION II

WASHINGTON

Seattle Pacific University
Seattle, WA 98119
AD: Alan Graham
(206) 281-2085

WEST VIRGINIA

Alderson-Broaddus College
Philippi, WV 26416
AD: Paul A. Bennett
(304) 457-1700, ext. 262

Bluefield State College
Bluefield, WV 24701
AD: Terry Brown
(304) 327-4191

Concord College
Athens, WV 24712
AD: Don Christie
(304) 384-5347

Davis & Elkins College
Elkins, WV 26241
AD: Will Shaw
(304) 637-1252

Fairmont State College
Fairmont, WV 26554
AD: Colin T. Cameron
(304) 367-4220

Glenville State College
Glenville, WV 26351
AD: Rich Rodriguez
(304) 462-4102

Salem-Teikyo University
Salem, WV 26426
AD: Mike Carey
(304) 782-5286

Shepherd College
Shepherdstown, WV 25443
AD: Monte Cater
(304) 876-5481

University of Charleston
Charleston, WV 25304
AD: Linda Bennett
(304) 357-4820

West Liberty State College
West Liberty, WV 26074
AD: James Watson
(304) 336-8046

**West Virginia Institute
of Technology**
Montgomery, WV 25136
AD: Terry Rupert
(304) 442-3121

West Virginia Wesleyan
Buckhannon, WV 26201
AD: George Klebez
(304) 473-8099

Wheeling Jesuit College
Wheeling, WV 26003
AD: Jay DeFruscio
(304) 243-2365

WISCONSIN

University of Wisconsin, Parkside
Kenosha, WI 53141-2000
AD: Lenny Klaver
(414) 595-2245

INTERCOLLEGIATE ASSOCIATIONS AND CONFERENCES

Despite the competitive fire that illumines college athletics, administrators of college sports like to get together. This clubbiness has produced no fewer than 325 intercollegiate associations and conferences. Shown here are some of the major organizations. All are good sources for internships.

ASSOCIATIONS

The National Collegiate Athletic Association (NCAA)

The origin of the NCAA goes back to the early years of the century, when playing football was a license to commit mayhem. Injuries and deaths were so numerous that President Theodore Roosevelt twice summoned college officials to the White House to persuade them to put a collar on the game. In 1906, to initiate changes in football playing rules, 62 colleges founded the Intercollegiate Athletic Association of the United States. Four years later, the organization adopted its present name.

In the years that followed, membership increased but the NCAA continued to serve mainly as a discussion group, occasionally issuing new playing rules in various sports. In 1921 it held its first national championship in track and field. More rules committees were formed and more championships were conducted, and all was calm until the post-World War II years, when amid an unsettled atmosphere nationwide, the NCAA found itself confronting a mounting series of crises. Guidelines on recruiting and financial aid were being widely abused, postseason football games were proliferating without control, unrestricted televising of football had member institutions worried about reduced gates.

There was more to come: public betting on basketball games had soared, leading to widespread rumors of game-fixing, which turned out to be true. Conditions clearly called for full-time professional leadership.

In 1951, Walter Byers, who had been working part-time, was named full-time executive director, and a year later a national headquarters was established in Kansas City, Missouri. With the blessings of its membership, the NCAA embarked on an expanded program of activities designed to bring cohesion and integrity to college sports. As its influence grew, the association moved aggressively against drug abuse and the shadowy intrusion of unscrupulous player agents. Most notably, it increased the vigor of its investigations of recruiting violations, grade doctoring, undercover payments, and other abuses of the code governing student athlete relations. In the 1980's, the association marshaled support for women's equity in sports. It also expanded national championships and developed one of those championships—the men's annual basketball tournament—into one of the nation's great sports attractions.

In what turned out to have dramatic consequences, the NCAA in 1984 created the Presidents Commission, which for the first time gave the heads of member colleges and universities a direct voice in the association's proceedings. Division I football and basketball coaches, who had long held sway in the association, did not react happily to this development. And as they feared, the college presidents began pressing for reforms in big-time sports, seeking, mainly, a reduction in the costs of sports programs and tougher academic standards for athletes.

Richard D. Schultz inherited this conflict when he succeeded Byers as executive director in 1987. He passed it on to his successor, Cedric W. Dempsey, former director of athletics at the University of Arizona, who became executive director in January 1994. Amid a good deal of rancor, delegates to the association's annual convention in January 1995 took a big step toward reform by voting to raise the academic eligibility standards for freshman athletes in Division I. Under new requirements beginning in August 1996, freshman athletes must attain a grade point average of 2.5 in 13 high school core courses and an SAT score of 700 (or 17 on the ACT). A special provision permits athletes with high school grade point averages as low as 2.0 to become eligible to compete if they score 900 on the SAT.

By 1996 the NCAA Presidents Commission was close to achieving a new governing structure for the NCAA that would give college presidents greater responsibility for athletic programs.

NCAA Scholarships and Internships for Minorities and Women

To help minorities and women prepare for careers in intercollegiate athletics, the NCAA has established a program of annual scholarships and internships.

Scholarships. Grants of $6,000 are awarded to 10 ethnic minorities and 10 women to be used for graduate work in a sports administration program or related program. To be considered for the grants, candidates must have a bachelor's degree and a record of academic achievement and extracurricular activity. In addition, they must be accepted into an NCAA member institution's graduate program. Financial need is not a factor.

Internships. The NCAA provides eight one-year internships at its national headquarters in Overland Park, Kansas, for minority and female college graduates who intend to pursue a career in intercollegiate sports. Interns receive a monthly stipend of $1,300. The NCAA provides hotel accommodations for five days while recipients seek permanent lodgings.

The scholarships and internships are made under the auspices of the NCAA's Minority Opportunities and Interests Committee and the Committee on Women's Athletics.

Additional information is available from Stanley D. Johnson, Director of Professional Development, NCAA, 6201 College Blvd., Overland Park, KS 66211-2422. Phone: (913) 339-1906.

The National Association of Intercollegiate Athletics (NAIA)

The second-largest association of 4-year colleges, the NAIA was the outgrowth of a national small-college basketball tournament held in 1937. It is composed now of more than 400 schools, including one in Canada, and conducts regional and national tournaments in a dozen sports, with 65,000 male and female student athletes taking part. The history of the NAIA is distinguished by the early racial integration of its teams and by its long support of women's participation in intercollegiate sports.

The National Junior College Athletic Association (NJCAA)

The NJCAA has been promoting the sports programs of two-year colleges since 1938, when 13 California schools signed on as charter members. Now encompassing about 550 junior colleges and community colleges nationwide, it is divided into 24 regional units, each with its own administrative corps.

The National Association of Collegiate Directors of Athletics (NACDA)

Founded in 1965 to establish standards in the operations of sports programs, the National Association of Collegiate Directors of Athletics (NACDA) today has a membership of close to 4,500 athletics administrators in the U.S. and Canada and a reputation as a first-rate organization.

Internship opportunities. The NACDA Foundation, funded by revenues from two preseason football games, the Kickoff Classic and the Disneyland Pigskin Classic, in 1985 added a program of student internships to its educational activities. It has proven to be extremely valuable.

The internship program provides training in athletics administration at NACDA's national office in Cleveland. It's available to undergraduate and graduate students, who may choose to attend for the summer months or for September through June. Their various projects include work on NACDA's magazine, *Athletics Administration.*

Full-time interns receive a stipend of $100 a week. For female interns, the program provides free housing.

NACDA's address is 24651 Detroit Rd., Westlake, OH 44145. In charge of the program is Melissa Dukov, who can be reached at (216) 892-4000.

Scholarships. These are grants of $1,000 for graduate study, and they are offered to an exceedingly slim category of college seniors. Recipients NACDA has in mind are people who have served as "athletic support personnel" in schools that have won a national championship of some kind. Support personnel are band members, cheerleaders, equipment managers, facility staff members, student assistants in the athletics department, etc. If you fall into this choice category, you can get more information from Laurie Garrison or Brian Horning in the NACDA office. Oh, one other thing: You've got to have a grade point average of at least 3.0 (based on a 4.0 scale).

CONFERENCES

Division I

The headquarters of the Southeastern Conference, a powerhouse among conferences, is a modern, two-story structure that occupies half a block in downtown Birmingham, Alabama. It was a gift from the city, which tells you what the conference means in that part of the country.

The building houses the SEC's 25-person staff and provides accommodations for the meetings of conference committees, coaches,

and administrative groups. It's also a conference showplace, featuring exhibits honoring the current champions in each of the 18 conference sports, along with displays of its 12 member institutions, and a colorful representation of the league's history.

In short, it's a pleasant setting for the staff's day-to-day business, which includes certifying the eligibility of all student athletes, managing all championship events, enhancing academic opportunities for student athletes, monitoring compliance with the rules and regulations of the NCAA and the conference, coordinating assignments of game officials, cultivating corporate sponsorships, handling media and public relations responsibilities, distributing conference revenue, and negotiating television contracts.

The last item—television deals—is by no means the least. In fact, a TV deal the SEC made in February 1994 was a high point in its 100-year history. The big transaction was a five-year agreement with CBS for the weekly televising of SEC football games starting in 1996. The price negotiated by Commissioner Roy Kramer: about $100 million.

The SEC staff, which consists of 15 professionals and 10 assistants, is one of the largest among the conferences in Division I. Most of the conferences have between seven and 12 professionals, plus several secretarial assistants. (Most, if not all, regularly engage one or more interns.)

While the overall operations of conference staffs are similar, the responsibilities of individual professionals do not always reflect their ranking. For example, the associate commissioner at the Pacific-10 Conference, second in authority, is concerned with compliance and the letter-of-intent program. At other conferences, the number-two person might be in charge of business affairs or the selection and evaluation of game officials.

Unvarying, however, is the role of the conference commissioner, who directs all activities and sets the tone for the conference. What qualities are needed for the job? When Commissioner Joe Kearney of the Western Athletic Conference announced his intention to retire, member institutions of the conference went looking for a successor who met these requirements: administrative experience in intercollegiate sports, including television marketing and negotiations; strong public relations skills; a commitment to NCAA rules and to gender equity; a knowledge of business procedures; and distinct leadership ability, accompanied by creativity and high energy.

And the pay? A conference commissioner draws—depending on the stature of the league—between $65,000 and $150,000. Salaries for associate commissioners range from $60,000 to $100,000. For assistant commissioners, including directors of media relations, the range is from $40,000 to $80,000.

Division II

The picture changes here. Rare is the conference that has more than three full-time professionals. Commonly, a Division II league is run by two or three full-timers—a commissioner and an assistant commissioner or two—and a secretary. Part-timers fill in the gaps. Part-timers usually include a publicity person who turns out news releases and stats, and a sports-wise person who is sent to observe game officials. Salaries for commissioners range from $35,000 to $65,000. For assistant commissioners, the range is from $25,000 to $40,000.

Division III

Only 10 of 32 conferences have paid commissioners, with salaries that run from $20,000 to $40,000. A few of the paid commissioners have full-time assistants. A number of the unpaid commissioners serve on a rotating basis. In some cases, a conference is headed by a person working on released time from a job at a member college.

A list of associations and a directory of conferences in Division I and Division II follows.

ASSOCIATIONS

National Collegiate
Athletic Association (NCAA)
6201 College Blvd.
Overland Park, Kansas 66211-2422
(913) 339-1906
President: Eugene F. Corrigan
Exec Director: Cedric W. Dempsey

National Association of Collegiate
Directors of Athletics (NACDA)
P.O. Box 16428
Cleveland, Ohio 44131
(216) 892-4000
Exec Director: Michael J. Cleary

Division I-A Athletics
Directors Association
P.O. Box 7401
Winston-Salem, N. Carolina 27109
(919) 723-6600
Exec Director: Gene Hooks

National Association of
Intercollegiate Athletics (NAIA)
6120 S. Yale, Suite 1450
Tulsa, Oklahoma 74136
(918) 494-8828
President/CEO: James R. Chasteen

College Football Association (CFA)
6688 Gunpark Dr., Suite 201
Boulder, Colorado 80301-3339
(303) 530-5566
Exec Director: Charles M. Neinas

National Junior College
Athletic Association (NJCAA)
P.O. Box 7305
Colorado Springs, Colorado 80933
(719) 590-9788
Exec Director: George E. Killian

College Athletic Business
Management Association
c/o Dep't of Athletics
University of Texas at El Paso
El Paso, Texas 79968
(915) 747-6780
President: John Giannoni

National Association of Collegiate
Marketing Administrators
P.O. Box 16428
Cleveland, Ohio 44116
(216) 892-4000
Contact: Bob Vecchione

Association of College
Licensing Administrators
638 Prospect Ave.
Hartford, Connecticut 06105-4298
(203) 232-4825
Exec Director: Sharon S. Bruce

National Association of
Athletic Development Directors
P.O. Box 16428
Cleveland, Ohio 44116
(216) 892-4000
Contact: Matt Wolfert

National Athletic Fund-Raisers
Association
P.O. Box 26202
Fresno, California 93729
(209) 436-0149
Exec Director: Lynn Eilefson

College Sports Information
Directors of America
P.O. Box 114A
Texas A&M University at Kingsville
Kingsville, Texas 78363
(512) 595-3908
Secretary: Fred Nuesch

National Association of Academic
Advisors for Athletics
Sports Medicine Bldg., Suite 254
East Carolina University
Greenville, N. Carolina 27858-4353
(919) 757-4550
Secretary: Pam Overton

National Association of Athletics
Compliance Coordinators
c/o Southland Conference
13098 W. 15th St., Suite 303
Plano, Texas 75075
(214) 424-4833
President: Greg Sankey

Athletic Equipment Managers
Association
6224 Hester Rd.
Oxford, Ohio 45056
(513) 523-2362
Exec Director: Jon Falk

NCAA Division I
Commissioners Association
Eugene F. Corrigan, President
Atlantic Coast Conference
P.O. Drawer ACC
Greensboro, N. Carolina 27419-6999
(919) 854-8787

NCAA Division II
Commissioners Association
Noel W. Olson, President
2400 N. Louise Ave., Ramkota Inn
Sioux Falls, S. Dakota 57107-0789
(605) 338-0907

NCAA Division III
Commissioners Association
Jack Swartz, President
Wheaton College Athletics Dep't
Wheaton, Illinois 60187
(708) 752-5167

American West Conference
5855 Brookline Lane
San Luis Obispo, CA 93401-8900
(805) 756-1412
Commissioner: Victor A. Buccola

Atlantic Coast Conference
P.O. Drawer ACC
Greensboro, NC 27419-6999
(910) 854-8787
President: Charles W. Ehrhardt

Atlantic-10 Conference
2 Penn Center Plaza, Suite 1410
Philadelphia, PA 19102
(215) 751-0500
Commissioner: Linda M. Bruno

Big East Conference
56 Exchange Terrace
Providence, RI 02903-1743
(401) 272-9108
Commissioner: Michael A. Tranghese

Big Sky Conference
P.O. Box 1459
Ogden, UT 84402
(801) 392-1978
Commissioner: Doug Fullerton

Big South Conference
Winthrop Coliseum
Eden Terrace
Rock Hill, SC 29733
(803) 817-63408
Commissioner: George F. Sasser

Big West Conference
2 Corporate Park, Suite 206
Irvine, CA 92714
(714) 261-2525
Commissioner: Dennis A. Farrell

Colonial Athletic Association
8625 Patterson Ave.
Richmond, VA 23235
(804) 754-1616
Commissioner: Thomas E. Yeager

Eastern College Athletic Conference
P.O. Box 3
Centerville, MA 02632
(508) 771-5060
Commissioner: Clayton W. Chapman

Ivy Group
120 Alexander St.
Princeton, NJ 08544
(609) 258-6426
Executive Director: Jeffrey H. Orleans

Metro Atlantic Athletic Conference
1090 Amboy Ave.
Edison, NJ 08837-2847
(908) 225-0202
Commissioner: Richard J. Ensor

Mid-American Conference
4 SeaGate, Suite 102
Toledo, OH 43604
(419) 249-7177
Commissioner: Jerry A. Ippoliti

Mid-Continent Conference
40 Shuman Blvd., Suite 118
Naperville, IL 60563
(630) 416-7560
Acting Commissioner: Jon Steinbrecher

Mid-Eastern Athletic Conference
102 N. Elm St.
Greensboro, NC 27420-1205
(919) 275-9961
Commissioner: Charles S. Harris

Midwestern Collegiate Conference
201 S. Capitol Ave., Suite 500
Indianapolis, IN 46225
(317) 237-5622
Commissioner: Jonathan B. LeCrone

Missouri Valley Conference
1000 St. Louis Union Station,
  Suite 333
St. Louis, MO 63102
(314) 421-0339
Commissioner: J. Douglas Elgin

Mountain Pacific Sports Federation
2 Corporate Park, Suite 206
Irvine, CA 92714
(714) 261-2525
Commissioner: Robert L. Halvaks

Northeast Conference
900 Route 9
Woodbridge, NJ 07095
(908) 636-9119
Commissioner: Chris Monasch

Ohio Valley Conference
278 Franklin Rd., Suite 103
Brentwood, TN 37027
(615) 371-1698
Commissioner: R. Daniel Beebe

Pacific-10 Conference
800 S. Broadway, Suite 400
Walnut Creek, CA 94596
(510) 932-4411
Commissioner: Thomas C. Hansen

Patriot League
3897 Adler Place, Bldg. C, Suite 310
Bethlehem, PA 18017-9000
(610) 691-2414
Executive Director: Constance
  H. Hurlbut

Pioneer Football League
1000 Union Station, Suite 333
St. Louis, MO 63103
(314) 421-2268
Commissioner: Patricia Viverito

Southeastern Conference
2201 Civic Center Blvd.
Birmingham, AL 35203
(205) 458-3000
Commissioner: Roy F. Kramer

Southern Conference
One W. Pack Sq., Suite 1508
Asheville, NC 28801
(704) 255-7872
Commissioner: Wright Waters

Southland Conference
8150 N. Central Expwy., Suite 930
Dallas, TX 75206
(214) 750-7522
Commissioner: Gregory Sankey

Southwestern Athletic Conference
1500 Sugar Bowl Dr.
New Orleans, LA 70112
(504) 523-7574
Commissioner: James Frank

Sun Belt Conference
One Galleria Blvd., Suite 2115
Metairie, LA 70001
(504) 834-6600
Commissioner: Craig Thompson

Trans America Athletic Conference
The Commons
3370 Vineville Ave., Suite 108-B
Macon, GA 31204
(912) 474-3394
Commissioner: William C. Bibb

West Coast Conference
400 Oyster Point Blvd., Suite 221
South San Francisco, CA 94080
(415) 873-8622
Commissioner: Michael M. Gilleran

Western Athletic Conference
9250 E. Costilla Ave., Suite 300
Englewood, CO 80112
(303) 799-9221
Commissioner: Karl D. Benson

Yankee Conference
University of Richmond
P.O. Box 8
Richmond, VA 23173
(804) 289-8371
Commissioner: Charles S. Boone

**California Collegiate
Athletic Association**
40 Via Di Roma
Long Beach, CA 90803
(310) 985-4051
Commissioner: Tom D. Morgan

**Central Intercollegiate
Athletic Association**
P.O. Box 7349
Hampton, VA 23666
(804) 865-0071
Commissioner: Leon G. Kerry

**Great Lakes Intercollegiate
Athletic Conference**
3250 W. Big Beaver, Suite 300
Troy, MI 48084
(810) 649-2036
Commissioner: Thomas J. Brown

Great Lakes Valley Conference
Pan Am Plaza
201 S. Capital Ave.
Indianapolis, IN 46225
(317) 237-5636
Commissioner: Carl McAlouse

Gulf South Conference
4 Office Park Cir., Suite 218
Birmingham, AL 35223
(205) 870-9750
Commissioner: Nathan N. Salant

Lone Star Conference
1221 W. Campbell Rd., Suite 217
Richardson, TX 75080
(214) 234-0033
Commissioner: Fred Jacoby

**Mid-America Intercollegiate
Athletics Association**
P.O. Box 508
Maryville, MO 64468
(816) 582-5655
Commissioner: Ken B. Jones

**New England Collegiate
Conference**
P.O. Box 1207
Farmington, CT 06034
(860) 677-1269
Commissioner: William M. Moore

**New York Collegiate Athletic
Conference**
3031 Arrowhead Lane
Norristown, PA 19401
(516) 877-4231
Commissioner: Tom Gallagher

**North Central Intercollegiate
Athletic Conference**
Ramkota Inn
2400 N. Louise Ave.
Sioux Falls, SD 57107
(605) 338-0907
Commissioner: Noel W. Olson

Northeast-10 Conference
P.O. Box 1197
Westfield, MA 01086
(413) 562-4789
Commissioner: F. Paul Bogan

**Northern Sun Intercollegiate
Conference**
6458 City West Pkwy., Suite 100
Eden Prairie, MN 55344
(612) 943-3929
Commissioner: Tom Wistrcill

Pacific West Conference
P.O. Box 2002
Billings, MT 59103
(406) 657-2932
Commissioner: Elwood B. Hahn

Peach Belt Athletic Conference
P.O. Box 204290
Augusta, GA 30917-4290
(706) 860-8499
Commissioner: Marvin Vanover

**Pennsylvania State Athletic
Conference**
105 Zimmerli Bldg.
Lock Haven University
Lock Haven, PA 17745
(717) 893-2512
Commissioner: Charles A. Eberle

**Rocky Mountain Athletic
Conference**
1631 Mesa Ave.
Copper Bldg, Suite B
Colorado Springs, CO 08906
(719) 471-0066
Commissioner: Kurt L. Patberg

South Atlantic Conference
McGregor Downs, Suite 201
10801 Johnston Rd.
Charlotte, NC 28226
(704) 543-1181
Commissioner: Doug Echols

**Southern Intercollegiate Athletic
Conference**
P.O. Box 92032
Atlanta, GA 30314
(404) 659-3380
Commissioner: Wallace Jackson

Sunshine State Conference
7061 Grand National Dr., Suite 138
Orlando, FL 32819
(407) 248-8460
Commissioner: Donald C. Landry

THE GOLF INDUSTRY

Golf accounts for more employment

than all other sports combined.

And its popularity continues to rise.

GOLF. IT'S BIG AND IT'S GROWING

The appeal of golf is extraordinary. According to the National Golf Foundation (NGF), the primary source of golf statistics, 25 million Americans are now playing the game. That's more than are engaged in any other sport. By a long shot.

And the sport continues to grow. The NGF says that 1,912 new courses were opened between 1991 and 1995, bringing the total number of courses in the country to 15,390. About 4,760 courses are owned by private country clubs and golf resorts. The rest are municipal and daily-fee courses.

The number of people employed in golf operations is 265,000, according to the NGF. By our reckoning, that means more people earn a living in golf than in baseball, football, basketball, hockey, and tennis combined.

Many of the jobs in the golf industry—jobs in organizing, marketing, and managing golf tournaments, and in representing touring golf professionals—are dealt with in our section on sports marketing and management. The material that follows covers other golf-related occupations.

COUNTRY CLUBS AND RESORTS

Golf pros who work at clubs and resorts have a big presence at these establishments (and often are the lure that draws clientele). The pros handle the daily schedule of play by club members and resort guests; they arrange competitions, run golf classes and give private lessons, and operate on-site golf shops, where golf equipment and attire can be purchased. If you're a scratch player and have an outgoing personality, you can look forward to earnings of about $30,000 at a small facility and an income of six figures at a nationally known club or resort. If you have an outgoing personality but play bogey golf at best, you might want to consider a job in club or resort management.

Even if you've never held a golf club in your hand, you can't ask for a more attractive and congenial atmosphere.

Country Club Management

Club managers supervise a wide variety of daily operations, from maintenance of athletic facilities to food service. Depending on the size and location of their clubs, their earnings range from $33,000 to well over $100,000. Assistant managers get between $25,000 and $35,000. So do assistant food-service managers. Clubhouse managers earn between $30,000 and $60,000.

New employees directly out of college are often hired at midmanagement level as assistant managers. Favored for these appointments are graduates with degrees in hotel and restaurant management or business administration, and particularly those who have picked up some experience in club operations, either through internships or summer work at clubs while in college.

More than a third of the clubs provide internships.

The Club Managers Association

An important source of job information is the Club Managers Association of America (CMAA), an organization of 5,000 managers of private clubs. (Almost 70 percent are managers of golf and country clubs; the others manage other types of private clubs, including city, athletic, and yacht clubs.)

The CMAA conducts an active program of assistance for college students planning to enter the private-club industry. As part of that program, it has established student chapters of the association in 27 colleges and universities, creating a networking system through which students are informed of association-sponsored scholarships, internships, and job openings. Chapter members can attend the association's workshops and regional meetings of club managers, and the industrywide annual conference. Chapters are located at these in-

stitutions:

Auburn University, Auburn, Alabama
California State Polytechnic University, Pomona
Cornell University, Ithaca, New York
Eastern Illinois University, Charleston
Florida State University, Tallahassee
Georgia State University, Atlanta
Iowa State University, Ames
Michigan State University, East Lansing
Northern Arizona University, Flagstaff
Oklahoma State University, Stillwater
Pennsylvania State University, University Park
Purdue University, Calumet, Indiana
Purdue University, West Lafayette, Indiana
University of Delaware at Newark
University of Denver, Colorado
University of Hawaii at Manoa, Honolulu
University of Houston, Texas
University of Massachusetts at Amherst
University of Missouri, Columbia
University of Nevada at Las Vegas
University of New Haven, Connecticut
University of New Orleans, Louisiana
University of North Texas at Denton
University of South Carolina at Columbia
University of Wisconsin-Stout at Menomonie
Washington State University, Pullman
Widener University, Chester, Pennsylvania

CMAA scholarships. The CMAA Foundation and many of the association's local professional chapters annually award thousands of dollars in scholarships to students who have demonstrated interest in the club management field. Requirements may vary but usually include at least one year of college study, a satisfactory grade point average, and work experience in a private club. Write or phone for more information.

CMAA job information services. The association produces a monthly listing of clubs with midmanagement openings that it sends to student chapter presidents, faculty advisors, and recent graduates. For the benefit of its members who are unemployed or who are looking for new opportunities, the association turns out a weekly list of openings for executive management personnel.

The address of the Club Managers Association of America is 1733 King St., Alexandria, VA 22314. Phone: (703) 739-9500.

Golf Resort Jobs

Resort managers carry a full load of responsibilities that include business management, marketing, personnel management, and public relations—plus the supervision of sports plant improvements, housekeeping functions, and the care and feeding of guests.

A bachelor's degree in hotel and restaurant administration is the usual preparation for a career in resort management. What students need to learn most of all is that they must be able to get along with all kinds of people, even in stressful situations. Managers also need to be able to organize and direct the work of others—a large resort may have a couple of hundred employees—and be able to solve problems.

A new college graduate begins as a trainee at low pay (perhaps $15,000). At large resorts, trainees who show promise are rotated among various departments to get a thorough knowledge of the resort's operation. Advancement comes with experience, but the process may be slow at independently owned establishments, where advancement depends on openings occurring higher up the administrative ladder. The best opportunities are offered by the large hotel chains, which have extensive career-ladder programs and give the aspiring manager a chance to transfer to other establishments.

Getting started. The route to jobs in golf resort management commonly begins with a college program in hospitality, as we've said, but the field is also open to graduates of other programs that have pertinence—business administration, for example, or sports management.

Jack Damioli, resident manager of the famous Greenbrier in Sulphur Springs, West Virginia, got his start in Ohio University's sports management program, which arranged an internship for him in the Greenbrier's golf department.

The internship was a nine-month deal. The work wasn't much of a challenge—it consisted mainly of storing golf bags and golf carts—but it met the primary purpose of an internship, a chance to look around and see what's happening. In any case, he made a nice impression and was invited to join the staff as a trainee.

His first job was at the front desk, where trainees often begin, learning to handle guests courteously and efficiently, resolving complaints and problems, and carrying out requests for special services. His next job brought him into conference services, helping to coordinate meetings and conventions of various organizations. He became sales manager, then assistant director of conference services. Nine years after arriving at the Greenbrier, at the age of 33, he was made resident manager, with complete responsibility for the supervision of the resort's complex day-to-day operations.

Damioli feels his interest in sports was a factor in his rise at the Greenbrier, because it gave him an understanding of the services and atmosphere that would make guests happy. But in evaluating job applicants, he says, he makes no distinction between graduates of sports management programs and hotel management programs.

"The right person can be trained to do the job," he says. And who is the right person? The one who has a genuinely pleasant disposition and is eager to be helpful to the guests. In the resort business, Damioli says, that's what it takes to get ahead.

Earnings. According to a 1995 survey, salaries of managers ranged from an average of about $40,000 at small resorts to an average of $82,000 at large establishments. In some places, managers can earn bonuses of up to 15 percent of their base salaries. In addition, they and their families usually get free lodging, meals, laundry, and other services. In 1995, salaries of assistant managers averaged $40,000, but salaries varied substantially because of differences in duties and responsibilities. Those involved in food service, for example, averaged close to $44,000.

For more information about careers in hotel management, write to: Information Center, American Hotel and Motel Association, 1201 New York Ave. NW, Washington, DC 20005-3931.

* * * * *

Florida State University has a resort and club management program that's designed for students interested in both sports and hospitality. Mark Bonn, director of the program, puts a heavy emphasis on paid internships ($4.25 an hour for a 40-hour week) and makes special efforts to bring recruiters from large resorts to the campus. The program makes a point of training students to be environmentally sensitive. (The overuse of pesticides is a matter of serious concern in Florida.)

GOLF COURSE SUPERINTENDENTS

A key figure in the management of club, resort, and public golf courses is the golf course superintendent, a specialist much esteemed in the industry (and paid accordingly).

Primarily, the superintendent is responsible for the playing conditions at a golf facility. But there's much more to the job.

Superintendents manage all golf playing areas and surrounding grounds, manage the equipment and facilities used in maintenance operations, and hire, train, and supervise the maintenance staff. They prepare an annual budget for all operations and oversee expenditures. They keep records of pest outbreaks and weather conditions. They are responsible for

HE'S PROBABLY THE RICHEST ENTREPRENEUR IN THE WORLD OF SPORTS, AND CERTAINLY THE BIGGEST EMPLOYER.

Robert H. Dedman of Dallas has been very good for the game of golf, and golf has returned the favor by helping him build a Texas-size fortune.

Dedman is the founder of ClubCorp International, a company that owns and operates about 250 private clubs, resorts, and public-fee golf courses around the world.

It all began in 1957, when Dedman, then a lawyer working for Texas oilman H. L. Hunt, got the idea of building a country club that would offer membership at low rates to Dallas's growing middle-income population. Two years after the Brookhaven Country Club opened, he opened a second club in Los Angeles. And he just kept going, building new clubs and then acquiring existing clubs that were in financial trouble, including grand old establishments like the Firestone Country Club in Ohio and the Pinehurst Hotel & Country Club in North Carolina. With golf as the catalyst, he added sports resorts to his string of properties, along with about 40 public golf courses around the country, and at the same time developed private city dining clubs for business executives.

The world's largest operator of clubs and resorts, ClubCorp is a $1.2 billion company employing 18,000 people, among them club managers, architects, agronomists, and golf personnel.

The company is widely respected for its efficient management, and is given credit for raising the standards of the entire industry.

Dedman grew up in modest circumstances in Rison, Arkansas. After service in the Navy, he collected degrees in business, engineering, and law at the University of Texas at Austin and a master's in law at Southern Methodist University. His many benefactions include a gift of $25 million to SMU. He is a member of the board of trustees of the university, where Dedman College and the Dedman Center for Lifetime Sports are named for him. At the University of Texas at Austin, 800 National Merit Scholars are named Dedman Merit Scholars in recognition of scholarship funds he has donated. A hospital in Dallas also bears his name.

any construction or renovation that takes place.

The superintendent may also be responsible for maintenance of the golf-car fleet, clubhouse grounds and landscaping, other recreational facilities, and, if it exists, a sod farm and nursery.

Requirements. The superintendent must have advanced knowledge of agronomy and turfgrass management, a working knowledge of the principles and methods of golf facility construction, and a thorough understanding of the rules and strategies of the game of golf. The abilities to communicate with the organization's top management and with the public and to work cooperatively with the facility's golf professional are also important.

The job also requires a knowledge of laws and regulations dealing with safety and environmental standards. Some states require certification or licensing as a pesticide applicator.

The pay. Salaries depend on the size and location of the golf facility. Most superintendents earn between $60,000 and $100,000. Some, at multicourse facilities, earn more.

Career preparation. To be competitive in the golf course management market, a bachelor's degree in turfgrass management is strongly recommended. If you already have a bachelor's degree in another field, you might

THE PRO AT PINEHURST

North Carolina's Pinehurst Hotel & Country Club, proud symbol of Robert Dedman's empire, bills itself as "the Golf Capital of the World," and who's to argue? With eight magnificent courses that stretch from the hotel's stately verandas to the golden horizon, and a golf tradition unmatched for the richness of its lore, Pinehurst is, indeed, something special.

Don Padgett, director of golf operations, and himself something of a legend among club professionals, takes it all in stride. A plain-spoken man from New Castle, Indiana, who has made his living in golf for almost half a century, he knows just what he's there for. "This is a business," he says. "And the business is to provide a place for people to relax and enjoy the game of golf."

Working for him in the golf department are 145 to 150 people. They include 22 pros (14 PGA members, eight apprentices). Padgett recruits his professionals through PGA job listings.

Many of the others in the department work in the golf shop, a busy retail operation that employs managers, assistant managers, and clerks. Filling other nonprofessional jobs are starters, rangers, driving-range personnel, and locker-room personnel. Entry-level employees start at about $275 a week and graduate to about $400 a week or more, depending on the job.

For Padgett, who worked as club pro at four resorts around the country before getting his plum appointment at Pinehurst in 1986, every member of the golf department is important to the overall operation, including the clerks in the golf shop. "Do you know," he said with obvious satisfaction, "we sell 15,000 golf shirts a year."

dent after graduation. To qualify as a head superintendent, you'll need several years of experience as an assistant.

Prospects. Although competition for the better positions in golf course management will always be intense, the prospects for employment in the years ahead look very good. New courses are being built at a rapid pace—about 125 a year—and there's no sign of a letup. In fact, the National Golf Foundation estimates that to meet the demand for play by the year 2000 nearly 400 new courses will be needed each year.

Incidentally, your studies won't end when you graduate. Virtually all superintendents participate in continuing education programs to keep up with scientific and technological advances affecting their work.

Golf Course Superintendents Association of America

The GCSAA is a powerhouse organization with 16,000 members in the U.S. and abroad and a program of services that extends from student assistance to a membership retirement plan. Its educational services include more than 60 different seminars on turfgrass and management topics, along with correspondence courses and special training courses for irrigation technicians and chemical applicators. Its International Golf Course Conference and Show is one of the biggest expositions in the U.S. Its monthly magazine, *Golf Course Management*, is the leading publication in the golf industry and one of the best trade journals in the country. The association also runs an employment assistance service for its members.

It does a lot, too, for students interested in careers as golf course superintendents.

To begin, the GCSAA invites students into the organization, a step that gives them networking access to 110 chapters throughout the country. For student members about to

consider taking a two-year turfgrass program for an associate degree. Many community colleges offer it. (See page 178 for information about programs in turfgrass management and the colleges that offer these programs.) You can increase your marketability by getting a summer or part-time job with a superintendent while you're in school. If a job isn't available, talk to the head of your department, or the appropriate faculty member, about arranging an internship. Many superintendents—not all—employ interns (often with a stipend). On-the-course training, coupled with your academic work, will help set you up for a position as an assistant superinten-

graduate, the GCSAA offers a special service: it gives them a free listing in the "Student Directory" section of *Golf Course Management*, alerting superintendents to their availability for jobs.

In addition, the association provides the following:

Scholarships and fellowships. The GCSAA Scholars Program funds awards from $500 to $3,500 to outstanding undergraduate and graduate students who are planning careers as golf course superintendents. Students must have completed the first year of an appropriate associate's or bachelor's degree program (in turfgrass science, agronomy, horticulture, etc.). The awards are made annually and are based on academic achievement, career preparation, and leadership potential.

The James Watson Fellowships provide up to four awards of $5,000 to candidates for master's and doctoral degrees in fields related to golf course management. The aim of this program is to identify tomorrow's leading teachers and researchers. Awards are based on academic achievement, professional preparation, peer recommendations, and potential to make an important contribution in science and/or education related to golf course management. The program is sponsored by the Toro Company.

The O. M. Scott Scholarship Program funds an internship/scholarship program that offers work experience and an opportunity to compete for a limited number of $2,500 financial aid awards. Students are selected for paid summer internships based on academic ability, interest in a "green industry" career, and other factors. A primary goal of the program is to attract women and minorities to this field. The program is sponsored by the O. M. Scott & Sons Co.

The Ambassador Award, a $3,500 scholarship, was created to recognize outstanding students from outside the United States.

The Robert Trent Jones Endowment Fund, honoring golf course architect Robert Trent Jones Sr., finances student scholarships from revenue generated by the endowment.

The GCSAA also runs a student essay contest (on the subject of golf and the environment) that's open to undergraduate and graduate students.

For more information on all of the above, contact GCSAA Development Department, 1421 Research Park Dr., Lawrence, KS 66049-3859. Phone: (913) 841-2240.

GOLF COURSE ARCHITECTS

If you've seen one football field, you've seen them all.

If you've seen one basketball court, you've seen them all.

If you've seen one hockey rink, you've seen them all.

If you've seen one golf course, you've seen one golf course.

Interesting, isn't it. Golf is the only major sport that does not have a playing area of specific length and width or a common setting. No two golf courses are exactly alike.

Baseball diamonds aren't forever; golf courses are. Stadiums that house baseball and other sports are old and tired after 25 years. But many of America's greatest golf courses are almost 100 years old and going strong. Oakmont, in Pittsburgh, host of the 1994 U.S. Open, was built in 1903. It is an official National Historic Landmark.

The name of Oakmont's creator, Henry C. Fownes, endures to this day. That's the way it is in golf. The designer of a great course is forever enshrined in the romance of the game. If you're looking for immortality, you might remember that when you're considering a career choice.

Every golf course has a character—a personality of its own. But each must be, in the words of the American Society of Golf Course Architects, "an enjoyable layout that challenges golfers of all abilities and exemplifies the highest standards and traditions of golf."

Creating a golf course is a collaboration of golf course designer and nature. Nature supplies the basic setting, which might be a verdant plain, a desert oasis, an ocean shore. The rest is up to the designer, who comes equipped with the following:

• A thorough knowledge of the game of golf. Aesthetic values must be combined with an understanding of what makes the game challenging without going beyond the limits of human athleticism. (Hazards, for example, should be punishing but not lethal.)

• Competence in landscape architecture. Sculpting a golf course must be done in compatibility with the natural landscape.

• A familiarity with civil engineering, turf culture, and the uses of heavy construction equipment.

• The ability to develop detailed plans and specifications covering all phases of construction, including clearing, grading, irrigation, and the planting of grass and trees. Plus, cost estimates that do not put golf course owners in shock.

Golf course architects work not only on designing new courses but also—and probably more frequently—on renovating existing courses. Theirs is an elite profession, meaning that their numbers are small. The American Society of Golf Course Architects, the dominant professional organization, has only 93 members. (Designers may not join until they have worked on at least five projects.)

For access to this profession, a degree in landscape architecture is recommended.

The address of the American Society of Golf Course Architects is 221 N. LaSalle St., Chicago, IL 60601. Phone: (312) 372-7090.

USGA MUSEUM AND LIBRARY (GOLF HOUSE)

Far Hills, New Jersey

The museum, known as Golf House, occupies a majestic Georgian colonial mansion in north central New Jersey. *Annual visitors:* 20,000. *Employees:* 200 full-time and part-time, with a "possible position" for an intern. *Director:* David B. Fay. *Address:* P.O. Box 708, Far Hills, NJ 07931. *Phone:* (908) 234-2306.

H O W   T H E Y   G O T   T H E R E

REES LEE JONES
Golf Course Designer

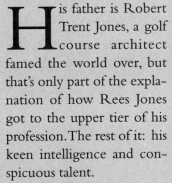

His father is Robert Trent Jones, a golf course architect famed the world over, but that's only part of the explanation of how Rees Jones got to the upper tier of his profession. The rest of it: his keen intelligence and conspicuous talent.

Rees Jones graduated from Yale with a degree in history in 1963 and went on to study landscape architecture at Harvard's Graduate School of Design. In 1965, following his brother, Bobby, he joined his father's firm and was involved in the design or supervision of more than 50 golf courses. He set up his own shop in 1974 and before long developed an inde-

pendent reputation as a creator of eye-arresting and eminently playable layouts. In 1978, at age 36, he became the youngest person to serve as president of the American Society of Golf Course Architects.

His triumphs include major remodeling projects at the Country Club at Brookline, Massachusetts, the Hazeltine Golf Club in Minnesota, and the Congressional Country Club in Maryland, and new courses at the Pinehurst in North Carolina, the Marriott's Griffin Gate in Kentucky, and the Country Club of Hilton Head in South Carolina.

Home base for Jones is Montclair, New Jersey, where he was born in 1941.

From Rees Jones, Some Career Tips

An undergraduate degree in landscape architecture or civil engineering is enough to get you started—but the degree won't be worth much unless you pick up work experience. And the way to get that experience is by getting summer jobs with contractors (golf course builders) while you're in college. Real, hard-work jobs. You have to know how a golf course is built before you can think of designing one. The time to apply for a job with a design firm is after you have worked for a contractor.

Skill in designing comes only by doing— by working with the land. Every kind of terrain, every kind of climate. It will take five years before you have a grasp of all the possible ways of using the land.

A beginning position with a design firm (starting pay is usually about $20,000) almost always means working at a drafting table. Don't allow yourself to get comfortable at the table—you must get out on a project as soon as possible.

The single most important requirement in this profession: you must have a true love for the game of golf.

*　*　*　*　*

Note: If you're interested in getting a summer job with a golf course contractor, the Golf Course Builders Association of America may be able to help you find contractors in your area. The association's address is 920 Airport Rd., Suite 210, Chapel Hill, NC 27514. Phone: (919) 942-8922.

MAJOR U.S. GOLF ORGANIZATIONS

**American Society
of Golf Club Architects**
221 N. LaSalle St.
Chicago, IL 60601
(312) 372-7090
Exec Sec: Paul Fullmer

**Club Managers Association
of America**
1733 Kings St.
Alexandria, VA 22314
(703) 739-9500
Pub Affairs Dir: Kathi Driggs

**Golf Course Builders
Association of America**
920 Airport Rd., Suite 210
Chapel Hill, NC 27514
(919) 942-8922
Exec VP: Phil Arnold

**Golf Course Superintendents
Association of America**
1421 Research Park Dr.
Lawrence, KS 66049-3859
(913) 841-2240
CEO: Stephen Mona

**International Association
of Golf Administrators**
3740 Cahuenga Blvd.
N. Hollywood, CA 91609
(818) 980-3630
Dir: Kevin Heaney

**Ladies Professional
Golf Association**
100 International Golf Dr.
Daytona Beach , FL 32124
(904) 274-1099
Comm: Jim Ritts
Has a staff of 40 at Daytona Beach
Headquarters. LPGA Tour membership is
over 300. Teaching and Club Professional
Division has almost 700 members.

National Club Association
3050 K St. NW
Washington, DC 20007
(202) 625-2080
Represents the common business interests
of private clubs in tax, legal, and
legislative matters.

**National Golf Course Owners
Association**
1470 Ben Sawyer Blvd.
Mt. Pleasant, SC 29464
(803) 881-9956
Exec Dir: Mike Hughes

National Golf Foundation
1150 S. U.S. Highway One
Jupiter, FL 33477
(407) 744-6006
Pres: Joe Beditz
The primary source for research and
statistical information on the golf
industry. Has a membership of more than
6,500, representing every aspect of the
industry.

**Professional Golfers
Association of America**
100 Ave. of the Champions
P.O. Box 109601
Palm Beach Gardens, FL 33410
(407) 624-8400
Exec Dir: Jim L. Awtrey
Composed of about 23,000 golf
professionals. Maintains educational,
recertification, insurance, and financial
programs for members.

PGA Tour
112 TPC Blvd., Sawgrass
Ponte Vedra Beach, FL 32082
(904) 285-3700
Comm: Tim Finchem

United States Golf Association
P.O. Box 708
Far Hills, NJ 07931-0708
(908) 234-2300
Exec Dir: David B. Fay
Governing body of golf in the U.S.
Sponsors 13 national championships.
Writes and interprets the rules of the
games, maintains national handicapping
and course rating systems, sponsors
turfgrass and environmental research,
tests equipment, distributes films and
publications on all aspects of golf, and
maintains Golf House museum
and library.

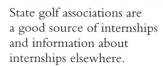

State golf associations are a good source of internships and information about internships elsewhere.

ALABAMA

Alabama Golf Association
P.O. Box 20149
Birmingham, AL 35216
(205) 979-1234
Exec Dir: Buford R. McCarty

ALASKA

Anchorage Golf Association
P.O. Box 112210
Anchorage, AK 99511
(907) 349-4653

ARIZONA

Arizona Golf Association
7226 N. 16th St., Suite 200
Phoenix, AZ 85020
(602) 944-3035
Exec Dir: Ed Gowan

Arizona Women's Golf Association
11001 N. Tatum Blvd., Suite 247
Phoenix, AZ 85044
(602) 953-5996
Exec Dir: Lorraine Theis

ARKANSAS

Arkansas State Golf Association
2311 Biscayne Dr., Suite 308
Little Rock, AR 72207
(501) 227-8555
Exec Dir: Jay Fox

CALIFORNIA

Northern California Golf Association
P.O. Box NCGA
Pebble Beach, CA 93953
(408) 625-4653
Exec Dir: Bill Paulson

Southern California Golf Association
3740 Cahuenga Blvd., Suite 100
N. Hollywood, CA 91609
(818) 980-3630
CEO: Newell O. Pinch

COLORADO

Colorado Golf Association
5655 S. Yosemite, Suite 101
Englewood, CO 80111
(303) 779-4653
Exec Dir: Warren Simmons

Colorado Junior Golf Association
5655 S. Yosemite, Suite 101
Englewood, CO 80111
(303) 779-4653

Colorado Women's Golf Association
5655 S. Yosemite, Suite 101
Englewood, CO 80111
(303) 779-4653

CONNECTICUT

Connecticut State Golf Association
35 Cold Spring Rd., Suite 212
Rocky Hill, CT 06067
(203) 257-4171
Exec Dir: Russell C. Palmer

DELAWARE

Delaware State Golf Association
7234 Lancaster Pike, Suite 302-B
Hockessin, DE 19707
(302) 257-4171
Exec Dir: J. Curtis Riley

FLORIDA

Florida State Golf Association
P.O. Box 21177
Sarasota, FL 34276-4177
(813) 921-5695
Exec Dir: Cal Korf

GEORGIA

Georgia State Golf Association
121 Village Pkwy., Bldg 3
Marietta, GA 30067
(404) 955-4272
Exec Dir: Stephen F. Mona

HAWAII

Hawaii Golf Association
1859 Alaweo St.
Honolulu, HI 96821
(808) 521-6622
Exec Dir: Dr. Richard Ho

IDAHO

Idaho Golf Association, Inc.
P.O. Box 3025
Boise, ID 83703
(208) 342-4442
Exec Dir: Lyman Gallup

ILLINOIS

Western Golf Association
One Briar Rd.
Golf, IL 60029
(708) 724-4600
Exec Dir: Donald Johnson

INDIANA

Indiana Golf Association
P.O. Box 516
Franklin, IN 46131
(317) 844-7271
Exec Dir: Mike David

KANSAS

Kansas Golf Association
3301 Clinton Pkwy. Court, Suite 4
Lawrence, KS 66047
(913) 842-4833
Exec Dir: Brett Marshall

KENTUCKY

Kentucky Golf Association—PGA
P.O. Box 18396
Louisville, KY 40261-0396
(502) 449-7255
Exec Dir: Mike Donahoe

LOUISIANA

Louisiana Golf Association
1305 Emerson St.
Monroe, LA 71201
(318) 342-1968
Exec Dir: R. L. "Bob" DeMoss

MAINE

Maine State Golf Association
P.O. Box 8
Gardiner, ME 04345
(207) 782-4158
Exec Dir: Ralph Noel Jr.

MARYLAND

Maryland State Golf Association
P.O. Box 16289
Baltimore, MD 21210
(301) 467-8899
Exec Dir: John Emich

MASSACHUSETTS

Massachusetts Golf Association
190 Park Rd.
Weston, MA 02193
(617) 891-4300
Exec Dir: Richard Haskell

MICHIGAN

Golf Association of Michigan
37935 Twelve Mile Rd., Suite 200
Farmington Hills, MI 48331
(810) 553-4200
Exec Dir: Brett Marshall

MINNESOTA

Minnesota Golf Association
6550 York Ave. S, Suite 405
Edina, MN 55435
(612) 927-4643
Exec Dir: Ross Galarneault

MISSISSIPPI

Mississippi Golf Association
1019 N. 12th Ave., Suite A3
Laurel, MS 39441
(601) 649-0570
Exec Dir: Billy D. Cass

MISSOURI

Missouri Golf Association
P.O. Box 104164
Jefferson City, MO 65110
(314) 636-8994
Exec Dir: Bill Wells

Metropolitan Amateur Golf Association
12225 Clayton Rd.
St. Louis, MO 63131

MONTANA

Montana State Golf Association
P.O. Box 3389
Butte, MT 59701
(406) 782-9208
Exec Dir: Fraser MacDonald

STATE GOLF ASSOCIATIONS

NEBRASKA

Nebraska Golf Association
5625 O St., Suite "Fore"
Lincoln, NE 68510
(402) 486-1440
Exec Dir: Virgil Parker

NEVADA

Nevada State Golf Association
P.O. Box 5630
Sparks, NV 89432-5630
(702) 673-4653
Exec Dir: John Whalen

NEW HAMPSHIRE

New Hampshire Golf Association
45 Kearney St.
Manchester, NH 03104
(603) 623-0396
Exec Dir: Robert Elliott

NEW JERSEY

New Jersey State Golf Association
100 Broad St.
Bloomfield, NJ 07003
(201) 338-8334
Exec Dir: Steve M. Foehl

NEW YORK

New York State Golf Association
P.O. Box 3459
Elmira, NY 14905
(607) 733-0007
Exec Dir: Thomas Reidy

Long Island Golf Association
66 Magnolia Ave.
Garden City, NY 11530

NORTH CAROLINA

Carolinas Golf Association
P.O. Box 428
West End, NC 27376
(919) 673-1000
Exec Dir: Jack Nance

NORTH DAKOTA

North Dakota State Golf
Association
930 Arthur Dr.
Bismarck, ND 58501
(701) 255-0242
Exec Dir: Gordon Benrud

OHIO

Ohio Golf Association
5300 McKitrick Blvd.
Columbus, OH 43235
(614) 457-8169
Exec Dir: Nicholas Popa

OKLAHOMA

Oklahoma Golf Association
629 Timber Lane
Edmond, OK 73083
(405) 340-6333
Exec Dir: Bill Barrett

OREGON

Oregon Golf Association
8364 S.W. Nimbus Ave., Suite A-1
Beaverton, OR 97005
(503) 643-2610
Exec Dir: Jim Cowan

PENNSYLVANIA

Golf Association of Philadelphia
P.O. Drawer 808
Southeastern, PA 19399
(215) 687-2340
Exec Dir: James D. Sykes

Keystone Public Golf Association
P.O. Box 160
Murraysville, PA 15668

Western Pennsylvania Golf
Association
1360 Old Freeport Rd., Suite 1BR
Pittsburgh, PA 15238
(412) 963-9806
Exec Dir: A. J. Luppino

RHODE ISLAND

Rhode Island Golf Association
10 Orms St., Suite 326
Providence, RI 02904
(401) 272-1350
Exec Dir: James J. Sprague

SOUTH CAROLINA

South Carolina Golf Association
145 Birdsong Trail
Chapin, SC 29036
(803) 732-9311
Exec Dir: Happ Lathrop

SOUTH DAKOTA

South Dakota Golf Association
509 S. Holt
Sioux Falls, SD 57103
(605) 338-7499
Exec Dir: Jay Huizenga

TENNESSEE

Tennessee Section, PGA
1500 Legends Club Lane
Franklin, TN 37064
(615) 790-7600
Exec Dir: Dick Horton

TEXAS

Dallas District Golf Association
4321 Live Oak
Dallas, TX 75204
(214) 823-6004
Exec Dir: Erik Fredricksen

Houston Golf Association
1830 S. Millbend
The Woodlands, TX 77380
(713) 367-7999
Exec Dir: Erik Fredricksen

San Antonio Golf Association
70 N.E. Loop 410, Suite 370
San Antonio, TX 78216
(512) 341-0823
Exec Dir: Nick Milanovich

UTAH

Utah Golf Association
1512 South 1100 East
Salt Lake City, UT 84105
(801) 466-1132
Exec Dir: Joe Watts

VERMONT

Vermont Golf Association
P.O. Box 1612, Station A
Rutland, VT 05701
(802) 773-8364
Exec Dir: James Bassett

VIRGINIA

Virginia State Golf Association
830 Southlake Blvd., Suite A
Richmond, VA 23236
(804) 378-2300
Exec Dir: David Norman

Washington Metropolitan Golf
Association
8012 Colorado Springs Dr.
Springfield, VA 22153-2721
(703) 569-6311
Exec Dir: Robert B. Riley III

WASHINGTON

Washington State Golf
Association
155 N.E. 100th St., Suite 302
Seattle, WA 99125
(206) 526-8605
Exec Dir: John Bodenhamer

WEST VIRGINIA

West Virginia Golf Association
P.O. Box 8133
Huntington, WV 25705
(304) 525-0000
Exec Dir: W. Scott Moore

WISCONSIN

Wisconsin State Golf Association
P.O. Box 35
Elm Grove, WI 53122
(414) 786-4301
Exec Dir: Eugene R. Haas

WYOMING

Wyoming Golf Association
501 First Ave. S
Greybull, WY 82426
(307) 568-3304
Exec Dir: Jim Core

CLUBS AND RESORTS WITH MAJOR GOLF FACILITIES

The clubs and resorts listed here are places where the sport of golf is taken very seriously. All have at least 36 holes; many have considerably more. If you're interested in working in a golf environment, you'll find your best opportunities in these pages.

ARIZONA

Arizona Biltmore
Phoenix, AZ 85016
(602) 955-6600
36 holes
Internships: contact Dori John

Marriott's Camelback Golf Club
Scottsdale, AZ 85253
(602) 24-CAMEL
36 holes
8 internships: contact Claudia Gebreselassie

Moon Valley Country Club
Phoenix, AZ 85023
(602) 942-0000
36 holes
6 internships: contact Brad Frasier

Scottsdale Princess
Scottsdale, AZ 85255
(602) 585-4848
36 holes

Sheraton El Conquistador Resort & Country Club
Tucson, AZ 85737
(602) 544-5000
45 holes

Ventana Canyon Golf Club
Tucson, AZ 85715
(800) 828-5701, ext. 356
36 holes

The Wigwam
Litchfield, AZ 85340
(602) 935-3805
Three 18-hole courses

CALIFORNIA

Blackhawk Country Club
Danville, CA 94526
(510) 736-6500
36 holes
1 internship: contact Tom Ringer

Breamar Country Club
Los Angeles, CA 91356
(818) 345-6520
36 holes

Hyatt Grand Champions Resort
Indian Wells, CA 92210
36 holes

Ironwood Country Club
Palm Desert, CA 92260
(619) 346-0551, ext. 1248
36 holes
Internships: contact John Hendricks

La Costa Resort & Spa
Carlsbad, CA 92009
36 holes

La Quinta Hotel, Golf & Tennis
La Quinta, CA 92253
(619) 564-4111
54 holes
2–4 internships: contact Bruce McDonald

Los Angeles Country Club
Los Angeles, CA 90024
(310) 276-6104
36 holes

Marriott's Desert Springs Resort & Spa
Palm Desert, CA 92260
36 holes

Mission Hills
Rancho Mirage, CA 92270
(619) 328-2153
Three 18-hole courses

Monterey Peninsula Country Club
Pebble Beach, CA 93953
(408) 373-1556
36 holes

Olympic Club
San Francisco, CA 94102
(415) 587-4800
36 holes

Palm Valley Country Club
Palm Desert, CA 92260
(619) 345-2737
36 holes

PGA West
La Quinta, CA 92253
(619) 564-7100
Four 18-hole courses

Rancho Murieta Resort
Rancho Murieta, CA 95683
(916) 354-3400
36 holes

Sheraton Industry Hills Resort & Conference Center
City of Industry, CA 91744
36 holes

Silverado Country Club & Resort
Napa, CA 94558
(707) 257-0200
36 holes

Stouffer Esmeralda Resort
Indian Wells, CA 92210
36 holes

Torrey Pines
La Jolla, CA 92037
(619) 570-1234
36 holes

The Vintage Club
Indian Wells, CA 92210
(619) 340-0500
36 holes
1–2 internships: contact Paul Lempcke

Whispering Palms Lodge & Country Club
Rancho Santa Fe, CA 92067
36 holes

COLORADO

The Broadmoor
Colorado Springs, CO 80901
(719) 577-5790
Three 18-hole courses

DELAWARE

The DuPont Country Club
Wilmington, DE 19898
(302) 654-4435
Four 18-hole courses

Wilmington Country Club
Montchanin, DE 19710
(302) 655-3333
36 holes

FLORIDA

Amelia Island Plantation
Amelia Island, FL 32034
(904) 261-6161
45 holes of golf
9 internships: contact Barbara Ross

Bear Lakes Country Club
West Palm Beach, FL 33411
(407) 478-0001
36 holes

Boca West Club
Boca Raton, FL 33434
Four 18-hole courses
(407) 488-6990
36 holes

The Breakers Golf Club
Palm Beach, FL 33480
(561) 659-8470
36 holes
Internships: contact Denise Bober

Club Med: The Sandpiper
Port St. Lucie, FL 33452
36 holes

Doral Resort & Country Club
Miami, FL 33178
(305) 591-6434
81 holes
Internships: contact Human Resources

East Lake Woodlands Country Club
Palm Harbor, FL 33563
(813) 784-7270
36 holes
1 internship: contact Tom Roewer

Fiddlesticks Country Club
Ft. Myers, FL 33908
(941) 768-2332
36 holes

Fountains Country Club
Lake Worth, FL 33463
(407) 965-8400
Three 18-hole courses

Frenchman's Creek
North Palm Beach, FL 33408
(407) 622-8300
36 holes

Grenelefe Golf & Tennis Resort
Grenelefe, FL 33844
(941) 422-7511
54 holes
Internships: contact Gloria Terry

Harbour Ridge Yacht & Country Club
Palm City, FL 34990
(407) 336-3000
36 holes
Internships: contact Personnel

Hollybrook Golf & Tennis Club
Pembroke Pines, FL 33029
(954) 431-4545
36 holes
2 internships: contact Joel Hyman

CLUBS AND RESORTS WITH MAJOR GOLF FACILITIES

Hollywood Lakes Country Club Resort
Hollywood Lakes, FL 14800
(305) 431-8800
36 holes

Indian Spring Golf & Tennis Country Club
Boynton Beach, FL 33437
(561) 736-1663
36 holes

Innisbrook Resort & Golf Club
Tarpon Springs, FL 34286
(813) 942-2000
63 holes
2 internships: contact Recreation Dep't

Inverrary Country Club
Lauderhill, FL 33319
(954) 733-7550
54 holes

John's Island Club
Vero Beach, FL 32960
(407) 231-1700
Three 18-hole courses

Jonathan's Landing Golf Club
Jupiter, FL 33458
(407) 474-5558
Three 18-hole courses
Internships: contact Fred Harkness

Mariner Sands
Stuart, FL 33494
(561) 221-7307
36 holes
2 internships: contact Chuck Knebels

Marriott at Sawgrass Resort
Ponte Vedra Beach, FL 32082
99 holes

Marriott's Bay Point Resort
Panama City, FL 32407
36 holes

Meadows Golf & Tennis Resort
Sarasota, FL 33580
54 holes

Mission Inn Golf & Tennis Resort
Howey-in-the-Hills, FL 34737
(352) 324-3885
36 holes

Ocean Reef Club
North Key Largo, FL 33037
(305) 367-3611
Three 18-hole courses
Internships: contact Danny Miller

Palm-Aire Country Club of Sarasota
Sarasota, FL 33580
(813) 355-9733
36 holes

Palm-Aire Spa Resort & Country Club
Pompano Beach, FL 33069
(954) 975-6225
94 holes

Palm Beach Polo & Country Club
West Palm Beach, FL 33411
(407) 798-8276
45 holes

Pelican Bay Country Club North
Daytona Beach, FL 32019
(904) 759-0034
36 holes

PGA National Golf Club
Palm Beach Gardens, FL 33418
(407) 627-1800
90 holes
Internships: contact Human Resources

Ponce de Leon Resort & Convention Center
St. Augustine, FL 32085
(904) 829-5314
36 holes

Ponte Vedra Inn & Club
Ponte Vedra Beach, FL 32082
(905) 285-1111
36 holes

Quail Creek Country Club
Naples, FL 33941
(813) 597-2831
36 holes

Quail Ridge Country Club
Boynton Beach, FL 33436
(407) 737-5100
36 holes

Resort at Longboat Key Club
Longboat Key, FL 34228
(941) 383-8821
36 holes

Royal Poinciana Golf Club
Naples, FL 33939
(813) 261-2558
36 holes

Saddlebrook Golf & Tennis Resort
Tampa, FL 33543
(813) 973-1111
36 holes

Sandestin
Sandestin, FL 32541
(904) 267-8294
63 holes
5–6 internships: contact Keith Massengill

Sheraton Palm Coast Golf & Tennis Resort
Palm Coast, FL 32137
(904) 445-3000
Four 18-hole courses

Suntree Country Club
Melbourne, FL 32935
(407) 242-6230
36 holes

Tournament Players Club at Prestancia
Sarasota, FL 33583
(813) 922-2800
36 holes

Tournament Players Club at Sawgrass
Ponte Vedra Beach, FL 32082
(904) 273-3230
36 holes

Turnberry Resort & Club
Aventura, FL 33180
(305) 932-6200
36 holes

Walt Disney World Resort
Lake Buena Vista, FL 32830
(800) 722-2930
99 holes
Six 6-month internships, hired from their own college program: contact College Recruiting Dep't
Website: www.careermosaic.com/cm/wdw/wdw1.html

The Villas of Grand Cypress
Orlando, FL 32819
(407) 239-4700
45 holes
Internships: contact Human Resources

GEORGIA

Atlanta Athletic Club
Duluth, GA 30136
(404) 448-2166
36 holes

Callaway Gardens Resort
Pine Mountain, GA 31822
(706) 663-2281
63 holes
10 internships: contact Don Ferrone

Cherokee Town & Country Club
Atlanta, GA 30363
(404) 993-4407
36 holes

The Cloister
Sea Island, GA 31561
(912) 638-3611
54 holes
Internships: contact Scott Davenport

Evergreen Conference Center & Resort
Stone Mountain Park, GA 30086
36 holes

Reynolds Plantation
Greensboro, GA 30642
(706) 467-3151
36 holes

Stone Mountain Park Inn
Stone Mountain Park, GA 30086
(404) 498-5715
36 holes

HAWAII

Hyatt Regency Maui Resort
Kaanapali Beach, HI 96761
(808) 661-1234
36 holes

Hyatt Regency Waikoloa Resort
Waikoloa, HI 96743
36 holes

Kaanapali Golf Courses
Kaanapali Beach, HI 96761
(808) 661-3691
36 holes

Kaanapali Royal
Kaanapali Beach, HI 96761
36 holes

Kapalua Land Company
100 Kapalua Drive
Kapalua, HI 96761
(808) 669-6577
54 holes
Internships: contact Personnel

Maui Inter-Continental Resort
Wailea, HI 96753
36 holes

Maui Marriott
Kaanapali Beach, HI 96761
36 holes

Mauna Lani Bay Hotel & Bungalows
Kamuela, HI 96743
(808) 885-6622
36 holes

CLUBS AND RESORTS WITH MAJOR GOLF FACILITIES

The Prince Golf & Country Club
Princeville, HI 96722
(808) 826-5000
45 holes

Princeville Hotel
Princeville, HI 96722
45 holes

Waikoloa Golf Club
Waikoloa, HI 96743
(808) 885-4647
36 holes

Wailea Golf Club
Maui Wailea Kihie, HI 96753
36 holes

Westin Kauai
Kalapaki Beach, HI 96766
(808) 245-5050
36 holes

ILLINOIS

Cog Hill Country Club
Lemont, IL 60439
(630) 257-5872
Four 18-hole courses
1–2 internships: contact Nick Mokelke

Eagle Ridge Inn & Resort
Galena, IL 61036
(815) 777-2280
63 holes
2–4 internships: contact John
Schlamen III

Indian Lakes Resort
Bloomingdale, IL 60108
36 holes

Lincolnshire Country Club
Crete, IL 60417
(708) 672-5411
36 holes

Medinah Country Club
Medinah, IL 60157
(708) 773-1700
Three 18-hole courses

Olympia Fields Country Club
Olympia Fields, IL 60461-1572
36 holes

INDIANA

French Lick Springs Resort
French Lick, IN 47432
(812) 936-9300
36 holes

IOWA

Des Moines Golf & Country Club
West Des Moines, IA 50265
36 holes

KANSAS

Alvamar Country Club
Lawrence, KS 66046
(913) 842-0004
45 holes

KENTUCKY

Anderson/Lindsey Golf Club
Fort Knox, KY 40121
(502) 624-2717
45 holes
1–2 internships: contact Barry
Bonifeld, Diane Ratcliffe

MARYLAND

Congressional Country Club
Bethesda, MD 20817
(301) 469-2000
36 holes

**Turf Valley Hotel
& Country Club**
Ellicott, MD 21043
(410) 465-1500
45 holes

MASSACHUSETTS

**New Seabury Resort &
Conference Center**
New Seabury, MA 02649-0549
(508) 477-9111
36 holes

MICHIGAN

Bartley House Hotel
Harbor Springs, MI 49713
54 holes

Boyne Highlands Resort
Harbor Springs, MI 49713
(616) 526-3000
54 holes

Boyne Mountain
Boyne Falls, MI 49713
(616) 549-6000
45 holes

Canadian Lakes Country Club
Stanwood, MI 49346
(616) 972-8410
36 holes

Detroit Golf Club
Detroit, MI 48203
(313) 345-4400
36 holes

Garland Resort
Lewiston, MI 49756
63 holes

Grand Traverse Resort Village
Traverse City, MI 49610
(616) 938-2100
36 holes

**Shanty Creek–Schuss Mountain
Resort**
Bellaire, MI 49615
(616) 533-8621
36 holes (adding 18 more)
5–7 internships: contact Marc Cross

Treetops Sylvan Resort
Gaylord, MI 49735
(517) 732-6711
54 holes

MINNESOTA

Breezy Point Resort & Marina
Brainerd, MN 56472
(218) 562-7811
36 holes

Madden's on Gull Lake
Brainerd, MN 56401
(218) 829-2811
54 holes

Majestic Oaks Country Club
Ham Lake, MN 55304
(612) 755-2142
45 holes
2 internships (maintenance): contact
Bill Folkes

MISSISSIPPI

Broadwater Beach Hotel
Biloxi, MS 39533
(601) 388-2211
36 holes

MISSOURI

The Lodge of the Four Seasons
Lake Ozark, MO 65049
(314) 365-3000
45 holes
50+ internships: contact Dane Roller,
(314) 365-8530; Jamie Suttles,
(314) 365-8526

NEVADA

Angel Park Golf Club
Las Vegas, NV 89128
(702) 254-GOLF
36 holes
Internships: contact: Tom Vold,
(702) 254-4219

Incline Village Golf Resort
Incline Village, NV 89450
(702) 832-1144
36 holes
2 internships: contact Brian Eilders,
(702) 832-1144; Cal Swanson,
(702) 832-1296

NEW JERSEY

The Great Gorge Resort
Mamaroon, NJ 07120
36 holes

Marriott's Seaview Golf Resort
Absecon, NJ 08201
(609) 652-1800
36 holes

Montclair Golf Club
Montclair, NJ 07042
(201) 239-1800
36 holes

NEW YORK

Concord Resort Hotel
Kiamesha Lake, NY 12751
(914) 794-4000
36 holes

Westchester Country Club
Rye, NY 10580
(914) 967-6000
45 holes

Winged Foot Golf Club
Mamaroneck, NY 10543
(914) 698-8400
36 holes

NORTH CAROLINA

Country Club of North Carolina
Pinehurst, NC 28374
(919) 692-6565
36 holes

Foxfire Resort & Country Club
Pinehurst, NC 27281
(910) 295-5555
36 holes

Grandfather Golf & Country Club
Linville, NC 28646
(704) 898-4531
36 holes

Pinehurst Hotel & Country Club
Pinehurst, NC 28374
(910) 295-6811
144 holes
1–2 internships: contact Don Padgett

Raintree Country Club
Matthews, NC 28105
(704) 542-0800
36 holes
Internships: contact Rebecca Walker

Whispering Pines Country Club Villas
Whispering Pines, NC 28327
54 holes

OHIO

Avalon Inn
Warren, OH 44484
36 holes

Westfield Country Club
Westfield, OH 44251
(216) 887-0391
36 holes

OKLAHOMA

Shangri-La Resort
Afton, OK 74331
(800) 331-4060
36 holes

OREGON

Black Butte Ranch Resort
Black Butte, OR 97759
36 holes

Pumpkin Ridge Golf Club
Cornelius, OR 97113
(503) 647-4747
36 holes

Sunriver Lodge and Resort
Sunriver, OR 97702
(800) 962-1769
36 holes

PENNSYLVANIA

Hershey Country Club
Hershey, PA 17033
(717) 533-2360
36 holes

Pocono Manor Resort & Conference Center
Pocono Manor, PA 18349
36 holes

SOUTH CAROLINA

The Cottages Conference Resort
Hilton Head Island, SC 29928
63 holes

Hyatt Regency Hilton Head Resort
Hilton Head Island, SC 29928
72 holes

Kiawah Island Resort
Kiawah Island, SC 29412
(803) 768-6000
72 holes
2 internships: contact Mike Hain

Litchfield by the Sea Resort & Country Club
Litchfield Beach, SC 29585
(800) 922-6348
54 holes

Palmetto Dunes
Hilton Head Island, SC 29938
(803) 785-1161
Three 18-hole courses

Seabrook Island Resort
Charleston, SC 29417
(803) 768-1000
36 holes

Sea Pines Plantation
Hilton Head Island, SC 29938
(803) 671-4417
54 holes

TEXAS

Barton Creek Conference Resort
Austin, TX 78735
(512) 329-4616
54 holes
Internships: contact Human Resources

Brookhaven Country Club
Dallas, TX 75381
(214) 243-6151
36 holes

The Club at Sonterra
San Antonio, TX 78258
36 holes

Dallas Athletic Club
Dallas, TX 75228
(214) 279-3671
36 holes

Horseshoe Bay Resort & Conference Club
Horseshoe Bay, TX 78654
(210) 598-2511
Four 18-hole courses
6–8 internships: contact Scott McDonough

Kingwood Country Club
Kingwood, TX 77339
(713) 358-2171
54 holes

Las Colinas Sports Club
Irving, TX 75062
(214) 717-2500
36 holes

Quail Valley World of Clubs
Missouri City, TX 77459
54 holes

Rancho Viejo Resort & Country Club
Brownsville, TX 78520
36 holes

Sweetwater Country Club
Sugar Land, TX 77497
(713) 980-4100
36 holes

Tennwood Golf Club
Hockley, TX 77447
(713) 757-4000
36 holes

The Woodlands Inn & Country Club
The Woodlands, TX 77380
(713) 367-1100
Three 18-hole courses

VIRGINIA

Army Navy Country Club
Arlington, VA 22204
(703) 521-6800
45 holes

Country Club of Virginia
Richmond, VA 23226
(804) 288-2891
54 holes

The Homestead
Hot Springs, VA 24445
(703) 839-5500
54 holes
2–3 internships: contact Fred Reese,
    (703) 839-7781; Wayne Nooe,
    (703) 839-7506

Kingsmill Resort
Williamsburg, VA 23185
(804) 253-1703
64 holes
Internships: contact Molly Cruikshank

Virginia Hot Springs Golf & Tennis Club
Hot Springs, VA 24445
(703) 839-5500
Three 18-hole courses

Wintergreen Resort
Wintergreen, VA 22958
(800) 325-2200
36 holes

WEST VIRGINIA

The Greenbrier
White Sulphur Springs, WV 24986
(304) 536-1110
54 holes

Wilson Lodge at Oglebay
Wheeling, WV 26003
54 holes

WISCONSIN

The American Club
Kohler, WI 53044
(414) 457-8000
36 holes

Americana Lake Geneva Resort
Lake Geneva, WI 53147
(414) 245-7010
36 holes

Blackwolf Run
Kohler, WI 53044
(414) 457-4446
36 holes
1–2 internships: contact Paul Becker

CHAPTER SEVEN

SPORTS TURF MANAGEMENT

On the green fields of athletic endeavors,

there's the promise of a plenitude of jobs

for graduates of this college program.

The Grass Really Is Greener Here

Not to be overlooked are the career opportunities in the management of turfgrass, a specialization of rising importance in the construction and maintenance of golf courses and athletic fields. Job prospects are extremely bright.

The pages that follow provide a directory of colleges and universities that offer sports turf management programs on all levels.

On the availability of jobs: no problem. At Penn State, which has programs leading to the bachelor's, master's, and doctoral degrees, Prof. Tom Watschke reports, "We have more job offers than graduates." The answer was the same at the universities of Maryland, Kansas State, Washington State, and California State Poly at San Luis Obispo—100 percent placement of graduates.

About 85 percent of students who graduate with a bachelor's degree aim for jobs as golf course superintendents. They start as assistant superintendents, with salaries of $21,000 to $26,000. Graduates of two-year programs who also aspire to jobs as golf course superintendents generally start at a couple of thousand dollars less.

About half the graduates with master's degrees go into the chemical industry, where starting pay can be as high as $40,000.

Students who obtain Ph.D. degrees have no trouble getting appointments to college faculties or industrial jobs dealing with turf research. Most doctoral graduates opt for jobs in research, which begin at about $50,000. Faculty salaries begin at about $45,000. There has never been a better time for Ph.D. graduates, say department heads at North Carolina State, Ohio State, and Rutgers.

Prof. Mark Caroll, at the University of Maryland, says that about 200 graduates of his program have advanced to the position of golf course superintendent. Most, he says, earn up to $70,000 a year, and 25 make $75,000 and more. Two earn about $150,000.

About the Program

Institutions that offer turfgrass management set it up as a specialized program of training within a department that deals with agricultural studies. At many campuses the courses are given in the department of agronomy. The degree awarded is in agronomy with a specialization in turfgrass management.

Basic courses in the bachelor's degree program typically include botany, plant physiology, plant pathology, principles of turfgrass science, chemistry, and environmental studies. Basic also are such matters as weed identification and safe pesticide management. Business courses may include economics, accounting, business management, and computer science. Among useful electives: meteorology, water control and utilization, soil conservation and land use, surveying and planning, marketing, and personnel management.

Internships are required at most institutions.

Only a small number of turf students—about 7 percent, according to a recent survey—are women.

Some of the colleges and universities listed here as offering bachelor's degrees and higher degrees also have two-year associate degree programs. Jobs are also available for graduates of two-year programs.

Scholarships Available

There are two scholarship sources for turf management students.

Of primary importance is the **Golf Course Superintendents Association of America**, a powerhouse organization that provides many services for students who intend to make their career in the golf industry. For information about its scholarship program, and other services, see page 167.

The second source for scholarships is the **Sports Turf Managers Association**, a professional group with about 800 members across the country. For information about its scholarship program, write to the association at 1375 Rolling Hills Loop, Council Bluffs, IA 51503, or phone (712) 366-2669.

Incidentally, the organization invites student membership, and it would be a good idea to inquire about that too. (Objective: networking.)

More about the Sports Turf Managers Association:

The association, which proclaims its purpose as "promoting better and safer sports turf areas," has been growing in size and influence under the stewardship of its new executive director, Steve Truly.

A new service the association has put in place is a job hotline that allows members to call in to find out about job openings. Serving members also are a colorful monthly magazine and a bimonthly newsletter, helping keep them up-to-date on new developments in the industry. Also, steps have been taken to set up a system for certifying turf managers.

Rather than compete with the Golf Course Superintendents Association, which dominates the golf industry, the Sports Turf Managers Association has opted for its own turf, which consists of stadiums, universities, schools, parks, and sports complexes—a total of 40,000 facilities, not counting golf courses.

A survey by the association shows that two out of three sports turf managers have earned at least a bachelor's degree.

COLLEGES WITH TURF MANAGEMENT PROGRAMS

The colleges and universities that follow have programs ranging from associate degree to doctorate. The letters A, B, M, and D after their names indicate the degree or degrees each offers: A-associate, B-bachelor's, M-master's, D-doctorate. Each entry includes the department or school in which the program is given and the professor to contact for information.

ALABAMA

Auburn University — B, M
Auburn, AL 36849-5412
Beth Guertal
Dep't of Agronomy & Soils
(334) 844-3977

ARIZONA

University of Arizona — B, M
Tucson, AZ 85721
Kenneth Marcum
Dep't of Plant Sciences
(520) 321-7786

ARKANSAS

**University of Arkansas
— B, M, D**
Fayetteville, AR 72701
John W. King
Dep't of Agronomy
(501) 575-5723

CALIFORNIA

**California State Polytechnic
University, Pomona — A, B, M**
Pomona, CA 91768-4042
Kent W. Kurtz
Dep't of Horticulture/Plant & Soil
Science
(909) 869-2211

**California State Polytechnic
University, San Luis Obispo
— B**
San Luis Obispo, CA 93407
David Wehner
Dep't of Environmental &
Horticultural Science
(805) 756-2279

COLORADO

**Colorado State University
— B, M, D**
Ft. Collins, CO 80523
Tony Koski
Dep't of Horticulture
(970) 491-7070

CONNECTICUT

**University of Connecticut
— B, M**
College of Agriculture &
Natural Resources
Storrs, CT 06269
William M. Dest
(860) 486-0189

FLORIDA

Florida A & M University — B, M
Tallahassee, FL 32307
J. Muchovej
Dep't of Ornamental Horticulture
(904) 599-3429

University of Florida — B, M, D
Gainesville, FL 32611
Grady L. Miller, Undergraduate
A. E. Dudeck, Graduate
Dep't of Environmental Horticulture
(352) 392-7942

GEORGIA

**Abraham Baldwin Agricultural
College — A, B**
Tifton, GA 31794-2601
E. Dean Seagle, Lorie Felton
ABAC 19, Horticulture/Turfgrass
(912) 386-3449

University of Georgia — B, M, D
Athens, GA 30602
Keith J. Karnok
Dep't of Crop & Soil Science
(706) 542-2461

HAWAII

**University of Hawaii at Manoa
— B, M**
Honolulu, HI 96822
David Hensley
Dep't of Horticulture
(808) 956-2150

IDAHO

University of Idaho — B
Moscow, ID 83844-2339
Larry O'Keeffe
Plant Science Division
(208) 885-6930

ILLINOIS

**Southern Illinois University
— B, M**
Carbondale, IL 62901-4415
Ken Diesburg
Dep't of Plant & Soil Science
(618) 453-1787

University of Illinois — B, M
Urbana, IL 61801
Thomas W. Fermanian, Bruce E.
Branham
Dep't of Horticulture
(217) 244-5147

Western Illinois University — B
Macomb, IL 61455
Thomas Green
Dep't of Agriculture
(309) 298-1160

INDIANA

Purdue University — A, B, M, D
W. Lafayette, IN 47907-1150
Clark Throssell
Dep't of Agronomy
(317) 494-4785

IOWA

Iowa State University — B, M, D
Ames, IA 50011
Nick Christians
Dep't of Horticulture
(515) 294-0036

KANSAS

**Kansas State University
— B, M, D**
Manhattan, KS 66506-5506
Jack Fry
Dep't of Horticulture
(913) 532-6170

KENTUCKY

**Eastern Kentucky University
— A, B**
Richmond, KY 40475-3110
Dwight G. Barkley
Dep't of Agriculture
(606) 622-2228

Morehead State University — B
Morehead, KY 40351
Robert Wolfe
Dep't of Agricultural Sciences
(606) 783-2662

**Murray State University
— A, B, M**
Murray, KY 42071
Roger Macha
Dep't of Agriculture
(502) 762-6945

University of Kentucky — B, M
Lexington, KY 40546-0091
A. J. Powell Jr.
Dep't of Agronomy
(606) 257-5606

**Western Kentucky University
— A, B**
Bowling Green, KY 42101-3576
O. W. "Pete" Dotson
Dep't of Agriculture
(502) 745-2969

LOUISIANA

**Louisiana State University
— B, M**
Baton Rouge, LA 70803-2120
James N. McCrimmon
Dep't of Horticulture
(504) 388-1029

MARYLAND

**University of Maryland
— A, B, M**
College Park, MD 20742
Mark J. Carroll
Dep't of Agronomy
(301) 405-1339

**University of Maryland
— A, B, M**
College Park, MD 20742
Kevin Mathias
Institute of Applied Agriculture
(301) 405-4692

COLLEGES WITH TURF MANAGEMENT PROGRAMS

MASSACHUSETTS

University of Massachusetts — A, B, M, D
Amherst, MA 01003
William Torello
(413) 545-2860

MICHIGAN

Michigan State University — B, M, D
East Lansing, MI 48824-1325
James Crum, Trey Rogers
Dep't of Crop & Soil Sciences
(517) 355-0271
Michigan State also has a two-year certificate program at its East Lansing campus. Contact: John N. Rogers III at the university's Institute of Agricultural Technology, (517) 355-0190.

MINNESOTA

University of Minnesota — B, M, D
St. Paul, MN 55108
Donald B. White
Dep't of Horticultural Science
(612) 624-9206

MISSISSIPPI

Mississippi State University — B, M
Mississippi State, MS 39762
Jeff Krans, Michael Goatley
Dep't of Agronomy
(601) 325-2311

MISSOURI

University of Missouri — B, M
Columbia, MO 65211
John H. Dunn
Dep't of Horticulture
(573) 882-7511

MONTANA

Montana State University — B
Bozeman, MT 59717
George E. Evans
Dep't of Plant & Soil Science
(406) 994-5052

NEBRASKA

University of Nebraska — B, M, D
Lincoln, NE 68583-0724
G. L. Horst
Dep't of Horticulture
(402) 472-1142

NEW JERSEY

Rutgers University — A, B, M, D
Cook College
New Brunswick, NJ 08903
James Murphy
Dep't of Plant Sciences
(908) 932-9271

NEW MEXICO

New Mexico State University — B, M
Las Cruces, NM 88003-0003
LeRoy A. Daugherty
Dep't of Agronomy & Horticulture
(505) 646-3406

NEW YORK

Cornell University — B, M, D
Ithaca, NY 14853
A. Martin Petrovic
Dep't of Floriculture & Ornamental Horticulture
(607) 255-1796

State University of New York — A, B
Colbeskill, NY 12043
Robert Emmons
Dep't of Plant Science
(518) 234-5644

NORTH CAROLINA

North Carolina State University — A, B, M, D
Raleigh, NC 27695
Rich Cooper, Charles Peacock
Dep't of Crop Science
(919) 515-7600

NORTH DAKOTA

North Dakota State University — B
Fargo, ND 58105
Ronald C. Smith
Dep't of Horticulture & Forestry
(701) 231-8161

OHIO

Ohio State University — B, M, D
Columbus, OH 43210
Karl Danneberger
Dep't of Horticulture & Crop Sciences
(614) 292-8491
Ohio State also has a two-year associate degree program at its Agricultural Technical Institute in Wooster, Ohio (zip 44691). Contact: Mike Fulton, Dep't of Horticulture, (330) 264-3911.

OKLAHOMA

Oklahoma State University — B, M
Stillwater, OK 74078
James H. Baird, Dennis Martin
Dep't of Horticulture & Landscape Architecture
(405) 744-6424

OREGON

Oregon State University — B
Corvallis, OR 97331
Tom Cook
Dep't of Horticulture
(541) 737-5449

PENNSYLVANIA

Delaware Valley College — B
Doylestown, PA 18901-2697
Fred T. Wolford
Dep't of Agronomy & Environmental Science
(215) 345-1500

Penn State University — A, B, M, D
University Park, PA 16802
Tom Watschke, G. W. Hamilton
Dep't of Agronomy
(814) 865-3007

RHODE ISLAND

University of Rhode Island — B, M
Kingston, RI 02881
R. J. Hull
Dep't of Plant Sciences
(401) 874-5995

SOUTH CAROLINA

Clemson University — B, M, D
Clemson, SC 29634-0375
A. R. Mazur
Dep't of Horticulture
(803) 656-2607

SOUTH DAKOTA

South Dakota State University — B
Brookings, SD 57007
Paul Prashar
Dep't of Horticulture
(605) 688-5136

TENNESSEE

University of Tennessee — B, M
Knoxville, TN 37901-1071
Lloyd M. Callahan
Dep't of Ornamental Horticulture & Landscape Design
(423) 974-7324

TEXAS

Texas A & M University — B, M, D
College Station, TX 77843-2474
C. T. Hallmark
Dep't of Soil & Crop Sciences
(409) 845-4678

UTAH

Brigham Young University — B, M
Salt Lake City, UT 84602
Frank Williams
Dep't of Agronomy & Horticulture
(801) 378-2185

Utah State University — A, B, M
Logan, UT 84322-4820
Eric D. Miltner
Dep't of Plants, Soils & Biometeorology
(801) 797-0410

VIRGINIA

Virginia Polytechnic Institute & State University — A, B, M
Blacksburg, VA 24061-0404
David R. Chalmers
Dep't of Crop & Soil Environmental Sciences
(540) 231-9738

COLLEGES WITH TURF MANAGEMENT PROGRAMS

WASHINGTON

**Washington State University
— B, M, D**
Pullman, WA 99164-6420
William J. Johnston
Dep't of Crop & Soil Science
(509) 335-3620

WISCONSIN

**University of Wisconsin at
Madison — B, M**
Madison, WI 53706
Wayne Kussow
Dep't of Soil Science
(608) 263-3631

**University of Wisconsin at
Madison — B, M**
Madison, WI 53706-1590
Frank Rossi
(608) 262-1624

**University of Wisconsin at
River Falls — B**
River Falls, WI 54022
Don Taylor
Dep't of Plant Sciences
(715) 425-3395

Note: The following schools
are mainly community
colleges. Some have two-year
associate degree programs,
others have two-year or one-
year certificate programs or
shorter programs. Contact
persons are indicated.

ARIZONA

Mundus Institute
Phoenix, AZ 85014
Steve Wallace
(602) 248-8548

Northland Pioneer College
Holbrook, AZ 86025
Robert H. Parnell
(520) 537-2976

CALIFORNIA

College of the Desert
Palm Desert, CA 92260
Melvin J. Robey
(619) 346-6102

Mount San Antonio College
Walnut, CA 91789
Charles Hewitt
(909) 594-5611

San Joaquin Delta College
Stockton, CA 95204
Mike Snyder
(209) 474-5151

COLORADO

Front Range Community College
Westminster, CO 80030
Robert Wecal
(303) 466-8811

Northeastern Junior College
Sterling, CO 80751
Gail Donaldson
(970) 522-6600

FLORIDA

Lake City Community College
Lake City, FL 32055
John Piersol
(904) 752-1822

ILLINOIS

College of DuPage
Glen Ellyn, IL 60137
Judy Burgholzer
(708) 942-3095

**Danville Area Community
College**
Danville, IL 61832
Charles Schroeder
(217) 443-8793

Illinois Central College
East Peoria, IL 61635
Glenn Herold
(309) 694-5414

Joliet Junior College
Joliet, IL 60431
Lisa Perkins, Jim Ethridge
(815) 729-9020

Kishwaukee College
Malta, IL 60150
Larry Marty
(815) 825-2086

Lincoln Land Community College
Springfield, IL 62708
James F. Martin
(217) 786-2200

McHenry County College
Crystal Lake, IL 60012
Brian Sager
(815) 455-3700

William Rainey Harper College
Palatine, IL 60067
Randy Illg
(847) 925-6857

IOWA

**Des Moines Area Community
College**
Ankeny, IA 50021
Barb Hansen
(515) 964-6318

Hawkeye Institute of Technology
Waterloo, IA 50704
Scott Harvey
(319) 296-2320

Indian Hills Community College
Ottumwa, IA 52501
Fran Leding
(712) 382-2117

Iowa Lakes Community College
Emmetsburg, IA 50536
Grant T. Spear
(712) 852-5232

Kirkwood Community College
Cedar Rapids, IA 52406
Phil Thomas
(319) 398-5441

Western Iowa Tech
Sioux City, IA 51102
Gina S. Hart
(712) 274-8733

KANSAS

**Johnson County Community
College**
Overland Park, KS 66210
Jim VomHof
(913) 469-4437

MASSACHUSETTS

**Essex Agricultural & Technical
Institute**
Hathorne, MA 01937
Paul R. Harder
(508) 774-0050

**University of Massachusetts
at Amherst**
Stockbridge School of Agriculture
Amherst, MA 01003
Katherine Conway
(413) 545-2222

MICHIGAN

Ferris State University
Big Rapids, MI 49307
Michael Hendricks
(616) 592-2100

MINNESOTA

Anoka Technical College
Anoka, MN 55303
Richard Robinson
(612) 576-4930

**Minnesota Riverland Technical
College**
Rochester, MN 55904
Vern Bushlack
(507) 280-3150

**University of Minnesota
at Crookston**
Crookston, MN 56716
Phil Baird
(218) 281-8020

**University of Minnesota
at Waseca**
Waseca, MN 56093
Brad Pedersen
(507) 835-0600

MISSISSIPPI

Hinds Community College
Raymond, MS 39154
Martha G. Hill
(601) 857-3290

MISSOURI

Linn Technical College
Linn, MO 65051
Ben Evers
(573) 897-3603

Longview Community College
Lee's Summit, MO 64081
Jim Beisel
(816) 672-2367

**St. Louis Community College
at Meramec**
St. Louis, MO 63122
Paul R. Roberts
(314) 984-7714

COLLEGES WITH TURF MANAGEMENT PROGRAMS

NEBRASKA

Central Community College
Hastings, NE 68902
Moe Rucker
(402) 461-2495

NEW YORK

State University of New York
Agricultural & Technical College
Delhi, NY 13753
Dominic Morales
(607) 746-4413

State University of New York
College of Technology
Farmingdale, NY 11735
Massoud Hakimian
(516) 420-2023

NORTH CAROLINA

Catawba Valley Community College
Hickory, NC 28602
Jerry A. Queen
(704) 464-4106

Sandhills Community College
Pinehurst, NC 28374
Fred Garrett
(910) 695-3883

Wayne Community College
Goldsboro, NC 27530-8002
John Mills
(919) 735-5151

OHIO

Ohio State University
Agricultural Technical Institute
Wooster, OH 44691
Michael M. Fulton
(330) 264-3911

Clark State Community College
Springfield, OH 45501
Robert W. Boufford, Susan Everett
(513) 328-6063

OKLAHOMA

Rogers State College
Claremore, OK 74017-2099
Vic Osteen
(918) 341-7510

OREGON

Central Oregon Community College
Bend, OR 97701-5998
David L. Weinecke, Ray Hoyt
(541) 383-7281

Clackamas Community College
Oregon City, OR 97045
Elizabeth Howley
(503) 657-6958

Linn-Benton Community College
Albany, OR 97321
Gregory F. Paulson
(541) 917-4765

Portland Community College
Portland, OR 97219
Jim Meyer
(503) 244-6111

SOUTH CAROLINA

Horry-Georgetown Technical College
Conway, SC 29526
Mark Flanagan
(803) 347-3186

TENNESSEE

Walters State Community College
Morristown, TN 37813-6899
John Phillips
(423) 585-0828

TEXAS

Grayson County College
Denison, TX 75020
Randy Vernon
(903) 786-2393

Texas State Technical College
Waco, TX 76705
Tinker Clift
(817) 867-4867

Western Texas College
Snyder, TX 79549
Don Buckland
(915) 573-8511

WASHINGTON

Clover Park Technical College
Tacoma, WA 98499-4098
Jim Butler
(206) 589-5597

Spokane Community College
Spokane, WA 99207
Mike McMackin
(509) 533-7260

Walla Walla Community College
Walla Walla, WA 99362
William Griffith
(509) 527-4336

A Course With Holes

Turf management students at the College of Technology at Delhi, New York, are getting a rare educational experience. They're building a nine-hole extension to the school's nine-hole golf course.

Delhi, part of the State University of New York system, is the only two-year college in the Northeast with its own golf course. Construction of the additional nine holes was begun in 1994 and will be completed over a period of three to five years.

Graduates of Delhi's programs in golf course operations and turf management hold positions as golf course superintendents at a number of prominent country clubs in the state. The programs get financial support from the golf industry.

CHAPTER EIGHT

THE TENNIS INDUSTRY

The industry is more stable than it's been in years, but off-court jobs are as rare as cream-colored slacks.

Background

For professional tournament players, the tournaments offer greater riches than ever.

For professionals who teach tennis, there's an increasing number of clients.

But for just plain folks who love the sport and want to be part of it, the tennis industry, as always, doesn't offer much in the way of jobs.

Still, here are some possibilities to consider:

• The best-paying jobs for nonpros are with the sports marketing agencies that produce and market professional tennis tournaments. Some of the agencies—notably International Management Group, ProServ, and Advantage International—have a substantial influence in the sport. It's difficult to get an agency job without marketing experience, but many of the companies offer internships, and that, of course, is a foot in the door. (The business of the agencies is discussed in the chapter on Sports Marketing and Management.)

• The major tennis organizations have salaried staffs, but waiting for an opening requires extreme patience. The biggest, to be sure, is the United States Tennis Association, which organizes the U.S. Open and runs a hundred other projects. The USTA has a paid workforce of 135 people—plus an army of volunteers. The ATP Tour (men's professional tournaments) has about 100 paid staffers, some of whom work in Monte Carlo, Monaco, and Sydney, Australia. Both the USTA and ATP Tour invite applications for internships.

• Probably most reasonable are the prospects of getting a job as manager or assistant at a tennis club, or at one of the other kinds of establishments—country clubs, resorts, parks—that have multiple-court tennis facilities. There are several thousand tennis facilities around the country (nobody has a precise count). Some, in swanky settings that include well-stocked pro shops, pay good salaries; others are humble operations with salaries to match. Overall, according to a 1992 survey, the average annual salary of general managers was $32,320. Now here's a hitch: most of the openings for general manager at the more attractive facilities are filled by men and women who are certified teaching pros.

Have You Considered Working as a Teaching Pro?

You don't have to be a nationally ranked player to qualify. If you know the game and play it fairly well, and if you have a pleasant personality, you're just a couple of steps away from being a professional teacher of tennis. There are four ways to go:

1. *Certification by the United States Professional Tennis Association.* The USPTA, the largest organization of tennis teachers in the country, certifies a thousand new teachers a year. Certification is granted on the basis of a two-day exam given 85 times a year at various locations coast to coast. A one-day workshop, which is optional, is held before the exam.

The exam consists of teaching a group lesson, teaching a private lesson, grip analysis, stroke analysis, and a written test. If you want to take the exam, you've got to join the USPTA. The membership application fee is $150, annual dues are $177, and the cost of the optional one-day workshop is $75. Nineteen percent of USPTA members are women.

2. *Certification by the United States Professional Tennis Registry.* The USPTR is an international organization of 7,500 tennis teaching professionals in 117 countries. It conducts certification exams 150 times a year in the U.S., at various sites. Exams, which include a tennis drill test and an error detection test, are preceded by a two-day workshop. Depending on how well they do, exam takers are classified as associate instructor, instructor, or professional. Again, you've got to join the organization to take the exam. The application fee is $100, annual dues are $95, and the preexam workshop fee is $75. Twenty-one percent of the USPTR members are women.

3. *An intensive, month-long period of training offered by Peter Burwash International.* PBI is a well-known tennis management firm that handles tennis operations for scores of posh clubs and hotels in the U.S., the Caribbean, Europe, Asia, and the Middle East. A key part of its services is recruiting and training tennis instructors—both men and women—for positions in those places. Recruits vary widely in playing talent (although a 4.5 rating on the National Tennis Rating Program scale is generally expected), but they are evaluated mainly on their grace and effectiveness as teachers. The training program, which includes classes in club and resort business as well as in the techniques of teaching, is conducted at the company's headquarters in Texas, at no charge (but participants have to cover a month's board and lodging). Earnings in the PBI circuit range from $25,000 to $60,000 and more—and often include free lodging. Many of the pros spend as much as 80 percent of their time on management responsibilities and are paid accordingly, says Dan Aubuchon, who heads the training program. Aubuchon, incidentally, says he's always looking for the right people.

4. *College programs in professional tennis management.* For information about these specialized programs, see page 8.

Addresses and phone numbers for USPTA, USPTR, and PBI are in the tennis directory that follows shortly.

The State of the Industry

Recreational tennis. In the late 1970s, a boom time for tennis, more than 30 million Americans were playing the game, and just dressing like a tennis player was a national fad. But then, quite suddenly, tennis went into a decline, losing players in droves to aerobics and other activities. By the end of the 1980s, however, there were signs of a turnaround, and in 1992, a survey sponsored by the Tennis Industry Association produced the cheerful news that some 11.6 million Americans were on the courts, at least occasionally. Industry sources say that if the current rate of recovery continues, tennis will have a record number of players by the end of the decade.

Professional tennis. The pros aren't playing catch-up, they're ahead of the game. The U.S. Open, the largest tennis tournament in the world, in 1996 set a record for paid attendance with 506,012 tickets sold for two weeks of events. Prize money in 1996, said the USTA, which runs the tournament, was a record $10,893,890.

Prize money for men's tournaments in 1995, said the ATP Tour, was up to a record total of $57,492,000. For comparison: the total for 1990 was $40,496,000.

The figures were up in women's professional tennis too. Tournament prize money in 1995 totaled $35,000,000, up from $23,000,000 in 1990.

INTERNATIONAL TENNIS HALL OF FAME

Newport, Rhode Island

Officially sanctioned in 1954 by the U.S. Tennis Association, this elegant facility was the original home in 1881 of the U.S. Championships, now the U.S. Open. *Annual visitors:* 80,000. *Employees:* 12 full-time, 2 part-time, a dozen summer temporaries, and 10 paid interns over the course of the year. *Director:* Mark Stenning. *Address:* 194 Bellevue Ave., Newport, RI 02840. *Phone:* (401) 849-3990.

TENNIS ORGANIZATIONS

United States Tennis Association
National headquarters:
70 W. Red Oak Lane
White Plains, NY 10604
(914) 696-7000
Exec Dir/COO:
    M. Marshall Happer III
The USTA is the national governing
    body of tennis and the very soul of
    the sport. Internships available.

USTA's Player Development offices:
7310 Crandon Blvd.
Key Biscayne, FL 33149
(305) 365-8782

USTA's National Tennis Center
    offices:
Flushing Meadows-Corona Park
Flushing, NY 11368
(718) 760-6200

_____

17 sectional units of the USTA follow.
All are sources of internships.

Caribbean Tennis Association
P.O. Box 40439
Minillas Station
Santurce, Puerto Rico 00940
(809) 724-7425
Exec Dir: Lydia de la Rosa

Eastern Tennis Association
550 Mamaroneck Ave., Suite 505
Harrison, NY 10528
(914) 698-0414
Exec Dir: Doris Herrick

USTA/Florida Section
1280 S.W. 36th Ave., Suite 305
Pompano Beach, FL 33069
(305) 968-3434
Exec Dir: Doug Booth

Hawaii Pacific Tennis Association
2615 S. King St., Suite 2A
Honolulu, HI 96826
(808) 955-6696
Exec Dir: Jane Forester-Leong

Intermountain Tennis Association
1201 S. Parker Rd., Suite 200
Denver, CO 80231
(303) 695-4117
Exec Dir: Becky Lenhart

USTA/Mid-Atlantic
2230 George C. Marshall Dr.
Falls Church, VA 22043
(703) 560-9480
Exec Dir: Richard Fusco

USTA/Middle States
460 Glennie Circle
King of Prussia, PA 19406
(610) 277-4040
Exec Dir: Laura Canfield

**Missouri Valley Tennis
    Association**
722 Walnut St., Suite 1
Kansas City, MO 64106
(816) 556-0777
Acting Exec Dir: Sandra Crowley

USTA/New England
P.O. Box 587
Needham Heights, MA 02194
(617) 964-2030
Exec Dir: Jeff Waters

USTA/Northern California
1350 S. Loop Rd., Suite 100
Alameda, CA 94502
(510) 748-7373
Exec Dir: Peter Herb

Northwestern Tennis Association
5525 Cedar Lake Rd.
St. Louis Park, MN 55416
(612) 546-0709
Exec Dir: Marcia Bach

USTA/Pacific Northwest
4840 S.W. Western Ave.
Beaverton, OR 97005
(503) 520-1877
Exec Dir: Donna Montee

**Southern California Tennis
    Association**
P.O. Box 240015
Los Angeles, CA 90024
(310) 208-3838
Exec Dir: Robert Kramer

Southern Tennis Association
3850 Holcomb Bridge Rd., Suite 305
Norcross, GA 30092
(404) 368-8200
Exec Dir: John Callen

USTA/Southwest
6330-2 E. Thomas Rd., Suite 120
Scottsdale, AZ 85251
(602) 947-9293
Exec Dir: Carol Marting

Texas Tennis Association
2111 Dickson, Suite 33
Austin, TX 78704
(512) 443-1334
Exec Dir: Kenneth McAllister

Western Tennis Association
8720 Castle Creek Pkwy., Suite 329
Indianapolis, IN 46250
(317) 577-5130
Exec Dir: Patricia Freebody

*   *   *   *

**United States Professional Tennis
    Association**
3535 Briarpark Dr.
Houston, TX 77042
(713) 978-7782
CEO: Tim Heckler
The USPTA, a trade association for
    tennis pros, provides training in the
    techniques of teaching tennis.

**United States Professional Tennis
    Registry**
P.O. Box 4739
Hilton Head Island, SC 29938
(803) 785-7244
Exec Dir/CEO: Daniel Santorum
This too is a nonprofit organization
    that trains and certifies tennis
    teaching professionals. Internships
    are available here.

Peter Burwash International
2203 Timberloch Place, Suite 126
The Woodlands, TX 77380
(713) 363-4707
PBI trains tennis teachers and places
    them with clubs and resorts
    throughout the U.S. and many
    places abroad. Internships are
    available at its Texas headquarters.

*   *   *   *

Tennis Industry Association
200 Castlewood Dr.
North Palm Beach, FL 33408
(407) 848-1026
Exec Dir: Brad Patterson
The TIA is composed of companies
    that manufacture and distribute
    tennis equipment and apparel and
    provide services for the recreational
    tennis market.

ATP Tour
U.S. headquarters:
200 ATP Tour Blvd.
Pointe Vedra Beach, FL 32082
(904) 285-8000
CEO: Mark Miles
The international organization of
    men's professional tournament
    players and key tournaments.

WTA Tour
133 First St. NE
St. Petersburg, FL 33701
(813) 895-5000
CEO: Anne Person Worcester
    The organization of women tennis
    professionals.

CHAPTER NINE

SPORTS BROADCASTING

It helps if you've made

a name on the playing field.

Actually, it helps a lot.

Still, for every Terry Bradshaw

there's a Vin Scully.

THE MAIN JOBS

Not counting those boring sports shows based on interviews with athletes, coaches, and mavens from the press, sports broadcasting falls into these main categories:

- Daily sports news broadcasts (scores, trades, busted knees, etc.)
- All-sports radio (with listener call-ins)
- Live game broadcasts

Sports News Broadcasters

The U.S. has 4,945 AM radio stations, 6,613 FM stations, and 1,518 television stations. (The National Cable Television Association says there are 11,217 cable systems, but there is no information on the number of systems that have news coverage.)

The best chance of getting a beginning job is at a small station, which may take you on as a news department assistant (the work will not tax your intellect), or—if you've managed to get some writing experience during your college years—as a newswriter. In either case, the pay can be as low as $13,000. But it's a start. When you get to know your way around a newsroom, you can aim for a bigger station.

Earnings with experience. According to a 1992 survey by the National Association of Broadcasters, the average pay for a radio sports reporter was $24,729. A 1993 survey of television newscasters, conducted by the same organization, showed TV sportscasters earning an average of $46,330.

College preparation. Lee Hanna, a consultant on radio and television news operations, said colleges and universities in many parts of the country have developed excellent courses in broadcasting skills, with first-rate faculties and extensive broadcasting facilities. (Many of the schools are listed at the end of this section.) Take the courses, said Hanna, and by all means get involved in the school's broadcasting activities. The experience students get in working on campus broadcasts gives them an edge when they enter the job market, he added.

One of the immediate benefits of working at a campus station is the opportunity to make a tape of some of the better things you've done there, things calculated to impress a prospective employer, Hanna said.

Some tips on this subject: Your prospective employers are likely to be station news directors. They are busy people and they get a lot of tapes from job applicants, so you're advised to keep your tape short, perhaps five to eight minutes. With crisp editing, a factor that would not go unnoticed, you would be able to include material that demonstrates your ability to do a news report from the studio, a report from the field, an interview with a game hero, and a commentary on a campus issue of some sensitivity. Three or four segments would be enough to show your versatility.

Incidentally, even though you hope to devote your career to sports broadcasting, Lee Hanna recommends that you fit as many English and social science courses as possible into your college program. The logic of that advice seems to be that the better educated you are the better broadcaster you'll be.

Hatim Hamer, head of the Employment Clearinghouse at the National Association of Broadcasters that provides job information for people already in the industry, said that college students would be crazy not to take advantage of their school's broadcast facilities, especially in handling sports events. He adds, however, that writing experience can also be beneficial in landing a job. An applicant who can show that he or she has written for the college paper, or for a local weekly, gains an advantage. Assuming, of course, that the samples demonstrate an ability to write well. "Many broadcasters," said Hamer, "came from print journalism."

All-Sports Radio

For a lot of sports fans, especially those with car phones, the rise of 24-hour all-sports radio is the greatest thing that's happened in radio since the broadcast of the Dempsey-

Carpentier fight in Jersey City on July 2, 1921, when sports and radio were first wed.

What all-sports radio has done, of course, is give fans access to the airwaves for the free expression of their judgments, theories, and outrage relating to the conduct of sports events that have brought their lives to some critical pass. These call-ins are serious stuff, and they go on for most of the hours of the day and night, interrupted only by the broadcast of a ballgame or by a kindred syndicated spirit like Imus of "Imus in the Morning."

It's a great format, says Beverly Tilden, station manager of WEEI of Boston, and ever since WFAN in New York gave it a life a few years ago, it's been popping up all over the country.

From a business point of view, Tilden says, the format produces a very desirable target audience—upscale men between the ages of 25 and 44. (Yes, Tilden avers, the format tends to attract listeners of higher than average incomes.)

A station's success with this format obviously is dependent on the talents of its hosts—the people who handle the call-ins. Tilden describes the hosts as performers with strong personalities who can stir things up and generate calls from listeners who have never called a talk show. With regard to her own staff of hosts, she looks for bright, well-read people who can bring philosophical and psychological insights to an issue. A host, she feels, should have a broad knowledge of sports, but a person whose head is filled with sports stats does not impress her, especially if there's no room for thought processes that lead to stimulating discourse.

It isn't often that Tilden has to replace a WEEI host, but when she goes shopping for one she looks for a broadcaster who can take a fresh look at the day's events in sports and dish out observations that are unexpected and provocative. It takes a talent that is not in abundant supply, she says.

At WFAN, which introduced the all-sports

format in July 1987, program director Mark Chernoff takes a similar view. A broadcaster's encyclopedic memory doesn't count for much in this format if it isn't used entertainingly. Chernoff also favors hosts who are "opinionated." They make lively radio. But, he adds, they've got to be able to make a case for their opinions.

On breaking into this field. Before you can hope to make a dent, says Tilden, you need a background in communications generally and broadcasting specifically. Working at a college radio station is a good way to start. Then apply for an internship and "do anything and everything to meet people and learn the business."

The range of pay for this type of work is as wide as the radio landscape. In small markets, young broadcasters who are learning the techniques of handling call-ins generally earn about $20,000. On the next plateau (mid-sized markets), the pay can rise to $40,000. In big cities, sports talk hosts—especially those who have become recognizable personalities—make a lot of money. How much, exactly? Says Chernoff: "A lot."

(See directory beginning on page 195 for addresses and phone numbers of all-sports radio stations.)

Game Broadcasters

Here's where the name broadcasters are— at the center of the action, delivering play-by-play and commentary to local, regional, or national audiences. And having a great time.

How do you get there? It helps if you've achieved some measure of fame as a player or coach. But you don't get beyond the tryout if you don't bring some broadcasting talent to the mike. Frank Gifford, Dan Dierdorf, Jim Palmer, Dick Vermiel, Tony Trabert, Dick Vitale, Jim Kaat, Bob Griese, Terry Bradshaw, Lynn Swann, Tim McCarver, Joe Namath, Phil Rizzuto—all have earned their roles on merit, as did many others who came up to the booth from the playing field.

The two broadcasters widely recognized as outstanding in their particular sports are John Madden in football and Vin Scully in baseball. Madden came to CBS after 10 successful years as head coach of the Oakland Raiders. Scully joined the broadcast team of the Brooklyn Dodgers after graduating from Fordham University, where he had worked at the student radio station. Two vastly different backgrounds.

What makes Madden so great? His commentary is bright and colorful, but most of all it's his personality that lifts this behemoth to stardom. His jocularity and modesty and sheer hominess make viewers wish they had him as a friend. It's a quality that's worth the millions he receives now from Fox Sports.

What makes Scully so terrific? It's a combination of things: a keen eye for the subtleties of the game, a quick mind, a genial disposition, and, most important of all, a mastery of the English language. He is just a pleasure to listen to. And the years haven't hurt a bit. Scully has been a professional sportscaster for four and a half decades, and his work is as fresh as ever.

*   *   *   *

Internships

The broadcast industry is on your side. Radio and television stations, cable operations big and small, and national networks offer thousands of internship deals. Check the listings at the end of this section for sources you may find especially interesting.

Tune in to this. An internship program of more than passing interest is the College Conference and Summer Fellowship program, which is conducted in New York City under the auspices of the International Radio and Television Society Foundation.

The program, which runs for nine weeks during the summer, is designed for college students interested in working in the broadcasting, cable, or advertising business.

Summer Fellows (read interns) are given free round-trip transportation, free housing (in a New York University dorm), and an allowance (to defray the cost of food).

The first week is spent with industry professionals. Activities include lectures, discussions, field trips—plus social functions, for networking purposes.

After that, students are assigned to supervised work in an area of interest to them—sports, for example. Work sites, all in the heart of New York City, include the four major networks, local radio and television stations, cable operations, and advertising agencies (many of which are deeply involved in sports marketing projects).

More information and an application can be obtained from the IRTS Foundation at 420 Lexington Ave., Suite 1714, New York, NY 10170-0101. Phone: (212) 867-6650.

Be advised: Competition for these appointments is no romp in Central Park.

Programs for minority students. The Radio and Television News Directors Association has a scholarship program and an internship program for minority college students. Both programs are designed to train students in the day-to-day management of electronic news. They're not geared to sports news especially, but they're worth looking into. For information on either or both programs write to: RTNDF Scholarships/Internships, 1000 Connecticut Ave. NW, Suite 615, Washington, DC 20036.

More help. Still another source of internships is the National Association of Broadcasters, which is interested in helping minorities and women get a start in the industry. Get in touch with the Human Resources Development Office. The phone number is (202) 429-5498. The NAB address is 1771 N St. NW, Washington, DC 20036-2891.

A caution on private schools. Not all of the private vocational schools that offer training in broadcasting are what they're cracked up to be. Some provide legitimate programs, but others offer phony programs with outmoded equipment and false promises of job placements. Private vocational schools are not properly regulated, so be careful. If you're considering enrolling in one of these schools, call the personnel manager of a local radio or television station and ask about the school's reputation.

Sourcebook

Addresses, phone numbers, and key executives of the nation's radio and television stations and cable operations appear in the *Broadcasting & Cable Yearbook*. It's the most comprehensive sourcebook in the industry, and your local library is sure to have it.

* * * *

Quick Shots

We had a look at the backgrounds of 60 broadcasters employed by the networks and found that almost half got their jobs without the benefit of big reputations earned on the playing field. Here are some of them, pure civilians all, and how they got started:

Al Michaels, native of Brooklyn , , , Majored in radio and TV at Arizona State . . . First job: broadcasting games of Hawaii Islanders in Pacific Coast League in 1968. (Received an Emmy nomination for his quick-witted coverage of the San Francisco earthquake during the 1989 World Series.)

Jim McKay (real name McManus), born in Philadelphia in 1921 . . . Graduated from Loyola College in Baltimore . . . Gave up his job as reporter for *Baltimore Sun* newspapers to join that organization's new TV station, WMAR-TV, in 1947. His was the first voice heard on television in Baltimore. Received an Emmy and journalism's prestigious George Polk Award for his brilliant reporting of terrorists' attack on Israeli athletes in the Olympic Village in Munich in 1972 . . . In 1968 became the first sports commentator to win an Emmy Award. Won 12 more after that . . . Much respected in the industry.

Lesley Visser, a pioneer among women sports journalists, started as a member of the sports staff of the *Boston Globe* in 1974 . . .

Worked for CBS Sports before joining ABC Sports in 1994 . . . Voted the Outstanding Women's Sportswriter in 1983 and received the Women's Sports Foundation Award in 1992.

Jack Whitaker, winner of two Emmy awards . . . Began his career in 1947 producing sports, news, and music programming at a Philadelphia-area radio station . . . Best sports essayist since John Kieran.

Greg Gumbel, born in New Orleans, grew up in Chicago . . . Majored in English at Loras College . . . Was sports anchor at WMAQ-TV in Chicago . . . Winner of three Emmy awards.

Charlsie Cantey, graduate of George Washington University . . . Was working as an exercise rider at Belmont Park when she was selected to cohost a horse racing program on WOR-TV in New York.

Robin Roberts, communications major and basketball star at Southeastern Louisiana University . . . Between and after classes and basketball games was sports director at local radio station . . . After graduation in 1983, worked at WDAM-TV in Hattiesburg, moved on to WLOX-TV in Biloxi, then to WSMV-TV in Nashville, where she won a Sportscaster of the Year Award . . . That took her to WAGA-TV in Atlanta, thence to ESPN (in 1990) and more awards.

Hannah Storm, native of Oak Park, Illinois . . . Majored in political science and communications at Notre Dame . . . Started her career at WNDU-TV in South Bend and KNCN-FM in Corpus Christi, Texas.

Jim Nantz, born in Charlotte, North Carolina, grew up in Colts Neck, New Jersey . . . Majored in radio and television at University of Houston . . . Considered a career in golf, but playing on Houston golf team with Fred Couples discouraged him . . . Got his start in television at KSL-TV in Salt Lake City at the age of 23.

Keith Jackson, native of Georgia, made his start in the Northwest as a student broad-

The Newhouse School of Public Communications at Syracuse University turns out more than its share of sports broadcasters. Here are some of them:

Marv Albert
Len Berman
Bob Costas
Ian Eagle
Marty Glickman
Hank Greenwald
Sean McDonough
Andy Musser
Greg Papa
Dick Stockton
Mike Tirico

caster from Washington State University beginning in 1952 . . . Has been identified with college football ever since, with shelves of awards attesting to his skill and popularity . . . His broadcasting philosophy: "Amplify, clarify, and punctuate, and let the viewers draw their own conclusions."

A Word About the People Behind the Cameras...

The men and women who operate the television cameras at sports events are mostly freelancers who work on a per diem basis. Most acquire their skills through on-the-job training.

John Lunning, productions manager at Dimension Cable in Phoenix, is a typical employer of camera operators. Lunning brings Dimension viewers about 80 games a year (NBA basketball and IHL hockey), selecting his camera operators from a pool of freelancers in Phoenix. He also trains young people who come to him and say they want to learn the trade. Trainees have to show a good attitude, he says. He expects them to turn up at games not only to watch and learn but also to lend a hand when it's needed (for lugging cable, for example). When he feels they can be entrusted with the equipment and actually get behind the cameras in a game, he pays them $50 a shoot. It takes beginners about two years to become journeyman operators, he says.

Lunning says that he's not keen about the training programs offered by colleges and private technical schools. "They usually don't have the professional equipment we use," he says. He also has reservations about the techniques they teach. "I'd rather teach a trainee from scratch," he says.

Veteran camera operators make between $200 and $300 a shoot. How much work they get depends on the reputation they establish. Overall, their earnings range from $30,000 to $60,000 a year.

HOW THEY GOT THERE

BOB COSTAS
NBC Sports

Bob Costas is probably the most versatile announcer in the business. But one thing he is not: he is not a screamer. Whether he's doing play-by-play, or game commentary, or studio hosting, his delivery is calm, articulate, informative. And respectful of the adults in his audience.

Costas, a native New Yorker, took the customary route to a career in broadcasting. He selected a college that had broadcasting facilities (in his case, Syracuse University), worked at the campus radio and TV stations, and with the experience gained there, hooked up with KMOX Radio in St. Louis. Later, he took a job as the radio voice of University of Missouri basketball and also handled regional NFL and NBA assignments for CBS Sports. He joined NBC in 1980, covering a wide array of assignments with an adroitness that moved him quickly to the top of his profession. Assignments as prime-time host for the '92 Barcelona Olympics in Atlanta affirmed his stature.

Among his awards are seven Emmys.

NATIONAL SPORTS TV NETWORKS

All the networks have internship programs. Suggestion: Don't call the network president. Do call the personnel (or human resources) department.

ABC Sports
47 W. 66th St.
New York, NY 10023
(212) 456-7777
Steven M. Bornstein, President
Internships offered

CBS Sports
51 W. 52nd St., 30th Floor
New York, NY 10019
(212) 975-4321
Sean McManus, President
Internships offered

CNN/SI
One CNN Ctr
Atlanta, GA 30303
(404) 878-1648
Jim Walton, Sr Vice President
Internships: contact Russell
    Bissen

ESPN
ESPN Plaza
Bristol, CT 06010
(860) 585-2000
Steven M. Bornstein, President
    and CEO
Internships offered

ESPN International
605 Third Ave., 8th Floor
New York, NY 10158
(212) 916-9200
Jacques Kremer, Sr Vice
    President

Fox Sports
5746 Sunset Blvd.
Los Angeles, CA 90028
(213) 856-1234
David Hill, President
Internships offered

HBO Sports
1100 Ave. of the Americas
New York, NY 10036
(212) 512-1000
Seth Abraham, President

NBC Sports
30 Rockefeller Plaza
New York, NY 10112
(212) 664-4444
Dick Ebersol, President
Internships offered

Turner Sports
(Turner Broadcasting Inc.)
One CNN Center
Atlanta, GA 30303
(404) 827-1735
Harvey Schiller, President
Internships offered

USA Network
1230 Ave. of the Americas
New York, NY 10020
(212) 408-9100
Gordon Beck, Vice President

NATIONAL SPORTS RADIO NETWORKS

ABC Radio Sports
125 West End Ave., 6th Floor
New York, NY 10023
(212) 456-5187
Shelby Whitfield, Executive Producer

Capitol Sports Network
711 Hillsborough St.
Raleigh, NC 27605
(919) 890-6080
Jerry Reckerd, General Sales Manager

CBS Radio Network
51 W. 52nd St., Suite 1876
New York, NY 10019
(212) 975-4321
Dan Mason, President

ESPN Radio Network
935 Middle St.
Bristol, CT 06010
(860) 585-2000
Drew Hayes, Executive Producer

Prime Sports
125 John Carpenter Freeway, Suite
670
Irving, TX 75039
(214) 401-0972
Jeff Dorf, General Manager

Talk America Radio Network
354 Turnpike St.
Canton, MA 02021
(617) 828-4546
John Crohan, President

Telemedia Network Radio
40 Holly St.
Toronto, Ontario M4S 3C3
Canada
(416) 482-9383
Nelson Millman, Program Director

**Westwood One Entertainment
Sports**
1755 S. Jefferson Davis Hwy.
Arlington, VA 22202
(703) 413-8340
Larry Michael, Director of Sports

ALL-SPORTS RADIO STATIONS

The programming of the radio stations listed here is devoted to sports news, call-in sports shows, and live coverage of sports events.

Internships: Most of the stations employ interns with regularity; some do it occasionally (depending on the quality of the applicant). All are good targets.

ALABAMA

WJOX
236 Goodwin Crest Dr.
Birmingham, AL 35209
(205) 945-4646
Gen Mgr: Davis Hawkins
Internships: contact Kelly Cruise

WSPZ
5200 Flatwoods Rd.
Northport, AL 35476
(205) 339-3700
Program Dir: Fred Nelson
Internships: contact Rick Jones

ARIZONA

KGME-AM
4745 N. Seventh St., Suite 410
Phoenix, AZ 85014
(602) 266-1360
Station Mgr: Reid Reker
Internship contact: Marlene Naubert

CALIFORNIA

KGEO-AM
P.O. Box 260
Bakersfield, CA 93302
(805) 631-1230
Gen Mgr: Rogers Brandon
Internships offered

XTRA
4891 Pacific Hwy.
San Diego, CA 92110
(619) 291-9191
Producer: Eric Ehnstrom

COLORADO

KYBG
5660 Greenwood Plaza Blvd.,
    Suite 400
Englewood, CO 80111
(303) 721-9210
Gen Mgr: Ron Jamison

FLORIDA

WFNS
7201 E. Hillsborough Ave.
Tampa, FL 33610
(813) 620-9100
Gen Mgr: Brent Harmon

WNZS
8386 Baymeadows Rd.
Jacksonville, FL 32256
(904) 636-0507
Program Dir: Tommy Charles

ALL-SPORTS RADIO STATIONS

WQAM
9881 Sheridan St.
Hollywood, FL 33024
(305) 431-6200
Gen Mgr: Greg Reed
Internships: contact Greg Reed

WSUN-AM
877 Executive Center Dr. W, Suite 300
St. Petersburg, FL 33702
(813) 576-1073
Sales Mgr: Dave Pecchia
Internships: contact Dep't Head

WZTM-AM
11300 Fourth St. N
St. Petersburg, FL 33716
(813) 577-7131
Gen Mgr: Drew Rashbaum
Internships: contact Dep't Head

GEORGIA

WCNN
209 CNN Center
Atlanta, GA 30303
(404) 688-0068
Gen Mgr: Len Dickey Jr.

WIBB
2525 Pio Nono Ave.
Macon, GA 31206
(912) 781-1063
Gen Mgr: Diana Smith

ILLINOIS

WMVP-AM
875 N. Michigan Ave., Suite 3750
Chicago, IL 60611
(312) 440-5270
Gen Mgr: Doug Stern
Internships: contact Gerri Wells

WSCR
4949 W. Belmont Ave.
Chicago, IL 60641
(312) 777-1700
Gen Mgr: Harvey Wells
Internships: contact Henry Henderson

IOWA

KJOC
1229 Brady St.
Davenport, IA 52803
(319) 326-2541
Program Dir: Dan Burich
Internships: contact Dan Burich

MARYLAND

WTEM
11300 Rockville Pike
Rockville, MD 20852
(301) 770-5700
Gen Mgr: Robert Snyder
Internships: contact Steve Lieberman

WTGM
P.O. Box U
Salisbury, MD 21802
(410) 742-1923
Gen Mgr: Ron Gillenardo
Internships: contact Doug Weldon

MASSACHUSETTS

WEEI
116 Huntington Ave.
Boston, MA 02116
(617) 375-8000
Station Mgr: Beverly Tilden

MICHIGAN

WDFN-AM
2930 E. Jefferson
Detroit, MI 48207
(313) 259-5440
Gen Mgr: Peter Connolly
Internships: contact Ronah Danzinger

WSFN
875 E. Summit Ave.
Muskegon, MI 49444
(616) 733-2126
Gen Mgr: Bob Goodrich

WVFN
2517 E. Mount Hope Ave.
Lansing, MI 48910
(517) 487-5986
Station Dir: Dennis Lemon

MINNESOTA

KBUN
P.O. Box 1656
Bemidji, MN 56601
(218) 751-4120
Gen Mgr: Lou Buron

KFAN
7900 Xerxes Ave. S, Suite 102
Minneapolis, MN 55431
(612) 820-4200
Gen Mgr: Mick Anselmo
Internships: contact Eric Webster

MISSOURI

KFNS
7711 Carondelet St., Suite 304
St. Louis, MO 63105
(314) 727-2160
Gen Mgr: Pat McMann
Internships: contact Steve Moore

NEVADA

KVEG
1455 E. Tropicana, Suite 250
Las Vegas, NV 89119
(702) 262-6600
Gen Mgr: Tom Humm
Internships: contact Cindy Johnson

NEW HAMPSHIRE

WCQL
P.O. Box 150
Portsmouth, NH 03802
(603) 430-9500
Gen Mgr: Rob Knight
Internships: contact Jeff Laurence

WTMN-AM
815 LaFayette Rd.
Portsmouth, NH 03801
(603) 430-9500
Gen Mgr: Rob Knight
Internships: contact Glenn Stewart

NEW MEXICO

KDEF
2117 Menaul NE
Albuquerque, NM 87107
(505) 888-1022
Station Dir: Henry Tafoya
Internships: contact Henry Tafoya
(Half sports, half conservative talk)

NEW YORK

WCMF-AM
3136 S. Winton Rd., Suite 300
Rochester, NY 14623
(716) 272-7260
Gen Mgr: Robert Morgan
Internships: contact Lori Baster

WFAN
34-12 36th St.
Astoria, NY 11106
(718) 706-7690
Program Dir: Mark Chernoff

NORTH CAROLINA

WFNZ
915 E. Fourth St.
Charlotte, NC 28204
(704) 338-9970
Gen Mgr: Macon Moye
Internships: contact Tom Carey

OHIO

WASN
401 N. Blaine Ave.
Youngstown, OH 44505
(216) 746-1330
Gen Mgr: Larry Ward

WKNR
9446 Broadview Rd.
Cleveland, OH 44147
(216) 838-1220
Gen Mgr: James Glass
Internships: contact Marin Durent

WKYN-AM
225 E. Sixth St.
Cincinnati, OH 45202
(513) 721-1050
Gen Mgr: John Rohm
Internships: contact Tim Lewis

OKLAHOMA

WWLS
4000 W. Indian Hill Rd.
Norman, OK 73072
(405) 360-7000
Station Dir: Tony Sellars
Internships: contact John Fox

OREGON

KFXX
4614 S.W. Kelly
Portland, OR 97201
(503) 223-1441
Station Dir: Steve Arena
Internships: contact Mike Turner,
    Angie Buss

PENNSYLVANIA

WFXX
P.O. Box 5057
South Williamsport, PA 17701
(717) 323-3608
Station Dir: Warren Diggins

ALL · SPORTS RADIO STATIONS

WIP
441 N. Fifth St.
Philadelphia, PA 19123
(215) 922-5000
Station Dir: Tom Bigby
Internships: contact David Helfrich

TEXAS

KILT-AM
24 Greenway Plaza, Suite 1900
Houston, TX 77046
(713) 881-5100
Gen Mgr: Dickey Rosenfeld

KTCK-AM
5307 E. Mockingbird. Lane, Suite 500
Dallas, TX 75206
(214) 826-8425
Gen Mgr: Dan Bennett
Internships: contact Dep't Head

UTAH

KISN-AM
4001 S. 700 E, Suite 800
Salt Lake City, UT 84017
(801) 262-9797
Sports Dir: Chris Tunis
Internships: contact Prog Dir

VIRGINIA

WGH
281 Independence Blvd.
Virginia Beach, VA 23462
(804) 497-1310
Gen Mgr: Bill Whitlow

WRVH
P.O. Box 1516
Richmond, VA 23212
(804) 780-3400
Program Dir: Tim Farley

WASHINGTON

KJR
190 Queen Anne Ave. N
Seattle, WA 98109
(206) 285-2295
Gen Mgr: Michael O'Shea

WISCONSIN

WAUK
1021 Whitehall St.
Waukesha, WI 53186
(414) 544-6800
Station Mgr: Ed Walters
Internships: contact Ed Walters

WBIZ
P.O. Box 24
Eau Claire, WI 54702
(715) 835-5111
Gen Mgr: Rick Hencley
(Half sports, half country)

WKBH
P.O. Box 1624
La Crosse, WI 54602
(608) 784-9524
Station Mgr: Tim Scott
Internships: contact Tim Scott

REGIONAL CABLE SPORTS COMPANIES

Many of the cable sports companies have internship programs. They are identified.

ASPN
17602 N. Black Canyon Hwy.
Phoenix, AZ 85023
(602) 995-2711
Internships offered

ChicagoLand Television
2000 York Rd.
Oak Brook, IL 60521
(630) 368-4000

Empire Sports Network
795 Indian Church Rd.
West Seneca, NY 14224
(716) 827-4289

Fox Sports Americas
10000 Santa Monica Blvd., Suite 333
Los Angeles, CA 90067
(310) 282-7230

Fox Sports Midwest
700 St. Louis Union Station, Suite 100
St. Louis, MO 63103
(314) 421-0014

Fox Sports Northwest
3626 156th Ave. SE
Bellevue, WA 98006
(206) 641-0104

Fox Sports Pittsburgh
2 Allegheny Ctr., Suite 1000
Pittsburgh, PA 15212
(412) 322-9500

Fox Sports Rocky Mountain
44 Cook St., Suite 600
Denver, CO 80206
(303) 267-7200

Fox Sports Rocky Mountain
1251 E. Wilmington Ave., Suite 175
Salt Lake City, UT 84105
(801) 484-7262

Fox Sports Southwest
100 E. Royal Lane, Suite 200
Irving, TX 75039
(214) 868-1800

Fox Sports West
10000 Santa Monica Blvd.
Los Angeles, CA 90067
(310) 286-3800

Home Team Sports
7700 Wisconsin Ave., 2nd Floor
Bethesda, MD 20814
(301) 718-3200

Madison Square Garden Network
4 Penn Plaza, 4th Floor
New York, NY 10001
(212) 465-6000
Internships offered

Midwest Sports Channel
90 S. 11th St.
Minneapolis, MN 55403
(612) 330-2736
Internships offered

New England Sports Network
70 Brookline Ave.
Boston, MA 02215
(617) 536-9233
Internships offered

PASS Sports
550 W. Lafayette
P.O. Box 3040
Detroit, MI 48231
(313) 222-7277

PRISM
225 City Line Ave.
Bala Cynwyd, PA 19004
(610) 668-2210

SportsChannel Chicago
820 W. Madison
Oak Park, IL 60302
(708) 524-9444
Internships offered

SportsChannel Cincinnati
11311 Cornell Park Dr., Suite 406
Cincinnati, OH 45242
(513) 469-2006

SportsChannel Florida
7900 Glades Rd., Suite 150
Boca Raton, FL 33434
(954) 832-9555
Internships offered

SportsChannel New England
10 Tower Office Park
Woburn, MA 01801
(617) 933-9300
Internships offered

SportsChannel New York
200 Crossways Park Dr.
Woodbury, NY 11797
(516) 364-3650
Internships offered

SportsChannel Ohio
6500 Rockside Rd., Suite 340
Independence, OH 44131
(216) 328-0333
Internships offered

SportsChannel Pacific
901 Battery St., Suite 204
San Francisco, CA 94111
(415) 296-8900
Internships offered

SportsChannel Philadelphia
225 City Line Ave.
Bala Cynwyd, PA 19004
(610) 668-2210
Internships offered

SportSouth Network
One CNN Center
Box 740080
Atlanta, GA 30374
(404) 827-4100
Internships offered

Sunshine Network
390 N. Orange Ave., Suite 1075
Orlando, FL 32801
(407) 648-1150
Internships offered

The Sports Network
2225 Sheppard Ave. E, Suite 100
Willowdale, Ontario M2J 5C2
Canada
(416) 494-1212

Wisconsin Sports Network
P.O. Box 3099
Milwaukee, WI 53201
(414) 933-4114

SPORTS PROGRAMMING AND PRODUCTION COMPANIES

All the companies listed here hire interns or, occasionally, part-time workers.

44 Blue Productions
4040 Vineland Ave., Suite 206
Studio City, CA 91604
(818) 760-4442
Internships: contact
  Lasta Drachkovitch

American Sports Network
P.O. Box 6100
Rosemead, CA 91770
(818) 292-2222
Internships: contact
  Louis Zwick

B.A.S.S., Inc.
5845 Carmichael Rd.
Montgomery, AL 36117
(334) 272-9530
Internships: contact
  Dave Precht

Chirkinian Communications
200 E. Broward Blvd., Suite 1330
Fort Lauderdale, FL 33301
(954) 847-3800
Internships: contact
  Frank Chirkinian

Creative Response
11500 Olympic Blvd., Suite 400
Los Angeles, CA 90064
(310) 473-7444
Internships: contact
  Michael Cohen

Creative Sports
7621 Little Ave., Suite 516
Charlotte, NC 28226
(704) 541-6600
Internships: contact
  Jeff Schmidt

Golden Gaters Productions
400 Tamal Plaza
Corte Madera, CA 94925
(415) 924-7500
Internships offered

Global Television Sports
15 E. Ridge Pike, Suite 500
Conshohocken, PA 19428
(610) 825-4000
Internships: contact
  Jim Drucker

High Bar Productions
250 W. 57th St., Suite 501
New York, NY 10107
(212) 307-7077
Internships: contact
  Amy Zuckerman

Intersport Television
414 N. Orleans Plaza, Suite 600
Chicago, IL 60610
(312) 661-0616
Internships: contact
  Peter Rudman

Learfield Communications
505 Hobbs Rd.
P.O. Box 104180
Jefferson City, MO 65110
(573) 893-7200
Internships: contact
  Chuck Zimmerman

Liberty Sports
100 E. Royal Lane
Irving, TX 75039
(214) 868-1000
Internships: contact
  Public Relations

NFL Films
330 Fellowship Rd.
Mt. Laurel, NJ 08054
(609) 778-1600
Internships: contact
  Denise Moser

OCC Sports
605 Third Ave.
New York, NY 10158
(212) 916-9200
Internships: contact
  (860) 585-2317

Paxson Networks
601 Clearwater Park Blvd.
West Palm Beach, FL 33401
(561) 659-4122
Internships may be offered

Phoenix Communications
3 Empire Blvd.
S. Hackensack, NJ 07606
(201) 807-0888
Internships: contact
  Denise Meola

ProServ Television
1101 Wilson Blvd., Suite 1800
Arlington, VA 22209
(703) 276-3030
Internships: contact
  Julie Kennedy

Raycom, Inc.
P.O. Box 33367
Charlotte, NC 28233
(704) 378-4400
Internships: contact
  Human Resources

Rick Scott & Associates
2509 152nd Ave. NE, Suite D
Redmond, WA 98052
(206) 867-9397
Internships: contact
  Rick Scott

SportsTicker
Harborside Financial Ctr. 600, Plaza 2
Jersey City, NJ 07311
(201) 309-1200
For paid part-time positions
  in newsroom, contact Jon Mastro

Tabler Communications
310 W. Liberty St., Suite 302
Louisville, KY 40202
(502) 585-2299
Internships: contact
  Grant Schomer

**Titan Sports/World Wrestling
Federation**
1241 E. Main St.
Stamford, CT 06902
(203) 352-8600
Internships: contact
  Human Resources

Trans World International
22 E. 71st St.
New York, NY 10021
(212) 772-8900
Internships: contact
  Deborah Dash

Winner Communications
6120 S. Yale, 2nd Floor
Tulsa, OK 74136
(918) 496-1900
Internships: contact
  Doug Wren

World Championship Wrestling
1 CNN Center
P.O. Box 105366
Atlanta, GA 30348
(404) 827-2066
Internships: contact
  Georgia Davidson

COLLEGES WITH FULL BROADCASTING FACILITIES

The institutions listed here have extensive radio and TV facilities. The level of their academic programs is shown by the letters B, M, and D, for bachelor's, master's, and doctoral degrees.

ALABAMA

University of Alabama — B, M, D
Tuscaloosa, AL 35487-0172
College of Communication
Edward Mullins, Dean
(205) 348-5520

ALASKA

University of Alaska — B
Fairbanks, AK 99775-0940
Dep't of Journalism and Broadcasting
Bruce L. Smith, Head
(907) 474-7761

ARIZONA

University of Arizona — B, M
Tucson, AZ 85721
Dep't of Journalism
Jim Patten, Head
(602) 621-7556

Arizona State University — B, M
Tempe, AZ 85287-1305
*Walter Cronkite School of Journalism and
  Telecommunication*
Douglas A. Anderson, Director
(602) 965-5011

ARKANSAS

Arkansas State University — B, M
Jonesboro, AR 72467
College of Communications
Russell E. Shain, Dean
(501) 972-2468

**University of Arkansas at
  Fayetteville — B, M**
Fayetteville, AR 72701
Walter J. Lemke Dep't of Journalism
Patsy Watkins, Chair
(501) 575-3601

CALIFORNIA

**California State University at
  Chico — B, M**
Chico, CA 95929
College of Communication
Stephen King, Dean
(916) 898-4015

COLLEGES WITH FULL BROADCASTING FACILITIES

California State University at Fresno — B, M
Fresno, CA 93740
Dep't of Journalism
Paul D. Adams, Chair
(209) 278-2087

California State University at Fullerton — B, M
Fullerton, CA 92634
Dep't of Communications
Terry Hynes, Chair
(714) 773-3517

California State University at Northridge — B, M
Northridge, CA 91330
Dep't of Journalism
Tom Reilly, Chair
(818) 885-3135

Pepperdine University — B, M
Malibu, CA 90263
Communication Division
Donald L. Shores, Chair
(213) 456-4211

San Diego State University — B, M
San Diego, CA 92182
Dep't of Journalism
Glen M. Broom, Chair
(619) 265-6635

University of California, Los Angeles — B
Los Angeles, CA 90024
Dep't of Theatre, Film and Television
Gil Cates, Dean
(310) 825-5761

University of Southern California — B, M
Los Angeles, CA 90089-1695
School of Journalism
William J. Woestendiek, Director
(213) 740-3914

COLORADO

University of Colorado — B, M, D
Boulder, CO 80309
School of Journalism and Mass Communication
Willard. D. Rowland Jr., Dean
(303) 492-5007

University of Denver — B, M
Denver, CO 80208
Dep't of Mass Communications and Journalism Studies
Michael O. Wirth, Chair
(303) 871-2166

DISTRICT OF COLUMBIA

American University — B, M
Washington, DC 20016
School of Communication
Sanford. J. Ungar, Dean
(202) 885-2060

Howard University — B
Washington, DC 20059
Dep't of Journalism
Lawrence N. Kaggwa, Chair
(202) 806-7855

FLORIDA

Edward Waters College — B
Jacksonville, FL 32218
Mass Communications Program
Emmanuel C. Alozie, Coord.
(904) 366-2502

University of Florida — B, M, D
Gainesville, FL 32611-2084
College of Journalism and Communications
Ralph L. Lowenstein, Dean
(904) 392-0466

University of Miami — B, M
Coral Gables, FL 33124
School of Communication
Edward. Pfister, Dean
(305) 284-2265

University of South Florida — B, M
Tampa, FL 33620
School of Mass Communications
Donna Lee Dickerson, Director
(813) 974-2591

University of West Florida — B, M
Pensacola, FL 32514
Communication Arts
Churchill L. Roberts, Chair
(904) 474-2874

GEORGIA

University of Georgia — B, M, D
Athens, GA 30602
Henry W. Grady College of Journalism and Mass Communication
J. Thomas Russell, Dean
(404) 542-1704

HAWAII

University of Hawaii at Manoa— B
Honolulu, HI 96822
Dep't of Journalism
John Luter, Chair
(808) 956-8881

IDAHO

University of Idaho — B
Moscow, ID 83843
School of Communication
Peter Haggart, Director
(208) 885-6458

Idaho State University —B
Pocatello, ID 83209
Mass Communication Program
Janet House, Assoc. Prof.
(208) 236-3295

ILLINOIS

Bradley University — B
Peoria, IL 61625
Dep't of Communication
John Schweitzer, Dep't Chair
(309) 676-7611

Eastern Illinois University — B
Charleston, IL 61920
Dep't of Journalism
John David Reed, Chair
(217) 581-6003

Northwestern University — B, M, D
Evanston, IL 60208
Medill School of Journalism
Michael C. Janeway, Dean
(708) 491-5091

Southern Illinois University at Carbondale — B, M
Carbondale, IL 62901
School of Journalism
Walter B. Jaehnig, Director
(618) 536-3361

Southern Illinois University at Edwardsville — B, M
Edward.sville, IL 62026
Dep't of Mass Communications
Barbara C. Regnell, Chair
(618) 692-2230

University of Illinois at Urbana — B, M, D
Urbana, IL 61801
College of Communications
James W. Carey, Dean
(217) 333-2350

INDIANA

Ball State University — B, M
Muncie, IN 47306
Dep't of Journalism
Earl L. Conn, Chair and Director
(317) 285-8200

Indiana University — B, M, D
Indianapolis, IN 46223
School of Journalism
Trevor R. Brown, Dean
(317) 274-2773

Purdue University — B, M, D
West Lafayette, IN 47907
Dep't of Communication
Charles J. Stewart, Head
(317) 494-3429

IOWA

Iowa State University — B, M
Ames, IA 50011
Dep't of Journalism and Mass Communication
J. Thomas Emmerson, Chair
(515) 294-4340

University of Iowa — B, M, D
Iowa City, IA 52242
School of Journalism and Mass Communication
Ken Starck, Dir
(319) 335-5821

KANSAS

Kansas State University — B, M
Manhattan, KS 66506-1501
A.Q. Miller School of Journalism and Mass Communications
Carol Oukrop, Dir
(913) 532-6890

University of Kansas — B, M
Lawrence, KS 66045
William Allen White School of Journalism and Mass Communications
Mike Kautsch, Dean
(913) 864-4755

Wichita State University — B, M
Wichita, KS 67208-1595
Elliott School of Communication
Vernon A. Keel, Dir
(316) 689-3185

KENTUCKY

Eastern Kentucky University — B
Richmond, KY 40475
Dep't of Mass Communications
Glen Kleine, Chair
(606) 622-1871

Morehead State University — B, M
Morehead, KY 40351
Dep't of Communications
W. David Brown, Journalism Coord.
(606) 783-2694

COLLEGES WITH FULL BROADCASTING FACILITIES

Murray State University — B, M
Murray, KY 42071
Dep't of Journalism and Radio-TV
Robert H. McGaughey III, Chair
(502) 762-2387

Western Kentucky University — B
Bowling Green, KY 42101
Dep't of Journalism
Jo-Ann Huff Albers, Dep't Head
(502) 745-4143

LOUISIANA

**Louisiana State University
— B, M**
Baton Rouge, LA 70803
Manship School of Journalism
John M. Hamilton, Dir
(504) 388-2336

**Southwestern Louisiana
University — B, M**
Lafayette, LA 70506-3600
Dep't of Communication
Paul Barefield, Head
(318) 231-6103

MAINE

University of Maine — B
Orono, ME 04469
*Dep't of Journalism and Mass
    Communication*
Stuart J. Bullion, Chair
(207) 581-1283

MARYLAND

Towson State University — B, M
Towson, MD 21204
Dep't of Speech and Mass Communication
Ronald J. Matlon, Chair
(410) 830-2891

University of Maryland — B, M, D
College Park, MD 20742
College of Journalism
Reese Cleghorn, Dean
(301) 405-2379

MASSACHUSETTS

Boston University — B, M
Boston, MA 02215
College of Communication
Brent Baker, Dean
(617) 353-3450

Emerson College — B, M
Boston, MA 02116
Mass Communication Division
A. David Gordon, Chair
(617) 578-8800

Northeastern University — B, M
Boston, MA 02115
School of Journalism
LaRue W. Gilleland, Dir
(617) 437-3236

MICHIGAN

Central Michigan University — B
Mount Pleasant, MI 48859
Dep't of Journalism
James Wieghart, Chair
(517) 774-3196

**Wayne State University
— B, M, D**
Detroit, MI 48202
Dep't of Journalism
Richard. A. Wright, Dir
(313) 577-2627

MINNESOTA

**University of Minnesota
— B, M, D**
Minneapolis, MN 55455
*School of Journalism and Mass
    Communication*
Daniel B. Wackman, Dir
(612) 625-9824

Winona State University — B
Winona, MN 55987
Dep't of Mass Communication
Dennis H. Pack, Chair
(507) 457-5230

MISSISSIPPI

University of Mississippi — B, M
University, MS 38677
Dep't of Journalism
Don Sneed, Chair
(601) 232-7147

MISSOURI

**Central Missouri State University
— B, M**
Warrensburg, MO 64093
Dep't of Communication
Daniel B. Curtis, Chair
(816) 543-4840

University of Missouri — B, M, D
Columbia, MO 65205
School of Journalism
Mike McKean, Chair
(314) 882-4823

NEBRASKA

**University of Nebraska at Lincoln
— B, M**
Lincoln, NE 68588
College of Journalism
Will Norton Jr., Dean
(402) 472-3041

**University of Nebraska at Omaha
— B, M**
Omaha, NE 68182
Dep't of Communication
Hugh P. Cowdin, Chair
(402) 554-2600

NEVADA

**University of Nevada at Las Vegas
— B, M**
Las Vegas, NV 89154
Greenspun School of Communication
Gage Chapel, Dir
(702) 739-3325

NEW JERSEY

Rutgers University — B
New Brunswick, NJ 08903-0270
Dep't of Journalism and Mass Media
Tony Atwater, Chair
(908) 932-8567

NEW MEXICO

University of New Mexico — B
Albuquerque, NM 87131
Dep't of Journalism
Everett Rogers, Dean
(505) 277-2326

NEW YORK

Syracuse University — B, M, D
Syracuse, NY 13244-2100
*S.I. Newhouse School of Public
    Communications*
David Rubin, Dean
(315) 443-2301

NORTH CAROLINA

**University of North Carolina
— M, D**
Chapel Hill, NC 27599-3365
*School of Journalism and Mass
    Communication*
Richard R. Cole, Dean
(919) 962-1204

NORTH DAKOTA

**University of North Dakota
— B, M**
Grand Forks, ND 58202
School of Communication
Dennis Davis, Director
(701) 777-2159

OHIO

**Bowling Green State University
— B, M**
Bowling Green, OH 43403
Dep't of Journalism
Hal Fisher, Chair
(419) 372-2076

Kent State University — B, M
Kent, OH 44242
*School of Journalism and Mass
    Communication*
Timothy D. Smith, Acting Director
(216) 672-2572

Miami University — B, M
Oxford., OH 45056
Dep't of Mass Communication
Jack Rhodes, Chair
(513) 529-3621

Ohio State University — B, M
Columbus, OH 43210
School of Journalism
Pamela J. Shoemaker, Director
(614) 292-6291

Ohio University — B, M, D
Athens, OH 45701-2979
E.W. Scripps School of Journalism
Ralph Izard, Director
(614) 593-2590

OKLAHOMA

**Oklahoma State University
— B, M**
Stillwater, OK 74078-0195
School of Journalism and Broadcasting
Marlan D. Nelson, Director
(405) 744-6354

COLLEGES WITH FULL BROADCASTING FACILITIES

University of Oklahoma — B, M
Norman, OK 73019
Herbert School of Journalism and Mass
Communication
David Dary, Director
(405) 325-2721

PENNSYLVANIA

Duquesne University — B, M
Pittsburgh, PA 15282
Dep't of Communication
Nancy Harper, Chair
(412) 434-6460

Pennsylvania State University
— B, M, D
University Park, PA 16802
School of Communications
Brian Winston, Dean
(814) 865-6597

Temple University — B, M, D
Philadelphia, PA 19122
Dep't of Journalism
David L. Womack, Chair
(215) 204-7433

SOUTH CAROLINA

University of South Carolina
B, M
Columbia, SC 29208
College of Journalism and Mass
Communications
Judy VanSlyke Turk, Dean
(803) 777-4102

SOUTH DAKOTA

University of South Dakota
— B, M
Vermillion, SD 57069
Dep't of Mass Communication
William A. Nevious, Chair
(605) 677-5477

South Dakota State University
— B, M
Brookings, SD 57007-0596
Dep't of Journalism and Mass
Communication
Richard. W. Lee, Head
(605) 688-4171

TENNESSEE

Memphis State University — B, M
Memphis, TN 38152
Journalism Dep't
Dan Lattimore, Chair
(901) 678-2401

University of Tennessee
— B, M, D
Knoxville, TN 37996
College of Communications; School of
Journalism
Dwight L. Teeter Jr., Dean
(615) 974-3031

TEXAS

Abilene Christian University
— B, M
Abilene, TX 79699
Journalism and Mass Communication
Dep't
Charles H. Marler, Chair
(915) 674-2298

Baylor University — B, M
Waco, TX 76798
Dep't of Journalism
Loyal N. Gould, Head
(817) 755-3261

Texas Christian University
— B, M
Fort Worth, TX 76129
Dep't of Journalism
Anantha S. Babbili, Chair
(817) 921-7425

Texas Tech University — B, M
Lubbock, TX 79409-3082
School of Mass Communications
Jerry C. Hudson, Director
(806) 742-3371

University of Houston— B, M
Houston, TX 77204-4072
School of Communication
Kenneth R. M. Short, Director
(713) 749-1745

University of Texas — B, M, D
Austin, TX 78712
Dep't of Journalism
Wayne Danielson, Chair
(512) 471-1845

UTAH

Brigham Young University
— B, M
Provo, UT 84602
Dep't of Communications
David P. Forsyth, Chair
(801) 378-2997

University of Utah — B, M, D
Salt Lake City, UT 84112
Dep't of Communication
James A. Anderson, Chair
(801) 581-6888

Utah State University — B, M
Logan, UT 84322-4605
Dep't of Communication
Scott Chisholm, Head
(801) 750-3292

WASHINGTON

University of Washington
— B, M, D
Seattle, WA 98195
School of Communications
Edward. P. Bassett, Director
(206) 543-2660

Washington State University
— B, M, D
Pullman, WA 99164-2520
Edward. R. Murrow School of
Communication
Alexis S. Tan, Director
(509) 335-1556

WEST VIRGINIA

Marshall University — B, M
Huntington, WV 25701
W. Page Pitt School of Journalism and
Mass Communications
Harold C. Shaver, Director
(304) 696-2360

West Virginia University — B, M
Morgantown, WV 26506-6010
Perley Isaac Reed School of Journalism
Emery L. Sasser, Dean
(304) 293-3505

WISCONSIN

Marquette University — B, M
Milwaukee, WI 53233
College of Communication, Journalism and
Performing Arts
Sharon M. Murphy, Dean
(414) 288-7133

University of Wisconsin at
Madison — B, M, D
Madison, WI 53706
Dep't of Journalism and Mass
Communication
Bob Drechsel, Dir
(608) 262-3691

WYOMING

University of Wyoming — B, M
Laramie, WY 82071
Dep't of Communication and Mass Media
Frank E. Millar, Head
(307) 766-3122

FROM NEAL PILSON, SOME TIPS ON MAKING YOUR WAY IN SPORTS

The comments that follow are those of Neal Pilson, former president of CBS Sports and now head of Pilson Communications, from an address he made at a Sports Career Conference.

———

The chance to work and earn a living in a field as dynamic and entertaining as sports is a life's dream. But you're not the only one seeking a job in this industry.

The key to getting a job in sports is to understand that it is a collection of many different businesses and is *not* a profession or a single industry.

Unlike law, or medicine, or engineering, you can't study a curriculum for sports. There is simply no common thread or denominator between doing promotion work for the

Florida Marlins, being a sports information director or assistant athletic director at the University of Illinois, doing sports production work as a broadcast associate at CBS or NBC or ABC, or planning sports media buys for Nike or Budweiser. The fact that all those jobs have sports as the subject really has no relevance in terms of your ability to prepare for such employment.

Unless you are a talented athlete whose endorsement or face will sell a product—and there are very few such folks—you *must* bring to the sports dance a hard, measurable, definable *skill!* Loving sports won't do it; being a college athlete won't do it. Teaching tennis or golf isn't enough. Attending every home baseball game this summer doesn't qualify you for anything.

We need skills—not athletes or sports junkies. We need people who can write, we need people with financial backgrounds, we need lawyers, we need press and communications people. In TV and radio we need people with experience in production and broadcasting, and, most of all, the sports businesses need people who can *sell!*

I can't emphasize too strongly that sales and marketing skills are talents always in demand and if they are coupled with a knowledge of the product line and an enthusiasm for dealing with people, you become an attractive job candidate.

In keeping with my theme on being prac-

A graduate of Hamilton College and Yale Law School, Neal H. Pilson worked at Metromedia, Inc. and the William Morris Agency before joining CBS in 1976 as director of business affairs for CBS Sports. From 1981 to 1983 and again from 1986 to 1994 he was president of CBS Sports, and he later became senior vice president of the CBS Broadcast Group. His new firm, Pilson Communications, specializes in TV sports consultation services.

tical, rather than inspirational, let me mention a few very basic and very practical thoughts I have had during years of reading resumes and interviewing job applicants.

*   *   *   *

Don't be a spear thrower. By that I mean don't target a particular job or company and invest all your energy chasing a specific opportunity. Also, don't worry too much about a near miss—you may scare up a job offer that's close to what you want, perhaps with the company you are looking for but not the division or department you want. My advice? Take it. It's far easier to move within a company once you are employed there than to get initial employment. Your career is going to have many twists and turns, and you simply cannot anticipate what will develop in the future. Your exact fit, meshing skills and aptitude and desire, may not take place for five or 10 or 15 years, but in the meantime try to *pyramid* your career decisions.

By that I mean try to make the various pieces and jobs fit together. Try to avoid a job in one area that has no relation to the last job somewhere else. You screw up your learning curve.

Contrary to popular belief, most senior executives I know don't look to hire "good athletes" who have had a general but not very intensive background in several areas.

To carry forward the sports analogy, when there is a job opening, we are looking for the best left tackle we can find who has solid experience at left tackle—not the terrific athlete who perhaps we can teach to play left tackle. We don't have time for that.

If you can, try to develop your career sequentially so that the skills learned in job one help you to get and do well in job two and continue that linkage in jobs three and four, etc. Try not to wander over the landscape with jobs that don't relate to or build on each other.

*   *   *   *

Set an *agenda* for the day, the week, the month. Do it for your personal life and your business.

Even if the list starts with "call Mom" and includes "buy toothpaste," you will save time, energy, and psychic resources (in other words, you will forget less—and as you grow older, forgetting less is the key to life).

Have an agenda for every meeting you attend—even if you are the junior person in the room and have no assigned responsibilities. I always welcome and appreciate the volunteered comment or question from young attendees such as "Have we considered X?" or "Why aren't we going in this direction?" It shows people are tracking and thinking along with you—and that's a big plus.

Speaking of tracking and thinking, my next practical suggestion is to *develop a point of view.*

This is a sensitive area. It doesn't mean on every occasion you should tell your boss what *you* think should be done. That can get a bit tiresome, particularly if your senior has 20 years of experience and you have six months.

But too many young people in the job setting tend to drift through business meetings or conversations, content to accept the directions of seniors. You assume they know what they are talking about. Don't make that assumption.

Now, I'm not suggesting you become a contentious pain in the ass. Nor am I recommending that you voice your thoughts on every occasion. But do sit there and assess the situation. Think to yourself: How would I handle it? What would I do here? What decision would I make? This is great training for the time *you* may have to run the ship.

And if you have something to contribute based on your preparation for the meeting, do so!

*   *   *   *

Finally, and take this as gospel from a network guy—*network.* Use your friends, your professors, alumni from your school, business associates, and social acquaintances to develop leads and contacts as you job hunt.

CHAPTER TEN

ATHLETIC TRAINERS

Kinesiology?

As athletes get richer, so does

the language of the professionals

who look after their health.

The Profession Has Been Upgraded

There was a time when the main tools of the trade were a bottle of liniment and a few rolls of inch-and-a-half adhesive tape, and the measure of an athletic trainer's worth was how fast he could bind an injured ankle without getting wrinkles in the tape.

Adroitness with a roll of tape is now taken for granted. The new standard by which trainers are judged is their knowledge of things like human anatomy, physiology, kinesiology, psychology, hygiene, nutrition, first aid (including CPR), and therapeutic exercises.

In short, trainers have achieved a loftier status. The turning point came in June 1990, when the American Medical Association formally recognized the athletic training specialization as an allied health profession.

Since that time, athletic training has become a popular career goal on the nation's campuses. But especially striking has been the growing number of women who have entered the profession. It is a trend that has changed markedly the composition of the National Athletic Trainers' Association (NATA), the profession's certifying organization. It wasn't until 1966 that NATA accepted its first female member, nor was there a rush of women in the next few years. Today, however, more than 40 percent of NATA's total membership of 21,000 are women.

Here's an even more interesting stat: Of all the athletic trainers certified since 1990 (between 1,200 and 1,500 a year), more than half have been women.

* * * *

The work. The athletic trainer works under the supervision of, or in consultation with, a physician and other health-care professionals. The basic responsibilities are these: (1) to recognize and evaluate injuries, (2) to provide immediate treatment and then determine if specialized care is needed, (3) to set up programs designed to prevent injuries, (4) to implement rehabilitation regimens, (5) to make sure athletes' equipment provides maximum safety, and to improvise improvements if needed, and (6) to counsel athletes on nutrition and other matters of general health.

Certain personal qualities are essential to the job. Trainers must be able to make instant decisions under pressure. They must be willing to work long and irregular hours, and have the stamina for it. And they must be able to establish close and trusting relationships with their athletes.

* * * *

Needed: certification. It's next to impossible to get an appointment as a trainer without certification. The certifying organization is NATA. (Trainers in good standing are permitted to add the letters ATC after their names to let the world know they are "athletic training certified.")

The steps to certification: NATA's minimum educational requirement is a bachelor's degree, with the completion of a program in athletic training that's accredited by the Division of Health Education and Accreditation of the American Medical Association. *(For the list of colleges with accredited programs, see page 210.)*

In addition to course work, however, NATA requires a minimum of 800 hours of supervised experience. Students usually meet that requirement by working for the head trainers at their colleges. But there's more. After graduation, candidates for certification have to pass a three-part examination—written, practical, and oral.

Moreover, to maintain certification, trainers must earn continuing education credits approved by NATA. The association says 70 percent of its members have master's degrees or doctorates.

And just so you won't be taken by surprise: In 27 states, athletic trainers are required to be registered, either as "licensed" or "certified."

The regulatory agencies of those states are listed here, after the directory of accredited college programs. In some states, you might care to know, trainers have to take another test to qualify for registration.

* * * *

Where the jobs are. Although job opportunities are increasing, it still takes effort and patience to get started, and still more patience to move on to better positions. About half the jobs for certified trainers are in the athletic programs of colleges and universities. Trainers are also employed in high schools, health clinics, and industrial settings, and, of course, in professional sports.

The best-paying jobs, as you might expect, are in the pro ranks—but it should be noted that only a little more than 5 percent of certified trainers are employed by professional teams, including those in the minor leagues.

According to NATA surveys, the range of pay for head trainers with professional teams is $40,000 to $110,000. For assistant trainers, it's $35,000 to $75,000.

In college sports (covering all levels again), head trainers earn between $22,000 and $80,000. For assistant trainers, the pay is $15,000 to $40,000.

Only about 10 percent of the nation's high schools employ trainers, and in almost all cases the trainers are required to be members of the teaching staff. In addition to their regular teaching salaries, trainers receive stipends ranging from $4,000 to $8,000.

In health clinics and industrial health programs, the pay ranges from $18,000 to $45,000.

Unlike their brethren in college sports, trainers with high-level professional teams usually work only one sport. The big ones are football, basketball, baseball, and hockey.

Job openings in college sports are announced with some frequency in the classified pages of the *NCAA News*. The pros don't advertise vacancies. How, then, do you break into—say—the NFL, which probably needs more trainers than any other league? Veteran trainers say you've got to be good at your work, take an active part in professional activities—and make friends. In other words, get into the network. Most of the people hired in the NFL, they say, come through the network after putting in several years in college sports.

However, despite all the carnage that takes place on the gridiron, the NFL is a small job market. In addition to the head trainer, each franchise has only one or two assistant trainers. In 1994, with 28 franchises in the league, the total number of trainers was 70.

But the NFL gives aggressive job seekers a special opportunity to gain visibility: During the six-week training-camp period, the head trainer of every team takes on temporary assistants. A number of trainers now in the NFL took advantage of that opportunity early in their careers, made a good impression, and got a leg up.

* * * *

How they got there. It's a quiet occupation. Trainers don't draw fans into the ballpark. Their names rarely appear in the sports pages. There are no stats or ratings connected with their work. So how did the trainers in top spots get there? Mainly by reputation, developed over years of hard work and passed around by word of mouth.

Trainers in big college sports programs built their reputations by their work in high schools and small college programs. Most of the trainers in the NFL, NBA, and NHL made the jump after long experience in the colleges or minor league operations. The pattern of ascension is clearest in baseball: Of the 56 trainers in the big leagues, all but two moved up from minor league clubs.

Putting Them Back Together

As head trainer of the Philadelphia Eagles, Otho Davis draws what most people would consider a handsome salary. He also gets a car, complimentary game tickets for his family, and a lot of respect. What he doesn't get is much time off from work.

The football season is only six months long, but Davis and his assistant work the full

Student membership in NATA is available to individuals enrolled in a full-time graduate program or participating in an internship. NATA's membership department is reachable at (214) 637-6282.

year. What keeps them busy in the off-season? "Putting the players back together for the next season," Davis says. The work of rehabilitating and conditioning those players can take rigorous 10-hour days.

It's in the off-season too that hundreds of college hopefuls show up for the annual "combine" to be checked out by all NFL teams as possible draft material. Along with other head trainers, Davis has to assess the fitness of a host of players and put them through tests of strength and agility to help his club avoid spending a precious draft pick on a player with an incipient hernia.

When Davis gets a little time to be alone with his thoughts, he uses it to plan the menus for training camp. That's another responsibility of pro trainers: supervising what the players eat.

With the opening of training camp, Davis's 10-hour day gets a few more hours heaped on it. The routine: At 6:30 he opens the training room and gets ready for the day's business. Players arrive at 7:30 for an hour and a half of treatments before morning practice. They return at 1:30 for more treatments before afternoon practice. After dinner, there's a team meeting, then it's back to the training room for some of the players, and Davis continues to work into the night.

Once the season begins, Davis and his assistant work a shorter day—only 12 to 14 hours. They open the training room at 7 and at 7:30 they're ready for a daylong procession of players suffering all manner of wrenches, rents, abrasions, contusions, and dislocations.

It's grueling work, "yet for some unknown reason," Davis says, laughing, "everybody wants to do this."

*　　*　　*　　*

Since the above was written, Otho Davis retired as active head trainer for the Philadelphia Eagles. He is now a consultant to the Eagles, with the special duty of evaluating the physical condition of players the club might be interested in acquiring.

Scholarships Plus

Lending a helping hand seems to come naturally to athletic trainers. Community work is one of their interests. Another is helping students who are preparing to join their profession.

The National Athletic Trainers' Association (NATA) not only welcomes students into the organization (there were more than 4,500 student members in 1996), it also awards $1,500 scholarships each year to 40 of those students.

There's more. NATA is divided into 10 districts across the U.S., and each of those districts also makes scholarship awards—ranging from $500 to $2,000—to student members of NATA.

Also helpful to students are these four organizations: the Professional Football Athletic Trainers Society, the National Basketball Trainers Association, the Professional Baseball Athletic Trainers Society, and the Professional Hockey Trainers Society. Each has a student-support program that offers one or more of these benefits: scholarships, internships, assistantships at preseason camps, and professional workshops.

(For addresses, see "Professional Organizations" below.)

A Word About Strength and Conditioning Coaches . . .

A generation ago athletes were warned against using weightlifting exercises to build their strength. The popular wisdom was that while these exercises might produce impressive muscles, the irons actually were detrimental to an athlete's flexibility and quickness. Besides, the critics said, weightlifting was dangerous. You could tear something.

That attitude has undergone a big change, thanks mainly to professional and college football teams, which now employ strength and conditioning coaches. The principal role of these specialists is working with athletes who have recovered from injuries and getting them into full playing shape through the use of weights and vigorous conditioning drills.

The National Strength and Conditioning Association, founded in 1978, has about 11,000 members. Some are engaged by individual athletes, like professional tennis players, boxers, and skiers.

According to the association, earnings for head coaches in college programs range from $10,000 to $65,000; for full-time assistant coaches, the range is $10,000 to $40,000. In pro sports earnings can rise to $75,000.

PROFESSIONAL ORGANIZATIONS

**National Athletic Trainers
  Association**
2952 Stemmons Freeway, Suite 200
Dallas, TX 75247-6117
(214) 637-6282

*The four organizations that follow
are affiliated with NATA.*

**Professional Baseball Athletic
  Trainers Society**
Secretary: David Labossiere
Trainer, Houston Astros
P.O. Box 288
Houston, TX 77001

**National Basketball Trainers
  Association**
Secretary: Chip Schaefer
Trainer, Chicago Bulls
500 Lake Cook Rd.
Deerfield, IL 60015

**Professional Football Athletic
  Trainers Society**
Secretary: John Norwig
Trainer, Pittsburgh Steelers
300 Stadium Cir.
Pittsburgh, PA 15212

Professional Hockey Trainers Society
Secretary-Treasurer: John Wharton
Trainer, Detroit Red Wings
Joe Louis Stadium
600 Civic Center Dr.
Detroit, MI 48226

**National Strength and
  Conditioning Association**
530 Communications Cir., Suite 204
Colorado Springs, CO 80905
(719) 632-6722

APPROVED COLLEGE PROGRAMS IN ATHLETIC TRAINING

The programs in athletic training at the institutions listed here are approved by the National Athletic Trainers Association or the Commission on Accreditation of Allied Health Education Programs. The letter U indicates an undergraduate program; G means the program is given also on a graduate level. Each entry includes the department or school in which the program is given and the professor to contact for information.

ALABAMA

Samford University — U
Birmingham, AL 35229
Dep't of Exercise Science & Sports Medicine
Christopher Gillespie
(205) 870-2574

University of Alabama — U
Tuscaloosa, AL 35487-0312
Dep't of Professional Studies
Kenneth E. Wright
(205) 348-8683

CALIFORNIA

California State University at Fresno — U
Fresno, CA 93740-0027
Dep't of P.E. & Human Performance
Ed Ferreira, Rebecca Crumpton
(209) 278-2400

California State University at Fullerton — U
Fullerton, CA 92634
Dep't of Kinesiology and Health Promotion
Julie Max
(714) 773-2219

California State University at Long Beach — U
Long Beach, CA 90840
Dep't of Physical Education
Keith Freesemann
(818) 885-4738

California State University at Northridge — U
Northridge, CA 91330
Dep't of Kinesiology
Alice McLaine
(818) 677-3205

California State University at Sacramento — U
Sacramento, CA 95819-2694
Dep't of Health & Physical Education
Doris E. Flores
(916) 278-6401

San Jose State University — G
San Jose, CA 95192-0054
Dep't of Human Performance
Jack Ransone
(408) 924-3019

COLORADO

University of Northern Colorado — U
Greeley, CO 80639
Dep't of Kinesiology & Physical Education
Dan Libera
(970) 351-2282

CONNECTICUT

Southern Connecticut State University — U
New Haven, CT 06515
Dep't of Physical Education
Sharon Misasi
(203) 392-6091

DELAWARE

University of Delaware — U
Newark, DE 19716
Dep't of Physical Education
Keith A. Handling
(302) 831-2287

FLORIDA

Barry University — U
Miami Shores, FL 33161
Sports Medicine/Athletic Training
Carl R. Cramer
(305) 899-3497

University of Florida — G
Gainesville, FL 32611
Dep't of Exercise and Sport Sciences
Mary Beth Horodyski
(352) 392-0584

GEORGIA

Valdosta State University — U
Valdosta, GA 31698
Sports Medicine
Jim Madaleno
(912) 333-7161

IDAHO

Boise State University — U
Boise, ID 83725
Dep't of Physical Education, Health & Recreation
John McChesney
(208) 385-3709

ILLINOIS

Eastern Illinois University — U
Charleston, IL 61920
Dep't of Physical Education & Athletics
Rob Doyle
(217) 581-3811

Southern Illinois University — U
Carbondale, IL 62901
Dep't of Physical Education
Sally Rouse Perkins
(618) 453-5482

University of Illinois — G
Urbana, IL 61801-3895
Dep't of Kinesiology
Gerald W. Bell
(217) 333-7699

Western Illinois University — U
Macomb, IL 61455
Dep't of Physical Education & Athletics
Roger D. Clark
(309) 298-2050

INDIANA

Anderson University — U
Anderson, IN 46012-1362
Dep't of Athletic Training
Steve Risinger
(317) 641-4491

Ball State University — U
Muncie, IN 47306
Dep't of Physical Education
Michael Ferrara
(317) 285-5128

Indiana State University — U
Terre Haute, IN 47809
Dep't of Physical Education
John Kovaleski
(812) 237-3961

Indiana State University — G
Terre Haute, IN 47809
Athletic Training Dep't
Ken Knight
(812) 237-8232

Indiana University — U
Bloomington, IN 47405
Dep't of Kinesiology
Katie Grove
(812) 855-4509

Indiana University — G
Bloomington, IN 47405
Dep't of Kinesiology
John W. Schrader
(812) 855-4509

Purdue University — U
West Lafayette, IN 47907
Dep't of HKLS
Larry Leverenz
(317) 494-3167

IOWA

University of Iowa — U
Iowa City, IA 52242
Dep't of Exercise Science & Physical Education
Dan Foster
(319) 335-9393

KANSAS

Kansas State University — U
Manhattan, KS 66605-0302
Secondary Education
Jeffrey P. Rudy
(913) 532-6991

KENTUCKY

Eastern Kentucky University — U
Richmond, KY 40475-3103
Dep't of Physical Education
Eva Clifton
(606) 622-2134

MARYLAND

Towson State University — U
Towson, MD 21252
Dep't of Athletic Training Education
Gail Parr
(410) 830-3174

APPROVED COLLEGE PROGRAMS IN ATHLETIC TRAINING

MASSACHUSETTS

Boston University — U
Boston, MA 02215
Dep't of Physical Therapy
Sara Brown
(617) 353-7507

Bridgewater State College — U
Bridgewater, MA 02325
Dep't of MAHPLS
Marcia Anderson
(508) 697-1215, ext. 2072

Northeastern University — U
Boston, MA 02115
Dep't of Athletic Training
Chad Starkey
(617) 373-4475

Springfield College — U
Springfield, MA 01109
*Dep't of Physical Education
& Health Fitness*
Charles Redmond
(413) 748-3231

MICHIGAN

Central Michigan University — U
Mount Pleasant, MI 48859
Dep't of Physical Education
David A. Kaiser
(517) 774-6687

Grand Valley State College — U
Allendale, MI 49401
*Dep't of Physical Education
& Athletics*
Deborah Springer
(616) 895-3140

Western Michigan University — G
Kalamazoo, MI 49008
*Dep't of Health, Physical Education
& Recreation*
Bob Moss
(616) 387-2678

MINNESOTA

Gustavus Adolphus College — U
St. Peter, MN 56082
Dep't of Physical Education
Gary D. Reinholtz
(507) 933-7612

Mankato State University — U
Mankato, MN 56002-8400
Dep't of Human Performance
Kent Kalm
(507) 389-6715

MISSISSIPPI

**University of Southern
Mississippi — U**
Hattiesburg, MS 39406-5142
*Dep't of Human Performance
& Recreation*
James B. Gallaspy
(601) 266-5577

MISSOURI

**Southwest Missouri State
University — U**
Springfield, MO 65804-0094
*Dep't of Sports Medicine
& Athletic Training*
Karen Toburen
(417) 836-8553

MONTANA

University of Montana — U
Missoula, MT 59812
*Dep't of Health & Human
Performance*
Scott Richter
(406) 243-5246

NEVADA

**University of Nevada
at Las Vegas — U**
Las Vegas, NV 89154-3032
*Dep't of Health Education
& Sports Injury Management*
Brent Mangus
(702) 895-3209

NEW HAMPSHIRE

University of New Hampshire — U
Durham, NH 03824
Dep't of Kinesiology
Daniel R. Sedory
(603) 862-1831

NEW JERSEY

Kean College of New Jersey — U
Union, NJ 07083
Dep't of Physical Education
Gary Ball
(908) 527-2103

**William Paterson College of New
Jersey — U**
Wayne, NJ 07470
Dep't of Movement Science
David Middlemas
(201) 595-2267

NEW MEXICO

New Mexico State University — U
Las Cruces, NM 88003-0001
*Dep't of Physical Education,
Recreation & Dance*
Leah Putman
(505) 646-5038

University of New Mexico — U
Albuquerque, NM 87131
*Dep't of Health, Physical Education
& Recreation*
Eric J. Kozlowski
(505) 925-5540

NEW YORK

Canisius College — U
Buffalo, NY 14208-1098
*Dep't of Athletic Training/Physical
Education*
Pete Kochneke
(716) 888-2952

Hofstra University — U
Hempstead, NY 11550
Dep't of HPER
Suanne S. Maurer
(516) 463-6952

Ithaca College — U
Ithaca, NY 14850
Dep't of Exercise & Sports Science
Kent Scriber
(607) 274-3178

**State University of New York at
Cortland — U**
Cortland, NY 13045
*Dep't of Physical Education &
Recreation*
John Cottone
(607) 753-4962

NORTH CAROLINA

Appalachian State University — U
Boone, NC 28608
*Dep't of Health Education, Physical
Education & Leisure Studies*
Jamie Moul
(704) 262-3140

East Carolina University — U
Greenville, NC 27858
Dep't of Health Education
Katie Walsh
(919) 328-4560

High Point University — U
High Point, NC 27262
Sports Medicine Program
Rick Proctor
(910) 841-9267

University of North Carolina — G
Chapel Hill, NC 27599-8700
Dep't of Physical Education
William E. Prentice
(919) 962-5174

NORTH DAKOTA

North Dakota State University — U
Fargo, ND 58105-5600
*Dep't of Health, Physical Education
& Recreation*
Elise Erickson
(701) 231-8093

University of Mary — U
Bismark, ND 58504
Dep't of Physical Education
Tim McCrory
(701) 255-7500, ext. 456

University of North Dakota — U
Grand Forks, ND 58202
Dep't of Sports Medicine
Jim Rudd
(701) 777-3102

OHIO

Capital University — U
Columbus, OH 43209-2394
Dep't of Health & Sport Sciences
Russ Hoff
(614) 236-6569

Marietta College — U
Marietta, OH 45750-3058
Dep't of Sports Medicine
Paul Spear
(614) 376-4772

Miami University of Ohio — U
Oxford, OH 45056
Dep't of PHS
Patricia Troesch
(513) 529-2015

Mount Union College — U
Alliance, OH 44601
*Dep't of Health, Physical Education
& Sports Management*
Dan Gorman
(330) 823-4882

Ohio University — U
Athens, OH 45701
Dep't of Recreation & Sport Sciences
Rich Deivert
(614) 593-0496

APPROVED COLLEGE PROGRAMS IN ATHLETIC TRAINING

University of Toledo — U
Toledo, OH 43606
Dep't of Health Promotion & Human
Performance
Jim Rankin
(419) 530-2752

OKLAHOMA

University of Tulsa — U
Tulsa, OK 74104-3189
School of Nursing
Greg Gardner
(918) 631-2316

OREGON

Oregon State University — U
Corvallis, OR 97331-3302
Dep't of Exercise & Sport Sciences
Rod Harter
(541) 737-6801

University of Oregon — G
Eugene, OR 97403
Dep't of Exercise & Movement Science
Rick Troxel
(541) 346-3394

PENNSYLVANIA

California University of
   Pennsylvania — U
California, PA 15419
Dep't of Sports Medicine
Bruce D. Barnhart
(412) 938-4562

California University of
   Pennsylvania — G
California, PA 15419
Dep't of Sports Medicine
William Biddington
(412) 938-4562

Duquesne University
Pittsburgh, PA 15282
Athletic Training
Paula Turocy
(412) 396-5695

East Stroudsburg University
   — U
East Stroudsburg, PA 18301
Dep't of Movement Studies &
Exercise Science
John Thatcher
(717) 424-3065

Lock Haven University — U
Lock Haven, PA 17745
Dep't of Health Science
James Scifers
(717) 893-2214

Mercyhurst College — U
Erie, PA 16546
Dep't of Sports Medicine
Bradley Jacobson
(814) 824-2526

Messiah College — U
Grantham, PA 17027
Dep't of Sports Medicine
Edwin Bush
(717) 691-6037

Pennsylvania State University
   — U
University Park, PA 16802
Dep't of Exercise Science
Craig Denegar
(814) 865-2725

Slippery Rock University — U
Slippery Rock, PA 16057
Dep't of Allied Health
Rick McCandless, Susan Hannam
(412) 738-2261

Temple University — U
Philadelphia, PA 19122
College of Health, Physical Education,
Recreation & Dance
Michael Sitler
(215) 204-1950

Temple University — G
Philadelphia, PA 19122
Dep't of Physical Education
Iris Kimura
(215) 204-8836

University of Pittsburgh — U
Pittsburgh, PA 15261
Dep't of HPER
Scott Lephart
(412) 648-8261

Waynesburg College — U
Waynesburg, PA 15370
Dep't of Sports Medicine
Jose E. Rivera
(412) 852-3295

West Chester University — U
West Chester, PA 19383
Dep't of Sports Medicine
Neil Curtis
(610) 436-2969

SOUTH CAROLINA

University of South Carolina — U
Columbia, SC 29208
Dep't of Physical Education
Malissa Martin
(803) 777-7301

SOUTH DAKOTA

South Dakota State University — U
Brookings, SD 57007
Dep't of Health, Physical Education
& Recreation
Jim Booher
(605) 688-5824

TENNESSEE

East Tennessee
   State University — U
Johnson City, TN 37614-0634
Dep't of Physical Education, Exercise
& Sport Science
Jerry Robertson
(423) 929-4208

TEXAS

Southwest Texas
   State University — U
San Marcos, TX 78666-4616
Dep't of Health, Physical Education &
Recreation
Bobby Patton
(512) 245-2561

Texas Christian University — U
Fort Worth, TX 76129-3292
Dep't of HPER
T. Ross Bailey
(817) 921-7984

UTAH

Brigham Young University — U
Provo, UT 84602
College of Physical Education
& Sports
Gaye Merrill
(801) 378-4670

VERMONT

University of Vermont — U
Burlington, VT 05405
College of Education
Denise Alosa
(802) 656-4456

VIRGINIA

James Madison University — U
Harrisonburg, VA 22807
Dep't of Health Sciences
Herbert Amato
(540) 568-3576

Old Dominion University — G
Norfolk, VA 23529-0197
Dep't of HPER
Marty Bradley
(804) 683-3383

University of Virginia — G
Charlottesville, VA 22903
Dep't of Human Services
David H. Perrin
(804) 924-6187

WASHINGTON

Washington State University — U
Pullman, WA 99164-1410
Dep't of Kinesiology, Sport
& Leisure Studies
Carol Zweifel
(509) 335-0307

WEST VIRGINIA

Marshall University — U
Huntington, WV 25755
Dep't of Health, Physical Education
& Recreation
Dan Martin
(304) 696-2412

University of Charleston — U
Charleston, WV 25304
Dep't of Sports Medicine
Jose Beckett
(304) 357-4902

West Virginia University — U
Morgantown, WV 26506-6116
Dep't of Health Promotion
Vince Stilger
(304) 293-3295, ext. 148

WISCONSIN

University of Wisconsin at
   LaCrosse — U
LaCrosse, WI 54601
Dep't of Exercise & Sport Science
Mark Gibson
(608) 785-8190

STATE REGULATORY AGENCIES FOR TRAINERS

To get a job in any of the 33 states shown here, trainers must be registered with the state. The trouble is, each state regulatory agency has its own set of requirements for registration. That's why the listing of agencies that follows includes phone numbers and contact persons (where available).

ALABAMA
Alabama Board of Athletic Trainers
415 Monroe St.
Montgomery, AL 36104

ARKANSAS
Arkansas Board of Physical Therapy
3 Financial Ctr., Suite 300
900 S. Shackleford
Little Rock, AR 72211
(501) 228-5535
Jennifer Coleman

DELAWARE
Delaware Board of Athletic Trainers
P.O. Box 1401
Dover, DE 19903
(302) 739-4522
Lena Corder

FLORIDA
Florida Department of Business and
Professional Regulation
Division of Professions
Northwood Ctr.
1940 N. Monroe St.
Tallahassee, FL 32399-0760
(904) 487-9824
Dot Faircloth

GEORGIA
Georgia Board of Athletic Trainers
166 Pryor St. SW
Atlanta, GA 30303
(404) 656-6719
Lilan Norton

IDAHO
Idaho State Board of Medicine
280 N. Eighth St.
State House, Suite 202
Boise, ID 83720
(208) 334-2822
Jackie Morris

ILLINOIS
Dep't of Professional Regulation,
Athletic Training
320 W. Washington, 3rd Floor
Springfield, IL 62786
(217) 782-8556

INDIANA
Health Professions Bureau
402 W. Washington St., Room 041
Indianapolis, IN 46204
(317) 232-2960
Barbara Marvel McNutt

IOWA
Iowa Department of Public Health
Lucas Bldg.
Des Moines, IA 50319-0075
(515) 242-5938
Marge Bledso

KANSAS
Kansas State Board of the Healing Arts
235 S. Topeka Blvd.
Topeka, KS 66603
(913) 296-7413
Charlene Abbott

KENTUCKY
Kentucky Board of Medical Licensure
310 Whittington Pkwy., Suite 1B
Louisville, KY 40222
(502) 429-8046
Angela Baker

LOUISIANA
Louisiana State Board of Medical
Examiners
P.O. Box 30250
New Orleans, LA 70190-0250
(504) 524-6763
Paula Mensen

MASSACHUSETTS
Board of Allied Health Professions
State Office Bldg., 15th Floor
100 Cambridge St.
Boston, MA 02202
(617) 727-3071

MAINE
Maine Department of Professional
and Financial Regulation
State House
Station 35
Augusta, ME 04333
(207) 624-8603

MINNESOTA
State Board of Medical Practice
2700 University Ave. W, Suite 106
St. Paul, MN 55114-1080
(612) 642-0533
Jeanne Hoffman

MISSISSIPPI
Mississippi State Dep't of Health
Office of Professional Licensure
P.O. Box 1700
2423 N. State St.
Jackson, MS 39215-1700
(601) 987-4153
David Kweller

MISSOURI
Missouri State Board
for the Healing Arts
P.O. Box 4
Jefferson City, MO 65102
(314) 751-0144
Karla Laughlin

NEBRASKA
Dep't of Health
Bureau of Examining Boards
301 Centennial Mall S
Lincoln, NE 68509-5007
(402) 471-2115
Irene Eckman

NEW HAMPSHIRE
Board of Registration in Medicine
Health and Welfare Bldg.
Hazen Dr.
Concord, NH 03301
(603) 271-4501

NEW JERSEY
The Board of Medical Examiners
140 E. Front St.
Trenton, NJ 08608
(609) 826-7100
Elizabeth Farlakas

NEW MEXICO
Regulation & Licensing Dep't
Athletic Training Practice Board
P.O. Box 25101
Santa Fe, NM 87504
(505) 827-7164
Becky Armijo

NEW YORK
State Board for Medicine
Room 3023, Cultural Education Ctr.
Albany, NY 12230
(518) 474-3842
Thomas Monahan

NORTH DAKOTA
Board of Athletic Trainers
113 Elm St.
Horace, ND 58047
(701) 280-3460
John R. Quick

OHIO
Executive Secretary
OT, PT, AT Board
77 S. High St., 16th Floor
Columbus, OH 43266-0317
(614) 466-3774
Carl Gabriel Williams

OKLAHOMA
Board of Medical Licensure
& Supervisions
P.O. Box 18256
Oklahoma City, OK 73154
(405) 848-6841
Robyn Kemp

OREGON
Licensure Program, Health Division
750 Front St. NE, Suite 200
Salem, OR 97310
(503) 378-8667, ext. 4322
Tricia C. Allbritton

PENNSYLVANIA
State Board of Physical Therapy
P.O. Box 2649
Harrisburg, PA 17105-2649
(717) 783-7134
Shirley Klinger

RHODE ISLAND
Rhode Island Dep't of Health
Professional Regulations
3 Capital Hill, Room 104
Providence, RI 02908
(401) 277-2827
Arthur L. Simonini

SOUTH CAROLINA
Dep't of Health & Environmental
Control
Center for Health Promotion
P.O. Box 10116, Mills Complex
Columbia, SC 29201
(803) 737-4120
Susan Provence

SOUTH DAKOTA
South Dakota Board of Medical
Examiners
1323 S. Minnesota Ave.
Sioux Falls, SD 57105
(605) 336-1965
Mitzi Turley

TENNESSEE
Board of Medical Examiners
State Dep't of Health
287 Plus Park Blvd.
Nashville, TN 37247-1010
(615) 367-6393 or 6231
Melissa Haggard

TEXAS
Texas Dep't of Health
Professional Licensing & Certification
Division
Advisory Board of Athletic Trainers
1100 W. 49th St.
Austin, TX 78756
(512) 834-6615
Becky Berryhill

WEST VIRGINIA
West Virginia Department of
Education
Bldg. 6, Room 309
1900 Kanawha Blvd. E
Charleston, WV 25305-0330
(304) 558-2691
John Ray

RECREATION MANAGEMENT

It reads "recreation,"

but a big part of this multibillion–dollar

industry is fitness.

AN OVERVIEW

It's not a small industry. The number of men and women who work at planning, organizing, and directing recreation activities is close to 222,000, says the U.S. Department of Labor.

Most people who seek full-time career positions in the recreation industry are college graduates who majored in parks and recreation or leisure studies. The programs are available in about 340 colleges and universities. Some institutions bestow associate degrees, others have bachelor's, master's, and doctoral degree programs. Although most people now in supervisory jobs got there with a bachelor's degree, an increasing number of students who are looking forward to supervisory positions are going on for master's degrees, with an emphasis on business management. Nationwide, undergraduate and graduate programs have a total enrollment of about 60,000.

The Department of Labor reports that starting pay for new graduates with bachelor's degrees generally ranges from $18,000 to $24,000. Veteran recreation managers with heavy responsibilities can earn as much as $95,000.

It is an interest in sports that draws many people to this field, but it should be understood that the recreation industry also embraces many other activities, including those that involve arts, crafts, travel, and, of particular importance, physical fitness. In other words, job candidates need to be flexible.

Almost all jobs in recreation management fall into one of three categories: public parks and recreation, corporate recreation programs for employees, and commercial recreation.

1. Public Parks and Recreation

More than half the people in recreation management work for public agencies, mainly in the parks and recreation departments of local governments (towns, cities, counties).

Typically, the person in charge of recreation facilities is the *director of recreation and parks*, a public employee who has overall responsibility for operations, maintenance, personnel, and budget, and who is expected to promote the fullest use of the facilities. A bachelor's degree and several years of experience in organized recreation are considered minimum requirements for the job. The pay varies, of course, with the size of the program and with the financial condition of the local government. The average pay is $43,000.

The chief assistant to the director is the *recreation supervisor*, a public employee who handles the day-to-day recreation programs and the administration of special events, which may include tennis tournaments, aquatic competitions, golf tournaments, and concerts and other entertainments. Average pay is $30,000.

Also in the employ of local governments is a *recreation center director*, whose work generally involves the management of an indoor facility that provides athletic, cultural, and entertainment activities that respond to a community's need. Average pay is $28,000.

Employment prospects for this category: not great. Even though the general economy has been on a rise, funds for public services have been tight and are likely to remain so in the foreseeable future.

But Prof. Dan McLean of Indiana University's Department of Recreation and Park Administration detects what may be a trend to privatization, with private companies taking over the administration of public recreation facilities. A widespread takeover is a few years away, if it happens at all, says Prof. McLean, but it could change the job picture.

* * * *

Also included in this category are state and federal agencies, which provide two types of employment. One is in outdoor recreation resources, such as state and national parks, forests, and wildlife areas. The other type of employment is with state and federal institutions serving special populations. Among those institutions: hospitals, prisons, mental health centers, rehabilitation centers, and schools for individuals with mental or physical disabilities. The main employer in this category is the U.S. Office of Personnel Management, 1900 E St., NW, Washington, DC 20415.

* * * *

Regarded as quasi-public agencies that offer opportunities in recreation management are voluntary nonprofit organizations such as the Ys, Boy Scouts, Girl Scouts, and 4-H Clubs. The largest employer among them is the YMCA. For job information, write to YMCA of the USA, 101 N. Wacker Dr., Chicago, IL 60606.

2. Corporate Programs for Employees

The idea of sponsoring recreation activities for employees came alive for U.S. companies in the 1970s, when recreation and fitness became a national obsession. Until then, company recreation programs consisted mainly of dressing the employee softball team or bowling team in the company name.

Today, says Kenneth Cammarata, director of member services of the National Employee Services and Recreation Association (NESRA), there are about 50,000 companies that have some form of employee program, designed for all employees—and often for their families as well.

Many of the companies have spent considerable sums on recreation facilities and equipment. One such company is Texas Instruments (TI), which has maintained recreation/fitness facilities for thousands of employees at each of 11 company locations. In January 1995 the company opened at its Dallas site an $8.4 million building that's the center of an eight-acre sports and fitness plant designed for TI employees, spouses, children, and retirees. The expanded facility includes an 8,736-square-foot gym, two aerobics rooms, a game room, six meeting rooms, a six-lane swimming pool, indoor and outdoor

running tracks, two volleyball courts, three tennis courts, a basketball court, and locker rooms. The company plans to keep the place open 106 hours a week, seven days a week. In addition to a staff of 12 professionals, the facility will employ five interns.

Much of the impetus for the rise of employee recreation programs in the past couple of decades has come from corporate human resource executives. The programs, they say, help recruit and retain valued personnel, raise morale and productivity, and keep employees fit.

Says Jerry Junkins, Texas Instruments board chairman: "We believe that a healthier employee will have a better outlook on life and the job, resulting in lower absenteeism for minor illness and, hopefully, lower health-care costs."

Does that mean there are lots of jobs available in these corporate programs? Not at the moment. Many big firms have been cutting operational costs to the bone, and employee programs in these companies have been curtailed. As Stuart Mann, director of Penn State's School of Hotel, Restaurant & Recreation Management, observes, the corporate programs at this time offer "limited opportunities."

But, says Ken Cammarata of NESRA, things are going to get better. His optimism is based on a NESRA survey that shows many companies expect to expand their employee programs by 1997 or '98.

In the meantime, Cammarata advises students to concentrate on business courses. Knowing how to manage a budget and being able to make a presentation in front of management can make a big impression, he says.

Cammarata affirms that starting salaries for applicants just out of college can be as high as $24,000. Program directors can earn from $60,000 to more than $70,000, he said.

3. Commercial Recreation

Commercial recreation, or the business of leisure activities, apart from what is covered in the other sections of this book, is so diverse and fragmented that another volume would be needed to encompass all the jobs in the industry. Some of the jobs: manager of health and fitness clubs, planner of college campus recreation, director of resort activities, and supervisory positions in such settings as hospitals, military bases, amusement parks, campgrounds, retirement communities, correctional institutions, church-sponsored youth programs, conventions, cruise lines, tour and travel agencies, and theaters and concert halls.

Professionals in commercial recreation point out that theirs is very much a people business. Important attributes for career seekers are interpersonal skills, including the ability to communicate easily and with patience. Also important: self-confidence, initiative, and an understanding of marketing and business procedures. But above all, you've got to like working with people.

Professional Organizations

Because of the diversity of this industry there are a great number of professional associations in it, most of them focused on a particular aspect of the industry. Many of those organizations are mentioned elsewhere in this book. The associations that follow have a broad focus, and each has an interest in helping newcomers to the field, offering networking opportunities, job placement services, and information on that precious boon to new job seekers—internships.

National Recreation and Park Association (NRPA)

The NRPA is a national service organization dedicated to promoting the importance of recreation and parks. It's the oldest and biggest organization in the industry.

Its membership is open to academic institutions and to individual students. Students can join for $25 a year, but check to see if your department is a member because institutional members get several interesting publications, including the *Job Opportunities Bul-*

letin, a listing of job vacancies across the country, and the *Employ* newsletter, a guide for students on how to approach potential employers.

Available to student members is a booklet describing internship opportunities around the country.

The association holds an annual convention—called the Congress for Recreation and Parks—that attracts more than 6,000 people, some from abroad. In conjunction with the convention, the association holds a Job Mart designed to bring employers and job seekers together.

Address of the NRPA: 2775 S. Quincy St., Suite 300, Arlington, VA 22206-2204. Phone: (703) 820-4940.

American Association for Leisure and Recreation (AALR)

The purpose of the AALR is to raise the quality of life of Americans by promoting "creative and meaningful" recreation activities. The organization is part of the American Alliance for Health, Physical Education, Recreation, and Dance, an educational octopus.

The AALR shares with the National Recreation and Park Association the responsibility of evaluating college programs in this field for accreditation. It is also involved in leisure research, legislation, and the publication of professional materials. In addition, it arranges regional and national meetings for its members, who include people engaged in recreation and leisure management, educators, and college students.

Address of the AALR: 1900 Association Dr., Reston, VA 22091. Phone: (703) 476-3471.

Association for Worksite Health Promotion (AWHP)

This organization is composed mainly of professionals who deal with the subject of employee fitness. Membership is open to college students who are taking courses in health promotion. The association has been cultivating college students and now has close to 20 campus chapters. Student membership is $70 a year; one of the benefits is a quarterly listing of internships.

Address of the AWHP: 60 Revere Dr., Suite 500, Northbrook, IL 60062. Phone: (708) 480-9574.

National Employee Services and Recreation Association (NESRA)

NESRA's purpose is to enhance the professionalism of managers of employee services, recreation, and health promotion. Like all professional organizations, it provides fertile ground for networking. For students, membership is $25 a year. They get a monthly magazine, a newsletter, invitations to conferences and exhibits, job placement assistance, and tips on internships.

Address for NESRA: 2211 York Rd., Suite 207, Oak Brook, IL 60521-2371. Phone: (708) 368-1280.

Resort and Commercial Recreation Association (RCRA)

RCRA represents recreation professionals in resorts, hotels, sports clubs, vacation home communities, campgrounds, theme parks, special-events companies, cruise lines, concessionaires, and universities. The association sponsors a four-day national conference and a number of regional workshops, all in a congenial atmosphere. It turns out a membership magazine seven times a year, a quarterly on management ideas, and, among other things, a bulletin on job openings.

The association welcomes student membership, priced at $50. Among its publications is a directory of available internships.

RCRA address: P.O. Box 1208, New Port Richey, FL 34656-1208. Phone: (813) 845-7373.

A Word About Recreational Therapists...

Recreational therapists, who usually work in cooperation with medical teams, help rehabilitate patients disabled by physical or mental problems using various leisure activities to bring them into the mainstream of life. The activities include sports, dance, arts and crafts, music, and dramatics, all with emphasis on social interaction.

As of 1994, recreational therapists held about 31,000 jobs. Most worked in hospitals or nursing homes. Others were associated with community mental health centers, adult day care programs, correctional facilities, community programs for people with physical disabilities, and substance abuse programs. Some therapists are self-employed, developing rehabilitation programs for nursing homes or community agencies for a fee.

A bachelor's degree in therapeutic recreation is the usual requirement for hospital and other clinical positions. The degree plus an internship and a passing grade on an exam given by the National Council for Therapeutic Recreation Certification leads to certification as a therapeutic recreation specialist. Some employers require job candidates to be certified.

There are 105 colleges and universities that have programs in recreational therapy. About half are accredited by a national council on accreditation. Most schools offer bachelor's degrees. Some offer master's degrees. Some have associate degree programs.

The Department of Labor reports the average annual salary for recreational therapists in 1994 was $31,472. In the federal government, the average in 1995 was about $35,954.

For further career information, write to:

American Therapeutic Recreation Association, P.O. Box 15215, Hattiesburg, MS 39402-5215.

National Therapeutic Recreation Society, 2775 S. Quincy St., Suite 300, Arlington, VA 22206-2204.

COLLEGE PROGRAMS IN RECREATION MANAGEMENT

The listing that follows contains the colleges and universities that offer bachelor's degree programs dealing, in the main, with the administration of parks, recreation, and leisure services, and bearing the stamp of approval of two professional organizations: the National Recreation and Park Association (NRPA) and the American Association for Leisure and Recreation (AALR). Most of the programs, as you will note, extend to graduate levels (indicated by the letter M for master's and D for doctorate), but the authority of the NRPA and AALR does not rise to such levels, so you're left to your own good judgment should you aspire to a graduate degree.

ARIZONA

Arizona State University — B, M
Main Campus
Tempe, AZ 85287-4905
Carlton Yoshioka, Chair
Dep't of Recreation Management
    & Tourism
(602) 965-7291

Arizona State University West — B
Phoenix, AZ 85069-7100
Richard Gitelson, Chair
Dep't of Recreation
    & Tourism Management
(602) 543-6603

ARKANSAS

Arkansas Tech University — B
Russellville, AR 72801
Theresa Herrick, Head
Dep't of Parks, Recreation
    & Hospitality Administration
(501) 968-0378

University of Arkansas — B, M, D
Fayetteville, AR 72701
Sharon Hunt, Chair
Dep't of Health Science, Kinesiology,
    Recreation & Dance
(501) 575-2870

CALIFORNIA

**Cal Poly State University,
    San Luis Obispo — B, M**
San Luis Obispo, CA 93407
Carolyn Shank, Coordinator
Dep't of Recreation Administration
(805) 756-2050

**California State University,
    Chico — B, M**
Chico, CA 95929-0560
Steve Dennis, Chair
Dep't of Recreation
    & Parks Management
(916) 898-6408

**California State University,
    Fresno — B, M**
Fresno, CA 93740-0103
Andrew Hoff, Head
Dep't of Physical Education
    & Recreation
(209) 278-2838

**California State University,
    Long Beach — B, M**
Long Beach, CA 90840-4903
Michael Blazey, Chair
Dep't of Recreation & Leisure Studies
(310) 985-4071

**California State University,
    Northridge — B, M**
Northridge, CA 91330
Robert Winslow, Chair
Dep't of Leisure Studies
    & Recreation
(818) 885-3202

**California State University,
    Sacramento — B, M**
Sacramento, CA 95819-6110
Steven W. Gray, Chair
Dep't of Recreation & Leisure Studies
(916) 278-6752

San Diego State University — B, M
San Diego, CA 92182-0368
Jesse Dixon, Chair
Dep't of Recreation
(619) 594-5110

**San Francisco State University
    — B, M**
San Francisco, CA 94132
Don Taylor, Chair
Dep't of Recreation & Leisure Studies
(415) 338-2030

San Jose State University — B, M
San Jose, CA 95192
Charles Whitcomb, Chair
Dep't of Recreation & Leisure Studies
(408) 924-3000

COLORADO

**Colorado State University — B,
    M, D**
Fort Collins, CO 80523
Glenn Haas, Chair
Dep't of Natural Resource Recreation
    & Tourism
(970) 491-6591

**Metropolitan State College
    of Denver — B**
Denver, CO 80217-3362
Cheryl Norton, Chair
Dep't of Human Performance,
    Sport & Leisure
(303) 556-3145

**University of Northern Colorado
    — B, M, D**
Greeley, CO 80639
N. R. VanDinter, Coordinator
Dep't of Recreation
(970) 351-2403

CONNECTICUT

University of Connecticut — B, M, D
Storrs, CT 06269-1110
Jay S. Shivers, Program Coordinator
Dep't of Sport, Leisure & Exercise
    Sciences
(860) 486-3623

DISTRICT OF COLUMBIA

Gallaudet University — B
Washington, DC 20002
Anne Simonsen, Coordinator
Recreation & Leisure Studies Program
(202) 651-5591

FLORIDA

Florida State University — B
Tallahassee, FL 32306-3001
Cheryl Beeler, Chair
Leisure Services & Studies
(904) 644-6014

Florida Int'l University — B
University Park Campus
Miami, FL 33199
Brenda Lux
Dep't of Health, Phys Ed, and
    Recreation
(561) 367-3654

University of Florida — B, M, D
Gainesville, FL 32611-2034
Paul Varnes, Chair
Dep't of Recreation, Parks
    & Tourism
(352) 392-4042

GEORGIA

Georgia Southern University — B, M
Statesboro, GA 30460-8077
Henry Eisenhart, Chair
Dep't of Recreation & Leisure
    Services
(912) 681-5462

University of Georgia — B, M, D
Athens, GA 30602-2303
Douglas Kleiber, Head
Dep't of Recreation & Leisure Studies
(706) 542-5064

IDAHO

University of Idaho — B, M, D
College of Forestry
Moscow, ID 83843
John D. Hunt, Head
Dep't of Resource Recreation
    & Tourism
(208) 885-7911

University of Idaho — B, M
College of Education
Moscow, ID 83843
Calvin Lathen, Division Director
Recreation Program Unit,
    Division of HPERD
(208) 885-6582

ILLINOIS

Aurora University — B, M
Aurora, IL 60506
Rita Yerkes, Chair
Recreation Administration Dep't
(708) 844-5404

College of St. Francis — B
Joliet, IL 60435
Ann Zito, Chair
Dep't of Recreation Administration
(815) 740-3691

Eastern Illinois University — B
Charleston, IL 61920
William Higelmire, Chair
Dep't of Leisure Studies
(217) 581-3018

Illinois State University — B, M
Normal, IL 61790-5121
Norma J. Stumbo, Director
Recreation & Park Administration
    Program
(309) 438-5608

COLLEGE PROGRAMS IN RECREATION MANAGEMENT

Southern Illinois University — B, M
Carbondale, IL 62901
Regina B. Glover, Chair
Dep't of Health Education
& Recreation
(618) 453-4331

University of Illinois — B, M, D
Champaign, IL 61820
William McKinney, Head
Dep't of Leisure Studies
(217) 333-4410

Western Illinois University — B, M
Macomb, IL 61455
Nick DiGrino, Chair
Dep't of Recreation, Park,
& Tourism Administration
(309) 298-1967

INDIANA

Indiana State University — B, M
Terre Haute, IN 47809
Owen R. Smith, Chair
Dep't of Recreation
& Sports Management
(812) 237-2183

Indiana University — B, M, D
Bloomington, IN 47405
Joel Meier, Chair
Dep't of Recreation
& Park Administration
(812) 855-4711

IOWA

University of Iowa — B, M
Iowa City, IA 52242
Bonnie Slatton, Chair
Dep't of Sport, Health, Leisure
& Physical Studies
(319) 335-9184

**University of Northern Iowa
— B, M**
Cedar Falls, IA 50614
Jane Mertesdorf, Coordinator
Leisure Services Division,
School of HPELS
(319) 273-2654

KANSAS

Kansas State University — B, M
Manhattan, KS 66506-4002
Thomas D. Warner, Head
Recreation Resources Division
(913) 532-6170

KENTUCKY

**Eastern Kentucky University
— B, M**
Richmond, KY 40475
Larry Belknap, Chair
Dep't of Recreation
& Park Administration
(606) 622-1833

**Western Kentucky University
— B, M**
Bowling Green, KY 42101
Alton Little, Chair
Curriculum in Recreation
& Park Administration
(502) 745-3591

LOUISIANA

Grambling State University — B
Grambling, LA 71245
Wallace Bly, Coordinator
Recreation Careers Program
(318) 274-2294

MAINE

University of Maine at Machias — B
Machias, ME 04654
Arthur McEntee, Chair
Program in Recreation Management
(207) 255-3313

**University of Maine at Presque
Isle — B**
Presque Isle, ME 04769
David B. Jones, Coordinator
Dep't of Recreation/Leisure
(207) 768-9415

MASSACHUSETTS

Springfield College — B, M
Springfield, MA 01109-3797
Matthew J. Pantera, Chair
Dep't of Recreation & Leisure
Services
(413) 748-3269

MICHIGAN

**Central Michigan University
— B, M**
Mt. Pleasant, MI 48859
Roger Coles, Chair
Dep't of Recreation, Parks
& Leisure Services
(517) 774-3858

Eastern Michigan University — B
Ypsilanti, MI 48197
Jerry L. Ricciardo, Chair
Recreation Division, Dep't of
HPERD
(313) 487-2338

**Michigan State University
— B, M, D**
East Lansing, MI 48824-1222
Joseph D. Fridgen, Chair
Dep't of Park, Recreation
& Tourism Resources
(517) 353-5190

MINNESOTA

Mankato State University — B, M
Mankato, MN 56002-8400
James Jack, Chair
Recreation, Parks
& Leisure Services
(507) 389-2127

University of Minnesota — B, M, D
Minneapolis, MN 55455
Stuart J. Schleien, Division Head
Division of Recreation, Park
& Leisure Studies
(612) 625-4073

MISSISSIPPI

**University of Southern
Mississippi — B, M**
Hattiesburg, MS 39406-5142
Sandra Gangstead, Director
Recreation Program
(601) 266-5386

MISSOURI

**Southeast Missouri State
University — B**
Cape Girardeau, MO 63701
Edward L. Leoni, Chair
Recreation Program,
Dep't of Health & Leisure
(314) 651-2470

**Southwest Missouri State
University — B**
Springfield, MO 65804-0089
Gary Shoemaker, Coordinator
Curriculum in Recreation
& Leisure Studies
(417) 836-5411

University of Missouri — B, M
Columbia, MO 65211
C. Randal Vessell, Chair
Dep't of Parks, Recreation
& Tourism
(573) 882-7088

MONTANA

University of Montana — B, M, D
Missoula, MT 59812
Steve McCool, Chair
Recreation Management Program
(406) 243-5521

NEW HAMPSHIRE

**University of New Hampshire
— B**
Durham, NH 03824
Lou Powell, Chair
Dep't of Recreation Management
& Policy
(603) 862-2391

NEW JERSEY

Montclair State College — B
Upper Montclair, NJ 07043
Tim Sullivan, Chair
Dep't of Physical Education,
Recreation & Leisure Studies
(201) 655-5253

NEW YORK

Ithaca College — B
Ithaca, NY 14850
Barbara DeWall, Chair
Dep't of Recreation & Leisure Studies
(607) 274-3335

**State University of New York
at Brockport — B**
Brockport, NY 14420
David L. Jewell, Chair
Recreation & Leisure Studies Dep't
(716) 395-5482

**State University of New York
at Cortland — B**
Cortland, NY 13045
Anderson B. Young, Chair
Dep't of Recreation & Leisure Studies
(607) 753-4941

NORTH CAROLINA

Appalachian State University — B
Boone, NC 28608
Paul L. Gaskill, Director
Leisure Studies Program,
Dep't of HLES
(704) 262-6336

East Carolina University — B, M
Greenville, NC 27858
Thomas Skalko, Chair
Dep't of Recreation & Leisure Studies
(919) 328-4640

COLLEGE PROGRAMS IN RECREATION MANAGEMENT

North Carolina State University — B, M
Raleigh, NC 27695-8004
Phillip S. Rea, Head
Dep't of Parks, Recreation
& Tourism Management
(919) 515-3276

University of North Carolina at Chapel Hill — B, M
Chapel Hill, NC 27599-3185
Charles C. Bullock, Chair
Curriculum in Leisure Services
& Recreation Administration
(919) 962-1222

University of North Carolina at Greensboro — B, M
Greensboro, NC 27412-5001
Kathleen Williams, Acting Chair
Dep't of Leisure Studies
(910) 334-3040

University of North Carolina at Wilmington — B
Wilmington, NC 28403-3297
Charles Lewis, Coordinator
Parks & Recreation Management,
Dep't of HPER
(910) 395-3251

Winston-Salem State University — B
Winston-Salem, NC 27102
Cynthia Stanley, Coordinator
Therapeutic Recreation Program
(910) 750-2580

OHIO

Bowling Green State University — B, M
Bowling Green, OH 43403-0248
Julie Lengfelder, Chair
Recreation & Tourism Division,
School of HPER
(419) 372-6908

Kent State University — B
Kent, OH 44242
Wayne W. Munson, Coordinator
Leisure Studies Program
(216) 672-2015

University of Toledo — B, M
Toledo, OH 43606
Steven L. Ranck, Coordinator
Division of Recreation
& Leisure Studies
(419) 530-2757

OKLAHOMA

Oklahoma State University — B, M, D
Stillwater, OK 74078
Jerry Jordan, Coordinator
Program in Leisure Studies,
School of HPELS
(405) 744-5493

PENNSYLVANIA

East Stroudsburg University — B
East Stroudsburg, PA 18301
Elaine Rogers, Chair
Dep't of Recreation
& Leisure Services Management
(717) 422-3297

Lincoln University — B
Lincoln University, PA 19352
James L. DeBoy, Chair
Dep't of Health, Physical Education
& Recreation
(610) 932-8300

The Pennsylvania State University — B, M, D
University Park, PA 16802
Stuart H. Mann, Director
School of Hotel, Restaurant
& Recreation Management
(814) 863-1851

Temple University — B, M, D
Philadelphia, PA 19122
Ira Shapiro, Chair
Dep't of Sport Management
& Leisure Studies
(215) 204-8706

York College — B
York, PA 17403-3426
Annette Logan, Coordinator
Recreation & Leisure Administration
(717) 846-7788

SOUTH CAROLINA

Clemson University — B, M, D
Clemson, SC 29634
Lawrence R. Allen, Head
Dep't of Parks, Recreation
& Tourism Management
(864) 656-3400

TENNESSEE

Middle Tennessee State University — B
Murfreesboro, TN 37132
Martha H. Whaley, Chair
Program in Recreation,
Dep't of HPER

(615) 898-2811

University of Tennessee — B
Knoxville, TN 37996-2700
Gene Hayes, Chair
Recreation & Leisure Studies
(423) 974-6045

TEXAS

Texas A & M University — B, M, D
College Station, TX 77843
Peter Witt, Chair
Dep't of Recreation, Park
& Tourism Sciences
(409) 845-5411

University of North Texas — B, M
Denton, TX 76203-6857
James R. Morrow, Chair
Dep't of Kinesiology,
Health Promotion & Recreation
(817) 565-2651

UTAH

Brigham Young University — B, M
Provo, UT 84602-2031
S. Harold Smith, Chair
Dep't of Recreation Management
& Youth Leadership
(801) 378-4369

University of Utah — B, M, D
Salt Lake City, UT 84112
Gary Ellis, Interim Chair
Dep't of Recreation & Leisure
(801) 581-3220

Utah State University — B, M, D
Logan, UT 84322-7000
Dennis A. Nelson, Chair
Parks & Recreation Program
(801) 797-1497

VERMONT

Green Mountain College — B
Poultney, VT 05764
Robert Riley, Chair
Dep't of Recreation & Leisure Studies
(802) 287-8000

Lyndon State College — B
Lyndonville, VT 05851
Catherine DeLeo, Chair
Dep't of Recreation & Leisure Studies
(802) 626-6475

VIRGINIA

Ferrum College — B
Ferrum, VA 24088
Dempsey Hensley, Coordinator
Recreation & Leisure Program
(703) 365-4494

Longwood College — B
Farmville, VA 23901
Pat Shank, Program Head
Therapeutic Recreation
Program, Dep't of HPER
(804) 395-2545

Old Dominion University — B, M
Norfolk, VA 23529-0196
Ladd G. Colston, Program
Coordinator
Recreation & Leisure Studies,
Dep't of HPER
(804) 683-4995

Radford University — B, M
Radford, VA 24141
Gerald O'Morrow, Chair
Dep't of Leisure Services
(540) 831-5221

Virginia Commonwealth University — B, M
Richmond, VA 23284-2015
Michael S. Wise, Program Head
Recreation, Parks & Tourism Program
(804) 828-1130

Virginia Wesleyan College — B
Norfolk, VA 23502
Douglas Kennedy, Coordinator
Recreation & Leisure Studies
Program
(804) 455-3305

WASHINGTON

Central Washington University — B, M
Ellensburg, WA 98926
Craig E. Rademacher, Director
Leisure Services Program
(509) 963-1969

Eastern Washington University — B
Cheney, WA 99004
Howard Uibel, Chair
Program in Recreation
& Leisure Services
(509) 359-2464

COLLEGE PROGRAMS IN RECREATION MANAGEMENT

Washington State University — B, M
Pullman, WA 99164
Edward Udd, Chair
Recreation Administration
   & Leisure Studies Curriculum
(509) 335-4593

Western Washington University — B
Bellingham, WA 98225
Ronald D. Riggins, Coordinator
Recreation Program, Dep't
   of PEHR
(360) 650-3782

WEST VIRGINIA

Marshall University — B
Huntington, WV 25755-2450
Raymond L. Busbee, Coordinator
Park Resources & Leisure Services,
   Dep't of HPER
(304) 696-2922

West Virginia State College — B
Institute, WV 25112
Ted Muilenburg, Program
   Coordinator
Recreation Program
(304) 766-3365

West Virginia University — B, M
Morgantown, WV 26506
Steve Hollenhorst, Program
   Coordinator
Recreation & Parks Management
(304) 293-2941

WISCONSIN

University of Wisconsin at LaCrosse — B, M
LaCrosse, WI 54601
George Arimond, Chair
Dep't of Recreation Management
   & Therapeutic Recreation
(608) 785-8207

The master's degree also is offered by the institutions that follow:
Alabama: University of South Alabama
Arizona: University of Arizona
California: Humboldt State University, University of Southern California
Colorado: University of Colorado
Florida: University of Miami, University of South Florida
Georgia: Georgia State University
Illinois: Chicago State University
Indiana: Ball State University, Purdue University

Iowa: Drake University
Kansas: Pittsburg State University, University of Kansas
Kentucky: Murray State University, University of Kentucky
Louisiana: Southern University
Maryland: University of Maryland
Massachusetts: Boston University, Northeastern University, University of Massachusetts at Amherst
Michigan: Northern Michigan University, University of Michigan, Wayne State University
Minnesota: University of Minnesota (St. Paul), Winona State University
Mississippi: Jackson State University, University of Mississippi
Missouri: Central Missouri State University
Montana: University of Montana
Nebraska: University of Nebraska (Omaha)
New Hampshire: University of New Hampshire
New Mexico: University of New Mexico
New York: Lehman College, Medaille College, New York University, St. Joseph's College, State University of New York at Brockport, State University of New York at Cortland
North Dakota: North Dakota State University
Ohio: Ohio State University
Oklahoma: University of Oklahoma, University of Tulsa
Oregon: Oregon State University, University of Oregon
Pennsylvania: Slippery Rock State University
Tennessee: Memphis State University
Texas: Baylor University, Texas Technical University
Vermont: University of Vermont
Virginia: George Mason University, Virginia Polytechnic University
Washington: University of Washington
Wisconsin: University of Wisconsin at Madison, University of Wisconsin at Milwaukee
Wyoming: University of Wyoming

AROUND THE HORN

At Ringside,
Prof. Harmon-Martin

When she isn't grading students at the University of the District of Columbia, Sheila Harmon-Martin, an assistant professor of political science, might be thousands of miles away grading professional boxers in a title bout.

Harmon-Martin is a professional boxing judge.

A boxing fan since her youth, she joined a training program for boxing officials in 1978 and two years later received a license as a professional judge. She is now the chief judge of the District of Columbia Boxing and Wrestling Commission and, in addition to her own work as a judge, oversees the training of apprentices.

Harmon-Martin is one of about a dozen women who are sanctioned internationally for professional bouts. She earns from $1,000 to $1,600 for title fights and as little as $50 for local fights. Money is not the only reward. As she likes to point out, "You get the best seat in the house."

Filmmaker With a Heart:
Bud Greenspan

At 21 he was sports director of radio station WMGM in New York and did the before and after broadcasts of Brooklyn Dodger games. He also covered hockey, basketball, track, and tennis from Madison Square Garden.

Bud Greenspan is in his 60s now, known the world over as a writer-producer-director of sports films, and acclaimed especially for his films of and about the Olympic Games. His latest, *Lillehammer '94: 16 Days of Glory*, a four-hour television special on the 1994 Winter Olympic Games, was the fifth in a series of Official Olympic Films. His earlier productions: the Games in Los Angeles in 1984; Calgary, 1988; Seoul, 1988; and Barcelona, 1992.

The films reveal Greenspan's affection for the athletes and his deep sentimentality about the purpose of the Olympics. A *New York Times* reviewer of *Lillehammer '94* described Greenspan's approach this way: "The standard style of Greenspan's Olympic films is unchanged—serious, respectful, loving, and abundant with the spirit of brotherhood and sportsmanship."

His company, Cappy Productions, is at 33 E. 68th St., New York, NY 10021. Phone: (212) 249-1800.

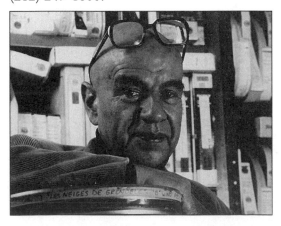

Track & Field:
No Lane for Job Seekers

USA Track & Field (formerly known as the Athletic Congress) rules over the entire domain of long-distance running, racewalking, and track and field in the U.S. The organization is composed of 56 regional associations with a membership of 2,500 clubs, schools, and colleges and 100,000 athletes. Its activities range from the sanctioning of grassroots events to the development of such major events as the 1995 USA Mobil Indoor Track & Field Series, telecast on NBC.

The various operations are run from offices in Indianapolis's RCA Dome (once the Hoosier Dome) with a paid staff of about 30, plus volunteers. Elsewhere in track and field, paid workers are about as numerous as 250-pound pole-vaulters.

A spokesman for USA Track & Field said that the organization does not use interns at its headquarters. The preference is for volunteers, especially retired persons who have been involved in track and field operations.

The mailing address of USA Track & Field is P.O. Box 120, Indianapolis, IN 46206. Phone: (317) 261-0500. Executive director is Ollan C. Cassell.

Volunteerism Lives!

Staging the 26.2-mile New York City Marathon for its 25,000 runners is a job and a half, as Rita Duffy of the New York Road Runners Club can tell you. Duffy is in charge of the marathon's corps of volunteers—all 13,315 of them.

If you'd like to join the world's biggest sports event—the race is run in November, but there's work to be done all year long—call (212) 423-2201 on Thursday evenings, 6 to 9.

Somebody Had to Do It

Jennifer Drury, a California lawyer and sports marketer, is a specialist in what she calls "alternative" sports—sports such as mountain biking, snowboarding, BMXing, and beach

The Center for the Study of Sport in Society

The mission of the Center for the Study of Sport in Society, at Northeastern University in Boston, is "to increase awareness of sport and its relation to society, and to develop programs that identify problems, offer solutions, and promote the benefits of sports." Perhaps most indicative of the seriousness of the Center's purposes is its periodic "Racial Report Card," a comprehensive analysis of hiring practices in professional sports.

Creator and director of the Center is Dr. Richard E. Lapchick. He is the son of Joe Lapchick, an outstanding player in the early days of professional basketball and later coach of the St. John's University basketball team and the New York Knicks.

The address of the Center for the Study of Sport in Society: Northeastern University, 360 Huntington Ave., 161 CP, Boston, MA 02115. Phone: (617) 373-4025.

volleyball. She has been especially successful in marketing Cheri Elliott, a professional mountain biker for whom Drury has negotiated sponsorships with 30 companies. Her firm is JED Sports Management and it's located at 3711 Almaden Court, Cameron Park, CA 95682.

The Business of Rodeo

It's a growing business. In 1975 the number of sanctioned rodeos was 594, with prize money totaling $6.4 million. By 1995 there were about 800 rodeos with more than $21.3 million in prize money. Now conducted in 43 states and four Canadian provinces, they attract 20 million customers a year. The 10-day National Finals Rodeo in Las Vegas has drawn so many overflow crowds in recent years that the city is considering building a 55,000-seat domed stadium to make sure it doesn't lose the event to another city.

The thing is, unless you aspire to be a professional rodeo cowboy, the sport offers little opportunity for a career. Each rodeo is a local affair, arranged either by a community's rodeo committee or by an independent producer. Most of the jobs are filled by part-timers or volunteers.

In addition to the rodeo producer, who hires the laborers, promotes the rodeo, and oversees the entire event, the key people are the stock contractor, who provides all the animals (and often acts also as producer); the rodeo announcer; timers; judges; pickup men, who help saddle-bronc and bareback riders get down from the horses; chute laborers; specialty acts; and the rodeo secretary, who keeps records of the event and pays the winning cowboys. And, of course, the cowboys themselves.

There are 8,000 professional rodeo cowboys in the U.S., about 1,000 of whom have national ranking. (Thousands more participate in small, unsanctioned rodeos.) Most ranked cowboys compete each year in as many as 125 rodeos, racing from one to the next, at their own expense, to be on time to pay their entry fees. It's not an easy life, but the romance of the sport is strong, and so is the lure of the prize money. In 1993, at the age of 24, world champion Ty Murray won $297,896, a record for annual earnings.

The governing body in the sport is the Professional Rodeo Cowboys Association (PRCA), which has a membership of almost 10,000 contestants, stock contractors, committees, and rodeo personnel. PRCA-sanctioned rodeos are required to observe standards of professionalism and safety and rules for the humane treatment of rodeo livestock.

Corporate sponsors have done a lot for the sport by expanding prizes and increasing its visibility. Among the sponsors considered especially important are Wrangler Jeans, Copenhagen/Skoal, Coors, Dodge Truck, Coca-Cola USA, Justin Boots, Resistol Hats, and Seagram.

The address of the Professional Rodeo Cowboys Association is 101 Pro Rodeo Dr., Colorado Springs, CO 80919. Phone: (719) 593-8840. Lewis A. Cryer is commissioner.

The other main organizations in the sport:

The International Professional Rodeo Association, 500 Tausick Way, Walla Walla, WA 99362. Phone: (509) 527-4212. Executive director: Tim Corfield.

The Women's Professional Rodeo Association, Route 5, Box 698, Blanchard, OK 73010. Phone: (405) 485-2277. Secretary-treasurer: Lydia Moore.

Horse Show Management

The ancient sport of competitive horsemanship is alive and well. Despite the continuing urbanization of the American landscape (and maybe because of it), interest in horses grows. The American Horse Shows Association, the chief regulatory body in equestrian competition, reports that it now sanctions as many as 2,500 shows a year. Attendance is edging up, as is TV exposure (thanks mainly to ESPN), and corporate sponsors are discovering the special benefits of entertaining business guests in this elite atmosphere. The AHSA itself has nearly 60,000 individual members, most of whom compete.

The country's largest hunter/jumper horse show is the Hampton Classic, held at summer's end in the town of Bridgehampton in eastern Long Island, where many of New York's rich and famous have summer homes. The seven-day, four-ring event draws more than 40,000 spectators, and for sponsors, patrons, and other special guests there's a 2,000-seat VIP tent, perhaps the largest of any U.S. sports event. Famed as a world-class competition, the Classic attracts about 1,200 horses and riders from all over North America and several countries abroad. Participating each year are the U.S. Olympic show-jumping team and individual competitors from other countries. The climax is the $100,000 Hampton Classic Grand Prix, which gets wide TV coverage.

Horse show jobs:

Show managers—Managing the competitions includes supervising the technical set-up (temporary stabling; preparation of the rings and schooling areas; feed, hay, and bedding provisions), overseeing the handling of show entries, contracting judges and other licensed officials, and arranging sponsorships. Many show managers put on several shows a year, each generally lasting four to six days, sometimes longer. Earnings: $40,000 to $80,000-plus.

Secretaries—They process all entries before, during, and after a competition. Major shows require working several weeks in advance and some days afterward. Pay: $100-plus per day.

Ring crews—The crew keeps rings and footing in good condition. For shows offering jumping events or Western trail events, setting up and tearing down a jumping course efficiently is extremely important. A crew may consist of seven or more individuals. Pay: $75-plus per day.

Course designers—The designer specifies which jumps are to be used and how they are to be placed. Pay: $250-plus per day.

Judges—All events are judged by officials licensed by the AHSA. (The association has issued more than 3,000 licenses.) Pay: $250-plus per day.

Stewards or technical delegates—These are AHSA-licensed personnel who make sure that all rules of the competition are observed. Pay: $125-plus per day.

Announcers—The announcer keeps the exhibitors aware of the timetable to keep the show running at a brisk pace and explains the events taking place. Pay: $125-plus per day.

Paddock masters—The paddock master is responsible for helping exhibitors prepare for events in a timely manner. Pay: $125-plus per day.

All personnel are compensated for travel expenses.

Involvement in horse shows means long days and weeks of travel, but it also means being around horses and congenial people, and for many there's no better life.

HORSE SHOW ORGANIZATIONS

American Horse Shows Association
(Also known as the National Equestrian
  Foundation of the United States)
Bonnie B. Jenkins, Executive Director
220 W. 42nd St.
New York, NY 10017-5876
(212) 972-2472
The AHSA is the principal sanctioning
  body in this sport.

**National Horse Show Association
  of America**
Henry L. Collins III, Executive Officer
680 Fifth Ave., Suite 1602
New York, NY 10019
(212) 757-0222
A repository of equestrian history founded
  in 1883. Sponsors major show annually.

**Intercollegiate Horse Show
  Association**
Robert E. Cacchione, Executive Director
Hollow Rd., Box 741
Stony Brook, NY 11790
(516) 751-2803
Promotes horsemanship through clinics
  and seminars, presents Grand
  Champion National Trophy at annual
  show, awards scholarships.

**Professional Horsemen's Association
  of America**
Hedda W. von Goeben, Secretary
254 S. Lake St.
Litchfield, CT 06759-3520
Promotes interest in the horse industry
  and proper care of horses. Sponsors
  horse shows and other activities. Has a
  scholarship fund.

A Final Tip on Internships: Local Sports Commissions

Scores of local sports commissions—municipally sponsored, for the most part—are hard at work trying to establish a reputation for their communities as the home of major sports events.

The effort to pull in events of high popularity is important to the economy of their communities and to the psychic well-being of the citizenry. Hosting these events not only is a boost to tourism, it also creates an atmosphere that marks a community as a good place to live and work, and that, in turn, helps to attract new industries (and new jobs for the populace).

The sports commissions, usually official or semiofficial city units, sometimes are independent operations organized by community movers and business interests. Occasionally, they are formed by regional authorities or by county or state governments.

However big their objectives, sports commissions are almost always small in terms of personnel. Not uncommon is a commission that has one regular employee, assisted by part-timers and volunteers. Other commissions may have five or six full-time people. Very few are bigger than that.

But virtually all the commissions have internship programs, and we suggest they're worth your consideration. A tour as an intern in any of the operations listed here could be a rich experience.

Many of the commissions are members of a networking organization, the National Association of Sports Commissions. Executive director is Don Schumacher and he is located at 300 Main St., Cincinnati, OH 45202. Phone: (513) 651-1330.

SPORTS COMMISSIONS

ALABAMA

Mobile Sports Commission
1 S. Water St.
Mobile, AL 36602
(334) 415-2000
Pres: Brenda Scott

ARIZONA

Maricopa County Sports Authority
1 E. Camelback Rd., Suite 610
Phoenix, AZ 85012
(602) 263-2333
Exec Dir: Mike Lawrence

CALIFORNIA

Los Angeles Sports Council
350 S. Bixel, Suite 250
Los Angeles, CA 90017
(213) 482-6333
Pres: David Simon

Sacramento Sports Commission
1030 15th St., Suite 250
Sacramento, CA 95814
(916) 264-5291
Dir: John M. McCasey

San Diego Int'l Sports Council
P.O. Box 601400
San Diego, CA 92160
(619) 682-3436
Contact: Ky Snyder

San Jose Sports Authority
99 Almaden Blvd., Suite 975
San Jose, CA 95113-1603
(408) 288-2931
Exec Dir: Dean Munro

COLORADO

Colorado Sports Council
1391 Speer Blvd., Suite 700
Denver, CO 80204
(303) 573-1995
Pres/CEO: Edmond F. Noel Jr.

Colorado Springs Sports Corp.
12 E. Boulder
Colorado Springs, CO 80903
(719) 634-7333
Exec Dir: Stephen D. Ducoff

FLORIDA

Gainesville Sports Organizing Committee
P.O. Box 1187
Gainesville, FL 32602-1187
(904) 338-9300
Exec Dir: J. Bruce Douglas

Miami Sports and Exhibition Authority
300 Biscayne Blvd. Way, Suite 1120
Miami, FL 33131
(305) 381-8261
Exec Dir/CEO: William R. Perry III

Orlando Area Sports Commission
P.O. Box 2969
Orlando, FL 32802
(407) 648-4900
Pres: Diane Hovenkamp

Palm Beach County Sports Authority
1555 Palm Beach Lakes Blvd., Suite 202
West Palm Beach, FL 33401
(407) 233-1015
Exec Dir: Pam Gerig

St. Petersburg-Clearwater Area Sports Organizing Committee
One Stadium Dr., Suite A
St. Petersburg, FL 33705-1706
(813) 582-7892
Dir: Carole Ketterhagen

GEORGIA

Atlanta Sports Council
P.O. Box 1740
Atlanta, GA 30301
(404) 586-8510
Exec Dir: Robert Dale Morgan

Gainesville-Hall County Sports Council
830 Green St.
Gainesville, GA 30501
(404) 536-5209
Exec Dir: Jack Hughes

Greater Augusta Sports Council
P.O. Box 1331
Augusta, GA 30903-1331
(706) 722-8326
Exec Dir: Charlie Obranowicz

HAWAII

Hawaii Pacific Sports
1493 Halekkoa Dr.
Honolulu, HI 96821
(808) 732-8805
Pres: Mark E. Zeug

INDIANA

Indiana Sports Corporation
201 S. Capitol Ave., Suite 1200
Indianapolis, IN 46225
(317) 237-5000
Pres: Dale E. Neuburger

LOUISIANA

Baton Rouge Area Sports Foundation
P.O. Box 4149
Baton Rouge, LA 70821
(504) 383-1825
Pres: Jerry Stovall

Greater New Orleans Sports Foundation
1520 Sugar Bowl Dr.
New Orleans, LA 70112
(504) 525-5678
Pres/CEO: Douglas Thornton

City of Shreveport Sports Commission
P.O. Box 1761
Shreveport, LA 71166
(318) 222-9391
Coord: Orvis Sigler

MASSACHUSETTS

Sports Marketing Division Greater Boston Convention & Visitors' Bureau
P.O. Box 990468
Boston, MA 02199
(617) 536-4100
Dir: Robert Mollica

Massachusetts Sports Partnership
One International Pl., Suite 825
Boston, MA 02110
(617) 443-4909
Exec Dir: Cindy Rowe Pelletier

MINNESOTA

Metro-Minneapolis Sports Council
33 S. Sixth St.
Minneapolis, MN 55402
(612) 661-4700
Dir: Bob McNamara

MISSOURI

Greater Kansas City Sports Commission and Foundation
1100 Pennsylvania Ave., Suite 1032
Kansas City, MO 64105
(816) 474-4652
Exec Dir: Kevin M. Gray

St. Louis Sports Commission
10 S. Broadway, Suite 1000
St. Louis, MO 63102
(314) 992-0687
Pres: Mike Dyer

NEBRASKA

Greater Omaha Sports Committee
666 Farnam Bldg.
1613 Farnam St.
Omaha, NE 68102
(402) 346-8003
Pres: Bob Mancuso

NEW JERSEY

New Jersey Sports & Exposition Authority
East Rutherford, NJ 07073-0700
(201) 460-4011
Pres/CEO: Robert E. Mulcahy III

NEW YORK

Albany Foundation for Sports & Special Events
23 Computer Dr. E
Albany, NY 12205
(518) 438-5195
Exec Dir: Lori Slezak

Long Island Sports Commission
80 Hauppauge Rd.
Commack, NY 11725-4495
(516) 493-3022
Dir: Regina Yagy

Nassau County Sports Commission
Administration Bldg., Eisenhower Park
East Meadow, NY 11554
(516) 794-2020
Exec Dir: Tauna Kay Vandeweghe

New York City Sports Commission
253 Broadway
New York, NY 10007
(212) 788-8389
Exec Dir: Arlene Weltman

Syracuse Sports Corporation
572 S. Salina St.
Syracuse, NY 13202-3320
(315) 470-1825
Sports Dir: Kristen J. Wood

NORTH CAROLINA

Charlotte Regional Sports Commission
301 S. Tryon, Suite 2260
Charlotte, NC 28282
(704) 332-7717
Exec Dir: Rich Sheubrooks

Greensboro Sports Commission
317 S. Greene St.
Greensboro, NC 27401
(910) 378-4499
Pres: Tom Ward

North Carolina Sports Development
430 N. Salisbury St.
Raleigh, NC 27603
(919) 733-3461
Dir: Bill Dooley

OHIO

Greater Cincinnati Sports & Events Commission
300 Main St., 1st Floor
Cincinnati, OH 45202
(513) 651-1330
Exec Dir: Don Schumacher

Greater Cleveland Sports Commission
P.O. Box 91654
Cleveland, OH 44101-3654
(216) 363-0695
Pres: Rick Bay

OKLAHOMA

Tulsa Sports Commission
616 S. Boston, Suite 100
Tulsa, OK 74119-1298
(918) 585-1201
Exec Dir: Diana D. Medders

OREGON

Portland Metropolitan Sports Authority
500 N.E. Multnomah, Suite 890
Portland, OR 97232
(503) 234-4500
Exec Dir: Craig Honeyman

PENNSYLVANIA

Philadelphia Sports Congress
1515 Market St., Suite 2020
Philadelphia, PA 19102
(215) 636-3417
Dir: Lawrence Needle

SOUTH CAROLINA

Metro Sports Council
P.O. Box 1360
Columbia, SC 29202
Fax: (803) 733-1125
Interim Exec Dir: Jeffrey T. Turgeon

TENNESSEE

Greater Chattanooga Sports Committee
P.O. Box 11508
Chattanooga, TN 37401-2508
(615) 756-8689
Pres: Merrill Eckstein

Knoxville Sports Corporation
900 E. Hill Ave., Suite 480
Knoxville, TN 37915
(615) 522-3777
Pres: Gloria S. Ray

TEXAS

Greater Austin Sports Council
P.O. Box 1967
Austin, TX 78767
(512) 322-5654
Exec Dir: Suzanne Hofmann

San Antonio Sports Foundation
P.O. Box 830386
San Antonio, TX 78283-0386
(210) 246-3480
Pres: William C. Hanson

VIRGINIA

Metropolitan Richmond Sports Backers
7275 Glen Forest Dr., Suite 204
Richmond, VA 23226
(804) 285-9495
Exec Dir: Jon Lugbill

WASHINGTON

Seattle-King County Sports & Events Council
1301 Fifth Ave., Suite 2400
Seattle, WA 98101-2603
(206) 389-7229
Pres: Michael Campbell

Tacoma-Pierce County Sports Commission
P.O. Box 1754
Tacoma, WA 98401-1754
(206) 627-2836
Com: Mike Shields

WISCONSIN

Wisconsin Sports Authority
901 N. Fourth St.
Milwaukee, WI 53203
(414) 277-6787
Pres: Joe Sweeney

The Student Intern Program of the U.S. Olympic Committee

The United States Olympic Committee has an attractive internship program for college students who have completed at least two years of college work in fields that have some relevance to USOC divisions.

The divisions: Athlete Support, Coaching Programs, Drug Control, International Games Preparation, Management Information Systems, National Events and Conferences, Media Relations, Broadcasting, Development (Marketing, Fund-Raising), Finance/Accounting, International Relations, Member Services and Grants, Training Center.

The program is conducted year-round and divided into fall, spring, and summer semesters. Up to 20 resident internships are awarded each semester at the USOC's Colorado Springs location. A smaller number of resident internships are also available at USOC centers in Chula Vista, California, and Lake Placid, New York.

Selection of a division is made with the help of Jan Schnitker, (719) 632-5551, ext. 2597.

Other aspects of the program:

Interns get a compensation package equal to the minimum wage. The cost of room and board is taken from the intern's earnings.

Travel expenses from an intern's home are the responsibility of the intern.

Interns work a minimum of 40 hours a week, which may include evening and weekend duties.

Students may receive academic credit for their work.

For an application to the program, write to: Student Intern Program, U.S. Olympic Committee, One Olympic Plaza, Colorado Springs, CO 80909-5760.

SPORTS ASSOCIATIONS AFFILIATED WITH THE USOC

Under the broad umbrella of the United States Olympic Committee are the 49 sports associations shown below. In the main, the function of the associations is to maintain a high level of competition in a manner that expresses the Olympic ideals of sportsmanship. Some of the associations use interns referred to them by the USOC; some recruit interns independently, and in these cases candidates for internships do not need to be college students.

ARCHERY

National Archery Association
One Olympic Plaza
Colorado Springs, CO 80909
(719) 578-4576
Thomas Stevenson Jr., President
8 employees
Internships: via USOC

BADMINTON

U.S. Badminton Association
One Olympic Plaza
Colorado Springs, CO 80909
(719) 548-4808
Diane Cornell, President
4 employees
Internships: via USOC

BASEBALL

USA Baseball
2160 Greenwood Ave.
Trenton, NJ 08609
(609) 586-2381
Mark Marquess, President
9 employees
Internships: via USOC

BASKETBALL

USA Basketball
5465 Mark Dabling Blvd.
Colorado Springs, CO 80918-3842
(719) 590-4800
C. M. Newton, President
20 employees
Internships: contact Caroline Williams

BIATHLON

U.S. Biathlon Association
P.O. Box 297
29 Church St., Lower Level #5
Burlington, VT 05402
(802) 862-0338
Maj. Gen. Donald Edwards, President
7 employees
Internships: via USOC

BOBSLED

U.S. Bobsled and Skeleton Federation
P.O. Box 828
421 Old Military Rd.
Lake Placid, NY 12946
(518) 523-1842
James S. Morris, President
30 employees
Internships: via USOC

BOXING

USA Boxing
1520 N. Union Blvd., Suite B
Colorado Springs, CO 80909
(719) 548-4506
Gary Toney, President
14 employees
Internships: via USOC

CANOE/KAYAK

American Canoe Association
7432 Alban Station Blvd., Suite B-226
Springfield, VA 22150
(703) 451-0141
Don Sorensen, Commodore
11 employees
Internships: contact Human Resources

CURLING

USA Curling
1100 Center Point Dr.
P.O. Box 866
Stevens Point, WI 54481
(715) 344-1199
Warren R. Lowe, President
5 employees
Internships: contact Human Resources

CYCLING

USA Cycling, Inc.
One Olympic Plaza
Colorado Springs, CO 80909
(719) 578-4581
Mike Plant, President
54 employees
Internships: contact Human Resources

SPORTS ASSOCIATIONS AFFILIATED WITH THE USOC

DIVING

United States Diving, Inc.
Pan American Plaza, Suite 430
Indianapolis, IN 46225
(317) 237-5252
Steve McFarland, President
5 employees
Internships: via USOC

EQUESTRIAN

American Horse Shows Association
220 East 42nd St., Suite 409
New York, NY 10017-5876
(212) 972-2472
Jane Forbes Clark, President
73 employees
Internships: via USOC

FENCING

U.S. Fencing Association
One Olympic Plaza
Colorado Springs, CO 80909-5774
(719) 578-4511
Stephen Sobel, President
8 employees
Internships: via USOC

FIELD HOCKEY

U.S. Field Hockey Association
1520 N. Union Blvd.
Colorado Springs, CO 80909
(719) 578-4567
Jenepher Shullingford, President
14 employees
Internships: via USOC

FIGURE SKATING

U.S. Figure Skating Association
20 First St.
Colorado Springs, CO 80906-3697
(719) 635-5200
Morry Stillwell, President
35 employees
Internships: via USOC

GYMNASTICS

USA Gymnastics
Pan American Plaza, Suite 300
201 South Capitol Ave.
Indianapolis, IN 46225
(317) 237-5050
Kathy Scanlan, President/Executive
    Director
45 employees
Internships: contact Julie Bejin,
    (317) 237-5050

ICE HOCKEY

USA Hockey, Inc.
4965 North 30th St.
Colorado Springs, CO 08919
(719) 599-5500
Walter L. Bush Jr., President
47 employees
Internships: via USOC

JUDO

United States Judo, Inc.
95 South Market St., Suite 220
San Jose, CA 95113
(408) 298-7551
Yoshihiro Ushida, President

LUGE

U.S. Luge Association
P.O. Box 651
35 Church St.
Lake Placid, NY 12946
(518) 523-2071
Dwight Bell, President
18 employees
Internships: contact Bob Hughes

MODERN PENTATHLON

**U.S. Modern Pentathlon
    Association**
530 McCullough, Suite 619
San Antonio, TX 78215
(210) 246-3000
Robert G. Marbut, President

ROWING

United States Rowing Association
Pan American Plaza, Suite 400
201 South Capitol Ave.
Indianapolis, IN 46225
(317) 237-5656
David Vogel, President
16 employees
Internships: send resume

SAILING

United States Sailing Association
P.O. Box 1260
15 Maritime Dr.
Portsmouth, RI 02871-1260
(401) 683-0800
David H. Irish, President
30 employees
Internships: contact Terry Harper

SHOOTING

USA Shooting
One Olympic Plaza
Colorado Springs, CO 80909
(719) 578-4670
Col. Stefan Richards, President
13 employees
Internships: contact Valerie Larabee

SKIING

U.S. Skiing
P.O. Box 100
1500 Kearns Blvd.
Park City, UT 84060
(801) 649-9090
Bill Marolt, President/CEO
89 employees
Internships: contact Deborah Engen

SOCCER

U.S. Soccer Federation
U.S. Soccer House
1801-1811 South Prairie Ave.
Chicago, IL 60616
(312) 808-1300
Alan Rothenberg, President
73 employees
Administrative internships: contact
    Dick Mosbey
Public relations internships: contact
    Tom Lang
Event management internships:
    contact Dan Flynn

SOFTBALL

Amateur Softball Association
2801 N.E. 50th St.
Oklahoma City, OK 73111-7203
(405) 424-6714
Wayne Myers, President
50 employees
Internships: contact Tim O'Toole

SPEED SKATING

U.S. Speedskating
P.O. Box 16157
Rocky River, OH 44116-6157
(216) 899-0128
Bill Cushman, President
9 employees

SWIMMING

U.S. Swimming, Inc.
One Olympic Plaza
Colorado Springs, CO 80909
(719) 578-4578
Carol Zaleski, President
53 employees
Internships: contact Cindy Hayes

SYNCHRONIZED SWIMMING

**U.S. Synchronized Swimming,
    Inc.**
Pan American Plaza, Suite 510
201 South Capitol Ave.
Indianapolis, IN 46225
(317) 237-5700
Nancy Wightman, President
7 employees
Internships: contact Laura LaMarca

TABLE TENNIS

USA Table Tennis
One Olympic Plaza
Colorado Springs, CO 80909
(719) 548-4583
Terry Timmins, President

TEAM HANDBALL

U.S. Team Handball Federation
One Olympic Plaza
Colorado Springs, CO 80909-5768
(719) 548-4582
Dr. Thomas T. Rosandich, President
3 employees

TENNIS

U.S. Tennis Association
70 West Red Oak Lane
White Plains, NY 10604-3602
(914) 696-7000
Dr. Lester M. Snyder Jr., President

TRACK AND FIELD

USA Track & Field
P.O. Box 120
One RCA Dome, Suite 140
Indianapolis, IN 46225
(317) 261-0500
Larry Ellis, President
30 employees
Internships: contact Patty Hogan

SPORTS ASSOCIATIONS AFFILIATED WITH THE USOC

VOLLEYBALL

USA Volleyball
3595 E. Fountain Blvd., Suite I2
Colorado Springs, CO 80909-1740
(719) 637-8300
Rebecca Howard, President
19 employees
Internships: via USOC

WATER POLO

United States Water Polo
1685 West Uintah
Colorado Springs, CO 80909-2921
(719) 634-0699
Richard Foster, President
5 employees
Internships: via USOC

WEIGHTLIFTING

U.S. Weightlifting Federation
One Olympic Plaza
Colorado Springs, CO 80909-5764
(719) 578-4508
Brian Derwin, President
9 employees
Internships: via USOC

WRESTLING

USA Wrestling
6155 Lehman Dr.
Colorado Springs, CO 80918
(719) 598-8181
Larry Sciacchetano, President
20 employees
Internships: via USOC

PAN AMERICAN SPORT ORGANIZATIONS

BOWLING

USA Bowling
5301 S. 76th St.
Greendale, WI 53129-0500
(414) 421-9008
Elaine Hagin, President
250 employees
Internships: contact Elaine Hagin

RACQUETBALL

American Amateur Racquetball Association
1685 West Uintah
Colorado Springs, CO 80904
(719) 635-5396
Van Dubolsky, President
13 employees
Internships: via USOC

ROLLER SKATING

U.S. Amateur Confederation of Roller Skating
P.O. Box 6579
4730 South St.
Lincoln, NE 68506
(402) 483-7551
Betty Ann Dianna, President
16 employees
Internships: via USOC

TAEKWONDO

U.S. Taekwondo Union
One Olympic Plaza, Suite 405
Colorado Springs, CO 80909
(719) 578-4632
Hwa Chong, President
12 employees
Internships: via USOC

AFFILIATED SPORT ORGANIZATIONS

KARATE

United States of America National Karate-Do Federation, Inc.
P.O. Box 77083
8351 15th Ave., NW
Seattle, WA 98177-7083
(206) 440-8386
Julius Thiry, President

ORIENTEERING

U.S. Orienteering Federation
P.O. Box 1444
Forest Park, GA 30051
Rick Worner, President

SPORTS ACROBATICS

United States Sports Acrobatics Federation
P.O. Box 8158
Riverside, CA 92515-8158
(909) 785-2293
Roger McFarland, President
Employees: all volunteer

SQUASH RACQUETS

U.S. Squash Racquets Association
P.O. Box 1216
23 Cynwyd Rd.
Bala Cynwyd, PA 19004
(610) 667-4006
Andre P. Naniche, President
5 employees

TRAMPOLINE AND TUMBLING

USA Trampoline and Tumbling
P.O. Box 306
Brownfield, TX 79316-0306
(806) 637-8670
Connie Mara, President

TRIATHLON

Triathlon Federation USA
3595 E. Fountain Blvd., Suite F-1
Colorado Springs, CO 80910
(719) 597-9090
Rick Margiotta, President
8 employees
Internships: via USOC

UNDERWATER SWIMMING

Underwater Society of America
64 N. Bascom Ave.
San Jose, CA 95128
(408) 286-8840
Michael Gower, President/Executive Director

WATER SKIING

American Water Ski Association
799 Overlook Dr., SE
Winter Haven, FL 33884
(941) 324-4341
Andrea Plough, President

United States Olympic Committee
One Olympic Plaza
Colorado Springs, CO 80909
Richard D. Schultz, Executive Director
(719) 578-4542

THE GROWTH OF WOMEN IN SPORTS-RELATED CAREERS

by Donna A. Lopiano, Ph.D.

Executive Director, Women's Sports Foundation®

There has never been a better time for women to consider sports-related careers. Over the past 25 years, barriers to the employment of women have diminished. Title IX of the 1972 Education Amendments Act eliminated quotas on the admission of women students to law, medical, and business schools, allowing them to pursue careers in everything from sports medicine to sports law. Title IX required that women get the same chance as men to play varsity sports and opened the high school and college coaching and athletic management professions to women. Similarly, equal opportunity employment laws of the '70s opened up job opportunities in the sporting goods manufacturing industry, which until that time had a workforce that was 95 percent male. In retail and in the world of sports sponsorships, the marketing of sports to the public also was basically a male domain.

Even though the sports industry is still predominantly male and subtle methods of discrimination remain, most of the overt barriers are down or in the process of coming down. Men and women who grew up in the '70s and after believe that their daughters could and should play sports and become anything they wish. These parents are now the 40-to-50 year olds in the workforce who hold the purse strings for sports sponsorships and the hiring and decision-making power in sports-related businesses. At this rate, most of the employment and other barriers should fall completely over the next decade.

The process of welcoming women into the sports-careers workforce has been hastened by these five developments:

1. The number of active female consumers is increasing. When women were given the opportunity to play sports through Title IX, they became a driving force for a major cultural revolution in the nature of the American woman. In 1971, only one in 27 high school girls played sports. That figure today is one in three. The active female is now a hot new market. Since 1991 women have outpurchased men in athletic shoes and apparel. Corporations are hiring women who can both understand what women consumers want and help them produce and sell products to this new large and lucrative market.

2. More and more women are watching men's sports. Close to 40 percent of the consumers of men's professional sports are women. Women are attending games, watching on TV, and purchasing licensed

Donna A. Lopiano is the executive Director of the Women's Sports Foundation, which has been in the vanguard of the campaign for equal opportunities for girls and women in sports. She is a graduate of Southern Connecticut State University and has a master's and a Ph.D. from USC. Lopiano has been an athlete in four sports and a college coach of men's and women's teams. She recently was ranked #46 of "The 100 Most Influential People in Sports" by *The Sporting News*.

products. They have been given the chance to play sports and understand them, and have developed into spectators just as passionate as their male counterparts. The NBA, NHL, MLB, NASCAR, and the NFL all have established special units to market to the female consumer, and they are all hiring women to give them an edge in understanding the needs of this market. The sports industry now believes that women customers will be half of their business, so women are increasingly accepted in men's sports.

3. Statistics show that both males and females watch women's sports. Men and women spectators have discovered that when women are given the chance to play, they become just as exceptionally skilled as their brothers—good enough to become professional athletes and to be sought after for product endorsements. During the 1996 Olympic Games, the U.S. television audience was 65 percent female. In the 12 months after the Games, three new professional leagues for women were established, two in basketball and one in fast pitch softball. All three leagues need everything from general managers to public relations directors to a ticket sales force, and are seeking a large women's presence to provide insight into this new market.

4. Women's sports are gaining acceptance by the sports media. In the 1970s coverage of women in the sports media was almost non-existent, with 99 percent of television hours and print column-inches devoted to men's sports. *Women's Sports & Fitness*, founded by Billie Jean King in 1974, was the only national magazine with a general women's sports focus until 1997, when two major publishing empires launched women's sports magazines: *Condé Nast Sports for Women* and *Sports Illustrated Woman*. These new publications hired predominantly female staffs to reach the female sports consumer. The niche sport magazines like *Runners World* and *Fitness Swimmer* are similarly increasing their coverage of women in their respective sports as

well as the number of women writers and editors on their staffs. The percentage of women in the heavily male dominated world of newspaper sports journalism doubled during the 1980s and should double again in the '90s.

5. Corporations are using sports to sell to women. From JCPenney to Evian, there are many major corporations outside the sporting goods manufacturing world that realize 70 to 80 percent of their consumers are women who have become more active, stronger, and more confident over the past two decades. Corporations seeking to appeal to the female consumer are developing messages that focus on active women. They are using female professional and Olympic athletes as inspirational advertising images. They are hiring female employees in their sports marketing units and are beginning to put money and female employees behind women's sports events. These corporations know that hiring females and funding women's events are important ways to generate customer loyalty.

These five developments have created exciting sports career opportunities for women. However, women must be prepared to face stiff job competition and the vestiges of gender discrimination in this historically male-dominated field. Therefore, the advice contained throughout this book applies doubly to young women seeking sports jobs: Join professional organizations. Attend regional and national conferences. Start a contact list. Find out how to gain access to key decision makers. Seek out a mentor—someone who can assist you in the process. And apply for internships. That's the most important way for you and your work to become known by people who can help you.

Twenty years ago, if a woman wanted a sports career she became a physical education teacher. Today she has a vast array of career choices. As the millennium approaches, the outlook for women in sports-related careers is bright.